Nature's Pharmacy

Unlocking the Power of **Medicinal Herbs**

Deaunna Marie Smith

Copyright © 2023 by Trient Press

All rights reserved. No part of this publication may be reproduced, distributed, or transmitted in any form or by any means, including photocopying, recording, or other electronic or mechanical methods, without the prior written permission of the publisher, except in the case of brief quotations embodied in critical reviews and certain other noncommercial uses permitted by copyright law. For permission requests, write to the publisher, addressed "Attention: Permissions Coordinator," at the address below.

Criminal copyright infringement, including infringement without monetary gain, is investigated by the FBI and is punishable by up to five years in federal prison and a fine of $250,000.

Except for the original story material written by the author, all songs, song titles, and lyrics mentioned in the novel Nature's Pharmacy: Unlocking the Power of Medicinal Herbsare the exclusive property of the respective artists, songwriters, and copyright holder.

Trient Press
3375 S Rainbow Blvd
#81710, SMB 13135
Las Vegas,NV 89180

Ordering Information:
Quantity sales. Special discounts are available on quantity purchases by corporations, associations, and others. For details, contact the publisher at the address above.
Orders by U.S. trade bookstores and wholesalers. Please contact Trient Press: Tel: (775) 996-3844; or visit www.trientpress.com.

Printed in the United States of America

Publisher's Cataloging-in-Publication data
Smith, Deaunna Marie
A title of a book :Nature's Pharmacy: Unlocking the Power of Medicinal Herbs
ISBN

Hard Cover	979-8-88990-098-6
Paper Back	979-8-88990-099-3
Ebook	979-8-88990-000-9

Disclaimer: The information provided in this book about herbs and their medicinal uses is for informational purposes only. It is not intended as a substitute for professional medical advice, diagnosis, or treatment. Herbs can have powerful effects and may interact with medications or other treatments. Before using any herb for medicinal purposes, it's important to speak with a qualified healthcare professional to ensure safety and to determine the appropriate use for your individual needs. The author and publisher of this book do not assume any liability for any adverse effects resulting from the use of any herbs mentioned in this book.

Table Of Contents

Prologue	1
Definition of Herbs	3
Brief History of Herbs	5
Different Types of Herbs & Their Uses	8
Understanding Herbs.	10
Herbs & The Human Body	39
Medicinal Herbs	57
Aloe Vera	58
Ashwagandha.	64
Astragalus	69
Bay Laurel	74
Black Cohosh	79
Burdock	83
Calendula	88
Catnip	93
Chaga Mushroom	98
Chamomile	103
Chickweed	109
Chives	113
Cinnamon	117
Cloves	121
Coltsfoot	127
Comfrey	132
Cordyceps	138
Dandelion	144
Echinacea	149
Elderberry	155
Eyebright	160
Fennel	165
Feverfew	172
Galangal	179
Garlic	185
Ginger	192
Ginkgo Biloba	198
Ginseng	204
Holy Basil	210
Hops	216

Hyssop	222
Juniper Berries	227
Kava Kava	233
Lady's Mantle	240
Lavender	246
Lemon balm	252
Licorice	258
Maca	265
Maitake Mushroom	270
Marshmallow Root	275
Milk Thistle	282
Mint	288
Mugwort	294
Muira Puama.	300
Nettle	305
Oregon Grape Root	311
Parsley	317
Passionflower	322
Peppermint	329
Red clover	334
Reishi Mushroom.	340
Rose Hips	347
Rosemary	354
Sage	360
Self-heal	366
Shiitake Mushroom	371
Siberian Ginseng	377
Skullcap	383
St. John's Wort.	388
Thyme.	394
Turmeric	399
Valerian	404
Wild yam	409
Yarrow	415
Growing Herbs At Home	421
Preparation Methods.	426
Safety Considerations.	440
Conclusion	444
References and Further Reading	446
General Recipes	449

Prologue

The world is filled with an abundance of plants and herbs, each with their own unique characteristics, properties, and uses. For thousands of years, humanity has turned to these herbs as a source of medicine, using them to heal ailments and promote wellness. From traditional medicine practices in China and India to the indigenous knowledge of the Americas and Africa, herbs have been a cornerstone of healthcare and well-being.

As a child, I was always fascinated with herbs and their medicinal properties. I found it incredible that these plants, which seemed so simple, could be so powerful in treating illness and promoting health. It was then that I realized that throughout history, humanity didn't always have access to modern medicine, but they relied on herbs and natural remedies to heal and stay healthy.

My fascination with herbs only grew as I got older. I began to study the properties and uses of different herbs, learning about their chemical makeup and how they interact with the human body. Eventually, I became a certified holistic herbalist, and my passion for herbs and natural medicine continues to grow every day.

This book is the culmination of my years of study and exploration into the world of herbs. In it, I hope to share my knowledge and passion for these plants with others who are curious about their medicinal uses.

In the following chapters, we'll explore the properties and uses of some of the most commonly used herbs, such as chamomile, lavender, and peppermint, as well as some lesser-known herbs like yarrow and elecampane. We'll delve into the history of these plants and how they've been used throughout the ages, as well as the scientific research that has been done to confirm their healing properties.

We'll also explore how to prepare and use herbs in a variety of forms, including teas, tinctures, and salves. With step-by-step instructions and helpful tips, you'll learn how to create your own herbal remedies at home, using simple ingredients and easy-to-follow techniques.

One of the most important things to understand about herbs is that they are not a replacement for modern medicine. While herbs can be incredibly powerful in treating many common ailments, it's important to seek professional medical advice for any serious conditions or illnesses.

That being said, incorporating herbs into your daily routine can be a wonderful way to support your overall health and wellness. Whether you're dealing with stress and anxiety, digestive issues, or just looking for ways to boost your immune system, there's an herb out there that can help.

Throughout this book, I hope to inspire you to explore the world of herbs and natural medicine. By learning about the properties and uses of these incredible plants, you'll be better equipped to make informed decisions about your health and well-being. So, grab a cup of herbal tea, sit back, and let's dive into the fascinating world of herbs!

Definition of Herbs

Herbs are a type of plant that is used for culinary, medicinal, and ornamental purposes. They are characterized by their soft, green stems and leaves, and they may produce flowers or seeds as well. Herbs have been used for thousands of years by different cultures around the world for their various benefits.

Culinary herbs are used in cooking to add flavor, aroma, or color to dishes. They are often added to soups, stews, salads, marinades, sauces, and other dishes, and can be used either fresh or dried. Some common culinary herbs include basil, rosemary, thyme, parsley, oregano, and sage. These herbs are often high in antioxidants, vitamins, and minerals, and can have a range of health benefits when consumed regularly in moderate amounts.

Medicinal herbs, on the other hand, are used for their therapeutic properties. These plants may be used in various forms, such as teas, tinctures, extracts, or capsules, and they may be used to treat a wide range of health conditions, including digestive issues, respiratory problems, anxiety, and inflammation. Some commonly used medicinal herbs include echinacea, chamomile, ginger, ginkgo biloba, and valerian. Many medicinal herbs contain active compounds such as alkaloids, flavonoids, terpenes, and essential oils, which have been shown to have various biological effects on the body.

In addition to their culinary and medicinal uses, herbs are also often used for ornamental purposes. These plants may be grown for their aesthetic qualities, such as their colorful flowers or attractive foliage. Some common ornamental herbs include lavender, rosemary, and thyme, which are often grown in gardens or containers for their beauty and fragrance.

Herbs are generally distinguished from other types of plants by their fragrant and flavorful leaves, stems, flowers, and roots. They can be annual or perennial, and can grow in a wide range of environments, from temperate forests to hot and arid deserts. Some herbs are native to specific regions or continents, while others have been introduced and cultivated around the world.

There are many different ways to classify herbs, based on their uses, botanical properties, or cultural traditions. One common distinction is between culinary herbs, which are used primarily for flavoring and seasoning food, and medicinal herbs, which are used to treat or prevent various health conditions.

However, many herbs have both culinary and medicinal properties, and their uses can overlap and vary depending on the context and culture.

Herbs have been used in traditional medicine systems around the world for thousands of years, and many of these practices continue to be used today. In Ayurvedic medicine, for example, herbs are used to balance the body's three doshas, or energies, and to treat a wide range of conditions, from digestive disorders to skin problems. In traditional Chinese medicine, herbs are used in combination with other therapies, such as acupuncture and massage, to treat various diseases and promote overall health.

Despite their long history of use and their many potential benefits, herbs can also have side effects and interactions with other medications or health conditions. Some herbs can be toxic in large amounts or when taken in certain forms, and some can interact with prescription drugs or cause allergic reactions in sensitive individuals. It is important to consult a healthcare professional or a qualified herbalist before using herbs for any purpose, and to carefully follow dosage and preparation instructions.

Herbs are a diverse and valuable group of plants that have been used for thousands of years for their culinary, medicinal, and ornamental properties. They are a rich source of nutrients and bioactive compounds that can support health and wellbeing in many ways. However, their use should be approached with caution and care, and it is important to seek professional

Brief History of Herbs

The use of herbs for medicinal purposes is a practice that dates back thousands of years and has been embraced by many cultures around the world. The earliest recorded evidence of herbal medicine comes from ancient China, where people have been using herbs to treat illnesses for over 3,000 years. In traditional Chinese medicine, herbal remedies are often prescribed in combination with other treatments such as acupuncture and massage therapy.

Some of the most commonly used herbs in traditional Chinese medicine include ginseng, ginger, and licorice root. Ginseng is believed to improve cognitive function and boost the immune system, while ginger is used to relieve nausea and promote digestion. Licorice root is often used to soothe coughs and sore throats.

The ancient Greeks also recognized the power of herbs for medicinal purposes, and their use of plants in medicine is well-documented. Hippocrates, often referred to as the father of modern medicine, believed that the body had the power to heal itself, and that herbs could help facilitate this healing process. He wrote extensively about the medicinal properties of herbs, and used them in his treatments.

During the Middle Ages, herbal medicine continued to be an important part of healthcare. Monks and nuns were often the ones who cultivated and prepared herbs, and they passed down their knowledge of herbal remedies from generation to generation. In fact, many of the most well-known herbal remedies today, such as lavender for relaxation and peppermint for digestion, have their roots in traditional herbal medicine from this time period.

In the 19th century, modern medicine began to emerge, and herbal medicine fell out of favor as people turned to pharmaceuticals. The development of synthetic drugs meant that doctors and patients could treat illnesses more quickly and effectively than ever before, but this came at the expense of natural remedies like herbs. However, in recent years, there has been a renewed interest in herbal medicine, and many people are now turning to herbs as a natural way to treat common ailments.

One of the most popular medicinal herbs today is echinacea, which is used to boost the immune system and prevent and treat colds and other respiratory infections. It is believed to work by stimulating the production of white blood cells, which play a key role in the body's immune response. Another commonly used herb is peppermint, which can soothe digestive issues such as gas, bloating, and stomach cramps. Chamomile is also a popular herb that is often used as a natural sleep aid.

In addition to these well-known herbs, there are many others that have been found to have medicinal properties. For example, turmeric is a spice that is often used in cooking, but it also has anti-inflammatory properties and is believed to be beneficial for conditions such as arthritis and heart disease. St. John's wort is an herb that is commonly used to treat mild to moderate depression, while valerian root is used as a natural remedy for anxiety and insomnia.

Research into the potential uses of herbs is ongoing, and new studies are constantly being conducted to uncover the medicinal properties of different plants. One area of research that is particularly promising is the use of herbs in cancer treatment. Many herbs contain compounds that have anti-cancer properties, and researchers are exploring how these compounds can be used in combination with traditional cancer treatments to improve outcomes for patients.

Despite the many benefits of herbs for medicinal purposes, it's important to note that not all herbs are safe for everyone to use. Some herbs can interact with medications or cause side effects, so it's important to talk to a healthcare professional before using herbs as a treatment for any condition. Additionally, herbs should never be used as a substitute for traditional medical treatments without the guidance of a qualified healthcare provider.

The history of herbs and their medicinal use is a long and fascinating one that spans thousands of years and numerous cultures. Throughout history, people have recognized the healing properties of plants and have used them to treat a wide range of ailments, from minor to severe.

One of the reasons herbs have been so widely used for medicinal purposes is their accessibility. Unlike pharmaceutical drugs, which often require a prescription and can be expensive, many medicinal herbs can be easily grown in a backyard garden or purchased at a local health food store.

Additionally, herbs often have fewer side effects than pharmaceuticals, which can make them a safer option for some people. Of course, as with any medication, it's important to use caution when taking herbs and to speak with a healthcare provider before starting any new treatment.

In recent years, there has been a growing interest in herbal medicine and a movement towards more natural and holistic forms of healthcare. As people become more aware of the potential benefits of herbs, they are seeking out natural remedies for everything from headaches to anxiety.

While some people may view herbal medicine as an alternative to conventional medicine, many practitioners believe that the two can be used together in a complementary way. For example, a person with high blood pressure may take medication prescribed by their doctor, but they may also incorporate hawthorn berry, an herb known for its ability to support heart health, into their daily routine.

As the use of herbs for medicinal purposes continues to grow, researchers are also studying the potential benefits of these plants. For example, studies have shown that curcumin, a compound found in turmeric, may have anti-inflammatory and antioxidant properties. And research has also suggested that garlic may help lower blood pressure and cholesterol levels.

Of course, not all herbs are safe for everyone, and some may interact with medications or cause allergic reactions. That's why it's important to do your research and speak with a healthcare provider before using any new herb or supplement.

The history of herbs and their medicinal use is a long and fascinating one that spans thousands of years and numerous cultures. From ancient China to modern-day America, people have recognized the healing properties of plants and have used them to treat a wide range of ailments. As we continue to learn more about the potential benefits of herbs, it's clear that they will continue to play an important role in healthcare for many years to come.

Different Types of Herbs and There Uses

There are countless herbs out there, but I'll touch on some of the most commonly used ones.

First up, let's talk about chamomile. Chamomile is often consumed as a tea and is known for its calming effects. It can help with anxiety, insomnia, and digestive issues. Some people also use chamomile topically to soothe skin irritations or wounds.

Next, we have ginger. Ginger is often used as a spice in cooking, but it also has medicinal properties. It can help with nausea, inflammation, and pain. Some people also use ginger to aid digestion or relieve cold and flu symptoms.

Peppermint is another popular herb with medicinal properties. It's often consumed as a tea or used in essential oils. Peppermint can help with digestive issues, headaches, and congestion.

Moving on to garlic. Garlic is a staple in many kitchens, but it also has a range of health benefits. It has antibacterial and antiviral properties, and can help with high blood pressure and cholesterol levels. Some people also use garlic to boost their immune system.

Echinacea is an herb that's often used to prevent or treat colds and flu. It can also help with inflammation and boost the immune system. Some people take echinacea supplements, while others consume it in tea form.

St. John's Wort is an herb that's often used to treat mild depression and anxiety. It can also help with nerve pain and sleep issues. However, it can interact with certain medications, so it's important to talk to a healthcare provider before using St. John's Wort.

Valerian root is an herb that's commonly used to aid with sleep issues. It can also help with anxiety and stress. Some people take valerian root supplements, while others consume it in tea form.

Milk thistle is an herb that's often used to support liver health. It can help with liver damage, inflammation, and detoxification. Some people also use milk thistle to lower cholesterol levels or aid digestion.

Turmeric is an herb that's often used as a spice in cooking. It has anti-inflammatory properties and can help with joint pain, digestive issues, and skin conditions. Some people take turmeric supplements, while others consume it in tea form.

Lastly, we have ginseng. Ginseng is an herb that's often used to boost energy and cognitive function. It can also help with stress and inflammation. Some people take ginseng supplements, while others consume it in tea form.

There are many more herbs out there with medicinal properties, but hopefully this gives you a good starting point. We will discuss more herbs later in this book. It's important to note that while herbs can have many health benefits, they can also interact with medications or have side effects. It's always a good idea to talk to a healthcare provider before using herbs for medicinal purposes.

Understanding Herbs

Herbs have been used for centuries for their medicinal and culinary properties. They are an integral part of various cultures and traditions, and continue to be popular to this day. In this chapter, we will delve into the fascinating world of herbs and explore their classification based on their use, as well as their structure and anatomy.

We will also discuss the factors that can affect the potency of herbs, including growing conditions, harvesting methods, and storage. Furthermore, we will explore the active ingredients in herbs and how they work to provide us with their medicinal benefits.

Whether you are a seasoned herbalist or someone who is just starting to explore the world of herbs, this chapter will provide you with a comprehensive understanding of these amazing plants and their potential benefits. So, let's begin our journey into the world of herbs and discover the secrets that they hold!

Classification Of Herbs Based On Their Use

Herbs are nature's treasures, providing us with a diverse range of uses and benefits. They have been used for centuries for their medicinal properties, culinary delights, aromatic fragrances, cosmetic benefits, and aesthetic value. The classification of herbs based on their use is an important aspect that helps us understand and utilize their properties effectively.

Each category of herbs serves a unique purpose and offers a plethora of benefits. Whether it's the tantalizing flavors and aromas of culinary herbs, the soothing and healing properties of medicinal herbs, or the beauty and elegance of ornamental herbs, there is no denying the versatility of these incredible plants. Understanding the various categories of herbs and their uses can help us incorporate them into our daily lives and reap the benefits they offer.

Herbs can be classified based on their use for different purposes such as culinary, medicinal, aromatic, cosmetic, and ornamental. Here is a detailed classification of herbs based on their use.
- Culinary Herbs
- Medicinal Herbs
- Aromatic Herbs

- Cosmetic Herbs
- Ornamental Herbs

Culinary Herbs:

Culinary herbs are the most common type of herbs used in cooking. These herbs are used to add flavor, aroma, and color to dishes. Culinary herbs can be further classified into three categories:

Flavoring Herbs:

These herbs are used to add flavor to dishes. Examples include parsley, basil, thyme, and oregano. Flavoring herbs are a popular category of culinary herbs that are used to add flavor, aroma, and depth to dishes. These herbs are essential for enhancing the taste of various cuisines and are widely used in many cultures worldwide. They can be used fresh or dried, depending on the recipe.

Parsley is one of the most commonly used flavoring herbs, known for its fresh and vibrant flavor. It is used in a variety of dishes such as soups, stews, sauces, and salads. Parsley is also a good source of vitamins and minerals, making it a healthy addition to any dish.

Basil is another popular herb used for its unique flavor profile. It has a sweet, slightly peppery taste and is commonly used in Italian cuisine, especially in dishes like pesto, caprese salad, and tomato-based pasta sauces. Basil also has antibacterial properties and is known for its anti-inflammatory effects.

Thyme is a herb that belongs to the mint family and has a strong, aromatic flavor. It is commonly used in Mediterranean and French cuisines and is an essential ingredient in many classic dishes such as beef stew, roast chicken, and tomato sauce. Thyme also has antimicrobial properties and is believed to have medicinal benefits for respiratory and digestive issues.

Oregano is a herb that has a pungent, slightly bitter taste and is commonly used in Mediterranean and Mexican cuisines. It is an essential ingredient in pizza and pasta sauces and is also used in marinades, dressings, and roasted vegetables. Oregano is also known for its antioxidant and antimicrobial properties, making it a popular herb in natural remedies.

Overall, flavoring herbs are an essential ingredient in many dishes and offer a variety of flavors and health benefits. They are easy to grow and can be used fresh or dried, making them a convenient and versatile ingredient for home cooking.

Aromatic Herbs:
These herbs are used to add aroma to dishes. Examples include rosemary, sage, and marjoram.

Aromatic herbs are a category of herbs that are known for their pleasing scents and are commonly used in cooking to add aroma and flavor to dishes. These herbs are often used in small quantities and can make a big difference in the overall taste and aroma of a dish.

Rosemary is a woody herb with needle-like leaves and a strong, fragrant aroma. It is commonly used in Mediterranean and Middle Eastern cuisines, especially in meat dishes like roasted lamb or chicken. Rosemary is also known for its antioxidant properties and has been shown to have anti-inflammatory effects.

Sage is an herb with soft, velvety leaves and a warm, earthy aroma. It is commonly used in Italian and Mediterranean cuisines and is an essential ingredient in classic dishes like sage butter sauce and sausage stuffing. Sage is also believed to have medicinal properties and has been used for centuries to treat digestive and respiratory issues.

Marjoram is a herb with delicate, sweet-smelling leaves and a subtle, floral aroma. It is commonly used in Mediterranean and Middle Eastern cuisines and is an essential ingredient in dishes like pizza, tomato sauce, and roasted vegetables. Marjoram is also believed to have antimicrobial properties and has been used for centuries to treat digestive and respiratory issues.

Other examples of aromatic herbs include thyme, bay leaves, and tarragon. These herbs are often used in combination with other herbs and spices to create complex and flavorful dishes.

In addition to their culinary uses, aromatic herbs are also commonly used in aromatherapy and as natural remedies for various ailments. They can be used in essential oils, herbal teas, and natural skincare products, among other things.

Garnishing Herbs:
These herbs are used to add color and decoration to dishes. Examples include chives, parsley, and cilantro.

Garnishing herbs are a category of herbs that are used to add color and visual interest to dishes. They are typically used in small quantities as a finishing touch to a dish, and their purpose is primarily aesthetic rather than adding flavor or aroma.

Chives are a type of onion that are commonly used as a garnish due to their mild flavor and bright green color. They are often used to top soups, salads, and baked potatoes. Chives are also a good source of vitamins A and C.

Parsley is a popular herb that is often used as a garnish due to its bright green color and delicate, fresh flavor. It is commonly used to top salads, soups, and meat dishes. Parsley is also a good source of vitamins A and C, as well as iron and calcium.

Cilantro, also known as coriander, is a herb with a distinct, pungent flavor and a bright green color. It is commonly used in Mexican and Asian cuisines, and is often used as a garnish for dishes like tacos, curries, and soups. Cilantro is a good source of vitamins A and C, as well as iron and calcium.

Other examples of garnishing herbs include dill, basil, and mint. These herbs are often used to add color and visual interest to dishes, and can also provide a subtle flavor that complements the other ingredients in a dish.

In addition to their culinary uses, garnishing herbs can also be used in decorative arrangements, such as in flower arrangements or as part of table settings.

Medicinal Herbs:

Medicinal herbs are used to treat various ailments and promote overall health and wellness. These herbs can be further classified based on their medicinal properties:

Anti-inflammatory Herbs:

These herbs help reduce inflammation in the body. Examples include turmeric, ginger, and chamomile.

Anti-inflammatory herbs are a category of herbs that have been shown to help reduce inflammation in the body. Inflammation is a natural response of the immune system to injury or infection, but chronic inflammation can contribute to a range of health problems, including heart disease, diabetes, and cancer. Anti-inflammatory herbs can be a natural way to help reduce inflammation and promote overall health and wellness.

Turmeric is a bright yellow spice that is commonly used in Indian and Middle Eastern cuisine. It contains a compound called curcumin, which has been shown to have potent anti-inflammatory effects. Studies have shown that curcumin can help reduce inflammation in the body and may be effective in treating conditions such as arthritis, heart disease, and Alzheimer's disease.

Ginger is a root that is commonly used as a spice in cooking and as a natural remedy for a range of health problems. It contains compounds called gingerols and shogaols, which have been shown to have anti-inflammatory effects. Ginger has been used to treat a range of conditions, including arthritis, digestive issues, and respiratory infections.

Chamomile is a flowering plant that has been used for centuries as a natural remedy for a range of health problems, including inflammation. Chamomile contains compounds called flavonoids, which have been shown to have anti-inflammatory effects. Chamomile tea is a popular way to consume chamomile and is often used to promote relaxation and improve sleep.

Other examples of anti-inflammatory herbs include garlic, rosemary, and green tea. These herbs have been shown to have anti-inflammatory effects and may help reduce the risk of chronic diseases associated with inflammation.

It's important to note that while anti-inflammatory herbs can be a natural way to help reduce inflammation in the body, they should not be used as a substitute for medical treatment. If you are experiencing chronic inflammation or other health problems, it's important to consult with a healthcare professional for diagnosis and treatment.

Digestive Herbs:
These herbs aid in digestion and help relieve digestive issues. Examples include peppermint, fennel, and ginger.

Digestive herbs are a group of herbs that have traditionally been used to support healthy digestion and relieve digestive issues. These herbs can help improve digestion by stimulating the production of digestive juices, increasing blood flow to the digestive system, and relaxing the muscles of the digestive tract.

Some of the most popular digestive herbs include:
Peppermint: Peppermint is a popular herb that has been used for centuries to aid digestion. It contains menthol, which helps to relax the muscles of the digestive tract and reduce bloating, gas, and cramps.

Fennel: Fennel is another herb that is commonly used to aid digestion. It contains compounds that help to relax the muscles of the digestive tract and reduce bloating, gas, and cramps.

Ginger: Ginger is a well-known digestive herb that has been used for centuries to treat nausea, vomiting, and other digestive issues. It contains compounds that help to stimulate digestion, increase blood flow to the digestive system, and reduce inflammation.

Chamomile: Chamomile is a soothing herb that can help to calm the digestive system and reduce inflammation. It is often used to relieve digestive issues such as bloating, gas, and indigestion.

Dandelion: Dandelion is a bitter herb that can help to stimulate digestion and increase the production of digestive juices. It is often used to relieve constipation and improve overall digestive health.

Licorice: Licorice is a sweet-tasting herb that has been used for centuries to treat digestive issues such as heartburn and indigestion. It contains compounds that help to soothe inflammation and protect the lining of the digestive tract.

Digestive herbs can be consumed in a variety of forms, including teas, tinctures, capsules, and powders. They can also be added to food and drinks to enhance their flavor and digestive benefits. It is important to consult with a healthcare practitioner before using digestive herbs, especially if you are pregnant, breastfeeding, or taking medication.

Immune-boosting Herbs:
These herbs help strengthen the immune system and protect against infections. Examples include echinacea, garlic, and elderberry.

Immune-boosting herbs are those that have been traditionally used to support and strengthen the immune system, helping to prevent and fight off infections. These herbs contain natural compounds that have anti-inflammatory, antibacterial, antiviral, and immune-boosting properties.

Here are some examples of immune-boosting herbs and their benefits:

Echinacea: Echinacea is a powerful immune-boosting herb that has been used for centuries to prevent and treat colds, flu, and other respiratory infections. It contains compounds that stimulate the production of white blood cells, which help to fight off infections.

Garlic: Garlic is a natural antibiotic that has been used for centuries to treat infections. It contains compounds that have antiviral, antibacterial, and immune-boosting properties. Garlic is also rich in antioxidants, which help to protect the body from damage caused by free radicals.

Elderberry: Elderberry is a powerful immune-boosting herb that has been used for centuries to prevent and treat colds, flu, and other respiratory infections. It contains compounds that help to stimulate the immune system and reduce inflammation in the body.

Astragalus: Astragalus is an adaptogenic herb that has been used in traditional Chinese medicine for thousands of years to support the immune system. It contains compounds that help to stimulate the production of white blood cells and enhance the body's ability to fight off infections.

Ginger: Ginger is a natural anti-inflammatory herb that has been used for centuries to treat digestive issues and other health problems. It contains compounds that help to reduce inflammation in the body and stimulate the immune system.

Turmeric: Turmeric is a potent anti-inflammatory herb that has been used for centuries to treat a variety of health problems. It contains compounds that help to reduce inflammation in the body and support the immune system.

These immune-boosting herbs can be used in a variety of ways, including as teas, tinctures, or supplements. However, it's important to talk to a healthcare professional before using any herbs or supplements, especially if you're pregnant, breastfeeding, or taking medication.

Aromatic Herbs:

Aromatic herbs are used for their pleasing scents and are commonly used in perfumes, soaps, and other cosmetic products. Aromatic herbs can be further classified based on their scent:

Floral Herbs:

These herbs have a sweet, floral scent. Examples include lavender, rose, and chamomile.

Floral herbs are a type of aromatic herbs that have a sweet, floral scent. They are commonly used in perfumes, soaps, and other cosmetic products for their pleasant aroma. However, they also have therapeutic properties and can be used for medicinal purposes.

Lavender is a popular floral herb that is known for its calming and relaxing properties. It is often used in aromatherapy to promote relaxation and relieve anxiety. Lavender oil can also be used topically to relieve pain, inflammation, and skin irritation.

Rose is another popular floral herb that is used in perfumes and other cosmetic products for its sweet and romantic scent. It is also used for its skin-benefiting properties. Rose oil is a natural astringent and can help tone and tighten the skin, reducing the appearance of wrinkles and fine lines.

Chamomile is a gentle and soothing floral herb that is commonly used in teas and other natural remedies. It is known for its calming properties and is often used to relieve stress and anxiety. Chamomile tea can also help relieve digestive issues and promote better sleep.

Other examples of floral herbs include jasmine, ylang-ylang, and neroli. These herbs are often used in aromatherapy for their mood-enhancing properties and can help promote relaxation, reduce stress, and improve overall wellbeing.

Woody Herbs:
These herbs have a strong, woody scent. Examples include cedarwood, sandalwood, and frankincense.

Woody herbs are a type of aromatic herbs that are known for their strong and woody scent. These herbs are often used in perfumes, candles, and incense, as well as in aromatherapy and skincare products. Some popular examples of woody herbs include:

Cedarwood: Cedarwood has a warm, woody scent that is often used in men's fragrances. It is also known for its insect-repelling properties and is commonly used in natural insect repellents.

Sandalwood: Sandalwood has a sweet, woody scent that is often used in perfumes and colognes. It is also known for its relaxing and calming properties and is commonly used in aromatherapy.

Frankincense: Frankincense has a sweet, resinous scent that is often used in incense and religious ceremonies. It is also known for its anti-inflammatory and anti-anxiety properties and is commonly used in aromatherapy.

Patchouli: Patchouli has a strong, earthy scent that is often used in perfumes and colognes. It is also known for its antifungal and antibacterial properties and is commonly used in skincare products.

Vetiver: Vetiver has a smoky, earthy scent that is often used in perfumes and colognes. It is also known for its grounding and calming properties and is commonly used in aromatherapy.

Overall, woody herbs have a wide range of uses and benefits, from their pleasant scent to their therapeutic properties. They are a popular choice in the fragrance and skincare industries and are also commonly used in natural remedies and alternative therapies.

Spicy Herbs:
   These herbs have a warm, spicy scent. Examples include cinnamon, clove, and nutmeg.

   Spicy herbs are a category of aromatic herbs known for their warm, spicy, and often pungent aroma. These herbs are commonly used in cooking, as well as in cosmetics and fragrances. Some popular examples of spicy herbs include:

   Cinnamon: Cinnamon is a versatile spice that can be used in both sweet and savory dishes. It has a warm, sweet, and spicy flavor that pairs well with apples, pears, and pumpkin.

   Clove: Clove has a strong, sweet, and spicy flavor that is often used in baking and cooking. It is also used in traditional medicine for its antiseptic and analgesic properties.

   Nutmeg: Nutmeg is a warm and aromatic spice with a slightly sweet and nutty flavor. It is often used in sweet dishes like pumpkin pie and eggnog, as well as in savory dishes like stews and curries.

   Ginger: Ginger has a warm and spicy flavor that adds depth and complexity to dishes. It is commonly used in Asian cuisine and is also known for its medicinal properties, including anti-inflammatory and digestive benefits.

   Cardamom: Cardamom is a fragrant spice with a sweet and slightly spicy flavor. It is commonly used in Indian and Middle Eastern cuisine and is also known for its digestive and detoxifying properties.

   Spicy herbs are often used in combination with other herbs and spices to create complex and flavorful dishes. They are also used in aromatherapy and other forms of alternative medicine for their various health benefits.

Cosmetic Herbs:

Cosmetic herbs are used in skincare and beauty products. These herbs can be further classified based on their skin benefits:

Moisturizing Herbs:

These herbs help hydrate and nourish the skin. Examples include aloe vera, rosehip, and shea butter.

Moisturizing herbs are commonly used in skincare and beauty products to help hydrate and nourish the skin. These herbs contain natural compounds that help to lock in moisture and prevent the skin from drying out.

Some examples of moisturizing herbs include:
Aloe vera: Aloe vera is a succulent plant that has been used for centuries for its medicinal properties. It contains a gel-like substance that is rich in vitamins, minerals, and antioxidants. Aloe vera is a popular ingredient in moisturizing lotions and creams due to its ability to soothe and hydrate the skin.

Rosehip: Rosehip is the fruit of the rose plant and is known for its high concentration of vitamin C and essential fatty acids. These nutrients help to moisturize and brighten the skin while reducing the appearance of fine lines and wrinkles. Rosehip oil is a popular ingredient in facial serums and moisturizers.

Shea butter: Shea butter is a fat extracted from the nuts of the African shea tree. It is rich in vitamins A and E, as well as essential fatty acids that help to moisturize and protect the skin. Shea butter is commonly used in body lotions, lip balms, and hair care products.

Jojoba oil: Jojoba oil is a liquid wax extracted from the seeds of the jojoba plant. It is similar in composition to the natural oils produced by the skin, making it an excellent moisturizer. Jojoba oil is commonly used in facial oils and hair care products due to its ability to hydrate and nourish without leaving a greasy residue.

Overall, moisturizing herbs are a great way to keep your skin healthy and hydrated, and they can be found in a variety of skincare and beauty products.

Anti-aging Herbs:

These herbs help reduce the signs of aging, such as wrinkles and fine lines. Examples include ginseng, green tea, and turmeric.

Anti-aging herbs are known for their ability to help reduce the signs of aging, including wrinkles, fine lines, and age spots. They work by protecting the skin from damage caused by free radicals, which are unstable molecules that can cause oxidative stress and damage to skin cells.

Here are some examples of anti-aging herbs and their benefits:

Ginseng: Ginseng is a popular anti-aging herb that has been used for centuries in traditional medicine. It contains compounds called ginsenosides, which have antioxidant and anti-inflammatory properties. These properties help to protect the skin from damage and reduce the appearance of fine lines and wrinkles.

Green tea: Green tea is rich in antioxidants, particularly a group of compounds called catechins. These antioxidants help to protect the skin from damage caused by free radicals and can help to reduce the appearance of fine lines and wrinkles. Green tea also has anti-inflammatory properties, which can help to reduce redness and inflammation in the skin.

Turmeric: Turmeric is a spice that has been used for centuries in traditional medicine. It contains a compound called curcumin, which has antioxidant and anti-inflammatory properties. These properties help to protect the skin from damage and reduce the appearance of fine lines and wrinkles. Turmeric also has antibacterial properties, which can help to prevent acne and other skin infections.

Overall, anti-aging herbs can be a great addition to a skincare routine, helping to protect the skin from damage and reduce the signs of aging.

Soothing Herbs:

These herbs help calm and soothe irritated skin. Examples include chamomile, calendula, and lavender.

Soothing herbs are commonly used in skincare products to calm and soothe irritated skin. These herbs contain anti-inflammatory and anti-irritant properties that help to reduce redness, itching, and inflammation.

Chamomile is a popular soothing herb that is often used in skincare products. It is known for its calming and anti-inflammatory properties, which help to soothe irritated skin. Chamomile is also rich in antioxidants that protect the skin from damage caused by free radicals.

Calendula is another popular soothing herb that is often used in skincare products. It is known for its anti-inflammatory, antibacterial, and antifungal properties, which help to soothe and heal irritated skin. Calendula is also rich in antioxidants that protect the skin from damage.

Lavender is a soothing herb that is often used in aromatherapy to promote relaxation and reduce stress. It is also known for its calming and anti-inflammatory properties, which make it a popular ingredient in skincare products. Lavender is also rich in antioxidants that protect the skin from damage caused by free radicals.

Other soothing herbs include aloe vera, witch hazel, and oatmeal. Aloe vera is a cooling and soothing herb that is commonly used to treat sunburn and other skin irritations. Witch hazel is an astringent herb that is used to soothe and tighten the skin. Oatmeal is a natural emollient that soothes and softens the skin.

Ornamental Herbs:

Ornamental herbs are grown for their aesthetic value and are commonly used in landscaping and gardening. Ornamental herbs can be further classified based on their appearance:

Flowering Herbs:

These herbs have beautiful flowers and are commonly used in flower gardens. Examples include lavender, daisy, and marigold.

Flowering herbs are a type of herb that is characterized by their beautiful flowers. These herbs are often grown for their ornamental value and are commonly used in flower gardens. They can also be used in culinary or medicinal applications.

Some popular examples of flowering herbs include:

Lavender: Known for its fragrant purple flowers, lavender is a popular herb that is often used in aromatherapy and skincare products. It is also used in cooking and baking, adding a floral flavor to dishes.

Daisy: Daisies are a common type of flowering herb that are often grown in gardens for their cheerful blooms. They can also be used in herbal remedies for their anti-inflammatory and pain-relieving properties.

Marigold: Marigolds are another popular flowering herb that are known for their bright orange and yellow blooms. They are often used in skincare products for their anti-inflammatory and healing properties.

Echinacea: Echinacea is a flowering herb that is commonly used for its immune-boosting properties. It is often taken as a supplement to help prevent colds and flu.

Chamomile: Chamomile is a flowering herb that is known for its calming properties. It is often used in herbal teas and skincare products to soothe irritated skin.

Overall, flowering herbs can add beauty and value to a garden, while also providing a range of medicinal and culinary benefits.

Foliage Herbs:
These herbs have attractive foliage and are commonly used in landscaping. Examples include rosemary, thyme, and sage.

Foliage herbs are those herbs that have attractive and distinctive foliage, making them ideal for use in landscaping, gardens, and container gardens. These herbs are often prized for their fragrant and ornamental leaves, which come in a variety of colors, shapes, and textures.

Rosemary is a popular foliage herb, known for its woody stems and needle-like leaves. It has a distinctive aroma and is commonly used in cooking.

Thyme is another popular foliage herb, with small, aromatic leaves that can be used fresh or dried in a variety of dishes. Sage is a foliage herb with a distinctively earthy, slightly bitter flavor that is often used in stuffing or as a seasoning for meats.

Other examples of foliage herbs include basil, which has large, tender leaves and a sweet, spicy flavor, and parsley, which has curly or flat leaves and is used as a garnish or seasoning. Many foliage herbs also have medicinal properties and are used in natural remedies and herbal medicine.

Foliage herbs are versatile and easy to grow, making them a popular choice for home gardens and landscaping projects. They can be grown in containers, raised beds, or directly in the ground, and require minimal care and maintenance.

Overall, herbs have a wide range of uses and benefits, and their classification based on their use can help in their selection and application in various contexts.

Herbs are versatile plants with various uses in cooking, skincare, and medicine. They are categorized into different groups based on their characteristics and properties. Flavoring, aromatic, and garnishing herbs add taste, aroma, and decoration to dishes, respectively. Anti-inflammatory, digestive, immune-boosting, anti-aging, and soothing herbs offer a range of health benefits. Floral, woody, and spicy herbs provide distinct scents for perfumes and aromatherapy.

Moisturizing herbs hydrate and nourish the skin, while flowering and foliage herbs are popular in gardening and landscaping. With their diverse properties and uses, herbs have become a valuable and essential part of our daily lives.

The Structure and Anatomy Of Herbs

The structure and anatomy of herbs are essential to their growth, survival, and usefulness to humans. Herbs have roots, stems, leaves, and flowers that all have specific functions. The roots absorb water and nutrients, the stem provides support and transport, the leaves produce energy through photosynthesis, and the flowers are responsible for reproduction. Herbs come in a variety of colors, shapes, and sizes, and each characteristic can provide insight into their properties and potential uses. By understanding the anatomy of herbs, we can better appreciate their value in various industries and cultivate them effectively for medicinal and culinary purposes.

Herbs are a type of plant that have been used for medicinal and culinary purposes for centuries. They come in a variety of shapes, sizes, and colors, but most have a similar basic structure.

The anatomy of herbs consists of several parts. The roots are the part of the plant that absorbs water and nutrients from the soil. The stem is the main body of the plant, providing support and transporting nutrients from the roots to the leaves.

The leaves are where photosynthesis occurs, and they are responsible for producing energy for the plant. The flowers of herbs are responsible for reproduction, and they contain the plant's reproductive organs.

The leaves of herbs are typically green and have a variety of shapes, ranging from round to elongated and pointed. The edges of the leaves can be smooth, serrated, or lobed, depending on the type of herb. Some herbs, such as mint and basil, have square stems, while others, such as rosemary and thyme, have woody stems.

The roots of herbs can vary in shape and size depending on the plant. Some herbs, such as ginger and turmeric, have fleshy, bulbous roots, while others, such as echinacea and goldenseal, have thin, fibrous roots.

In addition to varying in shape and size, the roots of herbs also play a vital role in the plant's overall health and survival. The roots of most herbs grow deep into the soil in search of water and nutrients. They are often densely branched to increase the surface area for absorption.

Fleshy roots, such as those found in ginger and turmeric, are specialized structures that store nutrients and water for the plant to use during times of drought or when nutrients are scarce. These types of roots are also capable of reproducing the plant through vegetative propagation, allowing new plants to grow from sections of the root.

Thin, fibrous roots, such as those found in echinacea and goldenseal, have a large surface area and are adapted for efficient absorption of nutrients and water from the soil. These roots are also important for stabilizing the plant in the soil and preventing erosion.

The roots of herbs play an essential role in the plant's growth and survival, and understanding the anatomy and function of the roots can help in the cultivation and harvesting of herbs for medicinal and culinary use.

The flowers of herbs can be various colors, such as purple, white, yellow, and pink. They can be shaped like cones, spikes, or clusters. Some herbs, such as chamomile and lavender, are known for their fragrant flowers.

The flowers of herbs are not only visually appealing but can also have various uses in different industries. For example, chamomile flowers are commonly used in tea and skincare products for their calming properties, while lavender flowers are often used in aromatherapy and as a natural remedy for anxiety and stress.

The colors of herb flowers can also indicate certain properties. For example, purple flowers often indicate anti-inflammatory properties, as seen in herbs such as lavender and echinacea. Yellow flowers are associated with digestive health, as seen in herbs such as dandelion and calendula.

The shape of herb flowers can also have practical uses. Spiky flowers, such as those seen in herbs like rosemary and thyme, can be used as skewers for grilling, while cone-shaped flowers, such as those seen in hops, are used in the brewing of beer.

The flowers of herbs play an important role in their uses and applications, and their colors and shapes can provide insight into their properties and potential uses.

Overall, the structure and anatomy of herbs are designed to support their growth and reproduction, as well as provide important medicinal and culinary benefits to humans. Understanding the anatomy of herbs can help us better appreciate their diversity and uses.

In summary, herbs are a diverse group of plants that have unique anatomical features. Their roots, stems, leaves, and flowers all have specific functions that contribute to the plant's overall health and survival. The roots absorb water and nutrients, while the stem provides support and transport of nutrients. The leaves produce energy through photosynthesis, and the flowers are responsible for reproduction. Herbs can have various colors, shapes, and sizes, and each of these characteristics can provide insight into their properties and potential uses. By understanding the structure and anatomy of herbs, we can better appreciate their value in different industries and cultivate them more effectively for medicinal and culinary purposes.

Factors Affecting The Potency Of Herbs

Herbs have been used for centuries for their medicinal and culinary properties. These plants contain various active compounds that can have therapeutic effects on the human body. However, the potency of herbs can be affected by several factors, which can impact their effectiveness. Understanding these factors can help to ensure that herbs are used safely and effectively. In this article, we will discuss the different factors that can affect the potency of herbs, including growing conditions, harvesting and processing, storage, age, plant part, and genetic variation. We will also explore how these factors can influence the effectiveness of herbs and how to maximize their potency.

The potency of herbs can be affected by various factors, including:

Growing conditions: The quality and potency of herbs can be affected by the environment in which they are grown. Factors such as soil quality, temperature, humidity, and sunlight can all impact the potency of herbs.

The quality and potency of herbs are influenced by a variety of factors related to the growing conditions in which they are cultivated. Here are some in-depth details about the various environmental factors that can impact the potency of herbs:

Soil quality: The soil in which herbs are grown plays a critical role in their potency and quality. The soil must be rich in nutrients and minerals to support healthy plant growth. If the soil lacks essential nutrients, the herbs may not develop to their full potential, resulting in lower potency. In addition, the pH of the soil can also impact the absorption of certain minerals, affecting the potency of the herbs. For example, if the soil is too acidic or alkaline, it may affect the absorption of essential minerals such as zinc, which can negatively impact the potency of the herbs.

Temperature: The temperature at which herbs are grown can impact their potency. Some herbs thrive in warmer climates, while others prefer cooler temperatures. High temperatures can cause some herbs to wilt, which can negatively impact their potency. On the other hand, some herbs, such as chili peppers, develop their spiciness when exposed to high temperatures.

Humidity: The amount of moisture in the air, or humidity, can also impact the potency of herbs. Excess moisture can encourage the growth of mold or mildew, which can negatively impact the quality of the herbs. High humidity can also cause some herbs to wilt or rot, which can affect their potency.

Sunlight: The amount of sunlight herbs receive can impact their potency. Some herbs require full sun exposure to develop to their full potential, while others prefer partial shade. Sunlight is essential for photosynthesis, which is the process by which plants convert sunlight into energy. Without adequate sunlight, herbs may not develop to their full potential, resulting in lower potency.

Water: The amount and quality of water herbs receive can also impact their potency. Overwatering can lead to waterlogged soil, which can cause root rot and negatively impact the quality of the herbs. Conversely, underwatering can cause herbs to wilt and negatively impact their potency. The quality of water used for irrigation can also impact the potency of herbs. For example, if the water is high in chlorine or other chemicals, it can negatively impact the quality of the herbs.

The quality and potency of herbs can be significantly impacted by the environmental conditions in which they are grown. Soil quality, temperature, humidity, sunlight, and water are all essential factors that can affect the potency and quality of herbs. By understanding the growing conditions that are optimal for specific herbs, growers can cultivate high-quality herbs with optimal potency.

Harvesting and processing: The timing and methods used for harvesting and processing herbs can also affect their potency. Herbs that are harvested at the right time and processed quickly tend to have higher levels of active compounds.

Harvesting and processing are crucial steps in ensuring the quality and potency of herbs. The timing of the harvest and the methods used to process the herbs can greatly impact the concentration and availability of the plant's active compounds.

The timing of the harvest is critical for optimal potency. Different parts of the plant, such as leaves, flowers, and roots, may contain different active compounds, and the timing of the harvest can affect their concentrations. For example, some herbs may be more potent when harvested before they bloom, while others may be more potent after blooming. Harvesting at the right time is important to ensure that the active compounds are at their highest levels.

In addition to timing, the methods used for harvesting can also impact the quality and potency of herbs. Ideally, herbs should be harvested by hand to minimize damage to the plant and ensure that only the mature parts are harvested. Mechanical harvesting methods can damage the plant and reduce its potency.

After the herbs are harvested, they must be processed quickly to maintain their potency. Drying is the most common method of processing herbs. Proper drying methods can help to preserve the plant's active compounds and prevent the growth of mold and bacteria. The herbs should be spread out in a single layer in a warm, dry, and well-ventilated area to dry. It is important to avoid exposure to direct sunlight or high heat, as this can cause the herbs to lose their potency.

Once the herbs are dry, they may be further processed by grinding, chopping, or extracting. The processing method used can depend on the intended use of the herb. For example, grinding may be used to create a powder for use in capsules, while extracting may be used to create a liquid extract for use in tinctures.

It is important to note that the potency of herbs can decrease over time, even with proper harvesting and processing methods. Therefore, it is essential to store herbs in a cool, dry, and dark place to prevent degradation. Proper storage can help to maintain the potency of the herbs for longer periods.

In summary, the timing and methods used for harvesting and processing herbs can greatly impact their potency. Herbs that are harvested at the right time and processed quickly tend to have higher levels of active compounds. Hand-harvesting and proper drying methods can help to preserve the plant's active compounds and prevent the growth of mold and bacteria. The processing method used can depend on the intended use of the herb. Proper storage is also essential to maintain the potency of herbs over time. By following proper harvesting and processing methods, one can ensure that the herbs are of the highest quality and potency for medicinal or culinary use.

Storage: The way herbs are stored can also affect their potency. Herbs should be stored in a cool, dark, and dry place to prevent moisture and light from degrading their active compounds.

The storage of herbs is an important factor in maintaining their potency and quality. If herbs are not stored properly, their active compounds can degrade and lose their effectiveness. To ensure that herbs retain their potency and flavor, it is essential to store them correctly.

One of the most important factors to consider when storing herbs is the level of moisture in the storage environment. Moisture can cause herbs to mold, decay, or lose their flavor and aroma. As such, herbs should be stored in a cool, dry place with low humidity. The ideal storage temperature for most herbs is between 60-70°F (15-21°C). This temperature range is low enough to prevent mold growth and high enough to prevent the herbs from becoming too dry.

Herbs should also be stored in airtight containers to prevent them from absorbing moisture or other odors from the surrounding environment. Glass jars with tight-fitting lids are often recommended for storing herbs. Plastic bags with zip-lock closures can also work well, as long as they are sealed tightly.

In addition to temperature and moisture, light can also affect the potency of herbs. Light exposure can cause the breakdown of certain compounds in herbs, leading to a loss of potency and flavor. Herbs should be stored in a dark environment, away from direct sunlight. A pantry or cupboard is an ideal storage location for herbs as it is typically dark and cool.

Another important factor to consider when storing herbs is the length of time they will be stored. Herbs should be used within a reasonable time frame to ensure their potency and flavor. As a general rule, dried herbs can be stored for up to a year, while fresh herbs should be used within a few days to a week. It is also important to check for signs of spoilage, such as mold, discoloration, or a rancid smell before using herbs that have been stored for an extended period.

The storage of herbs is an important factor in maintaining their potency and flavor. Herbs should be stored in a cool, dry, and dark environment to prevent the breakdown of active compounds. Airtight containers such as glass jars or plastic bags can be used to store herbs, and it is essential to check for spoilage before using herbs that have been stored for an extended period. By following these storage guidelines, the potency and quality of herbs can be maintained for longer periods.

Age: The age of the herbs can also affect their potency. Fresh herbs tend to be more potent than dried herbs, and the potency of dried herbs can decline over time.

The age of herbs is another factor that can affect their potency. Fresh herbs are generally considered more potent than dried herbs because they contain higher levels of essential oils and other active compounds that can degrade over time. However, fresh herbs are not always practical for storage and transportation, and they have a shorter shelf life than dried herbs.

Drying herbs is a common method of preserving them for later use. When herbs are dried, the water content is removed, and the essential oils and other active compounds become more concentrated.

Drying herbs can also help to prevent the growth of mold and bacteria, which can spoil fresh herbs.

However, the potency of dried herbs can decline over time due to exposure to light, air, and moisture.

Over time, the essential oils and other active compounds can evaporate or break down, reducing the potency of the herb. To prevent this, it is important to store dried herbs in a cool, dark, and dry place, such as a sealed jar in a pantry or cupboard.

The length of time that dried herbs remain potent can vary depending on the type of herb and how it is stored. Generally, herbs that are more delicate, such as basil or cilantro, tend to lose their potency more quickly than hardier herbs such as rosemary or thyme. It is recommended to use dried herbs within one to two years for optimal potency.

It is important to note that the age of herbs can also affect their flavor, aroma, and color, in addition to their potency. As herbs age, they can lose some of their distinct flavors and aromas, and the color of the herb can fade. To ensure the best flavor and aroma, it is recommended to use fresh herbs whenever possible, or use dried herbs that have been properly stored and are within their optimal shelf life.

Plant part: Different parts of the plant can have varying levels of potency. For example, the roots of some herbs may contain higher levels of active compounds than the leaves or flowers.

The potency of herbs can vary depending on which part of the plant is used. Here are some examples:

Roots: The roots of some plants, such as ginseng and valerian, are often used for medicinal purposes because they contain high levels of active compounds. These compounds are often more concentrated in the roots than in other parts of the plant.

The roots of certain plants contain higher levels of active compounds than other parts of the plant. For example, ginseng and valerian are two herbs commonly used for medicinal purposes that have roots with high concentrations of active compounds.

Ginseng is a perennial herb that has been used in traditional medicine for thousands of years. The root of the ginseng plant is known for its adaptogenic properties, which help the body cope with physical and mental stress. The active compounds in ginseng root are called ginsenosides, which have been shown to have a variety of health benefits, including boosting the immune system, improving cognitive function, and reducing inflammation.

Valerian is another herb that is commonly used for medicinal purposes. The root of the valerian plant contains a number of active compounds, including valerenic acid and valeranon. These compounds are known to have sedative and anxiolytic effects, making valerian root a popular natural remedy for anxiety and sleep disorders.

In general, the potency of roots can vary depending on the species of plant, the age of the plant, and the specific growing conditions. It is important to use herbs from a reputable source to ensure that the roots (or any other part of the plant) are of high quality and potency.

Leaves: Other plants, such as peppermint and sage, have leaves that contain high levels of active compounds. The leaves of these plants are often dried and used in teas or other preparations.

Leaves are an important part of many medicinal plants. They contain a variety of active compounds that can have medicinal properties. Different types of leaves can contain different compounds in varying amounts, which can affect their potency and potential uses.

Peppermint is one such plant whose leaves are known for their medicinal properties. Peppermint leaves contain menthol, a compound that has antispasmodic properties, making it useful for treating digestive issues such as irritable bowel syndrome (IBS) and nausea. The leaves of peppermint can also be used to treat headaches, cold and flu symptoms, and even bad breath.

Sage is another plant whose leaves are used for medicinal purposes. The leaves of sage contain compounds such as thujone, cineole, and camphor, which give it antibacterial, antifungal, and antiviral properties. Sage leaves can be used to treat sore throat, coughs, and other respiratory issues. It is also believed to help improve brain function and memory.

When using leaves for medicinal purposes, it is important to ensure that they are properly harvested and processed. Leaves should be harvested at the right time to ensure that they contain the highest levels of active compounds. They should also be dried and stored properly to prevent the loss of these compounds.

In addition to their medicinal properties, leaves can also be used for culinary purposes. Many herbs and spices, such as basil and oregano, have leaves that are used to add flavor to dishes. These leaves can be dried or used fresh, depending on the recipe.

Flowers: Some herbs, such as chamomile and lavender, have flowers that are used for medicinal purposes. These flowers contain essential oils that are believed to have a variety of health benefits.

Flowers of certain herbs have been used for medicinal purposes for centuries. They are often rich in essential oils, which contain volatile compounds that have a variety of therapeutic properties. These essential oils are extracted from the flowers and used in aromatherapy, as well as in other forms of herbal medicine.

Chamomile, for example, is a well-known herb that is commonly used to treat a variety of conditions, including anxiety, insomnia, and digestive problems. The flowers of chamomile contain essential oils that are believed to have a calming effect on the body and help to reduce inflammation.

Similarly, lavender is another popular herb that is often used in aromatherapy and herbal medicine. The flowers of lavender contain essential oils that have a relaxing effect on the body and are believed to help reduce stress and anxiety.

Other herbs that have flowers with medicinal properties include calendula, which is used to treat skin conditions such as eczema and dermatitis, and hibiscus, which is believed to help lower blood pressure and improve heart health.

Stems and Bark: In some plants, such as cinnamon and licorice, the stems or bark contain high levels of active compounds. These parts of the plant are often used in herbal preparations.

Stems and bark of some plants can contain high levels of active compounds that have medicinal properties. These plant parts are often used in traditional medicine and herbal remedies.

Cinnamon, for example, is a spice that is derived from the inner bark of several tree species in the Cinnamomum genus. The bark contains essential oils and other compounds, including cinnamaldehyde, which is believed to have anti-inflammatory and anti-diabetic properties. Cinnamon bark is often used in herbal preparations, such as teas and tinctures, and as a spice in cooking.

Licorice root, on the other hand, is derived from the roots of the Glycyrrhiza glabra plant. The root contains glycyrrhizin, a compound that has anti-inflammatory and anti-viral properties. Licorice root is often used in traditional medicine to treat coughs, sore throat, and other respiratory ailments. It is also used as a flavoring in food and beverages.

Other herbs that have stems or bark that are used for medicinal purposes include:
• Willow bark: contains salicin, a compound that is similar to aspirin and is used to relieve pain and inflammation.

• Cat's claw bark: contains compounds that have anti-inflammatory and immune-boosting properties and are used to treat a variety of ailments, including arthritis and digestive disorders.

• Slippery elm bark: contains mucilage, a substance that can soothe the digestive tract and is used to treat conditions such as irritable bowel syndrome and heartburn.

Stems and bark of certain plants can contain high levels of active compounds that have medicinal properties, and they are often used in traditional medicine and herbal remedies.

It is important to note that different plant parts may be more or less effective for different health conditions. It is always a good idea to consult with a healthcare professional before using any herbal remedies.

Genetic variation: The potency of herbs can also be affected by genetic variation. Different varieties of the same herb may have different levels of active compounds, depending on their genetic makeup.

Genetic variation refers to differences in the DNA sequences between individuals of the same species. In the case of herbs, different varieties of the same plant can have genetic variations that result in different levels of active compounds. For example, different varieties of chamomile may have varying levels of essential oils that contribute to their medicinal properties.

Plant breeders can use genetic variation to create new varieties of herbs with desired traits, such as higher levels of active compounds or improved growth characteristics. This is often achieved through selective breeding, where plants with desirable traits are bred together to create new varieties with those traits.

In addition to selective breeding, genetic engineering techniques can also be used to modify the genetic makeup of herbs. This can be used to introduce or enhance specific traits, such as increasing the levels of active compounds or improving resistance to pests and diseases.

However, it is important to note that genetic variation is just one of several factors that can affect the potency of herbs. Environmental factors, harvesting and processing techniques, and storage conditions can all play a role in determining the levels of active compounds in herbs.

It's important to keep in mind that the potency of herbs can also vary depending on the individual, as factors such as metabolism and health status can affect how the body responds to the active compounds in herbs.

Understanding Active Ingredients In Herbs And How They Work

Active ingredients in herbs refer to the specific compounds present in the plant that have medicinal properties and can be beneficial for health. These compounds can interact with the body in various ways to produce therapeutic effects. For example, some active ingredients in herbs can mimic the effects of certain hormones in the body, while others can stimulate the immune system or act as antioxidants.

To understand how active ingredients in herbs work, it is important to first identify and isolate the specific compounds responsible for the therapeutic effects. This can be done through laboratory testing and analysis. Once the active ingredients have been identified, researchers can study their mechanisms of action in the body.

Some common active ingredients in herbs include:

Alkaloids: These are nitrogen-containing compounds that have a variety of pharmacological effects. Examples include caffeine in coffee, morphine in opium poppy, and nicotine in tobacco.

Alkaloids are a class of organic compounds that contain at least one nitrogen atom in their chemical structure. They are found in a wide range of plants, including those used in traditional medicine and recreational drugs. Alkaloids can have a variety of pharmacological effects on the human body, ranging from stimulant to depressant to hallucinogenic.

Caffeine, which is found in coffee, tea, and some other plants, is a common example of an alkaloid. Caffeine is a central nervous system stimulant that can increase alertness, energy, and focus. Other alkaloids, such as morphine, which is found in the opium poppy, and nicotine, which is found in tobacco, can have more potent effects on the body, including pain relief and addiction.

Some alkaloids, such as ephedrine and pseudoephedrine, are used as decongestants and appetite suppressants. Others, such as quinine, are used to treat malaria. The alkaloids in some plants, such as the psychedelic compounds found in magic mushrooms and peyote, can cause hallucinations and altered states of consciousness.

The potency and effects of alkaloids can vary widely depending on the specific compound and the dose taken. Some alkaloids can be toxic or even lethal in high doses, while others can be used safely in medicine. Understanding the active ingredients in herbs, including alkaloids, is important for both medicinal and recreational use, as it can help people make informed choices about what they consume and how much.

Flavonoids: These are a class of plant pigments that have antioxidant properties and may have anti-inflammatory effects. Examples include quercetin in apples and onions, and catechins in green tea.

Flavonoids are a diverse class of plant pigments that are widely distributed in the plant kingdom. They are responsible for the bright colors of many fruits, vegetables, and flowers. Flavonoids have been studied for their potential health benefits, including their antioxidant and anti-inflammatory properties. They may also have anti-cancer, anti-diabetic, and anti-viral effects.

One of the most well-studied flavonoids is quercetin, which is found in many fruits and vegetables, including apples, onions, and berries. Quercetin has been shown to have anti-inflammatory effects, and may also have anti-cancer properties. Another important flavonoid is catechins, which are found in green tea. Catechins are believed to have antioxidant and anti-inflammatory effects, and may also help lower cholesterol levels.

Other flavonoids include anthocyanins, which give many fruits and vegetables their red, purple, or blue color. Anthocyanins have been shown to have antioxidant and anti-inflammatory effects, and may also have anti-cancer properties. Another flavonoid, called apigenin, is found in parsley, chamomile, and celery. Apigenin has been studied for its potential anti-cancer effects.

The potential health benefits of flavonoids are an active area of research, and many studies are being conducted to better understand their effects on human health. However, it's important to note that while flavonoids may have health benefits, they should not be considered a substitute for medical treatment, and individuals should always consult with a healthcare professional before making any changes to their diet or lifestyle.

Terpenes: These are a class of organic compounds that are responsible for the characteristic aroma and flavor of many herbs. They have a wide range of biological activities, including anti-inflammatory, antimicrobial, and antitumor effects. Examples include limonene in citrus fruits, and menthol in peppermint.

Terpenes are a diverse class of organic compounds that are commonly found in the essential oils of plants. They are responsible for the characteristic aromas and flavors of many herbs, as well as fruits and spices. Terpenes have a wide range of biological activities and are often used in aromatherapy, herbal medicine, and other natural remedies.

One of the most well-known terpenes is limonene, which is found in the essential oils of citrus fruits such as lemons, oranges, and grapefruits. Limonene has a fresh, citrusy aroma and is often used in cleaning products and air fresheners. It has also been studied for its anti-inflammatory, antioxidant, and anticancer effects.

Another terpene with significant health benefits is menthol, which is found in the essential oil of peppermint. Menthol has a cooling, minty aroma and is often used in cough drops, throat lozenges, and topical analgesic creams. It has been shown to have analgesic and anti-inflammatory effects and is often used to relieve pain and inflammation in conditions such as arthritis and muscle soreness.

Other terpenes that are commonly found in herbs include pinene, found in the essential oils of pine trees and many other plants, which has been shown to have antimicrobial and anti-inflammatory effects; eucalyptol, found in the essential oil of eucalyptus, which is often used to relieve respiratory symptoms such as coughs and congestion; and linalool, found in lavender and other herbs, which has been shown to have sedative and anxiolytic effects.

Terpenes are just one of the many active ingredients found in herbs, and their effects can vary depending on the specific terpene and the method of administration. However, research has shown that many terpenes have significant health benefits and may be useful in the treatment of a wide range of conditions.

Understanding how these active ingredients work in the body can help guide the use of herbs for medicinal purposes. For example, herbs that contain compounds with anti-inflammatory properties may be useful for treating conditions such as arthritis or asthma, while herbs with antioxidant properties may be helpful in preventing oxidative damage to cells and tissues.

Growing conditions such as soil quality, temperature, humidity, and sunlight can all impact the potency of herbs. The timing and methods used for harvesting and processing herbs can also affect their potency, with herbs that are harvested at the right time and processed quickly tending to have higher levels of active compounds. Additionally, the way herbs are stored, their age, and the specific plant part used (e.g. roots, leaves, flowers, stems, or bark) can also impact their potency. Finally, genetic variation among different varieties of the same herb can lead to varying levels of active compounds. Understanding these factors can help to ensure that the herbs used for medicinal or culinary purposes are of the highest quality and potency.

Herbs and the Human Body

Herbs have been used for thousands of years to support and promote the health and well-being of the human body. They are often used in traditional medicine systems, such as Ayurveda and Traditional Chinese Medicine, and have gained increasing attention in recent years as a complementary and alternative form of medicine.

Different herbs can affect various systems within the body in unique ways. Here are some examples of how different systems in the body can be influenced by the use of herbs:

Endocrine System and Herbs:
The endocrine system is a complex system responsible for producing and releasing hormones that regulate various bodily functions, including growth and development, metabolism, and mood. Hormonal imbalances can lead to a range of health problems, including thyroid disorders, diabetes, and infertility.

Herbs such as ashwagandha, ginseng, and licorice root have been used for centuries in traditional medicine to support and balance the endocrine system. These herbs contain compounds that can help regulate hormone production, reduce stress and anxiety, and boost energy levels.

Ashwagandha, for example, is an adaptogenic herb that has been shown to reduce stress and improve overall well-being by regulating cortisol levels. Cortisol is a hormone that is released in response to stress, and prolonged high levels of cortisol can have negative effects on the body.

Ginseng, another adaptogenic herb, has been shown to improve mental performance, reduce stress, and enhance physical endurance. It is also believed to have a positive effect on insulin sensitivity, which can help regulate blood sugar levels.

Licorice root, on the other hand, contains compounds that can help regulate estrogen and testosterone levels, making it beneficial for women with hormonal imbalances. It can also help improve adrenal function, which is important for overall health and well-being.

While herbs can be beneficial for supporting the endocrine system, it is important to consult with a healthcare provider before taking any herbal supplements, especially if you have a medical condition or are taking prescription medications. Some herbs may interact with medications or have side effects.

Digestive System and Herbs:

The digestive system is responsible for breaking down food and absorbing nutrients. Herbs such as ginger, peppermint, and fennel can help alleviate digestive issues such as nausea, bloating, and indigestion. Additionally, herbs like chamomile and marshmallow root can help soothe and heal the digestive tract.

The digestive system plays a crucial role in maintaining overall health by breaking down food and absorbing nutrients. Digestive issues such as nausea, bloating, and indigestion can be caused by a variety of factors, including poor diet, stress, and certain medical conditions.

Fortunately, several herbs have been shown to have beneficial effects on the digestive system. Ginger, for example, has anti-inflammatory properties and can help alleviate nausea and vomiting. It has also been shown to improve digestion by increasing the production of digestive enzymes.

Peppermint is another herb that can be beneficial for digestive health. It contains menthol, which has a relaxing effect on the muscles of the digestive tract, helping to relieve cramps, bloating, and indigestion. Peppermint has also been shown to have antimicrobial properties, which can help prevent the growth of harmful bacteria in the gut.

Fennel is another herb that can help relieve digestive issues. It contains compounds that help relax the muscles of the digestive tract, reducing bloating and cramps. Fennel also has anti-inflammatory properties, which can help soothe inflammation in the gut.

Chamomile is an herb that has been used for centuries to promote relaxation and soothe digestive issues. It has anti-inflammatory and antimicrobial properties and can help soothe and heal the digestive tract. Chamomile can also help alleviate symptoms of irritable bowel syndrome (IBS), including abdominal pain and bloating.

Marshmallow root is another herb that can be beneficial for digestive health. It contains mucilage, a substance that forms a protective layer over the mucous membranes of the digestive tract, helping to soothe inflammation and irritation. Marshmallow root can also help alleviate symptoms of gastroesophageal reflux disease (GERD), including heartburn and acid reflux.

While herbs can be helpful for digestive issues, it's important to talk to a healthcare provider before taking any herbal supplements, especially if you have a medical condition or are taking prescription medications. Some herbs may interact with medications or have side effects.

Respiratory System and Herbs:
The respiratory system includes the lungs, trachea, and bronchial tubes, and is responsible for breathing and oxygen exchange. Herbs like eucalyptus, thyme, and oregano can help support respiratory health by reducing inflammation and congestion, and promoting healthy breathing.

The respiratory system is crucial for breathing and oxygen exchange, and respiratory issues can be caused by a variety of factors such as allergies, infections, and environmental pollutants. Herbs can be used to support respiratory health and alleviate symptoms of respiratory issues.

Eucalyptus is an herb that has been used for centuries to promote respiratory health. It contains compounds called cineole, which have been shown to have anti-inflammatory, antibacterial, and antiviral properties. Eucalyptus oil can be used in a steam inhalation or diffuser to help reduce congestion and promote healthy breathing.

Thyme is another herb that can be beneficial for respiratory health. It contains compounds that have expectorant and antimicrobial properties, making it useful for clearing mucus and fighting infections. Thyme can be consumed as a tea or used in a steam inhalation to help alleviate respiratory symptoms.

Oregano is an herb that has antimicrobial and anti-inflammatory properties, making it useful for respiratory issues caused by infections. It can help fight off bacteria, viruses, and fungi that can cause respiratory infections. Oregano oil can be used in a diffuser or consumed as a supplement to support respiratory health.

In addition to these herbs, other herbs that can be beneficial for respiratory health include licorice root, mullein, and elecampane. Licorice root contains compounds that have expectorant properties and can help alleviate coughs and congestion. Mullein has been used to soothe respiratory issues for centuries and can help reduce inflammation in the respiratory tract. Elecampane has been shown to have antimicrobial properties and can help fight off respiratory infections.

It's important to talk to a healthcare provider before using any herbal supplements, especially if you have a medical condition or are taking prescription medications. Some herbs may interact with medications or have side effects.

Circulatory System and Herbs:

The circulatory system is responsible for transporting blood, oxygen, and nutrients throughout the body. Certain herbs, such as garlic, hawthorn berry, and cayenne, can help support cardiovascular health by improving circulation, reducing blood pressure, and promoting healthy cholesterol levels.

Yes, the circulatory system plays a vital role in maintaining overall health by transporting blood, oxygen, and nutrients throughout the body. Cardiovascular issues such as high blood pressure and cholesterol can increase the risk of heart disease and stroke.

Fortunately, several herbs have been shown to have beneficial effects on the circulatory system. Garlic, for example, has been used for centuries for its cardiovascular benefits. It contains compounds that can help reduce blood pressure, lower cholesterol levels, and improve circulation by dilating blood vessels.

Hawthorn berry is another herb that can be beneficial for cardiovascular health. It has been shown to help improve circulation by dilating blood vessels and can also help reduce blood pressure. Hawthorn berry has also been shown to have antioxidant properties, which can help protect against cardiovascular damage.

Cayenne is an herb that can help improve circulation by promoting the dilation of blood vessels. It contains capsaicin, a compound that has been shown to have cardiovascular benefits, including reducing blood pressure and improving cholesterol levels.

Other herbs that can be beneficial for cardiovascular health include ginger, turmeric, and ginkgo biloba. Ginger can help reduce inflammation in the cardiovascular system and improve circulation.

Turmeric contains compounds called curcuminoids, which have been shown to have antioxidant and anti-inflammatory properties that can help protect against cardiovascular damage. Ginkgo biloba has been shown to improve circulation by dilating blood vessels and reducing inflammation in the cardiovascular system.

It's important to note that while herbs can be beneficial for cardiovascular health, they should not be used as a substitute for medical treatment. If you have a cardiovascular condition, it's important to talk to a healthcare provider before using any herbal supplements, as some herbs may interact with medications or have side effects.

Nervous System and Herbs:
The nervous system includes the brain, spinal cord, and nerves, and is responsible for regulating bodily functions and responding to stimuli. Herbs like valerian, passionflower, and skullcap can help promote relaxation, reduce anxiety and stress, and improve sleep quality.

The nervous system plays a critical role in regulating bodily functions and responding to stimuli. Stress, anxiety, and sleep issues are some of the common problems that can affect the nervous system. Fortunately, there are several herbs that can help support nervous system health and alleviate these issues.

Valerian is an herb that has been used for centuries to promote relaxation and improve sleep quality. It contains compounds that can help increase levels of gamma-aminobutyric acid (GABA), a neurotransmitter that helps promote relaxation and reduce anxiety. Valerian root can be consumed as a tea or taken as a supplement to promote relaxation and improve sleep quality.

Passionflower is another herb that can be beneficial for nervous system health. It contains compounds that have been shown to have anxiolytic (anti-anxiety) and sedative effects. Passionflower can help reduce anxiety and promote relaxation, making it useful for stress-related nervous system issues. It can be consumed as a tea or taken as a supplement.

Skullcap is an herb that has been used for centuries to promote relaxation and reduce anxiety. It contains compounds that have been shown to have anxiolytic and sedative effects, making it useful for stress-related nervous system issues. Skullcap can be consumed as a tea or taken as a supplement.

Other herbs that can be beneficial for nervous system health include chamomile, lemon balm, and ashwagandha. Chamomile contains compounds that have been shown to have anxiolytic effects and can help reduce anxiety and promote relaxation. Lemon balm has been shown to have anxiolytic and sedative effects and can help promote relaxation and improve sleep quality. Ashwagandha is an adaptogenic herb that can help the body adapt to stress and improve nervous system function.

It's important to note that while herbs can be beneficial for nervous system health, they should not be used as a substitute for medical treatment. If you have a nervous system condition, it's important to talk to a healthcare provider before using any herbal supplements, as some herbs may interact with medications or have side effects.

Immune System and Herbs:
The immune system is responsible for defending the body against pathogens and disease. Herbs such as echinacea, elderberry, and astragalus can help boost immune function and reduce the severity and duration of illnesses.

Yes, the immune system is a complex network of cells, tissues, and organs that work together to defend the body against pathogens and disease. When the immune system is compromised or weakened, it can lead to a greater risk of infection and illness. Fortunately, there are several herbs that can help support and boost immune function.

Echinacea is an herb that has been used for centuries to support immune system health. It contains compounds that can help stimulate the production of white blood cells, which are responsible for fighting off infections. Echinacea can be consumed as a tea, taken as a supplement, or used topically in creams or ointments.

Elderberry is another herb that can be beneficial for immune system health. It contains compounds that have been shown to have antiviral and immune-boosting properties. Elderberry can help reduce the severity and duration of illnesses like the common cold and flu. It can be consumed as a syrup, tincture, or supplement.

Astragalus is an adaptogenic herb that has been used in traditional Chinese medicine to support immune system health. It contains compounds that can help stimulate the production of white blood cells and enhance immune system function. Astragalus can be consumed as a tea or taken as a supplement.

Other herbs that can be beneficial for immune system health include garlic, ginger, and turmeric. Garlic contains compounds that have been shown to have antibacterial, antiviral, and immune-boosting properties. Ginger has been shown to have anti-inflammatory and immune-boosting properties. Turmeric contains compounds that have been shown to have anti-inflammatory and immune-modulating effects.

It's important to note that while herbs can be beneficial for immune system health, they should not be used as a substitute for medical treatment. If you have a medical condition or are taking medication, it's important to talk to a healthcare provider before using any herbal supplements, as some herbs may interact with medications or have side effects.

Musculoskeletal System and Herbs:

The musculoskeletal system includes the bones, muscles, and joints, and is responsible for movement and support of the body. Herbs like arnica, turmeric, and ginger can help reduce inflammation and pain, promote healing, and support joint health.

The musculoskeletal system is responsible for providing support and movement to the body, and it is essential to maintain its health and function. Fortunately, there are several herbs that can help support and promote musculoskeletal health.

Arnica is an herb that has been used for centuries to treat muscle pain and inflammation. It contains compounds that can help reduce inflammation and relieve pain. Arnica can be applied topically in the form of creams or ointments, or taken orally as a homeopathic remedy.

Turmeric is another herb that can be beneficial for musculoskeletal health. It contains compounds called curcuminoids, which have been shown to have anti-inflammatory and antioxidant properties. Turmeric can help reduce inflammation and pain in the joints, as well as support joint health. It can be consumed as a spice in cooking, taken as a supplement, or used topically in creams or ointments.

Ginger is also known for its anti-inflammatory properties and can be helpful in reducing joint pain and inflammation. Ginger can be consumed as a tea or added to food, taken as a supplement or used topically in creams or oils.

Other herbs that can be beneficial for musculoskeletal health include devil's claw, boswellia, and white willow bark. Devil's claw has been shown to have anti-inflammatory and analgesic properties and is commonly used to treat joint pain and inflammation. Boswellia is also believed to have anti-inflammatory properties and can be beneficial in reducing joint pain and improving mobility. White willow bark is a natural source of salicylic acid, which is the active ingredient in aspirin and has been used for centuries as a natural pain reliever.

It's important to note that while herbs can be beneficial for musculoskeletal health, they should not be used as a substitute for medical treatment. If you have a medical condition or are taking medication, it's important to talk to a healthcare provider before using any herbal supplements, as some herbs may interact with medications or have side effects.

In summary, herbs have the potential to influence and support various systems within the body in unique ways. However, it is important to note that herbs should not be used as a substitute for medical treatment or prescribed medication without consulting with a healthcare professional.

Endocrine System and Herbs:
The endocrine system is a complex system of glands that produce and secrete hormones into the bloodstream to regulate various physiological functions and maintain homeostasis in the body. Hormones are chemical messengers that travel through the bloodstream to specific cells or organs to elicit a response.

Herbs can play a significant role in supporting and balancing the endocrine system. Here are some examples of herbs that are known to have an effect on the endocrine system:

Ashwagandha: Ashwagandha, also known as Withania somnifera, is an adaptogenic herb that has been used in Ayurvedic medicine for thousands of years. It is known to help reduce stress and anxiety by regulating cortisol levels, a hormone produced by the adrenal gland in response to stress. Additionally, ashwagandha has been shown to increase testosterone levels in men and improve fertility in women by regulating follicle-stimulating hormone (FSH) and luteinizing hormone (LH) levels.

Ginseng: Ginseng is a popular adaptogenic herb that has been used in Traditional Chinese Medicine for thousands of years. It is known to help boost energy levels, reduce stress, and improve cognitive function by regulating cortisol levels. Ginseng has also been shown to improve insulin sensitivity and glucose metabolism, making it a potential aid in managing diabetes.

Licorice root: Licorice root, also known as Glycyrrhiza glabra, has been used in traditional medicine for its anti-inflammatory and immune-boosting properties. It is known to help regulate cortisol levels and improve the function of the adrenal gland. Additionally, licorice root has been shown to have estrogen-like effects, making it a potential aid in managing menopausal symptoms.

Maca root: Maca root, also known as Lepidium meyenii, is an adaptogenic herb that has been used in traditional medicine for its energizing and libido-enhancing effects. It is known to help regulate hormone levels, particularly estrogen and progesterone in women, and testosterone in men. Additionally, maca root has been shown to improve fertility in both men and women by increasing sperm count and motility and regulating menstrual cycles.

Holy basil: Holy basil, also known as Ocimum tenuiflorum, is an adaptogenic herb that has been used in Ayurvedic medicine for its anti-inflammatory and immune-boosting properties. It is known to help regulate cortisol levels and improve the function of the adrenal gland. Additionally, holy basil has been shown to have anti-diabetic effects by regulating blood sugar levels and improving insulin sensitivity.

The endocrine system is a complex system of glands that produce and secrete hormones to regulate various physiological functions in the body. Herbs such as ashwagandha, ginseng, licorice root, maca root, and holy basil have been shown to have an effect on the endocrine system by regulating hormone levels and improving glandular function. However, it is important to consult with a healthcare professional before using herbs to support the endocrine system, particularly if you are already taking medication or have a pre-existing medical condition.

Digestive System and Herbs:
The digestive system is a group of organs that work together to break down food, absorb nutrients, and eliminate waste products from the body. The digestive system includes the mouth, esophagus, stomach, small intestine, large intestine, rectum, and anus. Herbs can play an important role in supporting and optimizing digestive function.

Here are some examples of herbs that are known to have an effect on the digestive system:

Ginger: Ginger has been used for centuries as a digestive aid. It is known to stimulate the production of digestive juices and enzymes, which can help improve digestion and relieve nausea and vomiting. Ginger also has anti-inflammatory properties, making it useful for relieving symptoms of inflammatory bowel disease and other digestive disorders.

Peppermint: Peppermint is a popular herb that is often used for its digestive properties. It is known to help relax the muscles in the digestive tract, which can help relieve symptoms of irritable bowel syndrome (IBS) and other digestive disorders. Peppermint can also help relieve nausea and indigestion.

Fennel: Fennel is an herb that has been used in traditional medicine for its digestive properties. It is known to help stimulate the production of digestive juices and enzymes, which can help improve digestion and relieve bloating and gas. Fennel can also help relieve symptoms of IBS and other digestive disorders.

Chamomile: Chamomile is an herb that is often used for its calming properties. It is known to help relieve anxiety and stress, which can be beneficial for people with digestive disorders. Chamomile can also help relieve symptoms of indigestion and IBS.

Dandelion: Dandelion is an herb that has been used for centuries as a digestive aid. It is known to help stimulate the production of digestive juices and enzymes, which can help improve digestion and relieve constipation. Dandelion can also help stimulate the liver and gallbladder, which can be beneficial for people with liver or gallbladder disorders.

Turmeric: Turmeric is an herb that is often used for its anti-inflammatory properties. It is known to help relieve symptoms of inflammatory bowel disease and other digestive disorders. Turmeric can also help improve digestion and relieve bloating and gas.

The digestive system is a complex system of organs that work together to break down food, absorb nutrients, and eliminate waste products from the body. Herbs such as ginger, peppermint, fennel, chamomile, dandelion, and turmeric can help support and optimize digestive function by stimulating the production of digestive juices and enzymes, relaxing the muscles in the digestive tract, and reducing inflammation. However, it is important to consult with a healthcare professional before using herbs to support digestive function, particularly if you have a pre-existing medical condition or are taking medication.

Respiratory System and Herbs:

The respiratory system is a complex network of organs and tissues that work together to enable breathing and gas exchange in the body. This system includes the nose, mouth, throat, larynx, trachea, bronchi, and lungs. Respiratory health is essential for overall wellbeing, and herbs can play a role in supporting and optimizing respiratory function.

Here are some examples of herbs that are known to have an effect on the respiratory system:

Eucalyptus: Eucalyptus is an herb that is often used for its respiratory properties. It contains compounds that can help loosen mucus and relieve coughs, making it useful for respiratory conditions such as bronchitis and asthma. Eucalyptus can also help relieve sinus congestion and promote easier breathing.

Thyme: Thyme is an herb that has been used for centuries as a respiratory aid. It contains compounds that can help loosen mucus and relieve coughs, making it useful for respiratory conditions such as bronchitis and pneumonia. Thyme can also help relieve congestion and promote easier breathing.

Licorice: Licorice is an herb that is often used for its anti-inflammatory properties. It can help reduce inflammation in the respiratory tract, making it useful for respiratory conditions such as asthma and bronchitis. Licorice can also help soothe sore throats and relieve coughs.

Mullein: Mullein is an herb that has been used for centuries as a respiratory aid. It can help soothe inflammation in the respiratory tract, making it useful for respiratory conditions such as asthma and bronchitis. Mullein can also help relieve congestion and promote easier breathing.

Ginger: Ginger is an herb that has anti-inflammatory properties, making it useful for respiratory conditions such as asthma and bronchitis. Ginger can also help relieve congestion and promote easier breathing. Ginger tea is a popular home remedy for colds and flu.

Peppermint: Peppermint is an herb that is often used for its respiratory properties. It can help relieve sinus congestion and promote easier breathing. Peppermint tea is a popular home remedy for colds and flu.

The respiratory system is a complex network of organs and tissues that work together to enable breathing and gas exchange in the body. Herbs such as eucalyptus, thyme, licorice, mullein, ginger, and peppermint can help support and optimize respiratory function by reducing inflammation, loosening mucus, relieving coughs, and promoting easier breathing. However, it is important to consult with a healthcare professional before using herbs to support respiratory function, particularly if you have a pre-existing medical condition or are taking medication.

Circulatory System and Herbs:
The circulatory system is responsible for transporting blood, oxygen, and nutrients throughout the body. It includes the heart, blood vessels, and blood. The circulatory system plays a vital role in maintaining overall health and wellness, and herbs can be used to support and optimize its function.

Here are some examples of herbs that are known to have an effect on the circulatory system:

Hawthorn: Hawthorn is an herb that is often used to support cardiovascular health. It contains compounds that can help dilate blood vessels, which can help improve blood flow and lower blood pressure. Hawthorn can also help reduce inflammation in the circulatory system, which can be beneficial for conditions such as atherosclerosis.

Garlic: Garlic is an herb that has been used for centuries for its cardiovascular benefits. It contains compounds that can help reduce cholesterol levels and lower blood pressure, which can help improve circulation and reduce the risk of cardiovascular disease. Garlic can also help reduce inflammation in the circulatory system.

Ginkgo: Ginkgo is an herb that is often used to support cognitive function, but it can also have benefits for the circulatory system. Ginkgo can help improve blood flow and reduce inflammation in the circulatory system, which can be beneficial for conditions such as atherosclerosis and peripheral artery disease.

Cayenne: Cayenne is an herb that contains capsaicin, which can help dilate blood vessels and improve blood flow. Cayenne can also help reduce inflammation in the circulatory system and lower blood pressure, which can be beneficial for cardiovascular health.

Turmeric: Turmeric is an herb that is known for its anti-inflammatory properties. It can help reduce inflammation in the circulatory system, which can be beneficial for conditions such as atherosclerosis and cardiovascular disease. Turmeric can also help improve blood flow and lower blood pressure.

Ginger: Ginger is an herb that has anti-inflammatory properties, which can be beneficial for the circulatory system. It can help reduce inflammation and improve blood flow, which can be helpful for conditions such as atherosclerosis and cardiovascular disease. Ginger can also help lower blood pressure.

The circulatory system is responsible for transporting blood, oxygen, and nutrients throughout the body. Herbs such as hawthorn, garlic, ginkgo, cayenne, turmeric, and ginger can help support and optimize circulatory function by improving blood flow, reducing inflammation, and lowering blood pressure. However, it is important to consult with a healthcare professional before using herbs to support circulatory function, particularly if you have a pre-existing medical condition or are taking medication.

Nervous System and Herbs:
The nervous system is a complex network of cells, tissues, and organs that coordinate the body's responses to internal and external stimuli. It includes the brain, spinal cord, and nerves. The nervous system plays a critical role in regulating many bodily functions, including movement, sensation, and cognition. Herbs can be used to support and optimize nervous system function.

Here are some examples of herbs that are known to have an effect on the nervous system:

Ashwagandha: Ashwagandha is an adaptogenic herb that is often used to support the nervous system. It can help reduce stress and anxiety, improve mood, and promote cognitive function. Ashwagandha can also help regulate the body's stress response system, which can be beneficial for conditions such as adrenal fatigue.

Ginkgo: Ginkgo is an herb that is often used to support cognitive function, but it can also have benefits for the nervous system. Ginkgo can help improve blood flow to the brain, which can enhance cognitive function and reduce the risk of age-related cognitive decline. Ginkgo can also help reduce inflammation in the nervous system, which can be beneficial for conditions such as multiple sclerosis.

St. John's Wort: St. John's Wort is an herb that is often used to support mood and emotional balance. It can help reduce symptoms of depression and anxiety and promote a sense of calm and relaxation. St. John's Wort can also help reduce inflammation in the nervous system, which can be beneficial for conditions such as neuropathy.

Skullcap: Skullcap is an herb that is often used to support the nervous system. It can help reduce anxiety and promote relaxation, making it beneficial for conditions such as insomnia and stress. Skullcap can also help reduce inflammation in the nervous system, which can be beneficial for conditions such as neuropathy.

Chamomile: Chamomile is an herb that is often used to promote relaxation and reduce anxiety. It can also help reduce inflammation in the nervous system, which can be beneficial for conditions such as multiple sclerosis.

Valerian: Valerian is an herb that is often used to promote relaxation and reduce anxiety. It can help improve sleep quality and reduce symptoms of insomnia. Valerian can also help reduce inflammation in the nervous system, which can be beneficial for conditions such as neuropathy.

The nervous system plays a critical role in regulating many bodily functions, and herbs can be used to support and optimize nervous system function. Herbs such as ashwagandha, ginkgo, St. John's Wort, skullcap, chamomile, and valerian can help reduce stress and anxiety, improve mood, promote cognitive function, and enhance relaxation.

However, it is important to consult with a healthcare professional before using herbs to support nervous system function, particularly if you have a pre-existing medical condition or are taking medication.

Immune System and Herbs:
The immune system is responsible for protecting the body against foreign invaders such as viruses, bacteria, and other pathogens. It is a complex system that involves various cells, tissues, and organs working together to defend against infections and diseases. Herbs can be used to support and strengthen the immune system, helping to enhance its ability to fight off infections and diseases.

Here are some examples of herbs that are known to have an effect on the immune system:

Echinacea: Echinacea is an herb that is often used to support the immune system. It can help boost the production of white blood cells, which are important for fighting infections. Echinacea is also known for its anti-inflammatory properties, which can help reduce inflammation in the body and support immune function.

Elderberry: Elderberry is an herb that is often used to support the immune system. It is rich in antioxidants and can help boost the production of cytokines, which are important for regulating the immune response. Elderberry has also been shown to have antiviral properties, making it a popular herb for preventing and treating viral infections such as the flu.

Garlic: Garlic is an herb that is often used for its immune-boosting properties. It contains a compound called allicin, which has antimicrobial properties that can help fight off infections. Garlic is also rich in antioxidants, which can help support immune function and reduce inflammation in the body.

Astragalus: Astragalus is an herb that is often used to support the immune system. It can help stimulate the production of white blood cells, which are important for fighting infections. Astragalus is also known for its anti-inflammatory properties, which can help reduce inflammation in the body and support immune function.

Andrographis: Andrographis is an herb that is often used to support the immune system. It contains compounds called andrographolides, which have been shown to have antimicrobial properties and can help boost the production of white blood cells. Andrographis is also known for its anti-inflammatory properties, which can help support immune function.

Ginger: Ginger is an herb that is often used for its immune-boosting properties. It contains compounds called gingerols and shogaols, which have antimicrobial properties and can help support immune function. Ginger is also known for its anti-inflammatory properties, which can help reduce inflammation in the body and support immune function.

The immune system plays a critical role in protecting the body against infections and diseases, and herbs can be used to support and strengthen the immune system. Herbs such as echinacea, elderberry, garlic, astragalus, andrographis, and ginger can help boost the production of white blood cells, reduce inflammation, and have antimicrobial properties that can help fight off infections. However, it is important to consult with a healthcare professional before using herbs to support immune function, particularly if you have a pre-existing medical condition or are taking medication.

Musculoskeletal System and Herbs:
The musculoskeletal system is composed of the bones, muscles, cartilage, ligaments, and tendons that provide support and movement to the body. Herbs can be used to support and maintain the health of the musculoskeletal system, including reducing inflammation, promoting bone health, and relieving pain and stiffness.

Here are some examples of herbs that are known to have an effect on the musculoskeletal system:
Turmeric: Turmeric is an herb that is often used for its anti-inflammatory properties. It contains a compound called curcumin, which has been shown to have anti-inflammatory effects that can help reduce inflammation in the body. Turmeric is often used to relieve joint pain and stiffness, making it a popular herb for supporting the health of the musculoskeletal system.

Boswellia: Boswellia is an herb that is often used for its anti-inflammatory properties. It contains compounds called boswellic acids, which have been shown to have anti-inflammatory effects that can help reduce inflammation in the body. Boswellia is often used to relieve joint pain and stiffness, making it a popular herb for supporting the health of the musculoskeletal system.

Ginger: Ginger is an herb that is often used for its anti-inflammatory properties. It contains compounds called gingerols and shogaols, which have been shown to have anti-inflammatory effects that can help reduce inflammation in the body. Ginger is often used to relieve joint pain and stiffness, making it a popular herb for supporting the health of the musculoskeletal system.

Devil's Claw: Devil's Claw is an herb that is often used to relieve pain and inflammation in the musculoskeletal system. It contains compounds called harpagosides, which have been shown to have analgesic and anti-inflammatory effects that can help relieve pain and inflammation in the body.

Horsetail: Horsetail is an herb that is often used for its high silica content, which can help support bone health. Silica is an important mineral that is essential for the development and maintenance of healthy bones, making horsetail a popular herb for supporting the health of the musculoskeletal system.

Nettle: Nettle is an herb that is often used for its anti-inflammatory properties. It contains compounds called flavonoids, which have been shown to have anti-inflammatory effects that can help reduce inflammation in the body. Nettle is often used to relieve joint pain and stiffness, making it a popular herb for supporting the health of the musculoskeletal system.

The musculoskeletal system is critical for movement and support of the body, and herbs can be used to support and maintain its health. Herbs such as turmeric, boswellia, ginger, devil's claw, horsetail, and nettle can help reduce inflammation, relieve pain and stiffness, and support bone health.

However, it is important to consult with a healthcare professional before using herbs to support musculoskeletal health, particularly if you have a pre-existing medical condition or are taking medication.

The human body is a complex system with multiple interrelated parts and functions. Each system plays an important role in maintaining overall health and well-being. Herbs can be used to support and maintain the health of various systems in the body, including the endocrine, digestive, respiratory, circulatory, nervous, immune, and musculoskeletal systems.

For example, herbs such as ashwagandha, licorice root, and ginseng can support the endocrine system by regulating hormones, while herbs such as ginger, peppermint, and chamomile can support the digestive system by reducing inflammation, promoting digestion, and relieving discomfort. Herbs such as eucalyptus, mullein, and thyme can support the respiratory system by reducing inflammation, promoting respiratory function, and relieving congestion.

Herbs such as hawthorn, garlic, and turmeric can support the circulatory system by reducing inflammation, improving blood flow, and promoting cardiovascular health. Herbs such as valerian, passionflower, and kava can support the nervous system by reducing stress and anxiety, promoting relaxation, and improving sleep. Herbs such as echinacea, astragalus, and elderberry can support the immune system by enhancing immune function, reducing inflammation, and promoting overall health.

Finally, herbs such as turmeric, boswellia, ginger, devil's claw, horsetail, and nettle can support the musculoskeletal system by reducing inflammation, relieving pain and stiffness, and supporting bone health. Overall, herbs can be a useful tool for supporting and maintaining the health of various systems in the body, but it is important to consult with a healthcare professional before using herbs, particularly if you have a pre-existing medical condition or are taking medication.

Medicinal Herbs

Aloe Vera	Ashwagandha	Astragalus	Bay Laurel
Black Cohosh	Burdock	Calendula	Catnip
Chaga Mushroom	Chamomile	Chickweed	Chives
Cinnamon	Cloves	Coltsfoot	Comfrey
Cordyceps	Dandelion	Echinacea	Elderberry
Eyebright	Fennel	Feverfew	Galangal
Garlic	Ginger	Ginkgo Biloba	Ginseng
Holy Basil	Hops	Hyssop	Juniper Berries
Kava Kava	Lady's Mantle	Lavender	Lemon balm
Licorice	Maca	Maitake Mushroom	Marshmallow Root
Milk Thistle	Mint	Mugwort	Muira Puama
Nettle	Oregon Grape Root	Parsley	Passionflower
Peppermint	Red clover	Reishi Mushroom	Rose Hips
Rosemary	Sage	Self-heal	Shiitake Mushroom
Siberian Ginseng	Skullcap	St. John's Wort	Thyme
Turmeric	Valerian	Wild yam	Yarrow

Aloe Vera

Herbal Identification:
- Common name: Aloe vera
- Latin binomial: Aloe barbadensis (also known as Aloe vera var. chinensis)
- Other common names: Barbados aloe, Curacao aloe, Indian aloe
- Plant family: Asphodelaceae (formerly known as Liliaceae)
- Botanical description: Aloe vera is a succulent plant that belongs to the Aloe family (Asphodelaceae). It is a perennial plant with thick, fleshy green leaves that are pointed at the tips and have serrated edges. The leaves can grow up to 50 cm long and 10 cm wide, and they contain a clear gel-like substance that is used for medicinal purposes.

The Aloe vera plant typically grows in hot, arid climates and is native to the Arabian Peninsula, but is now grown worldwide. It has shallow roots and can be propagated through offsets, which are small plantlets that grow from the base of the parent plant.

The flowers of the Aloe vera plant are tubular and can range in color from yellow to orange. They grow on long stalks that emerge from the center of the plant, usually in the summer.

Aloe vera has a slightly bitter and astringent taste, and is used in traditional medicine for its healing properties. The clear gel from the leaves is used to soothe and moisturize the skin, while the latex, found just beneath the skin of the leaf, is used as a laxative. It is also believed to have anti-inflammatory and immune-boosting properties.

Medicinal Properties:
- Recommended cultivars: There are no specific recommended cultivars for medicinal use.
- Parts used: The gel inside the leaves is used for medicinal purposes, while the outer leaf is often used for cosmetic purposes.
- Taste: The gel has a slightly bitter taste.
- Actions: Aloe vera is cooling, moisturizing, anti-inflammatory, antimicrobial, and astringent.
- Energetics: Aloe vera is considered cooling and moistening in traditional herbalism.

• Specific indications: Aloe vera has a wide range of medicinal indications, including:

Topical use:
- Burns: Aloe vera gel can help soothe and heal burns, including sunburns, thermal burns, and radiation burns.
- Skin irritation: Aloe vera gel can be used to soothe and heal skin irritation, including rashes, insect bites, and allergic reactions.
- Wound healing: Aloe vera gel can help promote wound healing, including surgical wounds, cuts, and abrasions.
- Acne: Aloe vera gel can help reduce inflammation and heal acne breakouts.

Oral use:
- Digestive health: Aloe vera juice can help support digestive health and reduce symptoms of conditions such as irritable bowel syndrome (IBS) and ulcerative colitis.
- Immune function: Aloe vera juice may help support immune function and reduce the risk of infections.
- Blood sugar management: Aloe vera juice may help regulate blood sugar levels in people with diabetes.
- Heart health: Aloe vera juice may help lower cholesterol levels and reduce the risk of heart disease.

It's important to note that aloe vera is not a substitute for medical treatment, and people with serious medical conditions should always seek the advice of a healthcare provider before using aloe vera or any other herbal preparation.

Medicinal preparations:
Aloe vera can be used topically or orally, and there are several medicinal preparations available:

Topical preparations:
- Aloe vera gel: The gel from the inner leaf of the aloe vera plant can be applied directly to the skin to soothe and heal burns, moisturize dry skin, and relieve sunburn.
- Aloe vera cream or lotion: These preparations often contain aloe vera gel as well as other ingredients to moisturize and soothe the skin.
- Aloe vera spray: Aloe vera spray can be used to soothe and heal sunburn or other skin irritations.
- Aloe vera juice: Aloe vera juice can be used topically as well as orally. It can be applied to the skin to soothe and heal burns, or taken orally to support digestive health and immune function.

Oral preparations:

- Aloe vera juice: Aloe vera juice is commonly used as a dietary supplement to support digestive health, immune function, and blood sugar management. It can be found in health food stores and online.
- Aloe vera capsules or tablets: Aloe vera capsules or tablets may be used to supplement the diet with the beneficial compounds found in aloe vera. It's important to follow the manufacturer's instructions for dosage and use.
- Aloe vera powder: Aloe vera powder can be used to add a nutritional boost to smoothies, juices, or other foods. It's important to follow the manufacturer's instructions for dosage and use.

It's important to use aloe vera preparations that are made from high-quality sources and that are free from contaminants or adulterants. It's also important to follow dosage instructions carefully, as high doses of aloe vera may have adverse effects. It's always best to consult with a healthcare provider before using aloe vera or any other herbal preparation for medicinal purposes.

- Ratio and dosage information: The dosage of aloe vera gel or juice will depend on the specific product and intended use. Follow the recommended dosage on the product label or consult with a qualified healthcare practitioner for guidance.

Medicinal uses:
Aloe vera has a wide range of medicinal uses, both topically and orally. Here are some of the most common medicinal uses of aloe vera:
Topical uses:
- Healing burns: Aloe vera gel has been traditionally used for its ability to soothe and heal burns. It may help to reduce pain, inflammation, and promote wound healing.
- Moisturizing skin: Aloe vera gel is commonly used as a moisturizer for dry skin. It may help to hydrate and nourish the skin, and may be particularly beneficial for people with eczema or psoriasis.
- Treating acne: Aloe vera gel may help to reduce inflammation and redness associated with acne, and may also have antimicrobial properties that can help to fight acne-causing bacteria.
- Relieving sunburn: Aloe vera gel may help to relieve the pain and inflammation associated with sunburn, and may also help to speed up the healing process.

Oral uses:

- Digestive support: Aloe vera juice has been traditionally used for digestive support, particularly for constipation. It may help to stimulate bowel movements and promote regularity.
- Immune support: Aloe vera juice may help to boost immune function, thanks to its high antioxidant content.
- Anti-inflammatory effects: Aloe vera juice may have anti-inflammatory effects, which may help to reduce inflammation throughout the body.

Blood sugar management: Aloe vera juice may help to lower blood sugar levels in people with type 2 diabetes, although more research is needed in this area.

It's important to note that aloe vera should only be used for medicinal purposes under the guidance of a healthcare provider, as it may interact with certain medications and may not be appropriate for everyone.

- Precautions and contradictions: While aloe vera is generally considered safe for most people when used topically or taken orally in small amounts, there are some precautions to keep in mind. Aloe vera may cause allergic reactions in some people, so it's important to do a patch test before using it topically. When taken orally, aloe vera may cause gastrointestinal side effects such as diarrhea and abdominal cramps, especially if consumed in large amounts. Aloe vera should not be taken by pregnant or breastfeeding women, as it may have abortifacient properties. Additionally, aloe vera should not be applied to open wounds or burns, as it may slow down the healing process.

Aloe vera is contraindicated in certain situations. Aloe vera should not be taken orally by people who are taking medications such as diuretics, steroids, and laxatives, as it may interact with these medications and cause adverse effects. Aloe vera should also be avoided by people with intestinal conditions such as Crohn's disease, ulcerative colitis, and hemorrhoids, as it may aggravate these conditions.

It's important to consult with a healthcare provider before using aloe vera for medicinal purposes, especially if you have any underlying health conditions or are taking any medications.

Cultivation:
- Native to: Aloe vera is believed to be native to the Arabian Peninsula, but is now widely cultivated in tropical and subtropical regions around the world.
- Zones: Aloe vera can be grown in USDA hardiness zones 9-11.

- Soil: Aloe vera prefers well-draining soil with a pH between 6.0 and 7.0. It is tolerant of poor soil conditions and drought, but will not tolerate waterlogged soil. Aloe vera plants prefer well-draining soil that is slightly acidic. You can use a cactus or succulent mix for planting Aloe vera.
- Propagation: Aloe vera plants can be propagated by removing offsets or "pups" that grow at the base of the plant. Allow the offsets to dry out for a few days, then plant them in well-draining soil. Also by seeds, or stem cuttings.
- Growing information and garden care: Aloe vera is a low-maintenance plant that requires minimal watering and fertilization. It prefers full sun or partial shade and can be grown indoors or outdoors in pots or in the ground. Protect the plant from frost and overwatering.
- Insects and disease: Aloe vera plants are relatively pest-resistant, but they can be affected by mealybugs or scale insects. If you notice any pests, you can remove them by wiping the leaves with a damp cloth. Aloe vera plants can also be affected by fungal diseases if they are overwatered or exposed to humid conditions. To prevent fungal diseases, be sure to plant Aloe vera in well-draining soil and avoid overwatering.
- Harvesting and preparations: The leaves of a mature aloe vera plant can be harvested for their gel at any time. To harvest, simply cut off one or more of the outer leaves close to the base of the plant, being careful not to damage the inner leaves. The gel can be extracted by cutting open the leaf and scooping out the clear, jelly-like substance inside. The gel can be used immediately or stored in the refrigerator for up to a week. Aloe vera gel can also be purchased pre-made in health food stores or online.

What medicines are made with this herb:

Aloe vera is used in a variety of medicinal and cosmetic preparations. Some of the most common medicines and products made with aloe vera include:

- Topical creams and lotions: Aloe vera is used topically in creams, lotions, and gels to soothe and moisturize the skin. It is commonly used to treat sunburns, rashes, and other skin irritations.
- Oral supplements: Aloe vera supplements are available in capsule, tablet, and liquid form. They are used to promote digestive health, support immune function, and reduce inflammation.
- Juice: Aloe vera juice is made by extracting the gel from the leaves of the plant and mixing it with water or other juices. It is used to promote digestive health and as a natural remedy for constipation.
- Shampoo and conditioner: Aloe vera is added to hair care products to moisturize and nourish the hair and scalp.
- Toothpaste: Aloe vera is added to toothpaste to help soothe and heal gum inflammation and promote oral health.

- Wound dressings: Aloe vera is used in wound dressings to promote healing and prevent infection.
- Eye drops: Aloe vera is used in some eye drops to soothe and moisturize the eyes.

What medicines this herb counteract:

Aloe vera is generally considered safe and does not typically counteract any specific medicines. However, if you are taking medications that can lower blood sugar levels, such as diabetes medications, it is important to monitor your blood sugar closely when using aloe vera internally as it may lower blood sugar levels.

Additionally, aloe vera can interact with certain medications that are broken down by the liver, so it is important to speak with your healthcare provider if you are taking any prescription or over-the-counter medications. Aloe vera should also be avoided during pregnancy, as it may cause uterine contractions.

Ashwagandha

Herbal Identification:
- Common name: Ashwagandha
- Latin binomial: Withania somnifera
- Other common names: Indian ginseng, winter cherry
- Plant family: Solanaceae
- Botanical description: Ashwagandha (Withania somnifera) is a perennial shrub that belongs to the Solanaceae family, which also includes tomatoes, eggplants, and potatoes. It is also known by other common names such as Indian ginseng and winter cherry.

The plant can grow up to 1.5 meters in height and has small green flowers and orange-red fruit. It is native to the dry regions of India, the Middle East, and parts of Africa.

The leaves of the ashwagandha plant are ovate or lanceolate, with a length of 5-10 cm and width of 2-6 cm. The flowers are small, green or yellow, and bell-shaped, and are arranged in clusters on the plant. The fruit of the ashwagandha plant is a small, round berry that turns red when it is ripe. The root of the ashwagandha plant is the primary part used for medicinal purposes and is usually harvested after the second year of growth.

Ashwagandha has a strong, earthy scent and taste, and is commonly used in Ayurvedic medicine as an adaptogen to help the body cope with stress and anxiety. It is also believed to have anti-inflammatory and immune-boosting properties.

Medicinal Properties:
- Recommended cultivars: Ashwagandha is typically grown from seed or propagated from cuttings.
- Parts used: The roots are the primary part of the plant used in herbal medicine.
- Taste: Bitter, astringent, and slightly sweet.
- Actions: Adaptogen, nervine, tonic, sedative, immune modulator.
- Energetics: Warming, moistening.
- Specific indications: Ashwagandha is known for its adaptogenic properties, meaning it helps the body adapt to stress and anxiety. It has been traditionally used for a variety of health conditions, including:

- Stress and Anxiety: Ashwagandha is known to reduce cortisol, the hormone associated with stress, and may help reduce anxiety and depression.
- Immune System Support: It has been shown to boost immune function and increase white blood cell count.
- Hormonal Balance: Ashwagandha may help regulate thyroid hormones and support reproductive health in both men and women.
- Cognitive Function: Some studies have shown that ashwagandha may improve memory, focus, and cognitive function.
- Inflammation and Pain: Ashwagandha has anti-inflammatory properties and may help reduce pain and inflammation associated with conditions such as arthritis.
- Insomnia: Ashwagandha may help improve sleep quality and reduce insomnia.
- Athletic Performance: Some studies suggest that ashwagandha may improve physical performance and increase muscle strength and endurance.

Medicinal preparations:
- Ashwagandha can be prepared and used in various forms, including:
- Powder: Ashwagandha root is dried and ground into a powder which can be mixed with warm water, milk, or honey and taken orally.
- Capsules and Tablets: Ashwagandha is available in capsule and tablet form, which can be taken orally with water or other liquids.
- Tincture: Ashwagandha root is steeped in alcohol to make a tincture, which can be taken orally.
- Tea: Ashwagandha can be used to make tea by boiling the root or leaves in water and steeping for 5-10 minutes before straining and drinking.
- Topical Creams and Ointments: Ashwagandha can be applied topically in the form of creams and ointments for treating skin conditions such as eczema and psoriasis.

The appropriate dosage and form of ashwagandha will vary depending on the specific health concern and individual needs. It is always best to consult with a healthcare professional before taking any new herb or supplement.
- Ratio and dosage information: Dosages may vary depending on the preparation and individual needs. It is recommended to follow dosage instructions on the product label or consult with a qualified healthcare provider.

Medicinal uses:
Ashwagandha has been used traditionally in Ayurvedic medicine for various medicinal purposes. Some of the potential medicinal uses of ashwagandha include:
- Stress and Anxiety: Ashwagandha is believed to have adaptogenic properties that help the body cope with stress and anxiety. It has been shown to reduce cortisol levels, a stress hormone, and improve overall mood.
- Depression: Ashwagandha may also have antidepressant properties. Studies have shown that it can improve symptoms of depression in people with mild to moderate depression.
- Cognitive Function: Ashwagandha may improve cognitive function and memory. It has been shown to improve reaction time, cognitive performance, and attention in healthy individuals and those with mild cognitive impairment.
- Immune System: Ashwagandha has been shown to boost immune system function by increasing white blood cell counts and enhancing immune cell activity.
- Sexual Function: Ashwagandha has been traditionally used as an aphrodisiac and may help improve sexual function in both men and women.
- Inflammation: Ashwagandha has anti-inflammatory properties that may help reduce inflammation in the body and improve conditions such as rheumatoid arthritis and osteoarthritis.
- Diabetes: Ashwagandha may help regulate blood sugar levels in people with diabetes by increasing insulin sensitivity and improving glucose metabolism.

It is important to note that while ashwagandha has potential medicinal benefits, more research is needed to fully understand its effects and to determine safe and effective dosages for various health conditions. As with any new supplement or herb, it is recommended to consult with a healthcare professional before use.

• Precautions and contradictions: Ashwagandha is generally considered safe for most people when taken in appropriate doses. However, there are some precautions to keep in mind. It is important to avoid ashwagandha if you are pregnant or breastfeeding, as it may have abortifacient properties. Additionally, ashwagandha may lower blood sugar levels and blood pressure, so people with diabetes or hypotension should use caution and monitor their levels closely if taking ashwagandha.

There are few known contraindications to ashwagandha, but it is recommended to avoid ashwagandha if you have autoimmune disorders such as multiple sclerosis, rheumatoid arthritis, or lupus, as it may stimulate the immune system and worsen symptoms. Ashwagandha may also interact with certain medications, such as sedatives, thyroid hormone replacement, and immunosuppressants, so it's important to consult with a healthcare provider before using ashwagandha if you are taking any medications.

As with any natural remedy, it's important to consult with a healthcare provider before using ashwagandha for medicinal purposes, especially if you have any underlying health conditions or are taking any medications.

Cultivation:
- Native to: India, Pakistan, Sri Lanka
- Zones: Ashwagandha is typically grown in zones 7-12.
- Soil: Ashwagandha prefers well-draining sandy or loamy soil with a pH range of 7.5-8.0.
- Propagation: Ashwagandha is typically grown from seed or propagated from cuttings.
- Growing information and garden care: Ashwagandha prefers full sun and requires regular watering during the growing season. It can be grown in containers or in the ground. Ashwagandha is a perennial plant and can be harvested after 1-2 years of growth.
- Insects and disease: Ashwagandha is generally pest-free, but can be susceptible to root rot if overwatered.
- Harvesting and preparations: The roots of ashwagandha can be harvested after 1-2 years of growth. The roots can be dried and used in herbal preparations or consumed as a tea or powder.

What medicines are made with this herb:
Ashwagandha is a popular herb used in traditional Ayurvedic medicine for its wide range of potential health benefits. Some of the medicines made with ashwagandha include:

- Capsules and tablets: Ashwagandha is commonly available in capsule or tablet form, which can be taken orally as a supplement.
- Tinctures: Ashwagandha tinctures are made by steeping the herb in alcohol or water and then straining it. The resulting liquid can be taken orally.
- Powders: Ashwagandha powder can be mixed into drinks or smoothies, or used to make herbal tea.
- Topical creams and ointments: Ashwagandha may be added to topical creams and ointments for its potential anti-inflammatory and skin-soothing effects.

- Ayurvedic preparations: Ashwagandha is a key ingredient in many traditional Ayurvedic formulas, such as Chyawanprash, which is a potent antioxidant and immune booster.

It is important to note that while ashwagandha is generally considered safe, it may interact with certain medications and supplements. Therefore, it is always important to speak with your healthcare provider before taking ashwagandha or any other herbal supplement.

What medicines this herb counteract:

Ashwagandha is generally considered safe and does not typically counteract any specific medicines. However, ashwagandha may interact with certain medications and supplements, including:

- Sedatives and anxiolytics: Ashwagandha may increase the effects of sedatives and anxiolytics, leading to excessive drowsiness or relaxation.
- Thyroid hormones: Ashwagandha may increase thyroid hormone levels, so it should be used with caution in individuals with thyroid disorders who are taking thyroid hormone medications.
- Immunosuppressant medications: Ashwagandha may increase immune system activity, so it should be used with caution in individuals taking immunosuppressant medications.
- Blood sugar lowering medications: Ashwagandha may lower blood sugar levels, so it should be used with caution in individuals taking medications for diabetes or other conditions that lower blood sugar levels.

It is important to speak with your healthcare provider before taking ashwagandha or any other herbal supplement, especially if you are taking prescription medications or have any underlying health conditions.

Astragalus

Herbal Identification:
- Common name: Astragalus
- Latin binomial: Astragalus membranaceus
- Other common names: Milk vetch, Huang qi
- Plant family: Fabaceae
- Botanical description: Astragalus is a plant species belonging to the legume family Fabaceae. It is a perennial herb that can grow up to 3 feet tall and has hairy stems with multiple branches. The leaves are composed of 12 to 18 small, oval-shaped leaflets that are silver-green in color. The plant produces small yellow flowers that bloom in late spring and early summer, followed by small seed pods.

The roots of the astragalus plant are the part typically used in herbal medicine. They are long, thin, and have a yellowish-white color. The roots have a sweet, slightly warming taste and are used in both traditional Chinese medicine and Western herbalism. Astragalus is also commonly grown as an ornamental plant due to its attractive foliage and delicate flowers.

Medicinal Properties:
- Recommended cultivars: There are several species of Astragalus used medicinally, but Astragalus membranaceus is the most commonly used.
- Parts used: The root of the astragalus plant is the primary part used for medicinal purposes. The root is harvested from mature plants that are at least four years old, as it takes several years for the root to develop the desired medicinal compounds. After harvesting, the root is typically cleaned, dried, and cut into small pieces or made into a powder for use in herbal preparations. Some herbalists may also use the leaves and stems of the plant in certain preparations, but the root is the most commonly used part.
- Taste: Sweet, slightly warm.
- Actions: Adaptogen, immunomodulating, tonic, diuretic.
- Energetics: Sweet, slightly warm.
- Specific indications: Astragalus is commonly used to support the immune system and prevent respiratory infections, such as the common cold and flu. It is also used as a tonic herb to improve overall vitality and energy levels, and to support the body during times of physical or emotional stress. Other specific indications for astragalus include:
  ➢ Chronic fatigue syndrome

- Chronic infections, such as Lyme disease or hepatitis
- Weakness or atrophy of muscles
- Allergies and asthma
- /Diabetes
- High blood pressure
- Heart disease
- Kidney disease
- Cancer

It is important to note that while astragalus may offer support for these conditions, it should not be used as a substitute for conventional medical treatment.

Medicinal preparations:
Astragalus can be prepared in various ways to extract its medicinal properties. Some common preparations include:
- Decoction: This involves simmering the dried root of astragalus in water for a prolonged period of time to extract its medicinal constituents. The resulting liquid can be consumed as a tea or used as a base for soups and stews.
- Tincture: Astragalus can be extracted in alcohol to create a concentrated liquid extract that can be added to water or taken directly in small doses.
- Capsules or tablets: Astragalus is also available in capsule or tablet form for convenience and easy dosing.
- Topical applications: Astragalus can be infused into oils or creams for external use, such as for skin irritations or wound healing.

Dosage and ratio information for astragalus will vary depending on the form of the herb and the specific condition being treated. It is always recommended to consult with a healthcare practitioner before using any herbal preparations.
- Ratio and dosage information: The typical dose of Astragalus root is 9-15 grams per day in decoction or 3-6 grams per day in capsules.

Medicinal uses:
Astragalus has a long history of use in traditional Chinese medicine for its immune-boosting properties. Some of the medicinal uses of astragalus include:
- Boosting the immune system: Astragalus is believed to stimulate the immune system and increase the production of white blood cells, which can help protect the body against infections and diseases.
- Supporting heart health: Astragalus may help improve heart function by reducing inflammation, lowering blood pressure, and improving blood flow.

- Improving respiratory health: Astragalus may help improve respiratory function by reducing inflammation and improving lung function, which can benefit people with respiratory conditions such as asthma and chronic obstructive pulmonary disease (COPD).
- Supporting kidney function: Astragalus is believed to support kidney function and may help protect against kidney damage caused by certain medications.
- Fighting fatigue: Astragalus may help combat fatigue and increase energy levels by supporting adrenal gland function.
- Managing diabetes: Astragalus may help regulate blood sugar levels and improve insulin sensitivity, making it potentially beneficial for people with diabetes.

It is important to note that more research is needed to fully understand the potential benefits and risks of using astragalus for medicinal purposes. It is always recommended to consult with a healthcare professional before using any herbal remedies.

- Precautions and contradictions: Astragalus is considered safe for most people when used appropriately. However, there are some precautions and contraindications to keep in mind.
  - Autoimmune diseases: Astragalus may stimulate the immune system, which could worsen symptoms in people with autoimmune diseases such as lupus, multiple sclerosis, and rheumatoid arthritis. It's best to avoid using astragalus if you have any of these conditions.
  - Immunosuppressant medications: Astragalus may interfere with the action of immunosuppressant medications, which are often used to prevent rejection of transplanted organs or to treat autoimmune diseases. If you're taking immunosuppressant drugs, avoid using astragalus unless under the guidance of a healthcare provider.
  - Pregnancy and breastfeeding: There's not enough research on the safety of astragalus during pregnancy and breastfeeding. It's best to avoid using it in these situations unless recommended by a healthcare provider.
  - Interactions with medications: Astragalus may interact with certain medications, including medications for diabetes, blood pressure, and blood thinning. If you're taking any medications, talk to your healthcare provider before using astragalus to avoid potential interactions.

Cultivation:
- Native to: China
- Zones: Astragalus is hardy in USDA zones 4-8.

- Soil: Prefers well-drained, sandy soil with a pH of 6.0-8.0.
- Propagation: Can be grown from seed or propagated by division in the spring or fall.
- Growing information and garden care: Astragalus prefers full sun to partial shade and is drought-tolerant once established. It should be planted in a location protected from high winds. It is a slow-growing plant and may take several years to reach maturity.
- Insects and disease: Astragalus plants are relatively hardy and not prone to many insect pests or diseases. However, some common problems that may occur include:
  - Root rot: This is a fungal disease that can affect astragalus plants if they are planted in soil that does not drain well. To prevent root rot, it is important to plant astragalus in well-draining soil and avoid overwatering.
  - Leaf spot: This is a fungal disease that can cause small, circular spots on the leaves of astragalus plants. It is usually not serious but can cause the leaves to yellow and drop prematurely. To prevent leaf spot, avoid getting the leaves wet when watering and remove any infected leaves promptly.
  - Aphids: These tiny insects can infest the leaves and stems of astragalus plants, sucking the sap and causing the leaves to curl and yellow. To control aphids, spray the plants with a strong jet of water or use insecticidal soap.
  - Spider mites: These are tiny arachnids that can infest astragalus plants, causing stippling or yellowing of the leaves. To control spider mites, spray the plants with a strong jet of water or use insecticidal soap.
  - Whiteflies: These are small, flying insects that can infest the leaves of astragalus plants, causing them to turn yellow and fall off prematurely. To control whiteflies, spray the plants with a strong jet of water or use insecticidal soap.
- Harvesting and preparations: The best time to harvest the roots of astragalus is in the fall, after the plant has died back and the energy has returned to the roots. The roots can be harvested by carefully digging around the base of the plant with a garden fork, being careful not to damage the roots.

Once harvested, the roots can be cleaned, dried, and sliced for use in teas, decoctions, tinctures, or capsules. To make a tea or decoction, simmer 1-2 teaspoons of dried root in 8 ounces of water for 20-30 minutes. Tinctures can be made by soaking the dried root in alcohol for several weeks before straining and bottling.

It is important to note that astragalus is often used in combination with other herbs to create synergistic effects. As with any medicinal herb, it is best to consult with a healthcare professional before using astragalus for medicinal purposes.

What medicines are made with this herb:

Astragalus is a commonly used herb in traditional Chinese medicine and is also used in Western herbal medicine. It is used in a variety of medicinal preparations, including:

- Tinctures: Astragalus tinctures are made by steeping the dried root in alcohol for several weeks. They are used to support immune function and promote overall health.
- Capsules: Astragalus capsules are made by grinding the dried root into a powder and encapsulating it. They are used to support immune function and reduce stress.
- Tea: Astragalus tea is made by steeping the dried root in hot water for several minutes. It is used to support immune function, reduce stress, and promote overall health.
- Topical preparations: Astragalus root powder can be used topically as a poultice or added to creams and lotions to soothe and nourish the skin.
- Soup: Astragalus root is sometimes added to soups and stews for its immune-supportive properties. It is often used in traditional Chinese soups like "huang qi" soup.
- Other herbal formulations: Astragalus is often used in combination with other herbs in traditional herbal formulations to support immune function, reduce stress, and promote overall health.

What medicines this herb counteract:

Astragalus is generally considered safe and does not typically counteract any specific medicines. However, if you are taking immunosuppressive medications, it is important to consult with your healthcare provider before using astragalus as it may interact with these medications. Astragalus may also interact with medications that are metabolized by the liver, so it is important to speak with your healthcare provider if you are taking any prescription or over-the-counter medications.

Bay Laurel

Herbal Identification:
- Common name: Bay Laurel
- Latin binomial: Laurus nobilis
- Other common names: Sweet Bay, Grecian Laurel
- Plant family: Lauraceae
- Botanical description: Bay Laurel, also known as sweet bay or bay tree, is a small evergreen tree or large shrub that belongs to the family Lauraceae. It is native to the Mediterranean region and can grow up to 10-18 meters tall in the wild. The leaves of the Bay Laurel are oval-shaped, glossy, and dark green in color, measuring about 6-12 cm in length and 2-4 cm in width. The tree also produces small yellow or greenish-yellow flowers that bloom in clusters from March to May, and its fruits are small, round, and black berries that ripen in the autumn. The bark of the Bay Laurel is smooth and grey, and the wood is hard and durable.

The Bay Laurel has a long history of culinary and medicinal use. Its leaves are commonly used as a spice in cooking, and the essential oil extracted from the leaves is used in aromatherapy and natural skincare products. The Bay Laurel also has a rich tradition of medicinal use, particularly in traditional European and Mediterranean herbal medicine.

Medicinal Properties:
- Recommended cultivars: No specific cultivars recommended.
- Parts used: Leaves and essential oil
- Taste: Aromatic, bitter, pungent
- Actions: Antimicrobial, antifungal, antioxidant, antispasmodic, carminative, diaphoretic, emmenagogue, expectorant, stimulant
- Energetics: Warming, drying
- Specific indications: Bay laurel (Laurus nobilis) has a wide range of traditional uses and potential health benefits. Some specific indications for using bay laurel include:
  - Digestive issues: Bay laurel has been traditionally used to aid digestion, relieve gas and bloating, and soothe stomach upset.
  - Respiratory issues: Bay laurel can help soothe respiratory congestion and coughs. It may also help alleviate symptoms of asthma, bronchitis, and other respiratory conditions.

- Skin conditions: Bay laurel has antibacterial and antifungal properties, making it useful for treating skin infections and irritations. It may also help relieve symptoms of eczema and psoriasis.
- Joint and muscle pain: Bay laurel has analgesic and anti-inflammatory properties, which can help reduce pain and inflammation in the joints and muscles.
- Stress and anxiety: Bay laurel has a calming effect on the nervous system and may help reduce symptoms of stress and anxiety. It is also believed to improve mental clarity and focus.
- Menstrual cramps: Bay laurel has been traditionally used to relieve menstrual cramps and regulate menstrual cycles.

It is important to note that bay laurel should not be used as a replacement for conventional medical treatment, and it is always recommended to consult with a healthcare provider before using any herbal remedies.

Medicinal preparations:

Bay laurel leaves can be prepared as a tea, infusion, tincture, or essential oil for medicinal purposes.

To make a bay leaf tea, add 1-2 teaspoons of dried bay leaves to 1 cup of boiling water and steep for 5-10 minutes. The tea can be consumed up to 3 times per day.

To make an infusion, use a larger quantity of dried bay leaves (around 4-5 teaspoons) and steep in a quart of boiling water for 30 minutes to an hour. This can be consumed in smaller amounts throughout the day.

Bay laurel tinctures can be made by steeping the leaves in alcohol for several weeks, shaking daily, then straining and bottling the liquid. The recommended dosage for a tincture is usually 1-2 dropperfuls up to 3 times per day.

Bay laurel essential oil can be added to carrier oils such as coconut or jojoba oil, and used for topical applications such as massage or as an inhalant for respiratory issues. However, it is important to note that essential oils are highly concentrated and should be used with caution, and should not be ingested.

As with any medicinal herb, it is recommended to consult with a healthcare professional before use, especially if pregnant, breastfeeding, or taking any medications.

• Ratio and dosage information: Infusion: 1-2 teaspoons of dried bay leaves per cup of boiling water, steep for 10-15 minutes; Tincture: 1-2 ml, 3 times per day; Essential oil: 1-2 drops in a diffuser or diluted in a carrier oil for topical use.

Medicinal uses: Bay Laurel (Laurus nobilis) has a long history of medicinal use. The plant has antimicrobial, antifungal, and anti-inflammatory properties. Some of the medicinal uses of Bay Laurel include:
- Digestive disorders: Bay Laurel has been traditionally used to treat digestive disorders such as indigestion, flatulence, and bloating. It helps to stimulate the production of digestive enzymes, which aids in digestion.
- Respiratory problems: Bay Laurel has been used to treat respiratory problems such as bronchitis, asthma, and coughs. Its essential oil has expectorant properties that help to loosen mucus and ease breathing.
- Arthritis and rheumatism: Bay Laurel has anti-inflammatory properties that make it useful in the treatment of arthritis and rheumatism. It can be used topically as a massage oil or added to bathwater for a relaxing soak.
- Skin conditions: Bay Laurel has been used to treat a variety of skin conditions such as eczema, acne, and psoriasis. Its antimicrobial properties can help to reduce inflammation and prevent infection.
- Headaches and migraines: Bay Laurel has been used to treat headaches and migraines. Its essential oil can be applied topically to the temples or used in aromatherapy.

It is important to note that Bay Laurel should not be used in large quantities or for extended periods of time. It should also not be used during pregnancy or by individuals with liver or kidney problems. As with any herbal remedy, it is recommended to consult with a healthcare provider before use.
• Precautions and contradictions: Bay Laurel, also known as Laurus nobilis, is generally considered safe when used in culinary amounts. However, when used in medicinal amounts, it can have some precautions and contraindications.

The essential oil of bay laurel should not be taken internally, as it can be toxic and cause serious side effects such as vomiting, confusion, and seizures. Pregnant and breastfeeding women should avoid using bay laurel in medicinal amounts due to potential risks to the fetus or infant.

Bay laurel may interact with certain medications, including blood thinners and diabetes medications, so it is important to speak with a healthcare provider before using bay laurel medicinally if you are taking any prescription medications. It is also important to note that some people may be allergic to bay laurel, and may experience allergic reactions such as skin rash, itching, or difficulty breathing.

Cultivation:
- Native to: Mediterranean region
- Zones: Bay Laurel is hardy in USDA zones 8-11.
- Soil: Bay Laurel prefers well-drained soil that is slightly acidic to neutral (pH 6.0-7.5).
- Propagation: Bay Laurel can be propagated from seeds or cuttings.
- Growing information and garden care: Bay Laurel prefers full sun to partial shade and requires moderate watering. It can be grown in pots or in the ground, and should be pruned regularly to maintain shape and size.
- Insects and disease: Bay laurel is generally a hardy plant with few issues with insects or diseases. However, it can occasionally be affected by scale insects, mites, and whiteflies. Fungal diseases, such as powdery mildew and leaf spot, can also occur if the plant is grown in damp, humid conditions.

Proper spacing and air circulation, as well as avoiding overhead watering, can help prevent these issues. If necessary, organic pesticides and fungicides can be used to control insect and disease problems.
- Harvesting and preparations: Bay Laurel leaves can be harvested throughout the year, but they are most potent when harvested in the morning during the spring or summer. It is best to use young leaves, as they have a higher concentration of essential oils.

To harvest, simply pick the leaves by hand, being careful not to damage the tree. It is recommended to only take a few leaves from each tree to ensure that the tree is not overharvested.

Once harvested, the leaves can be used fresh or dried for later use. To dry, spread the leaves out in a single layer in a well-ventilated area out of direct sunlight. The leaves can be stored in an airtight container once they are completely dry.

Bay Laurel leaves can be used fresh or dried in a variety of culinary dishes and as a flavoring agent in teas and other beverages. The essential oil extracted from the leaves can also be used topically as a massage oil or added to skincare products for its antimicrobial and antioxidant properties.

What medicines are made with this herb:

Bay Laurel (Laurus nobilis) is commonly used as a culinary herb and a fragrant ornamental plant. However, it also has some medicinal uses, including:
- Essential oil: Bay Laurel essential oil is extracted from the leaves and is used in aromatherapy and massage. It is believed to have a warming effect on the body and can help ease muscle aches and pains, as well as digestive issues.
- Herbal tea: Bay Laurel leaves can be used to make a tea that is believed to help relieve coughs, colds, and other respiratory issues.
- Poultice: Bay Laurel leaves can be crushed and applied to the skin to help ease pain and inflammation.
- Tincture: Bay Laurel leaves can be used to make a tincture that is believed to help boost the immune system and support overall health.

It is important to note that the medicinal uses of Bay Laurel have not been extensively researched, and it should not be used as a substitute for conventional medical treatment without consulting a healthcare professional.

What medicines this herb counteract:
Bay laurel is not typically known to counteract any specific medications. However, it is important to note that the essential oil and some of the chemical components of bay laurel may interact with certain medications or conditions. For example, the essential oil may cause skin irritation or allergic reactions in some individuals, and should be used with caution. Additionally, the chemical component eugenol found in bay laurel oil may interact with blood-thinning medications or cause issues for those with bleeding disorders. As with any herbal remedy, it is always best to consult with a healthcare provider before using bay laurel in medicinal preparations, particularly if you are taking any medications or have any underlying health conditions.

Black Cohosh

Herbal Identification:
- Common name: Black cohosh
- Latin binomial: Actaea racemosa
- Other common names: Black snakeroot, bugbane, bugwort, rattleroot, rattletop, rattleweed, and macrotys
- Plant family: Ranunculaceae
- Botanical description: Black cohosh (Actaea racemosa) is a herbaceous perennial plant that belongs to the buttercup family Ranunculaceae. It is native to eastern North America and typically grows in the understory of hardwood forests, reaching a height of 3-9 feet (1-3 meters). The plant has large, compound leaves with toothed edges and produces tall, showy spikes of small white or cream-colored flowers in the late summer to early fall. The plant's root and rhizome are the parts used for medicinal purposes.

Medicinal Properties:
- Recommended cultivars: Not applicable
- Parts used: The parts of the black cohosh plant that are typically used for medicinal purposes are the roots and rhizomes (underground stems).
- Taste: Slightly bitter, astringent
- Actions: Anti-inflammatory, antispasmodic, estrogenic, nervine, sedative
- Energetics: Cooling and moistening
- Specific indications: Black cohosh has traditionally been used for a variety of indications, including:
  - Menopausal symptoms: Black cohosh is commonly used to alleviate hot flashes, night sweats, mood swings, vaginal dryness, and other symptoms of menopause.
  - Premenstrual syndrome (PMS): Black cohosh can help relieve symptoms of PMS, including mood swings, irritability, breast tenderness, and cramping.
  - Pain relief: Black cohosh has anti-inflammatory and analgesic properties and can be used to alleviate pain associated with conditions such as arthritis, rheumatism, and muscle spasms.
  - Anxiety and depression: Black cohosh can help to reduce anxiety, nervousness, and depression.
  - Sleep disturbances: Black cohosh can improve the quality of sleep and alleviate insomnia.
  - Bone health: Black cohosh can help to prevent bone loss and improve bone density, reducing the risk of osteoporosis.

> Menstrual irregularities: Black cohosh can help to regulate menstrual cycles and alleviate symptoms of menstrual irregularities.

It is important to note that more research is needed to fully understand the effectiveness of black cohosh for these specific indications. As with any herbal remedy, it is recommended to consult with a healthcare professional before using black cohosh for medicinal purposes.

Medicinal preparations:
Black cohosh can be taken in various forms, including:
> Tea or infusion: Add 1-2 teaspoons of dried black cohosh root to a cup of hot water and let it steep for 10-15 minutes. Drink this tea up to three times per day.
> Tincture: A tincture is a liquid extract made by soaking black cohosh root in alcohol. It can be taken orally, usually in 1-2 ml doses up to three times per day.
> Capsules or tablets: These are available in health food stores and should be taken as directed on the label.
> 4opical cream: Black cohosh cream can be applied topically to the skin to relieve symptoms of menopause, such as hot flashes.

It is important to follow the recommended dosages on the product label or as advised by a healthcare provider.
• Ratio and dosage information: Dosage varies depending on the preparation and individual needs. Typical doses range from 20-40 drops of tincture, 1-2 grams of dried root in a tea, or 40-80 mg of standardized extract per day.

Medicinal uses:
Black cohosh (Actaea racemosa) is a popular herbal remedy that has been used traditionally for a variety of purposes. Some of its commonly known medicinal uses include:
> Menopause: Black cohosh is used to alleviate symptoms of menopause, such as hot flashes, vaginal dryness, and mood swings.
> Premenstrual syndrome (PMS): It may help reduce symptoms of PMS, such as cramping, mood swings, and breast tenderness.
> Pain relief: Black cohosh may have pain-relieving effects, and it is sometimes used to help alleviate pain associated with conditions such as osteoarthritis, rheumatoid arthritis, and neuralgia.
> Sleep disorders: It may help to improve sleep quality and duration.

- Anxiety and depression: Black cohosh may have mild anti-anxiety and anti-depressant effects.
- Menstrual irregularities: Black cohosh may help regulate menstrual cycles and reduce heavy bleeding.
- Bone health: It may help improve bone density and reduce the risk of osteoporosis.

However, it's important to note that research on the effectiveness of black cohosh for these uses is limited and more studies are needed to determine its potential benefits and risks. It is important to talk to a healthcare provider before using black cohosh as a medicinal herb.

• Precautions and contradictions: Black cohosh is generally safe for most people when taken appropriately for up to 6 months. However, long-term use is not recommended, as it may increase the risk of certain types of cancer. Pregnant and breastfeeding women should avoid taking black cohosh, as it may stimulate uterine contractions and affect hormone levels. People with liver disease should also avoid black cohosh, as it may worsen liver function. In addition, people taking medication for blood pressure, blood thinning, or hormone therapy should consult a healthcare professional before taking black cohosh. Finally, individuals with a history of breast cancer or estrogen-sensitive cancers should avoid using black cohosh.

Cultivation:
 • Native to: Eastern part of North America
 • Zones: 3-8
 • Soil (pH and type of soil): Prefers rich, moist, well-drained soil with a pH of 6.0-7.0
 • Propagation: Black cohosh can be propagated from seeds or by dividing the root ball in the fall or early spring.
 • Growing information and garden care: Black cohosh prefers partial shade and moist soil. It can be grown in a woodland garden or shaded perennial border. It is a low-maintenance plant that requires minimal care once established.
 • Insects and disease: Not particularly prone to pests or diseases.
 • Harvesting and preparations: The roots are typically harvested in the fall after the leaves have died back. They can be dried for later use or used fresh to make a tincture or tea.

What medicines are made with this herb:
Black cohosh is used in a variety of herbal remedies and dietary supplements, including:

- Menopausal symptom relief: Black cohosh is commonly used to alleviate hot flashes, mood swings, and other symptoms of menopause.
- Pain relief: Black cohosh is sometimes used to relieve menstrual cramps, headaches, and other types of pain.
- Anti-inflammatory agent: Black cohosh is believed to have anti-inflammatory properties, and is sometimes used to treat conditions such as arthritis.
- Mood disorders: Some studies suggest that black cohosh may have a positive effect on mood, and may be useful in treating anxiety and depression.

It is important to note that the U.S. Food and Drug Administration (FDA) does not regulate dietary supplements, and there is limited scientific evidence to support the effectiveness of black cohosh in treating these conditions. As with any herbal remedy or supplement, it is important to consult with a healthcare provider before using black cohosh.

What medicines this herb counteract:

Black cohosh may interact with some medications, such as hormonal contraceptives, antihypertensive drugs, and sedatives. It may also interact with supplements like St. John's wort and valerian. It's important to speak with a healthcare provider before taking black cohosh if you are on any medications or supplements.

Burdock

Herbal Identification:
- Common name: Burdock
- Latin binomial: Arctium lappa
- Other common names: Great burdock, edible burdock, gobo
- Plant family: Asteraceae or Compositae (daisy family)
- Botanical description: Burdock, also known as Arctium lappa, is a biennial plant in the Asteraceae family. It can grow up to 6 feet tall and has large, broad leaves that can reach up to 2 feet long. In its first year, burdock produces a rosette of large leaves close to the ground. In the second year, it produces a tall stem with smaller leaves and pink-purple flowers arranged in clusters. The plant produces a large taproot that can grow up to 3 feet long and is brown on the outside and white on the inside. The plant is native to Europe and Asia but has since been naturalized in other parts of the world, including North America.

Medicinal Properties:
- Recommended cultivars: None specified
- Parts used: Root, seeds, leaves
- Taste: Bitter, sweet
- Actions: Alterative, diuretic, mild laxative, diaphoretic, hepatic, tonic, antimicrobial, anti-inflammatory
- Energetics: Cooling and moistening
- Specific indications: Skin disorders (acne, eczema, psoriasis), urinary tract infections, constipation, liver and gallbladder disorders, arthritis and rheumatism, fever, respiratory infections, diabetes, cancer

Burdock has been traditionally used for a variety of medicinal purposes, including:

- Skin health: Burdock is believed to promote skin health and is commonly used to alleviate skin conditions such as acne, eczema, and psoriasis.
- Digestive health: Burdock is believed to promote digestive health by stimulating the production of digestive juices and enzymes. It is also used to alleviate digestive conditions such as constipation and bloating.
- Blood sugar control: Burdock is believed to help regulate blood sugar levels, making it a potential treatment for diabetes.
- Anti-inflammatory effects: Burdock is believed to have anti-inflammatory effects, which may make it useful in treating conditions such as arthritis.
- Immune system support: Burdock is believed to support immune system function, making it useful for fighting off infections.

- Detoxification: Burdock is believed to help support the liver and promote detoxification.

It is important to note that while burdock has been traditionally used for these purposes, more research is needed to fully understand its potential health benefits.

Medicinal preparations:
Burdock root can be prepared in a variety of ways for medicinal use. Some common preparations include:
- Infusion: A burdock root infusion can be made by steeping 1-2 teaspoons of dried root in 8 ounces of hot water for 10-15 minutes. This can be consumed up to three times a day.
- Decoction: A decoction can be made by simmering 1-2 teaspoons of dried root in 8 ounces of water for 10-15 minutes. This can also be consumed up to three times a day.
- Tincture: Burdock root tincture can be made by steeping chopped root in alcohol for several weeks. The tincture can be taken in 1-2 mL doses up to three times a day.
- Capsules: Burdock root capsules are also available and can be taken according to the manufacturer's instructions.
- Poultice: A burdock root poultice can be made by boiling fresh or dried roots, mashing them, and applying the resulting paste to the skin. This can help to relieve skin irritations and infections.

It's important to note that the appropriate preparation and dosage of burdock root may vary depending on the specific condition being treated and individual factors such as age, weight, and overall health. It's always best to consult with a healthcare practitioner before using any herbal remedies.

- Ratio and dosage information: Dried root: 2-6 g per day; tincture: 2-4 ml, 3 times per day; decoction: 2-3 cups per day

Medicinal uses:
Burdock (Arctium lappa) has a long history of medicinal use and is valued for its many health benefits. Some of the traditional medicinal uses of burdock include:
- Skin Health: Burdock root is used to promote healthy skin, clear up acne and eczema, and alleviate dry skin conditions. It can be taken internally or applied topically in the form of a poultice or salve.
- Detoxification: Burdock root is a blood purifier and helps to eliminate toxins from the body. It supports liver function and promotes the elimination of waste through the kidneys and digestive system.

- Digestive Health: Burdock root is a digestive tonic and can help to alleviate symptoms of indigestion, bloating, and constipation. It stimulates the production of digestive juices and supports the growth of beneficial gut bacteria.
- Immune System Support: Burdock root contains compounds that have been shown to boost the immune system and protect against bacterial and viral infections.
- Anti-inflammatory: Burdock root contains compounds that have anti-inflammatory properties and can help to reduce pain and inflammation in the body.
- 6ancer Prevention: Some studies have suggested that burdock root may have anti-cancer properties and may be effective in preventing certain types of cancer.

It is important to note that more research is needed to fully understand the medicinal uses and benefits of burdock, and that it should not be used as a substitute for medical treatment.

• Precautions and contradictions: Burdock is generally considered safe for most people when consumed in food amounts or taken as a dietary supplement. However, there are some precautions and potential side effects to be aware of:

- Allergic reactions: Some people may experience an allergic reaction to burdock, especially if they are also allergic to plants in the daisy family.
- Pregnancy and breastfeeding: Pregnant and breastfeeding women should avoid using burdock as there is not enough reliable information available on its safety during these times.
- Diabetes: Burdock might lower blood sugar levels, so people with diabetes or hypoglycemia should use burdock with caution and monitor their blood sugar levels closely.
- Surgery: Burdock might increase the risk of bleeding during surgery due to its blood-thinning properties, so it should be stopped at least two weeks before surgery.

It is always recommended to consult with a healthcare professional before using any new herbs or supplements, especially if you have a medical condition or take any medications.

Cultivation:
• Native to: Europe and Asia
• Zones: 3-9
• Soil (pH and type of soil): Well-drained soil with a pH between 5.5-7.0; prefers loamy or sandy soil

- Propagation: Burdock can be grown from seed or root cuttings.
- Growing information and garden care: Burdock is a hardy plant that prefers full sun to partial shade. It can be grown in a variety of soils but prefers rich, moist soil. Burdock can be invasive, so it is important to control its spread by harvesting the burrs before they mature.
- Insects and disease: Burdock is susceptible to a number of insect pests, including aphids, flea beetles, and Japanese beetles. It may also be affected by various plant diseases such as powdery mildew, leaf spot, and root rot. To prevent insect infestations and diseases, it's recommended to provide adequate soil drainage, maintain good air circulation, and practice crop rotation.
- Harvesting and preparations: Burdock roots are typically harvested in the fall of their first year or the spring of their second year. They should be dug up when the soil is moist and then washed, dried, and cut into small pieces. The leaves and seeds can also be used medicinally and are harvested in the summer.

Burdock root can be prepared in various ways, including as a decoction, tincture, or infusion. To make a decoction, the roots are simmered in water for 20-30 minutes. To make a tincture, the roots are soaked in alcohol for several weeks before being strained. To make an infusion, the dried leaves or seeds are steeped in hot water for 10-15 minutes.

Burdock root can also be used in cooking, particularly in Japanese and Korean cuisine. It can be sautéed, stir-fried, or boiled, and is often used in soups and stews. The young leaves of burdock can also be eaten raw or cooked, and the seeds can be roasted and used as a coffee substitute.

What medicines are made with this herb:
Burdock root is used as a traditional herbal remedy in various forms, including teas, tinctures, capsules, and extracts. Some specific medicines made with burdock include:
- Burdock root tea: Used to treat skin problems, boost liver function, and support the immune system.
- Burdock root tincture: Used to help treat skin conditions, promote detoxification, and boost liver function.
- Burdock root oil: Used topically to treat skin conditions such as eczema, psoriasis, and acne.
- Burdock root capsules: Used as a dietary supplement to promote overall health and well-being.

It's important to note that these uses have not been evaluated by the FDA, and burdock root should not be used as a substitute for medical treatment without consulting a healthcare professional.

What medicines this herb counteracts:

There is no known specific medicine that Burdock counteracts. However, as with any herbal medicine, it is important to consult with a healthcare professional before use, especially if you are taking any prescription medications or have a pre-existing medical condition. Burdock root may interact with some medications, including diuretics and blood thinners, so it is important to use caution and seek medical advice if you are considering using Burdock root as a medicinal herb.

Calendula

Herbal Identification:
- Common Name: Calendula
- Latin Binomial: Calendula officinalis
- Other Common Names: Pot marigold, English marigold, Marybud
- Plant Family: Asteraceae
- Botanical Description: Calendula, also known as pot marigold, is a plant species in the daisy family (Asteraceae). It is native to the Mediterranean region but has been widely cultivated throughout the world. Calendula plants typically grow 30 to 60 cm (12 to 24 in) tall, with bright yellow or orange flowers that bloom from early summer to early autumn. The leaves are bright green, oblong, and arranged oppositely on the stem. The plant has a hairy stem and leaves, and the flowers are made up of ray and disc florets. The fruit is a small achene with a curved shape. Calendula is an annual or short-lived perennial plant and is easy to grow in gardens.

Medicinal Properties:
- Recommended Cultivars: 'Lemon Zest', 'Radio', 'Indian Prince'
- Parts Used: Flower petals
- Taste: Bitter
- Actions: Anti-inflammatory, antispasmodic, astringent, lymphatic, vulnerary
- Energetics: Warming and drying
- Specific Indications: Calendula has a variety of potential health benefits and specific indications, some of which include:
  - Wound healing: Calendula has anti-inflammatory and antimicrobial properties that may help to speed up the healing of wounds, including cuts, burns, and bruises.
  - Skin irritation and rashes: Calendula has soothing properties that may help to reduce skin inflammation and irritation, including eczema, psoriasis, and dermatitis.
  - Menstrual cramps: Calendula has been used traditionally to help ease menstrual cramps and regulate menstrual cycles.
  - Digestive issues: Calendula may help to soothe digestive issues such as upset stomach, gastritis, and ulcers.
  - Oral health: Calendula may help to promote oral health by reducing inflammation and fighting bacteria that can cause gum disease and tooth decay.

- Immune system support: Calendula has immune-stimulating properties that may help to support overall immune function and reduce the risk of infections.

Medicinal Preparations:
Calendula can be prepared in a variety of ways for medicinal use. Here are a few examples:
- Infusion: Calendula flowers can be steeped in hot water to make an infusion. This can be used as a topical wash or taken internally as a tea.
- Oil: Calendula flowers can be infused in a carrier oil, such as olive or coconut oil, to make a soothing and healing oil. This can be used topically for a variety of skin conditions.
- Salve: Calendula oil can be mixed with beeswax to make a salve, which can be used topically on wounds, burns, and other skin irritations.
- Tincture: Calendula flowers can be infused in alcohol to make a tincture, which can be taken internally for digestive issues or used topically on wounds and skin irritations.

It's important to note that different preparations may be more effective for different conditions, and dosages can vary depending on the method of preparation and intended use. It's always best to consult with a qualified herbalist or healthcare provider before using any herbal preparations.
• Ratio and Dosage Information: For tea, steep 1-2 teaspoons of dried flowers in 8 ounces of hot water for 10-15 minutes, and drink up to three times per day. As a tincture, take 2-4 milliliters up to three times per day. For external use, apply as needed.

Medicinal Uses:
Calendula, also known as marigold, has a wide range of medicinal uses. Some of the most common uses include:
- Skin health: Calendula has anti-inflammatory and antibacterial properties, making it effective in treating a variety of skin conditions such as cuts, wounds, burns, and rashes. It can also be used to soothe dry or irritated skin.
- Menstrual cramps: Calendula has antispasmodic properties that can help to relieve menstrual cramps.
- Digestive health: Calendula can be used to stimulate digestion and relieve gastrointestinal problems such as indigestion, constipation, and stomach ulcers.

- Anti-inflammatory: Calendula has anti-inflammatory properties that can help to reduce inflammation throughout the body. It has been used to treat conditions such as arthritis, asthma, and inflammatory bowel disease.
- Immune system support: Calendula contains compounds that can help to stimulate the immune system and protect against infections.
- Oral health: Calendula can be used to treat oral health problems such as gingivitis and mouth ulcers. It has antibacterial and anti-inflammatory properties that can help to reduce inflammation and prevent the growth of harmful bacteria.
- Eye health: Calendula can be used to treat a variety of eye conditions such as conjunctivitis and dry eyes. It has anti-inflammatory and antibacterial properties that can help to reduce inflammation and prevent infections.

It is important to note that while calendula is generally considered safe, it may cause an allergic reaction in some individuals. It should also not be used during pregnancy without first consulting with a healthcare provider.

• Precautions and Contradictions: Calendula is generally considered safe for most people when used appropriately. However, individuals with allergies to plants in the Asteraceae/Compositae family (such as ragweed, chamomile, and echinacea) may experience allergic reactions to calendula.

Calendula may also cause skin irritation or a rash in some people when applied topically, especially if they have sensitive skin. It is recommended to do a patch test before using it extensively on the skin.

Pregnant and breastfeeding women should consult their healthcare provider before using calendula, as there is not enough scientific evidence about its safety during pregnancy and lactation.

Ingesting large amounts of calendula may cause nausea, vomiting, dizziness, and other symptoms. It is important to follow recommended dosages and consult a healthcare provider before taking calendula internally.

Cultivation:
• Native to: Mediterranean region
• Zones: 3-9
• Soil: Well-draining soil with a pH of 6.0-7.0
• Propagation: Seeds or cuttings

- Growing Information and Garden Care: Calendula is easy to grow and thrives in full sun to partial shade. It prefers cool temperatures and can be grown in containers or in the ground. Water regularly and fertilize lightly.
- Insects and Disease: Calendula is relatively resistant to pests and diseases. However, some pests that may occasionally affect calendula include aphids, slugs, snails, and spider mites. To prevent these pests, it is important to maintain good garden hygiene and to remove any plant debris regularly.

Fungal diseases such as powdery mildew and rust can also affect calendula, particularly in humid or wet conditions. To prevent these diseases, avoid over-watering and ensure adequate air circulation around the plants.

In general, calendula is a hardy and low-maintenance plant that is easy to grow and care for.
- Harvesting and Preparations: Calendula is a fairly easy plant to grow and harvest. Here are some tips for harvesting and preparing calendula:
  - Harvesting: Calendula flowers should be harvested in the morning when the dew has dried, but before the sun gets too hot. The flowers should be plucked off the stem, and any green or brown parts should be removed.
  - Drying: The flowers can be dried in a cool, dry place with good ventilation. Spread them out in a single layer on a clean, dry surface. They will shrink as they dry.
  - Infusion: Calendula flowers can be used to make an infusion. Pour boiling water over the dried flowers and let steep for 10-15 minutes. Strain and drink as desired.
  - Oil: Calendula flowers can also be used to make an infused oil. Combine dried flowers and a carrier oil such as olive or jojoba oil in a glass jar. Let the mixture sit in a warm place for 2-4 weeks, shaking occasionally. Strain the flowers and use the oil as desired.
  - Salve: Calendula oil can be used to make a healing salve. Melt beeswax in a double boiler, and add the calendula oil. Pour the mixture into tins or jars and let cool. Use as needed on cuts, scrapes, and other skin irritations.

Note: Always make sure to properly identify calendula before harvesting, as there are other plants that may look similar. Also, if you have any allergies or medical conditions, consult with a healthcare professional before using calendula medicinally.

What medicines are made with this herb:
Calendula is used to make various types of medicines, including:
- Topical preparations such as creams, ointments, and salves for treating skin conditions like rashes, burns, and wounds.
- Oral supplements in the form of capsules or tinctures for internal use to treat various health conditions like inflammation, infections, digestive disorders, and menstrual cramps.
- Homeopathic remedies for various health conditions.
- Essential oil for aromatherapy and topical use.

It's worth noting that the effectiveness of Calendula for different health conditions is not well established, and more research is needed to fully understand its potential uses. Consult a healthcare professional before using Calendula or any other herbal supplement for medicinal purposes.

What medicines this herb counteracts:
There are no known medications that Calendula counteracts. However, it is important to note that Calendula may interact with certain medications, such as those that slow blood clotting or drugs that are broken down by the liver. It is recommended to consult with a healthcare provider before using Calendula alongside any medications.

Catnip

Herbal Identification:
- Common name: Catnip
- Latin binomial: Nepeta cataria
- Other common names: Catmint, Catnep, Field Balm
- Plant family: Lamiaceae
- Botanical description: Catnip (Nepeta cataria) is a perennial herbaceous plant that belongs to the mint family (Lamiaceae). It is native to Europe, Asia, and Africa, but has been naturalized in other parts of the world, including North America. The plant typically grows to be 50-100 cm tall and has square stems with grayish-green leaves that are heart-shaped and toothed. The leaves and stems of the plant are covered in fine hairs and contain an essential oil that gives catnip its distinctive scent. In the summer, the plant produces clusters of white or pale purple flowers at the top of its stems.

Medicinal Properties:
- Recommended cultivars: None in particular
- Parts used: Leaves, stems, and flowers
- Taste: Aromatic, slightly bitter
- Actions: Antispasmodic, carminative, diaphoretic, nervine, sedative
- Energetics: Cooling
- Specific indications: Catnip has a variety of traditional uses, including:
  - Sedative and Relaxant: Catnip is often used as a mild sedative and relaxant, and is believed to help relieve anxiety, stress, and insomnia.
  - Digestive aid: Catnip is used to improve digestion, reduce bloating, and relieve gas.
  - Cold and flu: Catnip is believed to be effective in treating symptoms of cold and flu, such as fever, headache, and congestion.
  - Menstrual cramps: Catnip is believed to help relieve menstrual cramps and other symptoms associated with PMS.
  - Pain relief: Catnip has been used as a natural pain reliever for various types of pain, including headaches, toothaches, and muscle pain.
  - 6nsect repellent: Catnip is also believed to be a natural insect repellent and can be used to deter mosquitoes, flies, and other insects.

Medicinal preparations:
Catnip can be used in various medicinal preparations, including:

- Tea: Catnip tea is made by steeping 1-2 teaspoons of dried catnip leaves in a cup of boiling water for 10-15 minutes. It can be consumed 2-3 times a day for various purposes.
- Tincture: Catnip tincture can be made by soaking fresh or dried catnip in alcohol for several weeks. This tincture can be used in small doses to help relieve anxiety and promote relaxation.
- Catnip oil: Catnip essential oil can be used in aromatherapy to promote relaxation and calmness. It can be diffused or diluted with a carrier oil and applied to the skin.
- Catnip poultice: A catnip poultice can be made by mashing fresh catnip leaves and applying them directly to the skin to relieve pain and inflammation.

It is recommended to consult with a healthcare professional before using catnip for medicinal purposes.

• Ratio and dosage information: 1-2 teaspoons of dried herb per cup of water for tea, 2-4 ml of tincture three times daily, 1-2 drops of catnip essential oil per teaspoon of carrier oil for topical use

Medicinal uses:
Catnip (Nepeta cataria) has been used for various medicinal purposes, including:

- Sedative: Catnip can act as a mild sedative, helping to calm the nerves and promote relaxation.
- Digestive aid: Catnip can stimulate digestion and relieve gastrointestinal upset, including nausea, flatulence, and diarrhea.
- Anti-inflammatory: Catnip has anti-inflammatory properties that may help relieve pain and inflammation associated with arthritis, sore muscles, and other conditions.
- Fever reducer: Catnip can help reduce fever by promoting sweating and increasing circulation.
- Respiratory aid: Catnip can help relieve congestion and coughs by promoting the production of mucus and helping to loosen phlegm.
- Menstrual cramp relief: Catnip can help relieve menstrual cramps by promoting relaxation and reducing inflammation.
- Anxiety and stress relief: Catnip may help reduce anxiety and stress by promoting relaxation and calming the nerves.

It's worth noting that while catnip is generally considered safe, it may interact with certain medications and should be used with caution in pregnant or breastfeeding women. As with any herbal remedy, it's best to consult with a healthcare provider before using catnip for medicinal purposes.

• Precautions and contradictions: Catnip is generally considered safe when used appropriately, but there are a few precautions and potential contradictions to keep in mind:
- Pregnant or breastfeeding women should avoid using catnip as there is not enough information available regarding its safety during pregnancy or breastfeeding.
- People with allergies to plants in the mint family, such as peppermint or spearmint, may also be allergic to catnip and should avoid it.
- Catnip may cause drowsiness, so it is recommended to avoid driving or operating heavy machinery after using it.
- Catnip may interact with sedative medications or supplements, so it is important to talk to a healthcare provider before using catnip if you are taking any prescription medications or supplements.

As with any herbal remedy, it is always a good idea to talk to a healthcare provider before using catnip, especially if you have any underlying medical conditions or are taking medications or supplements.

Cultivation:
• Native to: Europe, Asia, and parts of Africa
• Zones: 3-9
• Soil: Catnip prefers well-draining soil that is rich in organic matter. It can tolerate a range of soil types and pH levels.
• Propagation: Catnip can be propagated from seed or by division. Seeds should be sown in the spring or fall, while divisions should be planted in the spring.
• Growing information and garden care: Catnip is an easy-to-grow herb that prefers full sun to partial shade. It should be watered regularly but not overwatered, as it is susceptible to root rot. Pruning the plant can help to promote bushy growth and prolong the flowering period.
• Insects and disease: Catnip is known for its insect-repelling properties and can help keep away mosquitoes, flies, and other insects. However, like most plants, catnip can be susceptible to various diseases and pests. Some common pests that can attack catnip include spider mites, aphids, and whiteflies. Diseases that can affect catnip include powdery mildew, root rot, and bacterial blight. Proper care, including regular pruning and keeping the plant well-drained, can help prevent these issues. If necessary, natural or chemical remedies can be used to control pests and diseases.

• Harvesting and preparations: Catnip can be harvested once the plant reaches a height of at least 12 inches (30 cm). The leaves and stems should be dried in a well-ventilated area and stored in an airtight container.

Catnip is a hardy perennial plant that is easy to grow and harvest. The best time to harvest catnip is just before the flowers open, which is usually in midsummer. At this point, the plant is at its most potent. The leaves, stems, and flowers can all be harvested for use in medicinal preparations.

To dry catnip, cut the stems and hang them upside down in a cool, dry, and dark place. Once the leaves and flowers are completely dry, they can be stripped from the stems and stored in an airtight container.

Catnip can also be used fresh. Simply chop the leaves and stems finely and add them to a tea or tincture.

What medicines are made with this herb:
Catnip is primarily used for its calming and relaxing properties and is not commonly used to make medicines. However, it can be used as an ingredient in some herbal remedies or teas. Catnip is also used in some natural pet remedies to help soothe and calm cats.

Some examples of herbal remedies or teas that may contain catnip include:
- Cold and flu remedies: Catnip can help relieve congestion and promote relaxation, making it a useful ingredient in teas or remedies for colds and flu.
- Digestive remedies: Catnip has been traditionally used to soothe the digestive system and can be included in digestive remedies or teas.
- Sleep remedies: Catnip's calming properties may also make it a useful ingredient in sleep-promoting teas or remedies.

It's important to note that more research is needed to fully understand the medicinal properties of catnip and its potential uses in herbal medicine.

What medicines this herb counteracts:

There are no known medications that are counteracted by catnip. However, catnip may interact with certain medications, particularly sedatives and central nervous system depressants, as it can have a mild sedative effect. It is recommended to speak with a healthcare provider before using catnip if you are taking any medications.

Chaga Mushroom

Herbal Identification:
- Common name: Chaga mushroom
- Latin binomial: Inonotus obliquus
- Other common names: Clinker polypore, birch canker polypore, black mass, cinder conk, and sterile conk trunk rot
- Plant family: Hymenochaetaceae (formerly in the family Polyporaceae)
- Botanical description: Chaga mushroom (Inonotus obliquus) is not a plant, but a parasitic fungus that grows mainly on birch trees in cold regions of the Northern Hemisphere. It is also commonly known as clinker polypore, black mass, or birch canker polypore.

Chaga mushrooms have a black, charcoal-like appearance on the outside with a hard, woody texture, and a yellow to orange-brown color on the inside. They can grow up to 30 cm in length and weigh up to 2.5 kg.

Chaga mushrooms are related to other polypore mushrooms, such as reishi (Ganoderma lucidum) and turkey tail (Trametes versicolor), but are distinguished by their distinct appearance and growth pattern.

Medicinal Properties:
- Recommended cultivars: Not applicable as chaga mushroom is typically found growing in the wild.
- Parts used: The main part of the chaga mushroom used for medicinal purposes is the sclerotium, which is the dark, hard mass that grows on the outside of birch trees.
- Taste: Chaga mushroom has a slightly bitter taste.
- Actions: Chaga mushroom is considered to have anti-inflammatory, antioxidant, and immune-stimulating actions.
- Energetics: Chaga mushroom is considered to have a warming and drying energy.
- Specific indications: Chaga mushroom is traditionally used for the following specific indications:
  - Immune system support: Chaga mushroom has immunomodulatory effects and may help to enhance the immune system's response to infections.
  - Antioxidant support: Chaga mushroom contains high levels of antioxidants, which may help to reduce oxidative stress and inflammation in the body.
  - Anti-inflammatory support: Chaga mushroom has anti-inflammatory properties and may be useful in managing conditions associated with chronic inflammation, such as arthritis.

- Digestive support: Chaga mushroom has been traditionally used to support digestive health, including reducing inflammation and irritation in the gut, and improving nutrient absorption.
- Liver support: Chaga mushroom has hepatoprotective properties and may help to protect and support the liver.
- Skin health support: Chaga mushroom has been traditionally used for its skin-healing properties and may help to reduce inflammation and promote healthy skin.

Medicinal preparations:
Chaga mushroom can be prepared in various ways, including:
- Tea: Chaga tea can be made by simmering chunks of the mushroom in hot water for several hours, or by using powdered Chaga. The tea can be sweetened with honey or flavored with other herbs.
- Tincture: Chaga tincture can be made by steeping the mushroom in alcohol for several weeks. The tincture can be taken by adding drops to water or other beverages.
- Powder: Chaga mushroom can be ground into a fine powder and added to smoothies, juices, or other beverages.
- Capsules: Chaga mushroom capsules are also available and can be taken as a daily supplement.

The recommended dosage for Chaga mushroom varies depending on the form and concentration of the preparation, as well as the individual's health status and needs. It is important to follow the manufacturer's instructions or consult with a healthcare provider before taking Chaga mushroom. • Ratio and dosage information: Dosage and preparation methods may vary depending on the individual and specific condition being treated. It is best to consult with a qualified healthcare practitioner for specific dosing recommendations.

Medicinal uses:
Chaga mushroom has been traditionally used for a wide range of medicinal purposes, and has been studied for its potential health benefits. Some of the reported medicinal uses of Chaga mushroom include:
- Immune system support: Chaga mushroom is believed to enhance the activity of the immune system, helping to fight infections and diseases.
- Anti-inflammatory effects: Chaga mushroom contains compounds that possess anti-inflammatory properties, which may help to reduce inflammation and swelling in the body.
- Antioxidant properties: Chaga mushroom is rich in antioxidants, which help to neutralize harmful free radicals and protect cells from oxidative damage.

- Digestive health: Chaga mushroom has been used traditionally to support digestive health, and may help to alleviate symptoms of gastrointestinal issues such as bloating, constipation, and indigestion.
- Anti-cancer effects: Some studies have suggested that Chaga mushroom may have anti-cancer effects, although more research is needed in this area.
- Cardiovascular health: Chaga mushroom may help to lower cholesterol levels and reduce blood pressure, which can improve cardiovascular health.
- Liver health: Chaga mushroom has been used traditionally to support liver health, and may help to protect the liver from damage.
- Skin health: Chaga mushroom may have benefits for the skin, and has been used in traditional medicine to treat skin conditions such as eczema and psoriasis.

It is important to note that while Chaga mushroom has been traditionally used for these purposes, more research is needed to fully understand its potential health benefits and to determine the most effective dosages and preparations. It is always recommended to consult with a healthcare provider before using any herbal supplement.

• Precautions and contradictions: Chaga mushroom is generally considered safe for most people when consumed in moderation as a food or supplement. However, there are a few precautions and contradictions to keep in mind:

- Allergic reactions: Some people may be allergic to chaga mushroom, particularly if they are allergic to other types of mushrooms.
- Blood thinning: Chaga mushroom may have blood-thinning effects, which can increase the risk of bleeding in people who take blood-thinning medications or have bleeding disorders. It is best to consult with a healthcare provider before taking chaga mushroom if you are on blood-thinning medications.
- Diabetes: Chaga mushroom may lower blood sugar levels, which can be beneficial for people with diabetes. However, people who take medications to lower blood sugar should be cautious when using chaga mushroom, as it may increase the risk of hypoglycemia (low blood sugar).
- Immune system suppression: Chaga mushroom may have immune system suppression effects, which can be harmful for people with autoimmune diseases or those who take medications that suppress the immune system.
- Pregnancy and breastfeeding: There is not enough information about the safety of chaga mushroom during pregnancy and breastfeeding. It is best to avoid using chaga mushroom during these times.

As with any supplement or herbal remedy, it is important to consult with a healthcare provider before using chaga mushroom, particularly if you have any underlying health conditions or are taking any medications.

Cultivation:
• Native to: Chaga mushroom is found in colder regions of the Northern Hemisphere, including Siberia, Canada, and northern parts of Europe and the United States.
• Zones: Chaga grows in colder regions, typically in USDA zones 3-8.
• Soil: Chaga grows on certain species of trees, particularly birch trees, and prefers acidic soil with a pH range of 4-6. It requires a host tree to grow.
• Propagation: Chaga cannot be propagated in the traditional sense, as it is a parasitic fungus that grows on host trees.
• Growing information and garden care: As mentioned, Chaga cannot be grown in a garden or on its own. Instead, it must be harvested from the wild on birch trees.
• Insects and disease: As a mushroom that grows on living trees, Chaga can be affected by various tree diseases and pests. In particular, it tends to grow on birch trees that are stressed or diseased. Some common diseases of birch trees include Birch Dieback, Birch Canker, and Birch Rust. These diseases can weaken the tree and make it more susceptible to pests such as the Bronze Birch Borer or Birch Leafminer.

In addition to tree-related issues, Chaga can also be affected by contamination from other fungi, bacteria, or molds. It's important to properly identify and harvest Chaga from healthy, living trees to avoid contamination and ensure its medicinal properties.
• Harvesting and preparations: Chaga mushrooms are harvested from the birch trees they grow on. The best time to harvest them is in the fall and winter, when they are most mature. When harvesting, it is important to leave a portion of the mushroom intact on the tree so it can continue to grow.

To prepare Chaga mushroom for medicinal use, it is typically dried and then ground into a powder or made into a tea or tincture. The powder can be encapsulated for ease of consumption. Chaga tea is made by steeping the mushroom in hot water for at least 30 minutes to release its medicinal compounds. A tincture can be made by steeping the powdered mushroom in alcohol for several weeks before straining and using the resulting liquid.

What medicines are made with this herb:

Chaga mushroom is commonly used in traditional medicine systems, especially in Russia, Siberia, and other parts of Asia, as a remedy for various ailments. Medicines made with Chaga mushroom are typically in the form of teas, tinctures, and extracts. Chaga mushroom is also available as a dietary supplement in capsule form.

Some of the popular medicines made with Chaga mushroom include:
- Chaga tea: A simple infusion of Chaga mushroom in hot water, often sweetened with honey or other natural sweeteners, and consumed as a daily tonic for overall health and wellbeing.
- Chaga tincture: A concentrated extract of Chaga mushroom in alcohol or glycerin, used to enhance immune function, reduce inflammation, and fight infections.
- Chaga extract: A highly concentrated liquid extract of Chaga mushroom, used to treat cancer, diabetes, and other chronic diseases.
- Chaga powder: A finely ground powder of Chaga mushroom, used in smoothies, juices, and other foods for its immune-boosting and anti-inflammatory properties.

It is important to note that while Chaga mushroom has a long history of traditional use and is generally considered safe, it is always advisable to consult a healthcare professional before using any new herbal remedies or supplements, especially if you have any pre-existing health conditions or are taking any medications.

What medicines this herb counter act:

Chaga Mushroom has been reported to interact with certain medications. It may increase the effects of certain anticoagulant medications such as warfarin, which could increase the risk of bleeding. Therefore, it is important to talk to a healthcare provider before taking Chaga Mushroom if you are taking any medications or have any medical conditions.

Chamomile

Herbal Identification:
- Common name: Chamomile
- Latin binomial: Matricaria chamomilla or Chamaemelum nobile
- Other common names: German chamomile, Roman chamomile, English chamomile, wild chamomile, sweet false chamomile, Hungarian chamomile, scented mayweed, ground apple, earth apple, camomyle
- Plant family: Asteraceae (daisy family)
- Botanical description: Chamomile, also known as Matricaria chamomilla or Chamomilla recutita, is an annual herb that belongs to the Asteraceae family. It is native to Europe and Western Asia but is now widely cultivated in other parts of the world, including North America.

The plant typically grows to a height of 15-60 cm (6-24 inches) and has a branched stem covered in fine hairs. The leaves are feathery and delicate, with a fern-like appearance, and are divided into thread-like segments.

The flowers are small, daisy-like, and have a yellow center surrounded by white petals that are deeply notched at the tips. Chamomile blooms in the summer months, and the flowers are harvested when they are fully open and the pollen is visible on the center disc. The flowers have a pleasant, apple-like fragrance and a slightly bitter taste.

There are two main types of chamomile: German chamomile and Roman chamomile. German chamomile (Matricaria chamomilla) is the more commonly used medicinal variety and is taller and more sparsely branched than Roman chamomile (Chamaemelum nobile), which is often used in cosmetics and for its essential oil.

Medicinal Properties:
- Recommended cultivars: German chamomile (Matricaria chamomilla) and Roman chamomile (Chamaemelum nobile)
- Parts used: Flowers
- Taste: Bitter, sweet, and slightly aromatic
- Actions: Anti-inflammatory, antispasmodic, carminative, digestive, sedative, nervine, vulnerary
- Energetics: Cooling and drying

- Specific indications: Chamomile has a wide range of traditional uses and is known for its calming and soothing properties. Some specific indications for chamomile include:
  - Digestive issues: Chamomile can help ease digestive discomfort, including bloating, gas, and indigestion.
  - Anxiety and stress: Chamomile can promote relaxation and calmness, making it useful for reducing anxiety and stress.
  - Sleep disorders: Chamomile can help improve the quality of sleep and reduce the time it takes to fall asleep.
  - Skin irritations: Chamomile can be used topically to soothe skin irritations, including rashes, eczema, and minor burns.
  - Menstrual cramps: Chamomile can help relieve menstrual cramps and other menstrual-related symptoms.
  - Oral health: Chamomile can help reduce inflammation and promote healing in the mouth, making it useful for conditions such as gum disease and canker sores.

It's important to note that while chamomile has been traditionally used for these indications, more research is needed to fully understand its therapeutic benefits. Chamomile should not be used as a substitute for medical treatment without consulting with a healthcare provider.

Medicinal preparations:
Chamomile can be prepared and consumed in various ways, including:
- Tea: Chamomile tea is a common preparation and can be made by steeping 1-2 teaspoons of dried chamomile flowers in hot water for 5-10 minutes.
- Tincture: Chamomile tincture is made by soaking the chamomile flowers in alcohol, typically for a few weeks, to extract the medicinal compounds. The tincture can then be taken orally in small doses.
- Capsules: Chamomile capsules, which contain dried chamomile flowers in powdered form, are available as a dietary supplement.
- Topical applications: Chamomile can be used topically in the form of creams, ointments, and poultices for skin irritations and wounds.
- Inhalation: Chamomile essential oil can be used for inhalation therapy or added to bath water for a calming and relaxing effect.

It's important to note that different preparations may have different strengths and dosage recommendations, and it's best to consult with a healthcare provider or an experienced herbalist for guidance on proper preparation and dosage.

- Ratio and dosage information: For tea, use 1-2 teaspoons of dried chamomile flowers per cup of water, steep for 5-10 minutes. Dosage varies depending on the form of chamomile used.

Medicinal uses:
Chamomile has been used for various medicinal purposes, including:
- Promoting relaxation and reducing anxiety: Chamomile contains compounds that may promote relaxation and reduce feelings of anxiety.
- Aiding digestion: Chamomile has been used as a digestive aid for centuries, and may help alleviate symptoms such as indigestion, gas, and bloating.
- Supporting sleep: Chamomile has a calming effect that may help improve sleep quality and reduce insomnia.
- Soothing skin irritation: Chamomile can be used topically to help soothe skin irritations such as eczema, psoriasis, and rashes.
- Supporting immune function: Chamomile has anti-inflammatory and antioxidant properties that may help support immune function and protect against chronic diseases.
- Alleviating menstrual cramps: Chamomile tea may help alleviate menstrual cramps due to its anti-inflammatory and antispasmodic effects.
- Supporting oral health: Chamomile may help support oral health by reducing inflammation, fighting bacteria, and promoting healing of oral ulcers and sores.

It's important to note that chamomile is not a substitute for medical treatment and should be used in conjunction with, not instead of, professional medical advice and treatment.

• Precautions and contradictions: While chamomile is generally considered safe when consumed in moderation, there are some precautions and contraindications to be aware of:
- Allergic reactions: Some people may experience allergic reactions to chamomile, particularly if they are allergic to plants in the Asteraceae family, which includes ragweed, chrysanthemums, and daisies.
- Interactions with medication: Chamomile may interact with certain medications, including blood thinners, sedatives, and drugs metabolized by the liver. It's important to speak with a healthcare provider before using chamomile if you are taking any medications.
- Pregnancy and breastfeeding: Chamomile is generally considered safe during pregnancy and breastfeeding when consumed in moderation, but it's still a good idea to speak with a healthcare provider before using it.
- Sedative effects: Chamomile has mild sedative effects and may cause drowsiness, particularly when taken in large amounts or combined with other sedatives. It's important to avoid operating heavy machinery or driving after consuming chamomile.

- Gastrointestinal issues: Chamomile may exacerbate gastrointestinal issues such as acid reflux or stomach ulcers in some individuals.
- Blood pressure: Chamomile may lower blood pressure, so individuals with low blood pressure should use chamomile with caution.

As with any herbal supplement or medication, it's important to speak with a healthcare provider before using chamomile, particularly if you have any underlying health conditions or are taking any medications.

Cultivation:
- Native to: Europe, North Africa, and some parts of Asia
- Zones: 3-9
- Soil (pH and type of soil): Chamomile prefers well-drained soils with a pH between 5.6 and 7.5. It can tolerate poor, sandy, or rocky soil.
- Propagation: Chamomile can be propagated from seed or by dividing the root ball in the spring or fall.
- Growing information and garden care: Chamomile prefers full sun but can tolerate partial shade. It should be watered regularly, but not overwatered. Chamomile is a self-seeding annual or perennial and can become weedy if not managed properly.
- Insects and disease: Chamomile plants are relatively hardy and not usually affected by many insect pests or diseases. However, some potential pests and diseases to watch out for include:
  - Aphids: These small insects can infest the leaves and stems of chamomile plants, sucking the sap and causing deformities in the foliage. Aphids can be controlled with insecticidal soap or neem oil.
  - Leafhoppers: These pests can cause yellowing and stunted growth in chamomile plants. They can be controlled with insecticidal soap or neem oil.
  - Powdery mildew: This fungal disease can cause a white powdery coating on the leaves of chamomile plants, leading to decreased growth and yield. It can be controlled by pruning affected leaves and applying a fungicidal spray.
  - Root rot: Overwatering or poorly drained soil can lead to root rot in chamomile plants, which can cause wilting, yellowing, and eventual death. To prevent root rot, make sure the soil is well-drained and avoid overwatering.

Overall, chamomile is a relatively low-maintenance herb that is resistant to many pests and diseases. With proper care and attention, chamomile plants can thrive and produce abundant blooms.

- Harvesting and preparations: Chamomile flowers are typically harvested in the summer when they are in full bloom. The flowers should be harvested early in the day after the dew has evaporated, but before the sun is too hot. To harvest chamomile flowers, gently snip the stems just below the flower heads, being careful not to crush or bruise the delicate petals.

Once harvested, chamomile flowers can be dried for later use. To dry chamomile flowers, spread them out on a clean, dry surface in a well-ventilated area out of direct sunlight. Turn the flowers regularly to ensure even drying. Once the flowers are completely dry, store them in an airtight container in a cool, dark place.

Chamomile flowers can be prepared as a tea by steeping 1-2 teaspoons of dried flowers in a cup of hot water for 5-10 minutes. The tea can be sweetened with honey or lemon to taste. Chamomile tea can also be made with fresh flowers, but you will need to use more since fresh flowers are more water-rich.

Chamomile flowers can also be used to make infused oil, which can be used in homemade skin care products. To make chamomile infused oil, fill a jar with chamomile flowers and cover them with a carrier oil such as olive oil or jojoba oil. Let the jar sit in a warm, sunny spot for 2-4 weeks, shaking it occasionally. Strain out the flowers and store the infused oil in a clean, dry container.

Overall, chamomile is a versatile herb with many medicinal and culinary uses, and can be easily grown and harvested in a home garden.

What medicines are made with this herb:
Chamomile is a popular herb used in a variety of medicinal and cosmetic preparations. Some of the medicines made with chamomile include:

- Chamomile tea: Chamomile tea is a popular herbal tea made from the flowers of the chamomile plant. It is often used as a natural remedy for insomnia, anxiety, and digestive issues.
- Chamomile essential oil: Chamomile essential oil is made from the flowers of the chamomile plant and is used in aromatherapy and as a natural remedy for inflammation, skin irritations, and muscle spasms.
- Chamomile tincture: Chamomile tincture is an alcohol-based extract of the chamomile plant. It is often used as a natural remedy for anxiety, sleep disorders, and digestive issues.
- Chamomile cream: Chamomile cream is a topical preparation that contains chamomile extract and is used to soothe and heal irritated or inflamed skin.
- Chamomile supplements: Chamomile supplements are available in capsule or tablet form and are used to promote relaxation, reduce anxiety, and improve sleep.

Chamomile is also used in various cosmetic and personal care products, such as shampoos, conditioners, and lotions, due to its soothing and anti-inflammatory properties.

What medicines this herb counteract:
Chamomile may interact with certain medications such as blood thinners, sedatives, and anti-anxiety medications. It is important to speak with a healthcare provider before using chamomile if you are pregnant or breastfeeding, have allergies or asthma, are taking medications or supplements that may interact with chamomile, or have any underlying health conditions.

It's important to note that chamomile is generally considered safe when used as directed, but some people may experience allergic reactions or side effects, such as drowsiness, nausea, or vomiting. If you experience any adverse effects, discontinue use and consult with your healthcare provider.

Overall, chamomile is a versatile and beneficial herb that has been used for centuries to promote health and wellness. Whether you drink chamomile tea to relax or use it topically to soothe skin irritations, this herb can be a valuable addition to your natural health toolkit.

Chickweed

Herbal Identification:
- Common name: Chickweed
- Latin binomial: Stellaria media
- Other common names: Starweed, Starwort, Mouse-ear chickweed
- Plant family: Caryophyllaceae
- Botanical description: Chickweed is an annual herb that grows low to the ground, typically reaching only 4-12 inches in height. The leaves are oval-shaped and grow opposite each other on the stem. The flowers are small and white, with five petals deeply divided, giving the appearance of ten petals. Chickweed is a cool-season plant and grows in moist, shaded areas.

Medicinal Properties:
- Parts used: Aerial parts (leaves, stems, flowers)
- Taste: Sweet, slightly salty
- Actions: Demulcent, expectorant, nutritive, vulnerary
- Energetics: Cooling, moistening
- Specific indications: Chickweed is known for its various health benefits, including:
  - Soothing skin irritations and inflammation
  - Relieving coughs and bronchitis
  - Reducing inflammation and pain in joints and muscles
  - Improving digestion and easing constipation
  - Helping with weight loss by suppressing appetite and boosting metabolism
  - Supporting immune function
  - Providing relief from menstrual cramps and premenstrual syndrome (PMS)
  - Easing anxiety and promoting relaxation

It's important to note that while chickweed has been used traditionally for these purposes, scientific evidence is limited and more research is needed to confirm its effectiveness. It's always a good idea to consult with a healthcare provider before using any new herb for medicinal purposes.

Medicinal preparations:
Chickweed can be used in various medicinal preparations such as:
- Infusion: A tea can be made by steeping 1-2 teaspoons of dried chickweed in 1 cup of boiling water for 10-15 minutes. This can be consumed up to 3 times per day.

- Tincture: Chickweed can be made into a tincture by steeping the dried herb in alcohol for several weeks. This can be taken in doses of 1-2 ml up to 3 times per day.
- Poultice: A poultice can be made by crushing fresh chickweed and applying it directly to the affected area. This can help soothe skin irritations and inflammation.
- Salve: Chickweed can be infused in oil and mixed with beeswax to make a salve that can be applied topically to the skin.
- 5apsules: Chickweed is also available in capsule form for easy consumption.

It is important to note that it is always recommended to consult with a healthcare professional before using any new herb for medicinal purposes.

• Ratio and dosage information: Infusion: 1-2 teaspoons of dried herb per cup of boiling water, steeped for 10-15 minutes. Tincture: 2-4 ml, three times per day. Poultice: Fresh herb applied directly to affected area.

Medicinal uses:
Chickweed has a long history of use in traditional herbal medicine for various health issues. Some of the medicinal uses of chickweed include:
- Skin health: Chickweed has a soothing and cooling effect on the skin and is used topically to relieve itching, rashes, eczema, psoriasis, and other skin irritations.
- Digestive health: Chickweed is known to stimulate digestion and improve bowel function. It is used to treat constipation, bloating, and indigestion.
- Respiratory health: Chickweed is a natural expectorant and is used to treat respiratory infections such as coughs, colds, and bronchitis.
- Anti-inflammatory: Chickweed has anti-inflammatory properties and is used to reduce inflammation in the body, including inflammation of the joints and muscles.
- Weight loss: Chickweed is believed to help with weight loss by reducing appetite and increasing metabolism.
- Nutritional support: Chickweed is a rich source of vitamins and minerals, including vitamin C, iron, calcium, and magnesium. It is often used as a general tonic to support overall health and well-being.
- Urinary tract health: Chickweed is a natural diuretic and is used to treat urinary tract infections and other urinary system disorders.

Chickweed can be used in various forms, including teas, tinctures, ointments, and poultices. It is often combined with other herbs to enhance its therapeutic effects. It is important to consult with a qualified healthcare practitioner before using chickweed for medicinal purposes.

• Precautions and contradictions: Chickweed is generally considered safe and non-toxic for most people when consumed in moderate amounts as food or used

topically. However, there are a few precautions and contradictions to keep in mind:
- People who are allergic to plants in the same family as chickweed, such as ragweed or daisy, may also be allergic to chickweed and should avoid it.
- Pregnant and breastfeeding women should avoid consuming chickweed as it may stimulate the uterus and cause complications.
- Chickweed may interact with certain medications, so it is best to consult with a healthcare provider before using it medicinally.

As with any herbal medicine, it is important to use chickweed under the guidance of a qualified healthcare practitioner.

Cultivation:
- Native to: Europe, Asia, and North America
- Zones: 3-9
- Soil: Moist, fertile soil with a pH of 6.0-7.0
- Propagation: Direct seeding, transplanting
- Growing information and garden care: Chickweed prefers cool, moist conditions and can be grown in full sun to partial shade. It can be sown in the spring or fall, and should be kept well-watered.
- Insects and disease: Chickweed is relatively resistant to pests and diseases. However, it can be susceptible to root rot if the soil is consistently waterlogged. To prevent this, it is important to ensure proper drainage and avoid overwatering. Chickweed may also attract aphids, spider mites, and other common garden pests, but these can typically be controlled with organic insecticidal soap or by encouraging natural predators like ladybugs and lacewings.
- Harvesting and preparations: Chickweed can be harvested year-round in mild climates, but the peak season is usually in the spring. The best time to harvest is in the morning when the dew has evaporated. The leaves, stems, and flowers can all be used.

Preparations:

Chickweed can be used fresh or dried for tea, tinctures, infused oils, and salves. Here are some specific preparations:
- Infused oil: Fill a jar with fresh chickweed and cover with oil. Let the mixture sit for 4-6 weeks, shaking occasionally. Strain and use as a massage oil or in a salve.
- Salve: Melt beeswax and mix with the infused chickweed oil until the desired consistency is reached. Use as a topical ointment for skin irritations.
- Tea: Steep 1-2 teaspoons of dried chickweed in hot water for 10-15 minutes. Drink up to 3 cups per day.

Note: Always consult with a qualified healthcare practitioner before using chickweed or any other herbal remedy.

What medicines are made with this herb:
　　Chickweed has been traditionally used for various medicinal purposes, although it is not commonly used in modern medicine. Some of the traditional medicinal uses of chickweed include:
- Topical application for skin irritations and itching: Chickweed has anti-inflammatory and soothing properties, which make it helpful for relieving skin irritations and itching. It can be applied topically in the form of a poultice, salve, or cream.
- Digestive issues: Chickweed has been used to help with digestive issues, such as bloating, indigestion, and constipation. It can be taken as a tea or tincture.
- Respiratory issues: Chickweed has been used as a traditional remedy for respiratory issues, such as coughs, colds, and bronchitis. It can be taken as a tea or tincture.
- Weight loss: Chickweed has been used to aid in weight loss by suppressing appetite and reducing cravings. It can be taken as a tea or tincture.
- Joint pain and inflammation: Chickweed has been used to relieve joint pain and inflammation associated with conditions like arthritis. It can be applied topically in the form of a poultice, salve, or cream.
- Eye irritations: Chickweed has been used as an eyewash to relieve eye irritations and conjunctivitis.

　　It is important to note that there is limited scientific evidence to support the effectiveness of chickweed for these purposes, and it is not a substitute for medical advice or treatment. Always consult with a healthcare professional before using chickweed or any other herbal remedies.

What medicines this herb counteract:
　　There is no information to suggest that chickweed counteracts any specific medicines. However, as with any herb, it is important to consult with a healthcare professional before using it in combination with any prescription or over-the-counter medications to avoid any potential interactions.

Chives

Herbal Identification:
- Common name: Chives
- Latin binomial: Allium schoenoprasum
- Other common names: None
- Plant family: Amaryllidaceae
- Botanical description: Chives are a perennial herb that grows in clumps, with narrow, cylindrical, hollow leaves that can reach up to 20 inches in height. The leaves are bright green and have a mild onion-like taste and aroma. The plant also produces small pink or purple flowers that are edible.

Medicinal Properties:
- Recommended cultivars: Common chives are the most widely cultivated variety.
- Parts used: The leaves and flowers are used in medicinal preparations.
- Taste: Mildly pungent and slightly sweet.
- Actions: Anti-inflammatory, antioxidant, diuretic, antibacterial, antifungal.
- Energetics: Warming and drying.
- Specific indications: Chives have traditionally been used to support digestive health and may help relieve digestive disorders such as indigestion, bloating, and gas. They also have anti-inflammatory properties and may be helpful in reducing inflammation in the body. Chives have been used in traditional medicine to help relieve coughs and colds, and may also have a mild diuretic effect, making them useful in treating urinary tract infections. Additionally, some studies have suggested that chives may help regulate blood pressure levels.

Medicinal preparations:
Chives are primarily used as a culinary herb, but they can also be used for medicinal purposes. Here are some common medicinal preparations of chives:
- Infusion: Chive leaves can be steeped in hot water to make an infusion. This is often used to treat digestive disorders and urinary tract infections.
- Poultice: Crushed chive leaves can be made into a poultice and applied topically to treat inflammation.
- Tincture: Chive leaves can be steeped in alcohol to make a tincture. This is often used to treat high blood pressure.
- Essential oil: Chive essential oil can be extracted from the plant and used for aromatherapy or added to topical treatments for its anti-inflammatory properties.

Dosage and ratio information will vary depending on the specific preparation and intended use. It is recommended to consult with a qualified healthcare practitioner before using chives for medicinal purposes.
- Ratio and dosage information: There is no established dosage for chives, but they are generally considered safe to consume as a food or in moderate amounts as a medicinal herb.

Medicinal uses:
Chives are primarily used as a culinary herb, but they also have some medicinal properties. Some of the medicinal uses of chives include:
- Digestive disorders: Chives contain compounds that help stimulate digestion and improve gut health. They can be used to alleviate digestive issues like bloating, gas, and constipation.
- Inflammation: Chives have anti-inflammatory properties that can help reduce inflammation in the body. This can be beneficial for conditions like arthritis, asthma, and allergies.
- Coughs and colds: Chives have antiviral and antibacterial properties that can help fight off infections that cause coughs and colds.
- Urinary tract infections: Chives have diuretic properties, which means they can help increase urine production and flush out bacteria that cause urinary tract infections.
- High blood pressure: Chives contain compounds that can help lower blood pressure and improve heart health.

It's important to note that while chives have some medicinal properties, they should not be used as a replacement for medical treatment. If you have a medical condition, it's important to consult with your healthcare provider before using chives or any other herb as a treatment.
- Precautions and contradictions: Chives are generally considered safe to consume and have no known toxicity. However, some people may experience an allergic reaction to chives, particularly if they are allergic to other members of the Allium family, such as onions or garlic. Symptoms of an allergic reaction may include itching, swelling, hives, and difficulty breathing.

It is also important to note that chives are high in vitamin K, which can interfere with blood thinning medications. Therefore, individuals taking blood thinners should consult with their healthcare provider before consuming large amounts of chives or chive supplements.

Cultivation:
- Native to: Europe, Asia, and North America
- Zones: Chives are hardy in USDA zones 3-10.

- Soil: Chives prefer well-draining, fertile soil with a pH between 6.0 and 7.0.
- Propagation: Chives can be propagated by division, seed, or transplanting.
- Growing information and garden care: Chives prefer full sun to partial shade and regular watering. They can be grown in pots or in the ground and benefit from occasional fertilization.
- Insects and disease: Chives are generally not prone to serious insect or disease problems, but some issues may occur. Insects that may affect chives include onion thrips, aphids, and onion maggots. These can be controlled by using insecticidal soap or other organic pest control methods.

Diseases that may affect chives include fungal diseases such as rust and leaf spot. These can be prevented by proper spacing of plants, good air circulation, and avoiding overhead watering. Fungal diseases can also be treated with copper-based fungicides or other organic treatments.
- Harvesting and preparations: Chives are a perennial herb that can be harvested from spring to fall. The leaves are the most commonly used part of the plant, and they should be harvested when they are young and tender. The flowers can also be used in cooking and have a milder onion flavor.

To harvest chives, use scissors or a sharp knife to cut the leaves about an inch from the base of the plant. Avoid cutting into the center of the plant, as this can damage the growing point and reduce future growth. Chives can be used fresh or dried for later use.

To dry chives, hang them in small bunches in a warm, dry, and well-ventilated area. Once the leaves are dry and crispy, remove them from the stems and store them in an airtight container in a cool, dark place.

Chives can be used in a variety of culinary dishes, such as soups, salads, dressings, and dips. They can also be added to scrambled eggs, baked potatoes, and grilled vegetables for added flavor.

What medicines are made with this herb:

Chives are primarily used as a culinary herb, but they are also used in some traditional medicines, particularly in Chinese and Korean herbal medicine. They are often included in herbal formulations for digestive disorders, respiratory infections, and immune support.

What medicines this herb counteract:

There is no specific information on what medicines chives may counteract. However, they may interact with certain medications due to their high content of vitamin K, which can affect blood clotting. As such, people taking blood thinners should consume chives in moderation and talk to their healthcare provider before using them medicinally.

Cinnamon

Herbal Identification:
- Common name: Cinnamon
- Latin binomial: Cinnamomum verum or Cinnamomum cassia
- Other common names: True cinnamon, Chinese cinnamon, Cassia bark, Ceylon cinnamon
- Plant family: Lauraceae
- Botanical description: Cinnamon is a small evergreen tree that grows up to 10-15 meters in height, with thick, leathery leaves and small white or yellow flowers. The bark of the tree is harvested and dried to make cinnamon. It is reddish-brown in color and has a rough texture, with thin layers that can be peeled off. The inner bark is the part of the plant used for culinary and medicinal purposes, and is known for its distinctive sweet and spicy aroma.

Medicinal Properties:
- Parts used: Bark
- Taste: Sweet, pungent, and slightly bitter
- Actions: Carminative, astringent, stimulant, tonic, antiseptic, antifungal, antibacterial, antiviral, and anti-inflammatory
- Energetics: Warming
- Specific indications: Cinnamon has been traditionally used for a variety of medicinal purposes, including:
  - Digestive issues: Cinnamon has been used to aid in digestion, reduce bloating and gas, and improve appetite.
  - Blood sugar regulation: Cinnamon may help to lower blood sugar levels and improve insulin sensitivity, making it useful for people with type 2 diabetes.
  - Anti-inflammatory properties: Cinnamon has anti-inflammatory properties and has been used to relieve pain and inflammation associated with conditions such as arthritis.
  - Anti-microbial and anti-fungal properties: Cinnamon has been shown to have antibacterial, antiviral, and antifungal properties, making it useful for fighting infections.
  - Cognitive function: Some studies suggest that cinnamon may improve memory and cognitive function, and help protect against neurological disorders such as Alzheimer's disease.
  - Menstrual cramps: Cinnamon has been used to alleviate menstrual cramps.
  - Respiratory infections: Cinnamon has been used to treat respiratory infections such as bronchitis and colds.

It's important to note that while cinnamon has been traditionally used for these purposes, more research is needed to confirm its effectiveness.

Medicinal preparations:
Cinnamon can be prepared in various ways for medicinal use, including:
- Infusion: Add 1-2 cinnamon sticks or 1-2 teaspoons of powdered cinnamon to 1 cup of boiling water. Steep for 10-15 minutes, then strain and drink.
- Tincture: Combine 1 part cinnamon bark with 5 parts alcohol (such as vodka) in a jar. Seal and let sit for 4-6 weeks, shaking the jar daily. Strain and store in a dark glass bottle.
- Essential oil: Cinnamon essential oil can be used in aromatherapy, diluted in a carrier oil and applied topically, or added to baths.
- Powder: Cinnamon powder can be used as a spice in cooking, or taken in capsule form as a dietary supplement.

It is important to note that the dosage and method of preparation may vary depending on the specific health condition being treated and the individual's age, weight, and overall health. It is recommended to consult with a healthcare provider or qualified herbalist before using cinnamon for medicinal purposes.

• Ratio and dosage information: Dosage varies depending on the form and intended use of cinnamon. For example, 1-2 teaspoons of cinnamon powder can be added to food or drinks, while a decoction of cinnamon bark may require 1-2 teaspoons of bark per cup of water, simmered for 10-15 minutes.

Medicinal uses:
Cinnamon has been used for various medicinal purposes for centuries. Some of its traditional uses include:
- Anti-inflammatory: Cinnamon contains compounds that have anti-inflammatory properties and may help reduce inflammation in the body.
- Anti-diabetic: Cinnamon may help lower blood sugar levels and improve insulin sensitivity in people with type 2 diabetes.
- Anti-microbial: Cinnamon has strong anti-microbial properties and may help fight various infections, including bacterial, fungal, and viral infections.
- Digestive aid: Cinnamon may help improve digestion by reducing gas and bloating, and increasing appetite.
- Heart health: Cinnamon may help reduce risk factors for heart disease, such as high blood pressure and high cholesterol levels.
- Brain function: Cinnamon may help improve cognitive function and memory, and reduce the risk of neurological disorders such as Alzheimer's and Parkinson's disease.
- Menstrual pain: Cinnamon may help reduce menstrual pain and cramps.

> Anti-cancer: Cinnamon has been shown to have anti-cancer properties in some studies, but more research is needed to confirm these effects.

Note that while cinnamon has many potential health benefits, more research is needed to confirm its effectiveness and safety for various uses. It is also important to use cinnamon in moderation, as high doses may be harmful.

• Precautions and contradictions: Cinnamon is generally considered safe when used in culinary amounts. However, taking cinnamon supplements in large doses or for a prolonged period may cause liver damage, mouth sores, or other adverse effects. It may also cause allergic reactions in some people.

Cinnamon may interact with certain medications, particularly blood-thinning drugs, and should be used with caution by people taking these medications. It may also lower blood sugar levels and should be used with caution by people with diabetes, particularly if taking medication to lower blood sugar levels.

Pregnant and breastfeeding women should also use cinnamon with caution, as there is not enough information available about its safety in these populations.

Cultivation:
• Native to: Sri Lanka, India, Bangladesh, and Myanmar
• Zones: 9-11
• Soil (pH and type of soil): Well-drained soil with a pH between 6.0-7.0
• Propagation: Cinnamon can be propagated through seeds or cuttings, but it is usually grown from root suckers.
• Growing information and garden care: Cinnamon trees prefer a warm, tropical climate with plenty of rainfall. They require regular pruning to maintain their shape and encourage new growth.
• Insects and disease: Cinnamon trees can be susceptible to a variety of pests and diseases, including bark beetles, mealybugs, and powdery mildew. It can be susceptible to root rot if the soil is kept too moist. Additionally, if grown in humid conditions, the leaves may be prone to fungal infections. To prevent these issues, it is important to provide well-draining soil and avoid overwatering.
• Harvesting and preparations: Cinnamon is harvested from the inner bark of cinnamon trees. The bark is peeled off and left to dry, which causes it to curl into the familiar cinnamon stick shape. It can also be ground into a fine powder for use in cooking and medicinal preparations.

Cinnamon is widely available in grocery stores and health food stores in both stick and powder form. When purchasing cinnamon, it is important to choose high-quality sources that are free from contaminants and adulterants. Organic and sustainably harvested cinnamon is also available.

To make a cinnamon tea or infusion, cinnamon sticks or powder can be steeped in hot water for several minutes. Cinnamon can also be added to a variety of foods and beverages, including oatmeal, smoothies, and baked goods.

What medicines are made with this herb:

Cinnamon is primarily used as a culinary spice, but it is also used in some traditional medicines, particularly in Ayurvedic and Chinese herbal medicine. It is often included in herbal formulations for digestive disorders, respiratory infections, and immune support. Some supplements containing cinnamon extract are marketed for their potential blood sugar-lowering effects in people with diabetes. Additionally, cinnamon oil is used in aromatherapy for its warming and stimulating properties.

What medicines this herb counteract:

Cinnamon may interact with certain medications, particularly blood-thinning drugs, and should be used with caution by people taking these medications. It may also lower blood sugar levels and should be used with caution by people with diabetes, particularly if taking medication to lower blood sugar levels. Additionally, cinnamon oil is not recommended for internal use, as it can cause irritation and inflammation of the skin and mucous membranes.

It is important to note that cinnamon is not a replacement for conventional medical treatment and should not be used to treat serious medical conditions without the supervision of a healthcare professional.

In terms of interactions with other herbs and supplements, cinnamon may enhance the effects of herbs and supplements with blood sugar-lowering properties, such as bitter melon and fenugreek. It may also interact with herbs and supplements with blood-thinning properties, such as garlic, ginkgo biloba, and turmeric.

As with any herbal remedy, it is important to consult with a healthcare professional before using cinnamon as a treatment for any medical condition or before combining it with other herbs or supplements.

Cloves

Herbal Identification:
- Common name: Cloves
- Latin binomial: Syzygium aromaticum
- Other common names: Caryophyllus aromaticus, Eugenia aromatica, clove
- Plant family: Myrtaceae
- Botanical description: Cloves are the aromatic flower buds of a tree in the Myrtaceae family. The tree grows up to 12 meters tall with large leaves and crimson flowers. The buds are harvested when they are still immature and then dried. The dried buds are dark brown and have a hard, woody texture.

Medicinal Properties:
- Recommended cultivars: None
- Parts used: Dried flower buds
- Taste: Spicy, pungent
- Actions: Analgesic, antiseptic, carminative, digestive, expectorant, stimulant, stomachic
- Energetics: Warm, drying
- Specific indications: Cloves have several specific indications including:
  - Toothache: Cloves are commonly used for their analgesic properties to alleviate toothache pain. Eugenol, a compound found in cloves, has a numbing effect on the nerves in the mouth.
  - Digestive problems: Cloves have carminative properties, which means they can help relieve digestive issues such as bloating, gas, and nausea.
  - Respiratory infections: Cloves have expectorant properties, which can help loosen phlegm and mucus in the lungs and promote coughing. They are commonly used to treat coughs, colds, and flu.
  - Fungal infections: Cloves have antifungal properties and can be used topically to treat skin infections caused by fungi.
  - Rheumatism: Cloves have anti-inflammatory properties and may be effective in reducing pain and inflammation associated with rheumatism.

Medicinal preparations:
Cloves can be prepared and used for medicinal purposes in various forms, including:
  - Infusion: To prepare an infusion, steep 1-2 teaspoons of crushed cloves in a cup of boiling water for 10-15 minutes. This infusion can be consumed up to three times a day to relieve digestive issues and respiratory infections.

- Decoction: To prepare a decoction, simmer 1-2 teaspoons of crushed cloves in a cup of water for 10-15 minutes. This decoction can be consumed up to three times a day to relieve toothache and as a digestive aid.
- Powder: Clove powder can be used to relieve toothache and as a digestive aid. The recommended dosage is 1-3 grams per day, divided into several doses.
- Tincture: A clove tincture can be made by steeping crushed cloves in alcohol or glycerin for several weeks. This tincture can be used to relieve digestive issues and respiratory infections. The recommended dosage is 1-2 mL up to three times a day.
- Essential oil: Clove essential oil can be used topically to relieve toothache and as an antifungal agent. It can also be used in aromatherapy to promote relaxation and relieve stress. The oil should be diluted before use and should not be ingested.

• Ratio and dosage information: 1-3 grams of dried cloves per day in divided doses. Essential oil should be diluted before use.

Medicinal uses:
Cloves have a long history of use in traditional medicine. They are commonly used for their analgesic and antiseptic properties, making them effective for treating toothaches and oral infections. They are also used for digestive issues such as bloating, gas, and nausea, and are helpful for coughs, colds, and flu. Cloves are sometimes used as an expectorant to help clear congestion in the lungs. Topically, cloves can be used as an antifungal and antiseptic for skin infections.

Cloves have several medicinal uses, including:
- Dental health: Cloves are commonly used for their analgesic and antibacterial properties to promote dental health. They can be used to relieve toothache and prevent dental decay.
- Digestive health: Cloves have carminative properties and can help relieve digestive issues such as bloating, gas, and nausea. They can also promote digestion and improve appetite.
- Respiratory health: Cloves have expectorant properties and can help loosen phlegm and mucus in the lungs. They are commonly used to treat coughs, colds, and flu.
- Anti-inflammatory effects: Cloves have anti-inflammatory properties and can be used to reduce pain and inflammation associated with conditions such as rheumatism and arthritis.
- Antifungal effects: Cloves have antifungal properties and can be used topically to treat skin infections caused by fungi.

- Antioxidant effects: Cloves contain compounds that have antioxidant properties and can help protect the body from oxidative stress.
- Stress and anxiety relief: Clove essential oil can be used in aromatherapy to promote relaxation and relieve stress and anxiety.

It is important to note that while cloves have many potential medicinal uses, they should not be used as a substitute for medical treatment. If you have a medical condition or are taking medications, consult with a healthcare professional before using cloves for medicinal purposes.

• Precautions and contradictions: While cloves are generally safe when used in moderation as a culinary herb, there are some precautions and contradictions to keep in mind when using cloves for medicinal purposes:
- Allergies: Some people may be allergic to cloves and may experience symptoms such as itching, swelling, and difficulty breathing. If you experience these symptoms, stop using cloves immediately and seek medical attention.
- Bleeding disorders: Cloves may increase the risk of bleeding in people with bleeding disorders or those taking blood-thinning medications.
- Pregnancy and breastfeeding: Cloves are not recommended for use during pregnancy or breastfeeding, as their safety has not been established.
- Diabetes: Cloves may lower blood sugar levels and should be used with caution in people with diabetes.
- Liver disease: Cloves may have hepatotoxic effects and should be used with caution in people with liver disease.
- Surgery: Cloves may increase the risk of bleeding during and after surgery and should be stopped at least two weeks before any surgical procedure.
- Other drug interactions: Cloves may interact with certain medications, including anticoagulants, antiplatelets, and insulin. Consult with a healthcare professional before using cloves if you are taking any medications.

It is important to note that using excessive amounts of cloves can be toxic and may cause symptoms such as nausea, vomiting, and abdominal pain. It is recommended to use cloves in moderation and follow dosage instructions carefully.

Cultivation:
• Native to: Indonesia
• Zones: 9-11
• Soil: Well-drained soil with a pH of 5.5-6.5
• Propagation: Seeds or cuttings
• Growing information and garden care: Clove trees prefer warm, humid climates and need regular watering. They should be planted in a location with

partial shade and protected from strong winds. Pruning is necessary to maintain tree shape and promote fruit production.

• Insects and disease: Clove plants are generally considered to be resistant to pests and diseases. However, they can be affected by some common garden pests such as aphids, mites, and mealybugs. These pests can be controlled through natural methods such as spraying the plants with a solution of water and soap or neem oil.

Clove plants can also be affected by fungal diseases such as anthracnose and powdery mildew. To prevent these diseases, it is recommended to plant cloves in well-draining soil and avoid overwatering. In case of an outbreak, affected plants should be removed and destroyed to prevent further spread.

Additionally, clove plants can be affected by nutrient deficiencies, particularly of nitrogen and phosphorus. Fertilization with a balanced fertilizer can help prevent these deficiencies.

Regular inspection of clove plants is important to detect and prevent any pest or disease outbreaks. • Harvesting and preparations: Clove plants are ready to harvest when the flower buds turn pink, which usually occurs between 6 to 8 months after planting. At this stage, the flower buds contain the highest concentration of essential oils and are ideal for culinary and medicinal use.

To harvest cloves, the flower buds are hand-picked before they open fully. The flower buds are then dried in the sun or in a dehydrator until they turn dark brown in color and become hard and brittle.

Once dried, cloves can be used whole or ground into a powder for culinary use. Cloves can also be used to make essential oil, which is extracted from the flower buds through steam distillation.

To make clove essential oil, the dried flower buds are placed in a distillation chamber with water and heated until steam is produced. The steam carries the essential oil from the flower buds and is then cooled and collected in a separate container.

Cloves are commonly used in a variety of culinary dishes, such as stews, curries, and baked goods, as well as in traditional medicine to treat various ailments. It is important to use cloves in moderation and follow dosage instructions carefully, as excessive use can be toxic.

What medicines are made with this herb:

Cloves are a commonly used medicinal herb and are used in various traditional medicines around the world. Some of the common medicinal preparations made from cloves include:

- Clove oil: Clove oil is extracted from the dried flower buds through steam distillation and is used as a natural remedy for toothache, sore throat, and respiratory infections.
- Clove tea: Clove tea is made by steeping dried cloves in hot water and is used to treat digestive issues, such as nausea, bloating, and gas.
- Clove tincture: Clove tincture is made by soaking dried cloves in alcohol or vinegar and is used to treat a variety of conditions, including fungal infections, digestive issues, and toothache.
- Clove poultice: A clove poultice is made by grinding dried cloves into a paste and applying it topically to the skin. It is used to relieve pain and inflammation associated with conditions such as arthritis, sore muscles, and insect bites.
- Clove cigarettes: Clove cigarettes, also known as kreteks, are cigarettes that contain a mixture of tobacco and ground cloves. They are commonly used in traditional medicine to treat respiratory infections and relieve coughing.

It is important to note that the medicinal uses of cloves have not been extensively studied, and the effectiveness of these preparations may vary depending on the individual and the specific condition being treated. As with any herbal medicine, it is important to consult with a healthcare professional before using cloves for medicinal purposes.

What medicines this herb counteract:

There are no known medicines that cloves specifically counteract. However, cloves can interact with certain medications and should be used with caution in individuals taking the following:

- Blood-thinning medications: Cloves contain eugenol, which can have blood-thinning effects. Individuals taking blood-thinning medications such as warfarin or aspirin should use cloves with caution, as they may increase the risk of bleeding.
- Diabetes medications: Cloves can lower blood sugar levels and may interact with diabetes medications such as insulin and metformin. Individuals taking these medications should monitor their blood sugar levels closely when using cloves.
- Antidepressants: Cloves can interact with certain antidepressant medications, including selective serotonin reuptake inhibitors (SSRIs) and monoamine

oxidase inhibitors (MAOIs). Individuals taking these medications should consult with a healthcare professional before using cloves.

- Liver medications: Cloves can interact with medications used to treat liver conditions such as hepatitis and cirrhosis. Individuals taking these medications should use cloves with caution and consult with a healthcare professional before use.

It is important to note that the interactions between cloves and medications have not been extensively studied, and individuals should always consult with a healthcare professional before using cloves for medicinal purposes.

Coltsfoot

Herbal Identification:
- Common name: Coltsfoot
- Latin binomial: Tussilago farfara
- Other common names: Coughwort, British tobacco
- Plant family: Asteraceae (daisy family)
- Botanical description: • Coltsfoot is a perennial herb that grows up to 30cm (12 inches) in height. It has large, round, and furry leaves that resemble a horse's hoof, hence its common name. The leaves grow in a basal rosette and can measure up to 30cm (12 inches) across. The plant produces bright yellow, daisy-like flowers on separate stems in early spring, before the leaves appear.

The flowers are composed of numerous small florets and can measure up to 3cm (1.2 inches) across. The plant produces rhizomes that spread rapidly, and it can become invasive if not controlled. The plant is native to Europe and Asia, but it has been naturalized in many other parts of the world, including North America.

Coltsfoot can sometimes be confused with other plants, such as butterbur (Petasites spp.), which also has large, round leaves. However, butterbur leaves are not furry like those of Coltsfoot, and the flowers appear after the leaves have emerged. It is important to properly identify Coltsfoot before using it, as other plants may have toxic properties.

Medicinal Properties:
- Recommended cultivars: N/A
- Parts used: Dried leaves, flowers, and/or root
- Taste: Bitter, mucilaginous
- Actions: Demulcent, expectorant, anti-inflammatory, astringent, emollient
- Energetics: Cool and dry
- Specific indications: Coltsfoot has been traditionally used for respiratory conditions, particularly those that involve excessive mucus production. Specific indications include:
  - Coughs: Coltsfoot has a soothing effect on the throat and can help to calm coughs. It is particularly useful for dry coughs and those caused by irritation.
  - Asthma: Coltsfoot can help to open up the airways and improve breathing, making it useful for asthma.

- Bronchitis: Coltsfoot is often used to treat acute bronchitis, as it helps to reduce inflammation and relieve coughing.
- Sinusitis: Coltsfoot can help to relieve congestion and reduce inflammation in the sinuses, making it useful for sinusitis.
- Sore throat: Coltsfoot has a soothing effect on the throat and can help to reduce inflammation, making it useful for sore throats.

It is important to note that coltsfoot should be used with caution, as it contains potentially harmful compounds called pyrrolizidine alkaloids. Therefore, it should only be used under the guidance of a qualified healthcare provider.

Medicinal preparations:

Coltsfoot can be used in a variety of medicinal preparations, including:
- Infusions: Coltsfoot leaves can be steeped in hot water to make an infusion. This is a good way to extract the plant's mucilage, which can soothe irritated mucous membranes. The infusion can be used as a tea, or as a gargle or mouthwash for sore throats and mouth sores.
- Decoctions: The root of the coltsfoot plant can be boiled in water to make a decoction. This is a good way to extract the plant's active compounds, including flavonoids and tannins. The decoction can be used as a cough syrup, or as a wash for skin conditions.
- Poultices: The leaves of the coltsfoot plant can be mashed and applied directly to the skin to soothe inflammation and irritation. This is a good way to treat skin conditions like eczema, psoriasis, and acne.
- Tinctures: Coltsfoot can be extracted in alcohol to make a tincture. This is a good way to preserve the plant's active compounds and make them more bioavailable. The tincture can be used as a cough syrup or to treat digestive issues.
- Capsules: Coltsfoot can be ground into a powder and encapsulated for easy ingestion. This is a good way to take the herb for respiratory issues, as it can be difficult to consume enough of the herb through teas or tinctures alone.

It is important to consult with a healthcare provider before using coltsfoot medicinally, as the plant can interact with certain medications and may not be appropriate for everyone.

- Ratio and dosage information: 1-2 teaspoons of dried herb per cup of water, up to 3 cups per day

Medicinal uses: Coltsfoot has been traditionally used for various medicinal purposes, including:

- Respiratory problems: Coltsfoot is known to help with coughs, bronchitis, asthma, and other respiratory issues. It can help to soothe inflammation in the respiratory tract and reduce mucus production.
- Digestive issues: Coltsfoot has been used to help with digestive problems such as constipation and indigestion. It is believed to have a mild laxative effect and can help to stimulate the digestive system.
- Skin conditions: Coltsfoot has been used topically to help with various skin conditions such as eczema and psoriasis. It is believed to have anti-inflammatory and antiseptic properties that can help to soothe and heal the skin.
- Pain relief: Coltsfoot has been used traditionally as a pain reliever. It is believed to have analgesic properties that can help to reduce pain and discomfort.
- Anti-inflammatory: Coltsfoot has been traditionally used as an anti-inflammatory herb. It is believed to help reduce inflammation in various parts of the body, including the respiratory tract, digestive system, and skin.
- Other uses: Coltsfoot has also been used to help with urinary tract infections, headaches, and fever.

It's important to note that scientific evidence for these uses is limited, and coltsfoot should not be used as a replacement for conventional medical treatment without consulting a healthcare provider.

• Precautions and contradictions: Coltsfoot contains pyrrolizidine alkaloids (PAs), which can be toxic to the liver in high doses or with long-term use. Therefore, it is not recommended for extended use or for use by individuals with liver disease. Pregnant and breastfeeding women should also avoid using coltsfoot. It is important to source coltsfoot from a reputable supplier and to ensure that it is free of contaminants, such as heavy metals, which can be harmful to health.

Cultivation:
• Native to: Europe and Asia
• Zones: 3-9
• Soil: Moist, well-drained soil with a pH of 6-7
• Propagation: Seeds or root division
• Growing information and garden care: Coltsfoot prefers moist soil and partial shade. It can be grown from seed or by dividing the rootstock. The plant spreads rapidly by rhizomes, so it can become invasive if not contained. Harvest leaves and flowers in early spring, and root in fall.
• Insects and disease: Coltsfoot is a relatively hardy plant and is not usually affected by serious insect pests or diseases. However, it can be susceptible to rust, a fungal disease that causes yellow-orange spots on the leaves, and powdery

mildew, a fungal disease that results in a white, powdery coating on the leaves. These diseases can be managed by removing infected leaves and improving air circulation around the plant.

In terms of pests, coltsfoot can be attacked by leaf miners, which are small, fly-like insects that lay their eggs on the underside of the leaves. The larvae tunnel through the leaves, leaving distinctive trails or "mines" behind. This damage is mostly cosmetic and doesn't usually harm the plant. If the infestation is severe, however, it can weaken the plant and make it more vulnerable to other problems. In this case, the affected leaves can be removed and destroyed to prevent the spread of the pest.

- Harvesting and preparations: Coltsfoot leaves and flowers should be harvested in early spring before the plant blooms. The root should be harvested in the fall after the leaves have withered. The plant can be dried for later use or used fresh. To dry the herb, it should be hung upside down in a dry, well-ventilated area out of direct sunlight. Once the leaves are dry, they can be stored in an airtight container in a cool, dry place.

Coltsfoot leaves can be made into a tea by steeping 1-2 teaspoons of dried leaves in a cup of hot water for 10-15 minutes. The tea can be consumed up to 3 times a day. A tincture can also be made by steeping the leaves in alcohol for several weeks and then straining. The recommended dosage of the tincture is 2-4 ml up to three times a day.

The fresh leaves can also be used to make a poultice or salve for topical application to soothe skin irritations, burns, and insect bites. The leaves should be crushed and mixed with a carrier oil, such as olive or coconut oil, and applied to the affected area. The poultice can be covered with a clean cloth or bandage to keep it in place.

What medicines are made with this herb:

Coltsfoot has been used in traditional herbal medicine for centuries to treat various ailments. It contains mucilage, which has a soothing effect on the mucous membranes in the respiratory tract. Coltsfoot is commonly used in cough syrups and expectorants to help relieve coughs and clear mucus from the lungs. It is also used as a natural remedy for sore throats, asthma, bronchitis, and other respiratory conditions.

Coltsfoot has been traditionally used in various medicinal preparations. Some of the medicines made with coltsfoot are:

- Herbal teas and infusions: Coltsfoot leaves can be used to prepare herbal tea or infusion, which is used to treat cough, bronchitis, and other respiratory problems.
- Syrups: Syrups made from coltsfoot are used to treat coughs and other respiratory ailments.
- Tinctures: Tinctures made from the leaves and flowers of coltsfoot are used to treat respiratory ailments, digestive problems, and skin conditions.
- Poultices: Poultices made from the leaves of coltsfoot are used to treat skin inflammation and irritation.
- Capsules and tablets: Capsules and tablets containing coltsfoot extracts are available in the market, which are used to treat respiratory problems such as asthma, bronchitis, and cough.

It is important to consult a healthcare provider before using any form of coltsfoot for medicinal purposes.

What medicines this herb counteract:

Coltsfoot may interact with certain medications, including diuretics, heart medications, and medications for diabetes. It may also cause allergic reactions in some people, especially those who are allergic to plants in the same family as coltsfoot, such as ragweed, daisies, and marigolds. It is important to speak with a healthcare provider before using coltsfoot, especially if you are taking medications or have any underlying health conditions. Pregnant and breastfeeding women should also avoid using coltsfoot as its safety in these populations has not been established.

Comfrey

Herbal Identification:
- Common name: Comfrey
- Latin binomial: Symphytum officinale
- Other common names: Knitbone, Bruisewort
- Plant family: Boraginaceae
- Botanical description: Comfrey (Symphytum officinale) is a perennial herbaceous plant that belongs to the Boraginaceae family. It is native to Europe and Asia but has been introduced to other parts of the world, including North America. Comfrey can grow up to 1.5 meters tall and has large, hairy leaves that are lance-shaped and up to 30 cm long. The leaves and stems are covered with fine hairs and have a rough texture.

The plant produces clusters of small, bell-shaped flowers that can be pink, purple, or white in color. The flowers are usually borne on a spike that can grow up to 1 meter in height. Comfrey flowers from May to August.

Comfrey has a deep, thick taproot that can reach up to 2 meters in length. The root is fleshy, black on the outside, and white on the inside. It has a high mucilage content, which gives it a slimy texture when crushed or boiled.

Comfrey is commonly used in herbal medicine as a poultice or salve to treat wounds, sprains, and other injuries. It is also used as a fertilizer in organic gardening due to its high nutrient content. However, comfrey contains pyrrolizidine alkaloids that can be toxic to the liver when consumed in large amounts, so it should be used with caution.

Medicinal Properties:
- Recommended cultivars: Bocking 14, Bocking 4
- Parts used: Leaves, roots
- Taste: Mucilaginous, slightly bitter
- Actions: Demulcent, astringent, vulnerary, expectorant, anti-inflammatory
- Energetics: Cooling, moistening
- Specific indications: Comfrey has been traditionally used for various medicinal purposes, particularly for its wound-healing and anti-inflammatory properties.

Here are some specific indications for comfrey:
- ➢ Wound healing: Comfrey has been used topically to help heal wounds, cuts, and burns. The high mucilage content of the plant helps to soothe and protect

damaged skin, while its allantoin content stimulates cell proliferation and helps to regenerate new tissue.
- Inflammatory conditions: Comfrey has anti-inflammatory properties that make it useful for treating conditions such as arthritis, gout, and other inflammatory disorders. The plant's high levels of rosmarinic acid, a natural compound with anti-inflammatory effects, make it an effective remedy for reducing pain and swelling.
- Bone fractures: Comfrey has been traditionally used to speed up the healing of bone fractures. Studies have shown that the plant's allantoin and rosmarinic acid can help to stimulate bone growth and repair.
- Skin conditions: Comfrey can be used topically to treat skin conditions such as eczema and psoriasis. The plant's high mucilage content and anti-inflammatory properties help to soothe irritated skin and reduce inflammation.

It's important to note that comfrey should not be taken internally, as it contains pyrrolizidine alkaloids that can be toxic to the liver. It should only be used topically under the guidance of a qualified healthcare practitioner.

Medicinal preparations:

Comfrey can be used to prepare a range of medicinal preparations, including:
- Comfrey salve: Comfrey salve is made by infusing comfrey leaves in oil and then combining it with beeswax to create a healing ointment. This salve can be applied topically to soothe and heal minor cuts, burns, and other skin irritations.
- Comfrey poultice: A comfrey poultice is made by crushing fresh comfrey leaves and applying them directly to the skin. The poultice can help to reduce pain and inflammation, and promote the healing of wounds, bruises, and sprains.
- Comfrey tea: Comfrey tea can be made by steeping dried comfrey leaves in hot water for 10-15 minutes. This tea can be used as a topical rinse for wounds or as a mouthwash to help relieve sore throats and mouth ulcers.
- Comfrey oil: Comfrey oil can be made by infusing comfrey leaves in a carrier oil, such as olive or coconut oil. This oil can be used topically to help relieve pain and inflammation in conditions such as arthritis and gout.

It's important to note that comfrey should only be used under the guidance of a qualified healthcare practitioner, as it can be toxic when taken internally. It should also not be used on open wounds or broken skin, as it may cause skin irritation or infection.

- Ratio and dosage information: For topical use, apply comfrey salve or oil to the affected area 2-3 times per day. For internal use, 1-2 teaspoons of dried leaf in a cup of hot water, steeped for 10-15 minutes, 3 times per day.

Medicinal uses:
Comfrey (Symphytum officinale) has a long history of use in traditional medicine for its healing properties. Here are some of the medicinal uses of comfrey:
- Wound healing: Comfrey is commonly used to help heal wounds, cuts, and burns. Its high mucilage and allantoin content help to soothe and protect damaged skin, while promoting cell growth and regeneration.
- Inflammatory conditions: Comfrey has anti-inflammatory properties that make it useful in the treatment of conditions such as arthritis, gout, and other inflammatory disorders. Its high levels of rosmarinic acid help to reduce pain and inflammation.
- Bone fractures: Comfrey has been traditionally used to speed up the healing of bone fractures. Studies have shown that its allantoin and rosmarinic acid content can help to stimulate bone growth and repair.
- Skin conditions: Comfrey can be used topically to help treat skin conditions such as eczema, psoriasis, and dermatitis. Its anti-inflammatory and soothing properties help to reduce itching and inflammation.
- Pain relief: Comfrey can be used to help relieve pain associated with conditions such as back pain, joint pain, and muscle strains. Its high mucilage and rosmarinic acid content help to reduce pain and inflammation.

It's important to note that comfrey should only be used under the guidance of a qualified healthcare practitioner, as it can be toxic when taken internally. It should also not be used on open wounds or broken skin, as it may cause skin irritation or infection.

• Precautions and contradictions: Comfrey (Symphytum officinale) has some potential health risks and precautions that should be considered before use. Here are some precautions and contradictions related to comfrey:
- Pyrrolizidine alkaloids: Comfrey contains pyrrolizidine alkaloids, which can be toxic to the liver when taken internally. For this reason, comfrey should not be taken orally.
- Allergy: Some people may be allergic to comfrey. It is advisable to perform a patch test before using comfrey topically.
- Pregnancy and breastfeeding: Pregnant or breastfeeding women should avoid using comfrey, as there is not enough evidence to determine its safety during pregnancy or while breastfeeding.
- Children: Comfrey should not be used on children, as it can be toxic if ingested or absorbed through the skin.
- Surgery: Comfrey should be avoided before and after surgery, as it can affect blood clotting and increase the risk of bleeding.
- Liver disease: Comfrey should not be used by individuals with liver disease or a history of liver disease.

- External use only: Comfrey should only be used topically on intact skin. It should not be used on open wounds or broken skin, as it may cause skin irritation or infection.

It is important to consult with a qualified healthcare practitioner before using comfrey, particularly if you have any medical conditions or are taking any medications.

Cultivation:
- Native to: Europe, Asia
- Zones: 3-9
- Soil: Comfrey prefers rich, moist soil with a pH between 6.0-7.0.
- Propagation: Comfrey can be propagated by root cuttings or crown divisions. It can also self-seed.
- Growing information and garden care: Comfrey prefers full sun to partial shade and can tolerate wet soil. It can become invasive, so it is recommended to contain it in a designated area of the garden.
- Insects and disease: Comfrey (Symphytum officinale) is generally a hardy plant that is not prone to many insect and disease problems. However, there are a few issues to be aware of:
  - Slugs and snails: Comfrey is a favorite food of slugs and snails, and they can quickly damage the young leaves and stems. To protect the plant, you can surround it with copper tape or use a slug and snail bait that is safe for organic gardening.
  - Rust: Comfrey can sometimes be affected by rust, which appears as yellow-orange spots on the leaves. To prevent rust, avoid overcrowding the plants and make sure they have good air circulation. If rust appears, remove the affected leaves and dispose of them away from the garden to prevent the spread of the disease.
  - Powdery mildew: Powdery mildew is a common fungal disease that affects many plants, including comfrey. It appears as a white powdery coating on the leaves and can cause them to become distorted and discolored. To prevent powdery mildew, avoid overhead watering and make sure the plants have good air circulation. If powdery mildew appears, remove the affected leaves and dispose of them away from the garden.
  - Aphids: Comfrey can sometimes be infested by aphids, which can cause the leaves to become distorted and discolored. To control aphids, spray the affected plants with a solution of water and insecticidal soap, or use a natural predator such as ladybugs or lacewings.

Overall, comfrey is a relatively low-maintenance plant that is not prone to many insect and disease problems. With proper care and attention, it can provide a bountiful harvest of leaves and flowers for use in medicinal preparations.

- Harvesting and preparations: Comfrey (Symphytum officinale) is a perennial herb that is typically harvested for its leaves and roots. Here are some guidelines for harvesting and preparing comfrey:
  - Harvesting: The leaves of comfrey can be harvested throughout the growing season, starting in late spring and continuing until the first frost. The leaves should be picked when they are young and tender, as older leaves can become tough and fibrous. The roots of comfrey should be harvested in the fall, after the plant has finished flowering.
  - Drying: To dry comfrey leaves, spread them out in a single layer on a drying rack or in a well-ventilated area out of direct sunlight. Turn them occasionally to ensure even drying. The leaves are dry when they are brittle and crumble easily. To dry comfrey roots, wash them thoroughly and cut them into small pieces. Spread them out in a single layer on a drying rack or in a well-ventilated area out of direct sunlight. Turn them occasionally to ensure even drying. The roots are dry when they are hard and brittle.
  - Preparations: Comfrey can be used fresh or dried in various medicinal preparations, such as teas, poultices, ointments, and tinctures. To make a comfrey tea, steep 1-2 teaspoons of dried leaves in hot water for 10-15 minutes. To make a comfrey poultice, crush fresh or dried leaves and apply them directly to the affected area. To make a comfrey ointment, simmer fresh or dried leaves in a carrier oil such as olive or coconut oil, strain, and mix with beeswax to create a salve. To make a comfrey tincture, steep fresh or dried leaves in alcohol for several weeks, strain, and store in a dark glass bottle.

It's important to note that comfrey should only be used under the guidance of a qualified healthcare practitioner, as it can be toxic when taken internally. It should also not be used on open wounds or broken skin, as it may cause skin irritation or infection.

What medicines are made with this herb:

Comfrey (Symphytum officinale) has been traditionally used for medicinal purposes, and various preparations can be made using this herb. Here are some of the medicines that are made with comfrey:
- Ointments and salves: Comfrey is often used topically to treat bruises, sprains, strains, and other musculoskeletal injuries. Ointments and salves made from comfrey leaves or roots can be applied directly to the affected area to promote healing.

- Poultices: Comfrey leaves can be crushed and applied directly to the skin as a poultice to treat skin inflammation, boils, and other skin conditions.
- Teas: Comfrey tea is believed to have a soothing effect on the digestive system, and it is sometimes used to treat stomach ulcers, diarrhea, and other gastrointestinal problems. It may also be used to treat respiratory infections and sore throat.
- Tinctures: Comfrey tincture is often used to treat joint pain, arthritis, and other inflammatory conditions. It may also be used as a general tonic to support overall health and well-being.

It's important to note that comfrey should only be used under the guidance of a qualified healthcare practitioner, as it can be toxic when taken internally. It should also not be used on open wounds or broken skin, as it may cause skin irritation or infection.

What medicines this herb counteract:

Comfrey (Symphytum officinale) has been traditionally used for medicinal purposes, but it is important to note that it can interact with certain medicines. Here are some medicines that comfrey may counteract:

- Blood thinners: Comfrey may have blood-thinning properties, so it may interact with blood-thinning medications like warfarin, aspirin, and heparin.
- Diuretics: Comfrey may have diuretic properties, so it may interact with medications that increase urine output, such as furosemide and hydrochlorothiazide.
- Liver medications: Comfrey contains pyrrolizidine alkaloids, which can be toxic to the liver. It may interact with medications that affect liver function, such as acetaminophen and statins.
- Sedatives: Comfrey may have sedative properties, so it may interact with medications that have a sedative effect, such as benzodiazepines and barbiturates.

It's important to note that comfrey should only be used under the guidance of a qualified healthcare practitioner, and it should not be taken internally due to its potential toxicity. It should also not be used on open wounds or broken skin, as it may cause skin irritation or infection.

Cordyceps

Herbal Identification:
- Common name: Cordyceps
- Latin binomial: Cordyceps sinensis
- Other common names: Caterpillar fungus, Dong Chong Xia Cao, Yartsa Gunbu
- Plant family: Ophiocordycipitaceae
- Botanical description: Cordyceps is a type of fungus that belongs to the Ascomycota division of fungi. The most well-known species of cordyceps is Cordyceps sinensis, which is native to the Tibetan plateau and other high-altitude regions of China, Nepal, and Bhutan.

The fruiting body of the cordyceps fungus resembles a small, elongated mushroom and grows out of the body of its host, typically a caterpillar. The fruiting body can range in color from brown to orange and is often curved or twisted.

Cordyceps has a unique life cycle in which it infects and consumes the body of its host insect or arthropod, eventually growing a fruiting body out of the host's body as it dies. This makes it an unusual and intriguing fungus to study.

Due to its medicinal properties and traditional use in Chinese medicine, cordyceps has become a popular ingredient in dietary supplements and functional foods. However, due to its unique life cycle and the difficulty of cultivating it in large quantities, cordyceps is a relatively expensive and rare ingredient.

Medicinal Properties:
- Recommended cultivars: Not applicable, as Cordyceps sinensis is a wild mushroom and cannot be cultivated in the same way as other mushrooms.
- Parts used: The fruiting body of Cordyceps sinensis is used for medicinal purposes.
- Taste: Not applicable, as Cordyceps sinensis is typically used in powdered form and does not have a distinctive taste.
- Actions: Adaptogen, immune modulator, anti-inflammatory, antioxidant, anti-cancer, anti-fatigue, and anti-aging.
- Energetics: Neutral to slightly warming.

- Specific indications: Cordyceps has a range of traditional medicinal uses and is believed to have many potential health benefits. Some specific indications for cordyceps include:
  - Immune system support: Cordyceps is believed to have immune-boosting properties and may be useful in supporting the body's natural defenses against infections and illnesses.
  - Athletic performance: Some studies suggest that cordyceps may improve athletic performance by increasing oxygen uptake and reducing fatigue. It is often used by athletes as a natural performance enhancer.
  - Anti-inflammatory effects: Cordyceps may have anti-inflammatory effects, which could make it useful in the treatment of inflammatory conditions such as arthritis and asthma.
  - Kidney disease: Cordyceps has been traditionally used in Chinese medicine to treat kidney disease, and some studies suggest that it may have potential as a treatment for chronic kidney disease.
  - Cancer: Some research has suggested that cordyceps may have potential as a treatment for certain types of cancer, although more research is needed in this area.

It is important to note that while cordyceps has many potential benefits, more research is needed to fully understand its effects on the body and to determine appropriate doses and formulations for specific conditions. It is also important to consult with a healthcare provider before using cordyceps to avoid any potential adverse effects or interactions with other medications.

Medicinal preparations:

Cordyceps can be consumed in various medicinal preparations, including:
- Capsules or tablets: Cordyceps supplements are available in capsule or tablet form and are often taken as a dietary supplement for general health and wellness.
- Extracts: Cordyceps extracts are made by boiling or steeping the dried fruiting body in water or alcohol. The resulting liquid is then concentrated to create a potent extract, which can be consumed as drops, added to drinks, or used in cooking.
- Tea: Cordyceps tea can be made by steeping the dried fruiting body in hot water for several minutes. The resulting tea can be consumed as is or sweetened with honey.
- Powders: Cordyceps powder can be added to smoothies, shakes, or other foods for easy consumption.

It is important to note that the potency and effectiveness of cordyceps preparations can vary depending on the extraction method and quality of the

starting material. It is important to choose high-quality products from reputable sources and to follow dosage instructions carefully.
- Ratio and dosage information: The recommended dosage of Cordyceps sinensis varies depending on the specific product and individual needs. It is important to follow the dosage instructions on the product label or to consult with a qualified healthcare practitioner for personalized dosage recommendations.

Medicinal uses:
Cordyceps is traditionally used in Chinese medicine for a variety of medicinal purposes. Some of the medicinal uses of cordyceps include:
- Boosting immune function: Cordyceps is believed to stimulate the production of white blood cells, which play a crucial role in the immune system's ability to fight infections and diseases.
- Improving respiratory function: Cordyceps has been used to treat respiratory conditions such as asthma and bronchitis. It is believed to help open up the airways and improve lung function.
- Supporting kidney function: Cordyceps has been used in Chinese medicine to treat kidney disease and to improve kidney function. Some studies suggest that cordyceps may have potential as a treatment for chronic kidney disease.
- Enhancing athletic performance: Some research has suggested that cordyceps may improve athletic performance by increasing oxygen uptake and reducing fatigue. It is often used by athletes as a natural performance enhancer.
- Anti-inflammatory effects: Cordyceps may have anti-inflammatory effects, which could make it useful in the treatment of inflammatory conditions such as arthritis and inflammatory bowel disease.
- Supporting heart health: Some research suggests that cordyceps may help reduce cholesterol levels and improve heart function, making it potentially useful in the prevention and treatment of cardiovascular disease.

It is important to note that while cordyceps has many potential health benefits, more research is needed to fully understand its effects on the body and to determine appropriate doses and formulations for specific conditions. It is also important to consult with a healthcare provider before using cordyceps to avoid any potential adverse effects or interactions with other medications.
- Precautions and contradictions: Cordyceps is generally considered safe when consumed in appropriate amounts, but it is important to exercise caution when using this herb, especially in certain situations:
- Pregnancy and breastfeeding: There is not enough information available about the safety of cordyceps during pregnancy and breastfeeding, so it is best to avoid using it during these times.

- Autoimmune diseases: Cordyceps may stimulate the immune system, which could potentially worsen symptoms of autoimmune diseases such as multiple sclerosis, lupus, and rheumatoid arthritis. It is important to consult with a healthcare provider before using cordyceps if you have an autoimmune disease.
- Bleeding disorders: Cordyceps may increase the risk of bleeding and should be used with caution in individuals with bleeding disorders or those taking anticoagulant medications.
- Surgery: Cordyceps should be discontinued at least two weeks before surgery to reduce the risk of bleeding.

It is important to choose high-quality cordyceps products from reputable sources and to follow dosage instructions carefully. Cordyceps may also interact with certain medications, so it is important to consult with a healthcare provider before using it, especially if you are taking any prescription or over-the-counter medications.

Cultivation:
- Native to: The high-altitude regions of the Himalayas, Tibet, and other parts of Asia.
- Zones: Not applicable, as Cordyceps sinensis is a wild mushroom that cannot be cultivated in the same way as other mushrooms.
- Soil (pH and type of soil): Not applicable.
- Propagation: Not applicable.
- Growing information and garden care: Not applicable, as Cordyceps sinensis cannot be cultivated.
- Insects and disease: Interestingly, cordyceps itself is a type of fungus that is known for its parasitic relationship with certain insects. The fungus invades the bodies of the insects, using them as hosts and eventually killing them. The resulting fruiting bodies of the fungus (the part used medicinally) grow from the dead insects.

However, in cultivation, cordyceps is grown without the presence of insects, so there are no major insect pests or diseases that affect its growth. Proper growing conditions, including appropriate temperature, humidity, and ventilation, can help prevent contamination by other fungi or bacteria that could potentially harm the crop.
- Harvesting and preparations: Cordyceps is typically harvested in the wild, but it can also be cultivated in controlled settings. In the wild, the fungus grows on the bodies of certain insects and is found in high-altitude regions in parts of Asia, including Tibet, Nepal, and Bhutan. Cultivated cordyceps is grown in specialized laboratories under controlled conditions, often using a substrate made from rice or other grains.

Once harvested, cordyceps can be prepared for use in a variety of ways. The most common forms of cordyceps used in traditional Chinese medicine are dried and ground into a powder or made into an extract. It can also be consumed in capsule form, or added to food or beverages.

Cordyceps extract is made by boiling the dried fungus in water to extract its active compounds, which are then concentrated through a process of evaporation. The resulting extract can be added to teas, soups, or other beverages.

When using cordyceps, it is important to follow dosage instructions carefully and choose high-quality products from reputable sources. Cordyceps preparations may interact with certain medications or have contraindications for certain medical conditions, so it is important to consult with a healthcare provider before using it.

What medicines are made with this herb:
Cordyceps sinensis is typically used in powdered form or as an extract in traditional Chinese medicine formulations, as well as in some dietary supplements. It is believed to have a range of health benefits, including boosting immune function, improving energy and endurance, and supporting respiratory and cardiovascular health.

In traditional Chinese medicine, cordyceps is often used in formulas for treating conditions such as fatigue, respiratory infections, kidney and liver disease, and sexual dysfunction. It is also sometimes used in cancer treatment protocols as an adjunct therapy to help alleviate symptoms and improve quality of life.

Cordyceps supplements are widely available in health food stores and online, and may be marketed for a variety of purposes, including improving athletic performance, enhancing sexual function, and reducing inflammation. However, scientific evidence supporting these uses is limited, and more research is needed to fully understand the potential health benefits of cordyceps.

Cordyceps is believed to have a range of medicinal properties, including immune system support, improved athletic performance, and anti-inflammatory effects. It is also thought to have antioxidant properties and may have potential as a treatment for certain cancers and kidney disease.

Some specific medicines made with cordyceps include Cordyceps sinensis polysaccharide, which is a water-soluble polysaccharide extracted from the fungus and is used as an immunostimulant. Another medicine is cordycepin, which is a compound found in cordyceps and has been studied for its potential antitumor and antiviral properties.

It is important to note that while cordyceps has many potential health benefits, there is still limited scientific evidence to support many of these uses, and more research is needed to fully understand its effects on the body.

What medicines this herb counter act:

There is limited information on specific medications that cordyceps may counteract or interact with. However, cordyceps may have the potential to interact with certain medications, such as immunosuppressants, blood thinners, and antidiabetic drugs. Therefore, it is important to consult with a healthcare provider before using cordyceps if you are taking any medications or have any underlying health conditions. Additionally, cordyceps should not be used as a replacement for conventional medical treatment, and it is important to seek appropriate medical care for any health concerns.

Dandelion

Herbal Identification:
- Common name: Dandelion
- Latin binomial: Taraxacum officinale
- Other common names: Blowball, Lion's tooth, Puffball, Wild Endive
- Plant family: Asteraceae (daisy family)
- Botanical description: Dandelion is a perennial herb that grows up to 30 cm tall. It has a rosette of toothed, lobed, and spatula-shaped leaves that can grow up to 30 cm long. The leaves are hairless and shiny, and the veins of the leaves are prominent. The plant produces yellow flowers that bloom from April to October. The flower heads are borne singly on hollow stems, and each head is made up of many small flowers. After flowering, the flowers turn into white, fluffy, spherical seed heads that are dispersed by the wind.

Medicinal Properties:
- Recommended cultivars: No specific cultivars recommended.
- Parts used: Leaves, roots, and flowers.
- Taste: Bitter.
- Actions: Diuretic, bitter tonic, cholagogue, anti-inflammatory, antioxidant.
- Energetics: Cooling and drying.
- Specific indications: Dandelion has been traditionally used for a variety of medicinal purposes, including:
  - Liver and gallbladder support: Dandelion is believed to stimulate the production and flow of bile, which helps to improve digestion and detoxification in the liver and gallbladder.
  - Digestive support: Dandelion may help to stimulate digestion and relieve constipation by increasing bowel movements.
  - Diuretic: Dandelion has been traditionally used as a natural diuretic to increase urine production and promote fluid elimination from the body.
  - Inflammation: Dandelion may help to reduce inflammation and swelling in the body due to its anti-inflammatory properties.
  - Skin health: Dandelion may help to improve the health of the skin by promoting detoxification and reducing inflammation.
  - Immune system support: Dandelion has been shown to have immunomodulatory effects, which may help to support the immune system.

It is important to note that while dandelion has been traditionally used for these indications, more research is needed to confirm its efficacy for each specific use.

Additionally, it is important to consult with a healthcare provider before using dandelion for medicinal purposes.

Medicinal preparations:
Dandelion can be used in various medicinal preparations, including:
- Infusions or teas: Dandelion leaves, flowers, and roots can be brewed in hot water to make a tea or infusion that can be consumed daily to promote digestive health, liver function, and overall wellness.
- Tinctures: Dandelion roots can be made into a tincture, which is a concentrated liquid extract that is taken orally to support liver and gallbladder function, improve digestion, and reduce inflammation.
- Capsules or tablets: Dandelion root extract can also be taken in capsule or tablet form as a dietary supplement to support liver function, digestion, and overall health.
- Topical preparations: Dandelion root extract can be added to skin care products, such as creams or ointments, to help soothe skin irritation and promote a healthy complexion.

It is important to note that the preparation and dosage of dandelion may vary depending on the specific use and individual needs. It is recommended to consult with a healthcare provider or a qualified herbalist for guidance on the appropriate preparation and dosage for your needs. • Ratio and dosage information: 1-2 teaspoons of dried leaves or roots per cup of water, up to 3 cups daily.

Medicinal uses:
Dandelion has a variety of medicinal uses, including:
- Liver support: Dandelion is believed to support liver function by promoting the production and flow of bile, which helps the liver to eliminate toxins from the body.
- Digestive aid: Dandelion can stimulate digestive function and promote healthy bowel movements, making it useful for constipation, bloating, and other digestive complaints.
- Diuretic: Dandelion is a natural diuretic, which means it can help to increase urine output and eliminate excess water and salt from the body. This can be helpful for reducing bloating and swelling, and may also be beneficial for individuals with high blood pressure or certain types of kidney problems.
- Anti-inflammatory: Dandelion contains compounds that have anti-inflammatory effects, making it potentially useful for reducing inflammation throughout the body and relieving pain.

- Immune support: Dandelion is rich in antioxidants, which can help to support the immune system and protect the body against damage from free radicals.
- Skin health: Dandelion may also be beneficial for promoting healthy skin, as it contains vitamins and minerals that are important for skin health and has anti-inflammatory and antibacterial properties that may help to reduce acne and other skin irritations.

It is important to note that while dandelion has a long history of traditional use and some scientific evidence to support its medicinal properties, more research is needed to fully understand its effects and determine its safety and efficacy. It is recommended to consult with a healthcare provider or a qualified herbalist before using dandelion for medicinal purposes.

• Precautions and contradictions: Dandelion is generally considered safe for consumption and has few known side effects. However, some precautions and contradictions should be noted:
- Allergic reactions: Some people may be allergic to dandelion, especially those who are allergic to plants in the Asteraceae family.
- Interaction with medications: Dandelion may interact with certain medications, such as diuretics, blood thinners, and antibiotics. It is important to consult with a healthcare provider before using dandelion if you are taking any medications.
- Gallbladder issues: People with gallbladder problems should avoid using dandelion as it may worsen their condition.
- Kidney problems: Dandelion has diuretic properties and may increase urine output, which can be harmful to people with kidney problems.
- Pregnancy and breastfeeding: There is insufficient evidence regarding the safety of dandelion during pregnancy and breastfeeding. It is best to avoid using dandelion in large amounts during these times.

Overall, it is important to consult with a healthcare provider before using dandelion for medicinal purposes, especially if you have any underlying health conditions or are taking any medications.

Cultivation:
• Native to: Europe and Asia, but now widely naturalized in North America.
• Zones: Hardy in USDA zones 3-9.
• Soil: Prefers well-draining soil with a pH of 6.0-7.5.
• Propagation: Can be propagated by seed, root cuttings, or division.
• Growing information and garden care: Dandelions are hardy plants that can grow in a wide range of conditions, but prefer full sun to partial shade. They are

often considered weeds, but can be cultivated in a garden setting by allowing some plants to flower and go to seed to propagate new plants.

• Insects and disease: Dandelions are relatively pest-free, and they are not usually affected by diseases. However, they can be invasive and compete with other plants in the garden. Dandelions can also be hosts to pests such as aphids and whiteflies, which can be harmful to other plants.

• Harvesting and preparations: Dandelion leaves and roots can be harvested at any time of the year, but the best time is in the spring when they are the most tender and have the highest nutrient content. The flowers can be harvested in the late spring and early summer when they are fully open.

To prepare dandelion leaves for consumption, they can be washed and chopped to add to salads or cooked like spinach. The roots can be washed, chopped, and roasted to make a coffee substitute or boiled to make a tea.

To make dandelion tea, pour boiling water over the dried or fresh roots or leaves and steep for about 5-10 minutes. Dandelion root can also be tinctured or made into a decoction by boiling it in water for about 20-30 minutes.

Dandelion leaves and flowers can also be used to make a infused oil, which is commonly used in topical preparations such as salves and lotions. To make the infused oil, fill a jar with fresh or dried dandelion leaves and/or flowers, cover them with oil, and let the mixture sit for a few weeks.

What medicines are made with this herb:
　　Dandelion is used in a variety of herbal preparations, including teas, tinctures, capsules, and extracts. It is also a common ingredient in many detox and cleansing formulas, as well as in digestive and liver support supplements. Additionally, dandelion leaves are sometimes used as a salad green or cooked vegetable, and the roots can be roasted and used as a coffee substitute. It is also used in some traditional medicine systems, such as Chinese and Ayurvedic medicine.

What medicines this herb counteract:
　　Dandelion is generally considered safe for most people when taken in appropriate amounts. It is not known to counteract any specific medicines, but it may interact with certain medications, including diuretics, lithium, and antibiotics. Therefore, if you are taking any prescription medications, it is best to consult with your healthcare provider before taking dandelion supplements. Additionally, people with certain medical conditions, such as gallbladder disease or kidney problems, should also exercise caution when using dandelion.

Echinacea

Herbal Identification:
- Common name: Echinacea
- Latin binomial: Echinacea purpurea
- Other common names: Purple coneflower, Kansas snakeroot
- Plant family: Asteraceae (Compositae)
- Botanical description: Echinacea is a perennial herb that grows up to 1.5 meters tall. It has hairy stems, rough leaves, and large, showy flowers with spiky centers. The flowers can be pink, purple, or white. There are nine species of Echinacea, including Echinacea angustifolia, Echinacea pallida, and Echinacea tennesseensis.

Medicinal Properties:
- Recommended cultivars: Echinacea purpurea 'Magnus', 'White Swan', 'Ruby Star'
- Parts used: Roots, leaves, and flowers
- Taste: Bitter, slightly sweet
- Actions: Immunomodulatory, anti-inflammatory, antimicrobial, lymphatic, vulnerary
- Energetics: Cooling, drying
- Specific indications: Echinacea is commonly used to support the immune system and to help prevent and treat colds, flu, and other respiratory infections. It is also used topically to treat wounds, burns, and skin infections. Echinacea can help stimulate lymphatic flow and is used to treat lymphatic congestion and swollen glands. Other specific indications for echinacea include:
  - Upper respiratory infections, such as bronchitis, sinusitis, and laryngitis
  - Urinary tract infections
  - Ear infections
  - Gum disease and other oral infections
  - Yeast infections, such as candida
  - Inflammatory conditions, such as rheumatoid arthritis and psoriasis
  - Allergies and asthma
  - Low white blood cell count due to chemotherapy or radiation therapy
  - Fatigue and low energy levels
  - Chronic fatigue syndrome
  - Lyme disease
  - Herpes simplex virus

- Canker sores
- Cold sores (herpes simplex labialis)
- Boils and abscesses
- Eczema
- Burns and other skin injuries
- Insect bites and stings

It is important to note that echinacea is not a cure for these conditions, but rather a supportive therapy that can help improve symptoms and overall immune function. Consult with a healthcare provider before using echinacea for any specific health condition.

Medicinal preparations:
Echinacea can be prepared in several ways for medicinal use, including:
- Tea: To make echinacea tea, steep 1-2 teaspoons of dried echinacea root, leaves, or flowers in a cup of hot water for 10-15 minutes. Strain and drink up to three times per day.
- Tincture: Echinacea tincture is made by extracting the medicinal compounds from the plant material using alcohol or glycerin. Follow the manufacturer's instructions for dosage or consult with a healthcare provider.
- Capsules: Echinacea capsules are widely available and can be taken orally. Follow the manufacturer's instructions for dosage or consult with a healthcare provider.
- Poultice: A poultice made from echinacea can be applied topically to treat wounds, burns, and skin infections. Crush fresh or dried echinacea leaves or flowers and apply directly to the affected area.
- Infused oil: Echinacea can be infused into oil and used topically for wound healing and skin infections. To make echinacea-infused oil, cover dried echinacea root, leaves, or flowers with a carrier oil such as olive or jojoba oil and let steep for several weeks. Strain and use as needed.

Dosages and specific preparations may vary based on the individual and the condition being treated. It is important to consult with a healthcare provider or an experienced herbalist for guidance on using echinacea medicinally.

- Ratio and dosage information: 1-2 grams of dried root per day, or 3-4 ml of tincture three times per day

Medicinal uses:
Echinacea has several medicinal uses, including:

- Immune system support: Echinacea is commonly used to support the immune system and to help prevent and treat colds, flu, and other respiratory infections.
- Upper respiratory infections: Echinacea can help treat respiratory infections such as bronchitis, sinusitis, and laryngitis.
- Wound healing: Echinacea can help speed up the healing process of wounds and skin infections due to its antimicrobial and anti-inflammatory properties.
- Urinary tract infections: Echinacea can be used to treat urinary tract infections due to its antibacterial and diuretic properties.
- Allergies and asthma: Echinacea can help alleviate symptoms of allergies and asthma due to its anti-inflammatory and immune-modulating properties.
- Anti-inflammatory: Echinacea has anti-inflammatory properties and can be used to treat inflammatory conditions such as rheumatoid arthritis and psoriasis.
- Low white blood cell count: Echinacea can help boost white blood cell counts and is used as a supportive therapy for individuals undergoing chemotherapy or radiation therapy.
- Fatigue and low energy levels: Echinacea can help increase energy levels and reduce fatigue.
- Oral health: Echinacea can help improve oral health by reducing inflammation and fighting oral infections such as gingivitis and periodontitis.
- Skin health: Echinacea can help improve skin health and appearance by reducing inflammation and fighting skin infections.

It is important to note that echinacea is not a cure for these conditions, but rather a supportive therapy that can help improve symptoms and overall immune function. Consult with a healthcare provider before using echinacea for any specific health condition.

- Precautions and contradictions: Echinacea is generally considered safe for most people when used in recommended doses. However, there are some precautions and contraindications to be aware of:
  - Allergic reactions: Some people may experience an allergic reaction to echinacea. Symptoms may include rash, itching, swelling, or difficulty breathing. Discontinue use if any allergic reactions occur.
  - Autoimmune disorders: Echinacea may stimulate the immune system, which can be problematic for individuals with autoimmune disorders such as lupus, rheumatoid arthritis, or multiple sclerosis. Consult with a healthcare provider before using echinacea if you have an autoimmune disorder.
  - Pregnancy and breastfeeding: The safety of echinacea during pregnancy and breastfeeding is uncertain. Consult with a healthcare provider before using echinacea if you are pregnant or breastfeeding.

- Drug interactions: Echinacea may interact with certain medications, including immunosuppressants, antipsychotics, and certain heart medications. Consult with a healthcare provider before using echinacea if you are taking any medications.
- Long-term use: Long-term use of echinacea may reduce its effectiveness over time. It is recommended to take echinacea for no more than 8 weeks at a time, followed by a break of at least 1-2 weeks before resuming use.
- Not for children under 12: Echinacea is not recommended for children under 12 years old.
- Not for individuals with ragweed allergies: Individuals with ragweed allergies may also be allergic to echinacea, as they belong to the same plant family.

It is important to consult with a healthcare provider or an experienced herbalist before using echinacea medicinally, especially if you have any pre-existing medical conditions or are taking any medications.

Cultivation:
- Native to: North America
- Zones: 3-9
- Soil: Well-drained, slightly acidic soil (pH 6-7)
- Propagation: Seeds or root cuttings
- Growing information and garden care: Echinacea prefers full sun to part shade and moderate watering. It is a hardy plant that can tolerate heat and drought. Deadheading spent flowers can encourage new blooms.
- Insects and disease: Echinacea is generally a hardy and disease-resistant plant, but like any plant, it can be affected by insects and diseases. Some of the common insects that can attack echinacea include aphids, spider mites, thrips, and leafhoppers. These insects can be controlled with insecticidal soap or neem oil.

Some of the common diseases that can affect echinacea include:
- Powdery mildew: A fungal disease that appears as a white powdery coating on the leaves and stems. It can be prevented by providing good air circulation and avoiding overhead watering.
- Septoria leaf spot: A fungal disease that appears as small brown or black spots on the leaves. It can be prevented by removing infected leaves and avoiding overhead watering.
- Botrytis blight: A fungal disease that causes the flowers and stems to rot. It can be prevented by providing good air circulation and avoiding overcrowding.

- Aster yellows: A viral disease that causes the plant to become stunted and the leaves to turn yellow. Infected plants should be removed and destroyed to prevent the spread of the disease.

To prevent disease and insect problems, it is important to provide echinacea with well-draining soil, plenty of sunlight, and good air circulation. Watering should be done at the base of the plant to avoid wetting the leaves. If insect or disease problems persist, it is recommended to consult with a professional or experienced gardener for advice on treatment options.

- Harvesting and preparations: Harvesting echinacea can be done when the plant has reached maturity and is producing flowers. It is best to harvest the plant early in the morning when the dew has dried but before the sun is too strong. The aerial parts of the plant (leaves, stems, and flowers) can be harvested by cutting the stems just above the second set of leaves.

The parts of echinacea that are used medicinally are the roots and the aerial parts of the plant. The roots are typically harvested in the fall, after the plant has finished flowering and the leaves have started to wither. The roots can be dug up, washed, and dried in a cool, dark place. The aerial parts of the plant can be harvested throughout the growing season and can be used fresh or dried.

Echinacea can be prepared in a variety of ways, depending on the intended use. Some common preparations include:

- Tea: To make echinacea tea, steep 1-2 teaspoons of dried echinacea root or aerial parts in a cup of hot water for 10-15 minutes. The tea can be sweetened with honey or other natural sweeteners.
- Tincture: Echinacea tincture is made by steeping dried echinacea root or aerial parts in alcohol for several weeks. The tincture can be taken orally or added to water.
- Capsules: Echinacea capsules contain powdered echinacea root or aerial parts and can be taken orally with water.
- Salve: Echinacea salve is made by infusing dried echinacea in a carrier oil (such as olive oil) and combining it with beeswax to create a healing ointment.

It is important to follow recommended dosage guidelines when using echinacea medicinally and to consult with a healthcare provider or experienced herbalist before using echinacea in combination with other medications or herbs.

What medicines are made with this herb:

Echinacea is used in a variety of herbal medicines, including:

- Immune support supplements: Echinacea is often used as a key ingredient in supplements designed to support the immune system and promote overall wellness.

- Cold and flu remedies: Echinacea is believed to help prevent and treat colds and the flu. It is often included in herbal remedies designed to alleviate symptoms such as congestion, cough, and sore throat.
- Wound healing products: Echinacea is believed to have antimicrobial and anti-inflammatory properties that may help promote healing of wounds, burns, and other skin irritations. It is often included in ointments and creams designed for topical application.
- Allergy relief products: Echinacea is believed to help reduce symptoms of allergies, such as congestion and inflammation. It is often included in natural allergy remedies.
- Anti-inflammatory supplements: Echinacea is believed to have anti-inflammatory properties that may help reduce inflammation throughout the body. It is often included in supplements designed to support joint health and reduce pain and swelling.

It is important to note that echinacea is not regulated as a drug by the FDA and there is limited scientific evidence to support its effectiveness for various health conditions. Therefore, it is important to consult with a healthcare provider or experienced herbalist before using echinacea or any other herbal medicine.

What medicines this herb counteract:

Echinacea may interact with certain medications, including:
- Immunosuppressants: Echinacea may interact with medications used to suppress the immune system, such as cyclosporine and corticosteroids. Taking echinacea with these medications may reduce their effectiveness and increase the risk of infection.
- Antiplatelet and anticoagulant medications: Echinacea may increase the risk of bleeding when taken with medications such as aspirin, warfarin, and heparin.
- Certain medications for heart conditions: Echinacea may interact with medications used to treat certain heart conditions, such as amiodarone and methotrexate.
- Certain medications for depression: Echinacea may interact with medications used to treat depression, such as amitriptyline and imipramine.

It is important to consult with a healthcare provider or experienced herbalist before using echinacea if you are taking any medications. It is also important to note that echinacea is not recommended for use in individuals with autoimmune diseases or certain allergies, as it may stimulate the immune system and worsen symptoms.

Elderberry

Herbal Identification:
- Common name: Elderberry
- Latin binomial: Sambucus nigra
- Other common names: Black elder, European elder, elderberry bush
- Plant family: Adoxaceae
- Botanical description: Elderberry is a deciduous shrub or small tree that can grow up to 30 feet tall. It has compound leaves with five to nine leaflets that are serrated and arranged opposite each other on the stem. The shrub produces clusters of small, white or cream-colored flowers in the late spring or early summer, which are followed by small, dark purple-black berries that are about 1/4 inch in diameter. The berries grow in clusters that can be up to 10 inches long and 6 inches wide.

The bark of elderberry is gray-brown and has shallow fissures, while the branches are greenish-brown and have a pithy center. The plant has a deep root system and can form dense thickets if left unchecked.

Medicinal Properties:
- Recommended cultivars: There are several cultivars of elderberry that are commonly used for medicinal purposes, including Sambucus nigra 'Adams' and Sambucus nigra 'Black Lace'.
- Parts used: The flowers and berries are the parts of the plant used for medicinal purposes.
- Taste: Elderflower has a sweet, floral taste, while elderberry is tart and slightly bitter.
- Actions: Antiviral, immune-stimulating, anti-inflammatory, diaphoretic, diuretic, laxative, and emetic.
- Energetics: Cooling and drying.
- Specific indications: Specific indications for Elderberry include:
  - Immune System Support: Elderberry is traditionally used to boost the immune system and help fight off colds, flu, and other respiratory infections. It has been shown to have antiviral and anti-inflammatory properties that may help reduce the duration and severity of cold and flu symptoms.
  - Upper Respiratory Infections: Elderberry has been traditionally used to help alleviate symptoms of upper respiratory infections, such as coughing, congestion, and sore throat. It has also been shown to have antibacterial properties that may help fight off infections.

- Inflammation: Elderberry contains compounds that have been shown to have anti-inflammatory properties, which may help reduce inflammation in the body and alleviate symptoms of conditions such as arthritis and other inflammatory conditions.
- Allergies: Elderberry has been shown to have antihistamine properties, which may help reduce allergy symptoms such as runny nose, itchy eyes, and sneezing.
- Skin Health: Elderberry has been traditionally used topically to help soothe skin irritations, such as rashes and eczema. It has also been shown to have antioxidant properties, which may help protect the skin from damage caused by free radicals.
- Digestive Health: Elderberry has been shown to have laxative properties and may help alleviate constipation. It has also been traditionally used to help alleviate symptoms of gastrointestinal distress, such as bloating, gas, and indigestion.

Medicinal preparations:
Elderberry can be used in various medicinal preparations, such as:
- Tea: Steep 1-2 teaspoons of dried elderberries in a cup of boiling water for 10-15 minutes.
- Syrup: Simmer 1 cup of dried elderberries in 4 cups of water for 30-45 minutes, strain and add 1 cup of honey. Store in a sterilized jar and refrigerate for up to 3 months.
- Tincture: Combine 1 part dried elderberries with 2 parts vodka or brandy. Allow to macerate for 4-6 weeks, shaking daily. Strain and bottle.
- Capsules: Elderberry can be found in capsule form at health food stores and online retailers.
- Gummies: Elderberry gummies are a popular way to consume elderberry, and can be found at health food stores and online retailers.

The dosage and ratio of elderberry preparations may vary depending on the intended use and individual factors. It is recommended to consult with a qualified healthcare practitioner before using elderberry as a remedy.

• Ratio and dosage information: The dosage of elderberry can vary depending on the preparation used. Generally, a typical dose is 1-2 teaspoons of elderberry syrup, or 500-1000 mg of elderberry extract, taken several times per day during acute illness.

Medicinal uses:

Elderberry has been used for centuries for its medicinal properties, and has been traditionally used for a variety of conditions. Some of the most common medicinal uses of elderberry include:
- Boosting the immune system: Elderberry has been found to stimulate the immune system, helping to fight off infections and diseases.
- Relieving cold and flu symptoms: Elderberry is commonly used to reduce the severity and duration of cold and flu symptoms such as fever, cough, and congestion.
- Reducing inflammation: Elderberry has anti-inflammatory properties and has been used to relieve pain and inflammation associated with conditions such as arthritis.
- Supporting cardiovascular health: Elderberry may help lower blood pressure and reduce the risk of heart disease.
- Relieving constipation: Elderberry has mild laxative properties and can help relieve constipation.
- 6mproving skin health: Elderberry has antioxidant properties and may help protect the skin against damage from UV rays and pollution.
- Fighting off bacterial and viral infections: Elderberry has antimicrobial properties and has been found to be effective against certain bacterial and viral infections.

It is important to note that while elderberry is generally safe for most people when consumed in moderate amounts, it is not a substitute for medical treatment and should not be used to self-treat serious health conditions without consulting a qualified healthcare practitioner.

• Precautions and contradictions: While elderberry has many health benefits, there are a few precautions and contraindications to keep in mind:
- Unripe or uncooked elderberries can be toxic, so it's important to only consume cooked or processed elderberries.
- Elderberry may interact with some medications, particularly immunosuppressants, and should not be taken in combination with these drugs.
- If you are pregnant or breastfeeding, it's best to avoid using elderberry as there is not enough research to determine its safety in these situations.
- If you have an autoimmune disease, such as lupus or rheumatoid arthritis, you should use elderberry with caution as it can stimulate the immune system.

As with any herbal remedy, it's important to consult with a healthcare provider before using elderberry, especially if you have any underlying health conditions or are taking medications.

Cultivation:
- Native to: Europe and North America
- Zones: Elderberry can grow in USDA zones 3-8.
- Soil: Elderberry prefers moist, well-drained soil with a pH between 5.5 and 6.5.
- Propagation: Elderberry can be propagated by seed or by stem cuttings.
- Growing information and garden care: Elderberry is a hardy plant that is relatively easy to grow. It prefers full sun to partial shade and needs regular watering.
- Insects and disease: Elderberry can be susceptible to fungal diseases such as powdery mildew and can attract pests such as aphids.
- Harvesting and preparations: The flowers and berries of the elderberry plant can be harvested in the summer and used fresh or dried for medicinal purposes.

What medicines are made with this herb:
Elderberry can be used to make a variety of medicinal preparations, including:

- Elderberry syrup: made by cooking elderberries with water and honey or another sweetener.
- Elderberry tincture: made by soaking dried elderberries in alcohol to extract their medicinal compounds.
- Elderberry tea: made by steeping dried elderberries in hot water.
- Elderberry capsules: made by encapsulating elderberry powder.

These preparations can be used to support the immune system, treat colds and flu, reduce inflammation, and alleviate respiratory symptoms. Additionally, elderberry extracts and syrups are often included in over-the-counter cold and flu remedies.

What medicines this herb counteract:
Elderberry can potentially interact with certain medications, including those that suppress the immune system and those used to treat diabetes. Some of the medications that elderberry may counteract or interact with include:

- Immunosuppressants: Elderberry may stimulate the immune system, which could potentially counteract the effects of drugs that suppress the immune system, such as those used to prevent transplant rejection or treat autoimmune disorders.
- Diabetes medications: Elderberry may lower blood sugar levels, so it could interact with medications used to treat diabetes and potentially cause hypoglycemia (low blood sugar).

If you are taking medications, it is important to consult with your healthcare provider before using elderberry or any other herbal remedies to avoid any potential interactions or negative effects.

Eyebright

Herbal Identification:
- Common Name: Eyebright
- Latin Binomial: Euphrasia officinalis
- Other Common Names: Euphrasia, Meadow eyebright, Red eyebright, Augentrost (German)
- Plant Family: Orobanchaceae
- Botanical Description: Eyebright is an annual herb that grows up to 30 cm in height. It has a square stem, small leaves, and produces small white or pink flowers with purple or yellow spots. The flowers bloom from July to September. The plant has a parasitic nature, which means it feeds on the roots of other plants. It grows in meadows, pastures, and grassy areas, and is native to Europe, western Asia, and northern Africa.

Medicinal Properties:
- Recommended Cultivars: There are no recommended cultivars of eyebright.
- Parts Used: The above-ground parts of the plant, including the flowers and leaves, are used for medicinal purposes.
- Taste: Bitter, astringent
- Actions: Anti-inflammatory, astringent, decongestant, expectorant
- Energetics: Cooling and drying
- Specific Indications: Eyebright is traditionally used for various eye-related conditions, including:
  - Conjunctivitis: Eyebright is believed to have astringent properties that can help reduce inflammation and irritation of the conjunctiva.
  - Blepharitis: Eyebright can be used to treat eyelid inflammation, also known as blepharitis.
  - Eye fatigue: Eyebright is said to help soothe and relieve eye fatigue, strain, and discomfort.
  - Hay fever: Eyebright is commonly used as a natural remedy for hay fever or allergic rhinitis, as it can help reduce inflammation and congestion of the mucous membranes.
  - Sinusitis: Eyebright can be used to relieve inflammation and congestion in the sinuses.
  - Headaches: Eyebright is believed to have pain-relieving properties, which makes it useful for treating headaches.

- Cataracts: Some people believe that eyebright can help prevent and treat cataracts, although there is limited scientific evidence to support this claim.

It is important to note that more research is needed to confirm the effectiveness of eyebright in treating these conditions. As with any herbal remedy, it is always best to consult with a healthcare professional before using eyebright for medicinal purposes.

Medicinal Preparations:
Eyebright can be prepared and used in several ways, including:
- Eyebright tea: Infuse 1 to 2 teaspoons of dried eyebright herb in 8 ounces of hot water for 5 to 10 minutes. Strain and drink up to three times a day.
- Eyebright eyewash: Mix 1 teaspoon of dried eyebright herb with 1 cup of boiling water. Let it steep for 5 minutes, then strain and let it cool. Use an eyedropper to put a few drops of the solution into each eye, up to twice a day.
- Eyebright compress: Steep 1 to 2 teaspoons of dried eyebright herb in 1 cup of boiling water for 10 minutes. Soak a clean cloth in the mixture and apply it as a warm compress to the affected area.
- Eyebright tincture: Take 2 to 4 ml of an eyebright tincture three times per day.

It is important to note that while eyebright is generally considered safe, it is always best to consult with a healthcare provider before using it, especially if you have an eye condition or are taking any medications.

- Ratio and Dosage Information: For an herbal infusion, use 1-2 teaspoons of dried herb per cup of hot water, and steep for 10-15 minutes. Drink up to three cups per day. For a tincture, take 2-4 ml three times per day.
- Medicinal Uses: Eyebright (Euphrasia officinalis) has been traditionally used as a medicinal herb for various eye problems. Some of the medicinal uses of eyebright include:
- Conjunctivitis: Eyebright is effective in treating conjunctivitis or pink eye, which is an inflammation of the conjunctiva (the thin, clear tissue that lines the inside of the eyelid and covers the white part of the eye). The herb is thought to help soothe and reduce inflammation in the eyes.
- Eye Strain: Eyebright has been used to relieve eye strain caused by prolonged computer use or reading. The herb is thought to help improve eye function and reduce eye fatigue.
- Allergies: Eyebright has been traditionally used as a natural remedy for seasonal allergies, hay fever, and other respiratory allergies. It is believed to help reduce inflammation and alleviate symptoms such as itchy eyes, runny nose, and sneezing.

- Sinusitis: Eyebright may also be used as a natural remedy for sinusitis or inflammation of the sinuses. It is believed to help reduce inflammation and relieve symptoms such as congestion, headache, and facial pain.
- Skin Conditions: Eyebright has been used topically as a remedy for various skin conditions such as acne, eczema, and psoriasis. It is believed to help reduce inflammation and soothe irritated skin.
- Digestive Issues: Eyebright has been used as a natural remedy for digestive issues such as indigestion, bloating, and flatulence. It is believed to help stimulate the production of digestive juices and enzymes, promoting better digestion.
- General Wellness: Eyebright has been traditionally used as a tonic to support overall wellness and boost the immune system. It is believed to have anti-inflammatory, antioxidant, and antimicrobial properties that can help protect the body against various diseases and infections.

It is important to note that while eyebright has a long history of use in traditional medicine, there is limited scientific evidence to support its effectiveness for these conditions. Always consult with a healthcare professional before using any herbal remedy, especially if you have an existing medical condition or are taking medication.

- Precautions and Contradictions: Eyebright is generally safe to use when taken in appropriate doses. However, some precautions and contradictions include:
- Avoid using eyebright if you are allergic to plants in the Scrophulariaceae family.
- There is limited information on the safety of using eyebright during pregnancy and breastfeeding, so it is best to avoid using it during these times.
- Eyebright can cause irritation and inflammation of the eyes if it comes into direct contact with them. Therefore, it is important to use only the recommended preparations and avoid getting the herb in your eyes.
- If you are taking medications that suppress the immune system, such as corticosteroids, or have an autoimmune disorder, it is important to consult with a healthcare professional before using eyebright as it may interact with these medications or exacerbate the condition.

As with any herb, it is important to consult with a healthcare professional before using eyebright if you have any underlying medical conditions or are taking any medications to avoid potential interactions.

Cultivation:
- Native to: Europe and western Asia
- Zones: 3-9
- Soil: Well-drained, loamy soil with a pH between 6.0 and 7.0
- Propagation: Eyebright can be propagated from seed or by dividing established plants in the spring or fall.
- Growing Information and Garden Care: Eyebright prefers cooler temperatures and partial shade. It should be watered regularly but not overwatered, as it is susceptible to root rot.
- Insects and Disease: Eyebright (Euphrasia officinalis) is relatively resistant to pests and diseases, making it a low-maintenance herb to grow. However, like all plants, it can still be affected by various issues. Some potential pests and diseases that can affect eyebright include:
  - Powdery mildew: This is a fungal disease that appears as a white, powdery coating on the leaves and stems of plants. It can be prevented by ensuring good air circulation around the plants and avoiding overhead watering.
  - Rust: Rust is another fungal disease that can cause yellowish or reddish spots on the leaves of plants. It can be prevented by removing any infected leaves and avoiding overcrowding of plants.
  - Aphids: Aphids are small, sap-sucking insects that can cause yellowing and distortion of leaves. They can be controlled through the use of insecticidal soap or by releasing natural predators like ladybugs or lacewings.
  - Spider mites: Spider mites are tiny, spider-like pests that can cause yellowing and stippling of leaves. They can be controlled through the use of insecticidal soap or by introducing natural predators like predatory mites.

Overall, keeping the growing area clean and avoiding overwatering can help prevent issues with pests and diseases in eyebright.
- Harvesting and Preparations: Eyebright can be harvested in the wild or cultivated in a garden. The aerial parts of the plant are the most commonly used in medicinal preparations, and they should be harvested when the plant is in bloom in the summer. The plant can be dried for later use or used fresh.

Eyebright can be prepared in a variety of ways, including:
- Eyewash: A strong infusion of eyebright can be used as an eyewash to soothe irritated eyes. The infusion can be made by steeping 1-2 teaspoons of dried herb in 1 cup of boiling water for 10-15 minutes. The mixture can be strained and used as an eyewash.
- Tea: Eyebright tea can be made by steeping 1-2 teaspoons of dried herb in 1 cup of boiling water for 10-15 minutes. The mixture can be strained and sweetened if desired.

- Tincture: A tincture of eyebright can be made by macerating the dried herb in alcohol for several weeks. The tincture can then be strained and used as needed.
- Capsules: Eyebright capsules are available commercially and can be taken according to the manufacturer's instructions.

It is important to note that eyebright is generally considered safe when used appropriately, but it should not be used as a substitute for professional medical advice. Consult a healthcare provider before using any herbal remedy, especially if you are pregnant, nursing, or taking medication.

What medicines are made with this herb:
Eyebright is used in a variety of commercial preparations including teas, tinctures, and homeopathic remedies. It is also used as an ingredient in eye drops and eyewashes. Some examples of commercially available products that contain eyebright include Similasan Allergy Eye Relief Drops, LifeSeasons Breathe-X, and Herb Pharm Eye Health Tonic.

What medicines this herb counteract:
There is not enough scientific evidence to determine what medicines Eyebright may counteract. However, it is known to have the potential to interact with certain medications and may increase the risk of bleeding if taken with blood-thinning drugs. It is always recommended to consult a healthcare provider before using any herbal remedies in combination with prescription medications.

Fennel

Herbal Identification:
- Common name: Fennel
- Latin binomial: Foeniculum vulgare
- Other common names: Sweet fennel, Bronze fennel, Florence fennel
- Plant family: Apiaceae (Umbelliferae)
- Botanical description: Fennel, also known as Foeniculum vulgare, is a flowering plant species in the carrot family Apiaceae. It is a perennial herb with a sweet, anise-like flavor and aroma, which is commonly used in cooking and herbal medicine.

The plant typically grows to a height of 1.5 to 2.5 meters (5 to 8 feet) and has finely dissected, feathery leaves that are bluish-green in color. Fennel also has a thick, bulbous base that can be eaten raw or cooked and has a crunchy texture similar to celery.

The plant produces small, yellow flowers in clusters known as umbels, which are about 10 to 15 centimeters (4 to 6 inches) in diameter. The flowers are followed by oblong, ridged seeds that are about 4 to 10 millimeters (0.2 to 0.4 inches) long and have a greenish-brown color.

Fennel is a hardy plant that prefers well-drained soil and full sun. It is native to the Mediterranean region but is now grown in many parts of the world, including Europe, Asia, and North America. It is commonly used in cooking as a flavoring for fish, vegetables, and soups, and is also used in herbal medicine to treat various ailments such as digestive issues and respiratory problems.

Medicinal Properties:
- Recommended cultivars: There are several cultivars of fennel, including Florence fennel, which is grown for its bulb, and bronze fennel, which is grown as an ornamental plant.
- Parts used: The seeds, leaves, and bulb of fennel are used for medicinal purposes.
- Taste: Sweet, aromatic, and slightly bitter.
- Actions: Carminative, antispasmodic, expectorant, galactagogue, diuretic, anti-inflammatory, antimicrobial.
- Energetics: Warm and dry.

- Specific indications: Fennel has been used for various medicinal purposes for centuries. Here are some specific indications for the use of fennel:
  - Digestive issues: Fennel is commonly used as a digestive aid to relieve symptoms such as bloating, gas, and indigestion. It has a carminative effect, which means it helps to ease the passage of gas through the digestive system, reducing discomfort.
  - Breastfeeding: Fennel has been traditionally used to increase milk production in breastfeeding mothers. Its galactagogue properties are attributed to the presence of anethole, a compound that stimulates the production of prolactin, a hormone responsible for milk production.
  - Menstrual cramps: Fennel has been used to relieve menstrual cramps due to its antispasmodic properties. It can help to relax the muscles in the uterus and reduce pain.
  - Respiratory problems: Fennel has expectorant properties and can be used to relieve respiratory issues such as coughs and bronchitis.
  - Eye health: Fennel contains high levels of vitamin A and antioxidants, which can help to improve eye health and prevent age-related eye diseases.

It is important to note that while fennel is generally considered safe, it may interact with certain medications and should be used with caution in some individuals. As with any herbal remedy, it is recommended to speak with a healthcare provider before using fennel for medicinal purposes.

- Medicinal preparations: Fennel can be used in various forms for medicinal purposes. Here are some common medicinal preparations of fennel:
  - Fennel tea: Fennel tea is a popular way to enjoy the benefits of fennel. To make fennel tea, steep 1 to 2 teaspoons of crushed fennel seeds in hot water for 5 to 10 minutes. Fennel tea can be enjoyed plain or sweetened with honey.
  - Fennel oil: Fennel oil is made by steam distilling the crushed seeds of the fennel plant. It can be used topically or ingested, depending on the intended use. Fennel oil is commonly used in aromatherapy for its calming and relaxing effects.
  - Fennel capsules: Fennel capsules are available in health food stores and can be used to relieve digestive issues, menstrual cramps, and other conditions. It is important to follow the recommended dosage on the packaging or as directed by a healthcare provider.
  - Fennel tincture: Fennel tincture is made by steeping fennel seeds in alcohol. It can be used topically or ingested for medicinal purposes. Fennel tincture is commonly used to relieve digestive issues and respiratory problems.
  - Fennel poultice: A fennel poultice can be made by crushing fresh fennel leaves or seeds and applying them directly to the affected area. Fennel

poultices can be used topically to relieve skin irritations or to ease breast engorgement in breastfeeding mothers.

It is important to note that while fennel is generally considered safe, it may interact with certain medications and should be used with caution in some individuals. As with any herbal remedy, it is recommended to speak with a healthcare provider before using fennel for medicinal purposes.

- Ratio and dosage information: For tea, steep 1-2 teaspoons of crushed fennel seeds in 1 cup of hot water for 10-15 minutes, and drink up to 3 times per day. For tincture, take 2-4 mL up to 3 times per day.

Medicinal uses:
Fennel has a variety of medicinal uses. Here are some of the most common:
- Digestive issues: Fennel has carminative properties, which means it can help to ease gas, bloating, and indigestion. It can also help to stimulate digestion and relieve constipation.
- Breastfeeding: Fennel has galactagogue properties, which means it can help to increase milk production in breastfeeding mothers.
- Menstrual cramps: Fennel has antispasmodic properties, which means it can help to relax the muscles in the uterus and reduce menstrual cramps.
- Respiratory problems: Fennel has expectorant properties, which means it can help to break up mucus and relieve coughs and bronchitis.
- Eye health: Fennel is a good source of vitamin A and antioxidants, which can help to improve eye health and prevent age-related eye diseases.
- Inflammation: Fennel contains anti-inflammatory compounds that may help to reduce inflammation and relieve pain associated with conditions such as arthritis.
- High blood pressure: Fennel has been shown to have a mild hypotensive effect, which means it may help to lower blood pressure.
- Anxiety and stress: Fennel has calming properties and may help to reduce anxiety and stress.

It is important to note that while fennel is generally considered safe, it may interact with certain medications and should be used with caution in some individuals. As with any herbal remedy, it is recommended to speak with a healthcare provider before using fennel for medicinal purposes.

- Precautions and contradictions: While fennel is generally considered safe, there are some precautions and contraindications to be aware of. Here are some of the most important:

- Allergic reactions: Some individuals may be allergic to fennel. If you experience symptoms such as itching, swelling, or difficulty breathing after consuming fennel, seek medical attention immediately.
- Pregnancy: Fennel is considered safe in small amounts during pregnancy, but larger amounts should be avoided as they may stimulate uterine contractions.
- Breastfeeding: While fennel is often used to increase milk production in breastfeeding mothers, excessive amounts may have the opposite effect.
- Medication interactions: Fennel may interact with certain medications, including blood thinners, hormone therapy, and some psychiatric medications. Speak with a healthcare provider before using fennel if you are taking any medications.
- Surgery: Fennel may have a mild blood-thinning effect and should be avoided for 2 weeks before and after surgery to reduce the risk of excessive bleeding.
- Children: Fennel should be used with caution in children, as there is limited research on its safety and efficacy in this population.
- Hormonal conditions: Fennel contains phytoestrogens, which may affect hormone levels in some individuals. It should be used with caution in individuals with hormonal conditions such as breast cancer, endometriosis, and uterine fibroids.

It is important to note that these precautions and contraindications are not exhaustive, and it is recommended to speak with a healthcare provider before using fennel for medicinal purposes.

Cultivation:
- Native to: Mediterranean region
- Zones: 5-10
- Soil: Fennel prefers well-draining soil with a pH of 6.0-8.0. It can tolerate poor soil conditions.
- Propagation: Fennel can be grown from seed or propagated by division.
- Growing information and garden care: Fennel prefers full sun and regular watering. It can be grown in containers or in the ground, and may require staking as it grows tall. Fennel attracts beneficial insects such as ladybugs and lacewings, but can also be a host plant for swallowtail butterfly larvae.
- Insects and disease: Fennel is generally resistant to pests and diseases. However, there are a few insects and diseases that may affect fennel plants, including:

- Aphids: Aphids are small insects that feed on the sap of fennel plants, causing stunted growth and deformation of the leaves. They can be controlled using insecticidal soap or by introducing natural predators such as ladybugs and lacewings.
- Fennel caterpillar: The fennel caterpillar is a common pest that feeds on the leaves of fennel plants, causing damage to the foliage. They can be controlled using insecticidal sprays or by handpicking them off the plants.
- Powdery mildew: Powdery mildew is a fungal disease that causes a white, powdery coating to form on the leaves of fennel plants. It can be controlled by removing infected leaves and using fungicidal sprays.
- Root rot: Root rot is a fungal disease that can affect fennel plants grown in poorly-drained soils. It causes the roots to rot and the plant to wilt and die. To prevent root rot, ensure that the soil is well-drained and avoid overwatering.

Overall, fennel is a hardy and low-maintenance plant that is relatively resistant to pests and diseases. Proper care and maintenance can help to keep fennel plants healthy and productive.

• Harvesting and preparations: Fennel can be harvested and prepared in a variety of ways. Here are some guidelines:
- Harvesting: Fennel bulbs can be harvested when they are about 2-3 inches in diameter. Cut the bulb off at the base of the plant, leaving a small amount of stem attached. The leaves and seeds can be harvested throughout the growing season.
- Storing: Fennel bulbs can be stored in a cool, dry place for up to a week. The leaves and seeds can be dried and stored in airtight containers for later use.
- Culinary uses: Fennel bulbs can be sliced and used in salads, roasted or grilled as a side dish, or used to make soups and stews. The leaves can be chopped and used as a garnish or in salads, and the seeds can be used to flavor dishes such as bread, fish, and sausages.
- Medicinal preparations: Fennel seeds can be brewed into a tea or infused into oil or alcohol to make tinctures. The essential oil of fennel can be used in aromatherapy or added to massage oils.
- Other uses: Fennel leaves and seeds can be used in natural insect repellents and as a natural dye for fabrics.

It is important to note that while fennel is generally safe to consume, some individuals may be allergic to it or experience side effects such as stomach upset or skin irritation. As with any herbal remedy, it is recommended to speak with a healthcare provider before using fennel for medicinal purposes.

What medicines are made with this herb:
Fennel is used in a variety of herbal medicines and remedies. Here are some examples:
- Digestive aid: Fennel seeds are commonly used as a natural remedy for digestive issues such as bloating, gas, and constipation. They can be brewed into a tea or taken in capsule form.
- Menstrual cramps: Fennel has been shown to have mild analgesic and anti-inflammatory properties, making it a popular natural remedy for menstrual cramps. It can be consumed as a tea or taken in capsule form.
- Breast milk production: Fennel is often used to stimulate milk production in breastfeeding mothers. It can be consumed as a tea or taken in capsule form.
- Respiratory issues: Fennel has been used for centuries to help alleviate coughs and congestion. It can be consumed as a tea or used in a steam inhalation.
- Skin care: Fennel essential oil is often used in skin care products due to its anti-inflammatory and anti-microbial properties. It can be added to massage oils, creams, and lotions.

It is important to note that while fennel has a long history of use in traditional medicine, more research is needed to fully understand its medicinal properties and potential side effects. As with any herbal remedy, it is recommended to speak with a healthcare provider before using fennel for medicinal purposes.

What medicines this herb counteract:
Fennel is generally considered safe when consumed in moderate amounts and is not known to have any major interactions with medications. However, there are some medications and conditions that may interact with fennel, including:
- Blood thinners: Fennel may have mild blood-thinning properties, so it is important to use caution if you are taking blood-thinning medications such as warfarin or aspirin.
- Estrogen-based medications: Fennel may have estrogenic effects and may interact with estrogen-based medications such as birth control pills or hormone replacement therapy.
- Seizure medications: Fennel may interact with seizure medications such as carbamazepine and phenytoin, so it is important to speak with a healthcare provider before using fennel if you are taking these medications.
- Allergies: Some individuals may be allergic to fennel, so it is important to use caution if you have a known allergy to this herb.
- Medical conditions: Fennel may exacerbate certain medical conditions such as gastroesophageal reflux disease (GERD) or inflammatory bowel disease

(IBD). If you have one of these conditions, it is important to speak with a healthcare provider before using fennel.

As with any herbal remedy, it is recommended to speak with a healthcare provider before using fennel if you are taking any medications or have any medical conditions.

Feverfew

Herbal Identification:
- Common name: Feverfew
- Latin binomial: Tanacetum parthenium (formerly known as Chrysanthemum parthenium)
- Other common names: Featherfew, Bachelor's button, Featherfoil, Flirtwort, Midsummer daisy
- Plant family: Asteraceae (Daisy family)
- Botanical description: Feverfew is a perennial herb that typically grows up to 60 cm in height, with erect, branching stems. The leaves are bright green and are pinnately compound, meaning that they are divided into many small leaflets. The leaflets are deeply lobed and toothed, giving them a feather-like appearance. The upper surface of the leaves is slightly hairy, while the lower surface is more densely hairy. The leaves are typically 5-10 cm long and 3-5 cm wide.

The flowers of feverfew are small and daisy-like, with white petals and a yellow center. They are borne on slender stems that arise from the axils of the leaves. The flowers bloom from June to October in the Northern Hemisphere, and they are attractive to bees and other pollinators. The fruits of the plant are achenes, which are small, dry, and one-seeded. The achenes are dispersed by wind or by sticking to the fur or feathers of animals.

Feverfew is similar in appearance to other members of the Asteraceae family, such as chamomile, yarrow, and tansy. However, feverfew can be distinguished by its deeply lobed leaves and its daisy-like flowers with yellow centers.

Medicinal Properties:
- Recommended cultivars: There are no specific recommended cultivars of feverfew.
- Parts used: Leaves and flowers
- Taste: Bitter
- Actions: Anti-inflammatory, analgesic, antispasmodic, emmenagogue, febrifuge, nervine, vasodilator
- Energetics: Cooling and drying
- Specific indications: Feverfew has traditionally been used for a variety of health conditions, although most commonly for its ability to reduce fever and relieve headaches. Some specific indications for feverfew may include:

- Migraines: Feverfew is perhaps most well-known for its ability to reduce the frequency and severity of migraines. Studies have shown that feverfew may help to prevent the constriction of blood vessels in the brain that can lead to migraines, and may also have anti-inflammatory and analgesic effects.
- Arthritis: Feverfew may have anti-inflammatory effects that can help to reduce pain and inflammation associated with arthritis.
- Menstrual cramps: Feverfew has been used traditionally to relieve menstrual cramps and other menstrual symptoms, although scientific evidence supporting this use is limited.
- Digestive issues: Feverfew may help to stimulate digestion and reduce inflammation in the digestive tract, making it potentially helpful for conditions such as indigestion and irritable bowel syndrome (IBS).
- •kin conditions: Feverfew may have anti-inflammatory effects that can help to reduce redness and irritation associated with conditions such as eczema and psoriasis. It may also help to soothe insect bites and other minor skin irritations.

It's important to note that while feverfew has been used for these and other health conditions, more research is needed to fully understand its effects and to determine appropriate dosages and formulations. It's always a good idea to speak with a healthcare provider before using any herbal remedies, especially if you have any underlying health conditions or are taking any medications.

Medicinal preparations:
Feverfew can be prepared and used in a variety of ways for medicinal purposes, including:
- Fresh leaves: Fresh feverfew leaves can be chewed or eaten to help relieve headaches or other symptoms. However, the leaves have a strong and bitter taste that some people may find unpleasant.
- Tea: Feverfew tea can be made by steeping fresh or dried leaves in hot water for several minutes. The tea can be sweetened with honey or another natural sweetener to improve its taste. Feverfew tea is often used to relieve headaches, menstrual cramps, and digestive issues.
- Tincture: A feverfew tincture can be made by soaking the plant in alcohol or vinegar for several weeks, then straining out the liquid. The tincture can be taken orally and is often used to relieve headaches and other symptoms.
- Capsules: Feverfew capsules are available in many health food stores and online. They contain dried feverfew leaves or extracts and are often used to help prevent migraines.
- Salve: A feverfew salve can be made by infusing the plant in oil, then combining the oil with beeswax and other ingredients to create a topical

ointment. The salve can be applied to the skin to help relieve minor skin irritations and inflammation.

Dosages and preparations may vary depending on the specific health condition being treated, as well as other individual factors such as age, weight, and overall health. It's important to follow dosing instructions carefully and to speak with a healthcare provider before using any herbal remedies.
- Ratio and dosage information: Infusion - 1 tsp of dried herb per cup of water, 1-3 cups per day; Tincture - 2-4 ml, 3 times per day; Capsule or tablet - follow manufacturer's instructions.

Medicinal uses:
Feverfew has been used for a variety of medicinal purposes, including:
- Headaches and migraines: Feverfew has long been used to help relieve headaches, including migraines. Studies have shown that feverfew may help to reduce the frequency and severity of migraines by preventing the constriction of blood vessels in the brain.
- Arthritis: Feverfew may have anti-inflammatory effects that can help to reduce pain and inflammation associated with arthritis.
- Menstrual cramps: Feverfew has been used traditionally to relieve menstrual cramps and other menstrual symptoms, although scientific evidence supporting this use is limited.
- Digestive issues: Feverfew may help to stimulate digestion and reduce inflammation in the digestive tract, making it potentially helpful for conditions such as indigestion and irritable bowel syndrome (IBS).
- Skin conditions: Feverfew may have anti-inflammatory effects that can help to reduce redness and irritation associated with conditions such as eczema and psoriasis. It may also help to soothe insect bites and other minor skin irritations.
- Fever: As its name suggests, feverfew has traditionally been used to help reduce fevers.
- Respiratory issues: Feverfew may help to relieve respiratory symptoms such as coughing and wheezing.

It's important to note that while feverfew has been used for these and other health conditions, more research is needed to fully understand its effects and to determine appropriate dosages and formulations. It's always a good idea to speak with a healthcare provider before using any herbal remedies, especially if you have any underlying health conditions or are taking any medications.

• Precautions and contradictions: Feverfew is generally considered safe for most people when used as directed, but there are some precautions and potential contradictions to keep in mind:
- Allergic reactions: Some people may be allergic to feverfew, especially those who are allergic to plants in the daisy family, such as chamomile, ragweed, or marigold. Symptoms of an allergic reaction may include rash, itching, swelling, and difficulty breathing.
- Pregnancy and breastfeeding: Feverfew may not be safe for use during pregnancy or breastfeeding, as it may cause contractions of the uterus and potentially harm the developing fetus or nursing baby.
- Blood-thinning effects: Feverfew may have blood-thinning effects, which can increase the risk of bleeding or interfere with blood-thinning medications such as warfarin or aspirin. It's important to speak with a healthcare provider before using feverfew if you are taking any blood-thinning medications or have a bleeding disorder.
- Surgery: Feverfew should be discontinued at least two weeks before any scheduled surgery or dental work, as it may increase the risk of bleeding.
- Other medications: Feverfew may interact with other medications, including nonsteroidal anti-inflammatory drugs (NSAIDs), antidepressants, and drugs that suppress the immune system. It's important to speak with a healthcare provider before using feverfew if you are taking any medications.

• Dosage: High doses of feverfew can cause mouth ulcers, skin irritation, and other side effects. It's important to follow dosing instructions carefully and not to exceed recommended doses.

As with any herbal remedy, it's important to speak with a healthcare provider before using feverfew, especially if you have any underlying health conditions or are taking any medications.

Cultivation:
• Native to: Balkan Peninsula
• Zones: 5-9
• Soil (pH and type of soil): Well-drained soil with a pH of 6.0-7.0
• Propagation: Seeds or division of established plants
• Growing information and garden care: Feverfew prefers full sun to partial shade and regular watering. It can be propagated by seed or division of established plants, and it self-seeds readily. The plant may become leggy and should be cut back to encourage bushier growth.

- Insects and disease: Feverfew is generally a hardy plant that is not particularly susceptible to pests or diseases. However, there are a few issues to watch out for:
  - Aphids: Aphids may occasionally infest feverfew plants, especially in humid conditions. They can be controlled with insecticidal soap or a strong stream of water.
  - Powdery mildew: Powdery mildew can be a problem in hot, humid conditions. It appears as a white, powdery coating on the leaves and can cause them to turn yellow and drop off. Good air circulation and proper spacing can help prevent powdery mildew, and affected plants can be treated with a fungicide.
  - Rust: Rust is a fungal disease that appears as orange or brown spots on the leaves. It can be treated with a fungicide, and affected leaves should be removed and destroyed.
  - Slugs and snails: Slugs and snails may occasionally feed on feverfew leaves. They can be controlled with slug bait or by placing copper tape around the base of the plants.

Overall, feverfew is a relatively low-maintenance plant that is easy to grow in most gardens. Regular monitoring and prompt treatment of any pest or disease issues can help keep your feverfew plants healthy and productive.

- Harvesting and preparations: The leaves of feverfew can be harvested throughout the growing season, starting in early summer and continuing until the first frost. Here are some tips for harvesting and preparing feverfew leaves:
  - Harvesting: To harvest feverfew leaves, simply snip off individual leaves or cut back entire stems to just above a set of leaves. Be sure to leave some leaves on the plant so that it can continue to grow and produce more leaves. The best time to harvest feverfew leaves is in the morning, after the dew has dried but before the sun is too hot.
  - Drying: To dry feverfew leaves, tie them into small bundles and hang them upside down in a warm, dry, well-ventilated place out of direct sunlight. Once the leaves are completely dry, strip them from the stems and store them in an airtight container in a cool, dark place.
  - Fresh use: Feverfew leaves can be used fresh in teas, tinctures, or other preparations. Simply chop the leaves finely and add them to boiling water, or use them as directed in your chosen recipe.
  - Infused oil: Feverfew leaves can be used to make an infused oil that is useful for treating headaches, muscle pain, and other conditions. To make an infused oil, fill a jar with fresh feverfew leaves and cover them with olive oil or another carrier oil. Place the jar in a sunny windowsill for two weeks,

shaking it daily. Strain the oil through a cheesecloth and store it in a dark bottle in a cool, dark place.
- Tincture: Feverfew leaves can be used to make a tincture that is useful for treating migraines and other conditions. To make a tincture, fill a jar with fresh feverfew leaves and cover them with vodka or another high-proof alcohol. Let the mixture steep for at least two weeks, shaking it daily. Strain the liquid through a cheesecloth and store it in a dark bottle in a cool, dark place. Dosage information for feverfew tincture will vary depending on the strength of the tincture and the condition being treated, so it's important to follow the manufacturer's instructions or speak with a healthcare provider before using.

What medicines are made with this herb:

Feverfew has been traditionally used for a variety of medicinal purposes, including treating migraines, headaches, fever, and arthritis. Today, it is primarily used for preventing migraines and other types of headaches.

Some common medicines made with feverfew include:
- Capsules: Feverfew capsules containing dried feverfew leaves are available as a dietary supplement. They are often marketed as a natural remedy for migraines and other types of headaches.
- Tinctures: Feverfew tinctures are made by steeping fresh or dried feverfew leaves in alcohol. They are often used to prevent migraines and other types of headaches.
- Teas: Feverfew tea can be made by steeping fresh or dried feverfew leaves in boiling water. It is sometimes used as a natural remedy for headaches and other conditions.
- Topical creams and ointments: Feverfew extract is sometimes used in topical creams and ointments to relieve pain and inflammation associated with conditions like arthritis.

It's important to note that while feverfew is generally considered safe, it can interact with certain medications and may cause side effects in some people. As with any herbal remedy, it's important to speak with a healthcare provider before using feverfew or any feverfew-containing products.

What medicines this herb counteract:

Feverfew may interact with certain medications, and it is important to speak with a healthcare provider before using feverfew if you are taking any prescription or over-the-counter medications. Some medications that feverfew may interact with include:

- Blood thinners: Feverfew may increase the risk of bleeding when taken with blood-thinning medications like warfarin or aspirin.
- Nonsteroidal anti-inflammatory drugs (NSAIDs): Feverfew may increase the risk of bleeding when taken with NSAIDs like ibuprofen or naproxen.
- Antidepressants: Feverfew may interact with certain antidepressant medications, including selective serotonin reuptake inhibitors (SSRIs), causing a risk of serotonin syndrome.
- Antiplatelet drugs: Feverfew may increase the risk of bleeding when taken with antiplatelet drugs like clopidogrel.
- Sedatives: Feverfew may interact with sedative medications, causing excessive drowsiness or other side effects.

It's also worth noting that feverfew may cause side effects in some people, including gastrointestinal upset, mouth ulcers, and allergic reactions. If you experience any side effects while using feverfew or any feverfew-containing products, stop use and speak with a healthcare provider.

Galangal

Herbal Identification:
- Common name: Galangal
- Latin binomial: Alpinia officinarum
- Other common names: Greater Galangal, Thai Ginger, Siamese Ginger
- Plant family: Zingiberaceae
- Botanical description: Galangal (Alpinia galanga) is a perennial herb belonging to the ginger family (Zingiberaceae). It has long, slender, and cone-shaped rhizomes that can grow up to 10-20 cm in length and 2-4 cm in diameter. The plant can reach a height of up to 2 meters and has large leaves that are lance-shaped and up to 30 cm in length. The flowers are small, white or pinkish, and have red-tipped petals. The fruit of the plant is a capsule that contains several seeds.

There are two main types of galangal: greater galangal (Alpinia galanga) and lesser galangal (Alpinia officinarum). Greater galangal has a more pungent flavor and is often used in cooking, while lesser galangal has a milder taste and is more commonly used in traditional medicine.

Medicinal Properties:
- Parts used: The root of the galangal plant is the part that is used for medicinal purposes.
- Taste: Galangal has a pungent and spicy flavor.
- Actions: Galangal has several medicinal properties, including anti-inflammatory, antimicrobial, digestive, and analgesic properties.
- Energetics: Galangal is warming and drying.
- Specific indications: Galangal has a wide range of medicinal properties and has been traditionally used to treat a variety of health conditions. Some specific indications for galangal include:
  - Digestive issues: Galangal is known to stimulate digestion, relieve bloating and flatulence, and improve appetite.
  - Respiratory infections: Galangal has antiviral and antibacterial properties that make it useful for treating respiratory infections such as colds, flu, and bronchitis.
  - Arthritis and joint pain: Galangal has anti-inflammatory properties that can help reduce pain and swelling associated with arthritis and other joint conditions.

- Nausea and motion sickness: Galangal has been used as a natural remedy for nausea and vomiting, and it is believed to be particularly effective for motion sickness.
- Menstrual cramps: Galangal has analgesic properties that can help relieve menstrual cramps and other types of pain.

It is important to note that while galangal has a long history of use in traditional medicine, more research is needed to fully understand its potential health benefits and to determine appropriate dosages and treatment protocols.

Medicinal preparations:
Galangal can be used in a variety of medicinal preparations, including:
- Tea: Galangal root can be steeped in hot water to make a tea that is used to treat digestive issues, respiratory infections, and other health conditions. To make galangal tea, finely chop or grate a small amount of fresh galangal root and steep it in hot water for several minutes before straining.
- Tincture: Galangal root can be used to make a tincture that is used to treat digestive issues, respiratory infections, and other health conditions. To make a galangal tincture, finely chop or grate fresh galangal root and soak it in alcohol for several weeks before straining.
- Essential oil: Galangal essential oil is made by steam distilling the roots of the plant. It can be used in aromatherapy to help relieve respiratory infections, muscle pain, and other health conditions.
- Powder: Galangal root can be dried and ground into a powder that is used to make capsules or added to food and drinks. The powder is often used to treat digestive issues, respiratory infections, and other health conditions.

It is important to note that the appropriate dosage and preparation of galangal will depend on the specific health condition being treated and individual factors such as age, weight, and overall health. It is always recommended to consult with a qualified healthcare practitioner before using galangal or any other herbal remedy.

• Ratio and dosage information: Dosage and ratio of galangal depends on the specific use and the form of the herb being used. Consult with a healthcare provider for appropriate dosage and use.

Medicinal uses:
Galangal has a variety of medicinal uses, including:
- Digestive health: Galangal is commonly used to treat digestive issues such as nausea, indigestion, bloating, and flatulence. It can help to stimulate digestion and improve the absorption of nutrients in the gut.
- Respiratory health: Galangal has traditionally been used to treat respiratory infections such as colds, flu, bronchitis, and asthma. It has anti-inflammatory and antimicrobial properties that help to reduce inflammation and fight off harmful bacteria and viruses.
- Pain relief: Galangal has analgesic properties that can help to reduce pain and inflammation in the body. It is often used topically to relieve muscle and joint pain.
- Immune system support: Galangal contains compounds that can help to boost the immune system and protect against illness and disease.
- Cancer prevention: Some research suggests that galangal may have anti-cancer properties and could be beneficial in the prevention and treatment of certain types of cancer.

It is important to note that more research is needed to fully understand the potential health benefits of galangal and its effectiveness as a natural remedy. It is always recommended to consult with a qualified healthcare practitioner before using galangal or any other herbal remedy.

• Precautions and contradictions: Galangal is generally considered safe for most people when consumed in moderate amounts as a food or in medicinal preparations. However, there are some precautions and contraindications to be aware of:
- Allergies: Some people may be allergic to galangal. If you experience symptoms such as hives, swelling, difficulty breathing, or other signs of an allergic reaction after consuming galangal, discontinue use and seek medical attention immediately.
- Pregnancy and breastfeeding: Galangal is not recommended for pregnant or breastfeeding women, as there is not enough research to determine its safety in these populations.
- Bleeding disorders: Galangal may increase the risk of bleeding, especially when consumed in large amounts. If you have a bleeding disorder or are taking medications that increase the risk of bleeding, such as blood thinners, speak with your healthcare provider before using galangal.
- Surgery: Galangal may also increase the risk of bleeding during and after surgery. It is recommended to stop using galangal at least 2 weeks before any scheduled surgery.

- Interactions with medications: Galangal may interact with certain medications, including blood thinners, diabetes medications, and drugs that are broken down by the liver. Speak with your healthcare provider before using galangal if you are taking any medications.

As with any herbal remedy, it is important to consult with a qualified healthcare practitioner before using galangal or any other herbal remedy, especially if you have any underlying medical conditions or are taking medications.

Cultivation:
- Native to: Galangal is native to Southeast Asia, including Indonesia, Malaysia, and Thailand.
- Zones: Galangal is a tropical plant that grows best in USDA zones 9-11.
- Soil: Galangal prefers well-drained soils that are rich in organic matter. It grows best in slightly acidic soils with a pH of 5.5-6.5.
- Propagation: Galangal is propagated by dividing the rhizomes in the spring or fall.
- Growing information and garden care: Galangal requires warm, humid conditions to grow well. It prefers partial shade and regular watering.
- Insects and disease: Galangal is generally not affected by many insects or diseases. However, here are some potential issues to be aware of:
  - Scale insects: Scale insects can be a problem for galangal, especially if it is grown in humid conditions. These insects feed on the sap of the plant, causing yellowing leaves and stunted growth. They can be treated with neem oil or insecticidal soap.
  - Root rot: Galangal is susceptible to root rot if the soil is poorly drained or if it is overwatered. Symptoms include wilting leaves and yellowing foliage. To prevent root rot, ensure that the soil is well-draining and that the plant is not overwatered.
  - Leaf spot: Leaf spot is a fungal disease that can affect galangal. Symptoms include small, dark spots on the leaves that eventually turn yellow and drop off. To prevent leaf spot, avoid overhead watering and ensure that the plant has good air circulation.

It is important to monitor your galangal plant for any signs of insects or diseases and take appropriate action to prevent or treat any issues that arise.
- Harvesting and preparations: Galangal can be harvested throughout the year, but the roots are most flavorful in the fall and winter. To harvest, dig up the entire plant or just the roots as needed.

Once harvested, the roots can be used fresh, dried, or frozen for later use. To dry the roots, wash them thoroughly and slice them thinly. Spread the slices out on a baking sheet and dry them in a warm, well-ventilated place for several days, or until they are completely dry and brittle. Store the dried slices in an airtight container.

To use galangal in cooking or for medicinal purposes, the root can be peeled and grated, sliced, or chopped finely. It has a pungent, spicy flavor and aroma and is commonly used in Southeast Asian and Indian cuisine, as well as in traditional medicine.

Galangal can be used fresh or dried in soups, stews, curries, and other dishes. It is also used to make tea, tinctures, and extracts for medicinal purposes. It is important to follow appropriate dosage and preparation guidelines when using galangal for medicinal purposes.

Medicines made with this herb:
- Galangal is used in traditional medicine and herbal remedies, and is an ingredient in some commercial medicines as well. Some medicines that use galangal as an ingredient include:
- Digestive aids: Galangal is believed to aid in digestion and is used in various digestive remedies and aids, such as digestive bitters, tonics, and teas.
- Anti-inflammatory and pain-relieving products: Galangal has anti-inflammatory properties and is used in some products that are intended to reduce inflammation and pain. It is also used topically in balms and salves for its analgesic properties.
- Respiratory remedies: Galangal is believed to help with respiratory issues such as coughs and colds, and is an ingredient in some cough syrups and respiratory aids.
- Skincare products: Galangal has antimicrobial and antioxidant properties, and is used in some skincare products to improve skin health and prevent acne.

It is important to consult with a qualified healthcare professional before using any herbal remedies or medicines containing galangal.

Medicines this herb counteracts:
There are no known medicines that galangal counteracts or interacts with in a negative way. However, as with any herb or medication, it is important to speak with a healthcare professional before using galangal, especially if you are taking any prescription medications or have any underlying medical conditions. Galangal may interact with certain medications or may not be safe for use in certain individuals, such as pregnant or breastfeeding women.

Garlic

Herbal Identification:
- Common name: Garlic
- Latin binomial: Allium sativum
- Other common names: Stinking rose, ajo, lahsun, rustre, knoblauch
- Plant family: Amaryllidaceae
- Botanical description: Garlic (Allium sativum) is a perennial plant in the Amaryllidaceae family, which is closely related to onions, leeks, and chives. It is native to Central Asia and has been cultivated for thousands of years for its culinary and medicinal properties.

Garlic bulbs consist of several small cloves enclosed in a papery, white or purple-tinged sheath. The leaves are long and slender, up to 30 cm in length, and emerge from the base of the plant. They are flat and narrow, with a slightly waxy texture, and a distinct garlic odor. The flowers are borne on a tall stem, up to 1 m in height, and are arranged in a spherical head or umbel. Each flower is small and star-shaped, with six petals that range in color from white to pink or purple.

Garlic prefers a sunny location with well-drained soil and moderate moisture. It is typically propagated by planting individual cloves in the fall, which then develop into new bulbs over the course of several months. Garlic is often harvested in the summer when the leaves begin to yellow and dry out, and the bulbs are then dried and stored for later use.

Medicinal Properties:
- Recommended cultivars: There are many different cultivars of garlic, including hardneck and softneck varieties. Some popular cultivars include Italian Late, Spanish Roja, and Purple Stripe.
- Parts used: The cloves are the most commonly used part of the garlic plant.
- Taste: Garlic has a pungent, spicy, and slightly sweet taste.
- Actions: Anti-inflammatory, antimicrobial, antifungal, antiviral, hypotensive, hypoglycemic, immune stimulant, expectorant, diaphoretic.
- Energetics: Warming, drying.
- Specific indications: Garlic has a long history of use in traditional medicine, and there is some evidence to support its use for various health conditions. Some of the specific indications for garlic include:

- Cardiovascular health: Garlic has been shown to have a positive effect on blood pressure, cholesterol levels, and overall cardiovascular health. It may also help reduce the risk of heart disease and stroke.
- Immune system support: Garlic has antimicrobial properties and may help boost the immune system, making it useful for preventing and treating infections.
- Cancer prevention: Some studies suggest that garlic may have a protective effect against certain types of cancer, including stomach and colon cancer.
- Anti-inflammatory effects: Garlic contains compounds that have anti-inflammatory properties, which may help reduce inflammation in the body and improve overall health.
- Digestive health: Garlic has been traditionally used to help support digestive health and may help reduce symptoms of gastrointestinal issues such as bloating and gas.

It is important to note that while garlic may be beneficial for certain health conditions, it should not be used as a replacement for medical treatment. As with any supplement or herb, it is best to speak with a healthcare provider before using garlic for medicinal purposes.

Medicinal preparations:
Garlic can be used in various medicinal preparations, including:
- Raw garlic: Raw garlic can be crushed and added to foods or taken in small amounts on its own to help support overall health.
- Garlic supplements: Garlic supplements are available in various forms, including capsules, tablets, and extracts. These supplements may provide a more concentrated dose of garlic and can be useful for individuals who may not enjoy the taste of raw garlic.
- Garlic oil: Garlic oil can be applied topically to the skin to help treat fungal infections, warts, and other skin conditions.
- Garlic tea: Garlic tea can be made by steeping garlic cloves in hot water and can be used to help treat respiratory infections and boost the immune system.
- Garlic poultice: A garlic poultice can be made by crushing garlic cloves and mixing them with a carrier oil, such as olive oil or coconut oil. This mixture can be applied topically to help relieve pain and inflammation.

It is important to note that while garlic can be beneficial for certain health conditions, it may also interact with certain medications, such as blood thinners. As with any supplement or herb, it is best to speak with a healthcare provider before using garlic for medicinal purposes.

- Ratio and dosage information: For general immune support, it is recommended to consume 1-2 cloves of garlic per day. For therapeutic use, dosage may vary depending on the condition being treated.

Medicinal uses:
Garlic has been used for centuries for its medicinal properties. Some of the common medicinal uses of garlic include:
- Cardiovascular health: Garlic has been shown to have a positive effect on blood pressure, cholesterol levels, and overall cardiovascular health. It may also help reduce the risk of heart disease and stroke.
- Immune system support: Garlic has antimicrobial properties and may help boost the immune system, making it useful for preventing and treating infections.
- Cancer prevention: Some studies suggest that garlic may have a protective effect against certain types of cancer, including stomach and colon cancer.
- Anti-inflammatory effects: Garlic contains compounds that have anti-inflammatory properties, which may help reduce inflammation in the body and improve overall health.
- Digestive health: Garlic has been traditionally used to help support digestive health and may help reduce symptoms of gastrointestinal issues such as bloating and gas.
- Skin health: Garlic oil can be applied topically to the skin to help treat fungal infections, warts, and other skin conditions.
- Respiratory health: Garlic tea can be made by steeping garlic cloves in hot water and can be used to help treat respiratory infections and boost the immune system.
- Wound healing: Garlic has antibacterial properties and may help speed up the healing of wounds and reduce the risk of infection.

It is important to note that while garlic may be beneficial for certain health conditions, it should not be used as a replacement for medical treatment. As with any supplement or herb, it is best to speak with a healthcare provider before using garlic for medicinal purposes.

- Precautions and contradictions: While garlic is generally safe when used in food and as a dietary supplement, there are some precautions and contraindications to consider:
  - Bleeding disorders: Garlic may increase the risk of bleeding, particularly in individuals with bleeding disorders or those taking blood-thinning medications.

- Surgery: Garlic should be avoided in the weeks leading up to surgery, as it may increase the risk of bleeding.
- Gastrointestinal issues: Garlic may irritate the digestive tract and cause gastrointestinal symptoms in some individuals, particularly when consumed in large amounts.
- Allergies: Some individuals may be allergic to garlic and experience allergic reactions, such as skin rash, hives, or difficulty breathing.
- Interactions with medications: Garlic may interact with certain medications, such as blood thinners, and should be used with caution in individuals taking these medications.
- Pregnancy and breastfeeding: Garlic should be used with caution during pregnancy and breastfeeding, as its safety has not been established in these populations.
- Odor: Garlic has a strong odor that may be unpleasant for some individuals, and may also cause bad breath.

It is important to speak with a healthcare provider before using garlic as a dietary supplement, particularly if you have a medical condition, take medication, or are pregnant or breastfeeding.

Cultivation:
- Native to: Central Asia and northeastern Iran
- Zones: Garlic is a cold-hardy plant and can be grown in most zones, but does best in zones 3-8.
- Soil: Garlic prefers well-drained soil with a pH between 6.0 and 7.5. It does best in soil that is high in organic matter and has good fertility.
- Propagation: Garlic is propagated by planting individual cloves in the fall, typically between September and November.
- Growing information and garden care: Garlic prefers full sun and moderate watering. It should be planted in the fall and overwintered. In the spring, it will begin to grow and can be harvested in the summer once the leaves begin to yellow and die back.
- Insects and disease: Garlic has been traditionally used as a natural insect and disease repellent in gardens and farms. Some of the benefits of using garlic in this way include:
  - Insect repellent: Garlic contains compounds that are known to repel insects, such as mosquitoes, ticks, and aphids. It can be used to create a natural insecticide or as a companion plant in gardens to help deter pests.
  - Fungal and bacterial disease prevention: Garlic contains natural antimicrobial compounds that can help prevent fungal and bacterial diseases

in plants. It can be used as a preventative measure or as a treatment for existing plant diseases.
- Nematode control: Garlic has been shown to have a toxic effect on nematodes, which are parasitic worms that can damage plant roots. It can be used as a natural nematode control in gardens and farms.
- Soil health: Garlic is a natural soil conditioner and can help improve soil health and fertility when used as a cover crop or composted.

It is important to note that while garlic can be useful in natural pest and disease control, it may also have negative effects on beneficial insects such as bees and other pollinators. As with any gardening or farming practice, it is important to use garlic and other natural remedies responsibly and with consideration for the environment.

- Harvesting and preparations: Garlic can be harvested and prepared for use in a few different ways:
- Harvesting: Garlic is typically harvested in the summer when the leaves begin to yellow and die back. It is important to harvest garlic at the right time to ensure proper curing and storage. Garlic bulbs can be gently dug up from the soil and hung to dry in a warm, dry location for several weeks.
- Cleaning: Once garlic has been harvested and dried, it can be cleaned by removing the outer layers of skin and trimming the roots. The bulbs can then be stored in a cool, dry location.
- Cooking: Garlic can be used in a variety of dishes to add flavor and nutritional benefits. It can be minced, chopped, or sliced and added to soups, stews, sauces, and other dishes. Garlic can also be roasted or grilled for a milder flavor.
- Pickling: Garlic can be pickled in vinegar or other acidic liquids for a tangy, flavorful addition to salads, sandwiches, and other dishes.
- Supplements: Garlic supplements are available in various forms, including capsules, tablets, and extracts. These supplements may provide a more concentrated dose of garlic and can be useful for individuals who may not enjoy the taste of raw garlic.

It is important to note that while garlic is generally safe when used in food and as a dietary supplement, it may interact with certain medications, and should be used with caution in individuals with certain medical conditions. As with any dietary supplement, it is best to speak with a healthcare provider before using garlic for medicinal purposes.

What medicines are made with this herb:
Garlic is used in a variety of medicinal preparations, including:
- Garlic oil: Garlic oil is made by steeping garlic cloves in vegetable oil or another carrier oil. It can be used topically to treat skin conditions and fungal infections.
- Garlic tincture: Garlic tincture is made by steeping garlic in alcohol. It can be used orally to boost the immune system and treat respiratory infections.
- Garlic supplements: Garlic supplements are available in various forms, including capsules, tablets, and extracts. They are often used to support cardiovascular health, boost the immune system, and lower cholesterol levels.
- Garlic ointment: Garlic ointment is made by combining garlic oil or extract with a carrier oil or other ingredients. It can be used topically to treat skin infections and insect bites.
- Garlic powder: Garlic powder is made by grinding dried garlic cloves. It can be used in cooking and as a supplement to support cardiovascular health and boost the immune system.

It is important to note that while garlic is generally safe when used in food and as a dietary supplement, it may interact with certain medications, and should be used with caution in individuals with certain medical conditions. As with any dietary supplement, it is best to speak with a healthcare provider before using garlic for medicinal purposes.

What medicines this herb counteracts:
Garlic may interact with certain medications, including:
- Blood thinners: Garlic may increase the risk of bleeding when taken with blood-thinning medications such as warfarin and aspirin.
- Hypertension medications: Garlic may lower blood pressure and can interact with medications used to treat hypertension.
- Immunosuppressants: Garlic may stimulate the immune system and can interact with medications used to suppress the immune system.
- Diabetes medications: Garlic may lower blood sugar levels and can interact with medications used to treat diabetes.
- Birth control pills: Garlic may reduce the effectiveness of birth control pills.

It is important to speak with a healthcare provider before using garlic or any other dietary supplement, especially if you are taking prescription medications or have any medical conditions.

Ginger

Herbal Identification:
- Common name: Ginger
- Latin binomial: Zingiber officinale
- Other common names: African Ginger, Jamaican Ginger, Shunthi
- Plant family: Zingiberaceae
- Botanical description: Ginger is a perennial herbaceous plant that belongs to the Zingiberaceae family, which also includes turmeric and cardamom. It can grow up to 1 meter in height and has lance-shaped leaves that can grow up to 20 cm long. The most commonly used part of the ginger plant is its rhizome, which is a thick, knobby, underground stem that can vary in size and shape depending on the cultivar. The rhizome is covered with a brownish skin and has a pale yellow interior that is highly aromatic and pungent. Ginger produces small, yellow-green flowers that grow on short stems and can be found at the base of the plant. Ginger is native to Southeast Asia and is now cultivated in many tropical and subtropical regions around the world.

Medicinal Properties:
- Recommended cultivars: There are many different cultivars of ginger, with varying levels of pungency and aroma. Some common cultivars include Jamaican ginger, Chinese ginger, and Indian ginger.
- Parts used: The rhizome is the part of the plant that is used medicinally.
- Taste: Ginger has a pungent and spicy taste.
- Actions: Anti-inflammatory, carminative, digestive, diaphoretic, expectorant, stimulant.
- Energetics: Warming and drying.
- Specific indications: Ginger is known for its many health benefits and has been traditionally used for a variety of specific indications, including:
  - Digestive issues: Ginger has been used for centuries to alleviate digestive problems such as nausea, vomiting, and bloating. It can help stimulate digestion, relieve gas, and reduce inflammation in the gut.
  - Cold and flu symptoms: Ginger has natural antiviral and antibacterial properties that can help boost the immune system and fight off infections. It is also a natural decongestant and can help relieve coughs and sore throats.
  - Inflammation and pain: Ginger has anti-inflammatory properties that can help reduce pain and swelling in the body. It is often used to treat conditions such as osteoarthritis, rheumatoid arthritis, and other inflammatory conditions.

- Menstrual cramps: Ginger can help alleviate menstrual cramps and other menstrual symptoms by reducing inflammation and pain.
- Motion sickness: Ginger has been shown to be effective in reducing the symptoms of motion sickness, including nausea and vomiting.
- Headaches and migraines: Ginger has natural pain-relieving properties and can help reduce the severity and frequency of headaches and migraines.
- High blood pressure: Ginger has been shown to have a mild blood pressure-lowering effect, which can help reduce the risk of heart disease and stroke.

Medicinal preparations:
Ginger can be prepared and consumed in a variety of ways to enjoy its medicinal properties. Here are some common medicinal preparations of ginger:
- Fresh ginger: You can peel and grate fresh ginger root and add it to your tea, smoothies, or meals.
- Ginger tea: Boil a few slices of fresh ginger in water and let it steep for 10-15 minutes to make ginger tea. You can add lemon or honey for taste.
- Ginger capsules: Ginger supplements in the form of capsules or tablets are available and can be taken orally.
- Ginger oil: Ginger oil can be used topically to relieve pain and inflammation. It can also be added to bathwater for a relaxing soak.
- Ginger compress: You can make a ginger compress by soaking a cloth in hot ginger tea and applying it to the affected area to relieve pain and inflammation.
- Ginger syrup: Ginger syrup can be made by simmering fresh ginger in water and adding honey or sugar for taste. It can be added to drinks or used as a sweetener for meals.

It is important to consult with a healthcare professional or a licensed herbalist to determine the appropriate dosage and preparation for your specific needs.

• Ratio and dosage information: The appropriate dose of ginger depends on several factors, including age, health status, and the condition being treated. It is generally safe to consume up to 4 grams of ginger per day.

Medicinal uses:
Ginger has a long history of medicinal use and has been traditionally used to treat a variety of health conditions. Here are some of the medicinal uses of ginger:
- Digestive issues: Ginger has been used for centuries to alleviate digestive problems such as nausea, vomiting, and bloating. It can help stimulate digestion, relieve gas, and reduce inflammation in the gut.

- Cold and flu symptoms: Ginger has natural antiviral and antibacterial properties that can help boost the immune system and fight off infections. It is also a natural decongestant and can help relieve coughs and sore throats.
- Inflammation and pain: Ginger has anti-inflammatory properties that can help reduce pain and swelling in the body. It is often used to treat conditions such as osteoarthritis, rheumatoid arthritis, and other inflammatory conditions.
- Menstrual cramps: Ginger can help alleviate menstrual cramps and other menstrual symptoms by reducing inflammation and pain.
- Motion sickness: Ginger has been shown to be effective in reducing the symptoms of motion sickness, including nausea and vomiting.
- Headaches and migraines: Ginger has natural pain-relieving properties and can help reduce the severity and frequency of headaches and migraines.
- High blood pressure: Ginger has been shown to have a mild blood pressure-lowering effect, which can help reduce the risk of heart disease and stroke.
- Cancer prevention: Some studies suggest that ginger may have anti-cancer properties and may help prevent certain types of cancer.

It is important to consult with a healthcare professional or a licensed herbalist to determine the appropriate use and dosage of ginger for your specific needs.

• Precautions and contradictions: Although ginger is generally considered safe, there are some precautions and contradictions that you should be aware of:
- Blood-thinning medications: Ginger may increase the risk of bleeding when taken with blood-thinning medications such as warfarin. It is important to consult with a healthcare professional before taking ginger if you are on blood-thinning medications.
- Gallstones: Ginger may increase the production of bile, which can worsen symptoms in people with gallstones. It is important to consult with a healthcare professional before taking ginger if you have a history of gallstones.
- Surgery: Ginger may interfere with blood clotting and should be avoided for at least two weeks before surgery to avoid excessive bleeding.
- Heart conditions: Ginger may lower blood pressure and heart rate, which may be problematic for people with certain heart conditions. It is important to consult with a healthcare professional before taking ginger if you have a heart condition.
- Allergic reactions: Some people may have allergic reactions to ginger, including skin rash, hives, and difficulty breathing. If you experience any allergic reactions, stop taking ginger immediately and seek medical attention.

> Pregnancy and breastfeeding: While ginger is generally considered safe during pregnancy and breastfeeding, it is important to consult with a healthcare professional before taking ginger in large amounts.

It is important to note that these precautions and contradictions apply to ginger supplements and concentrated extracts, and not to the amount of ginger commonly used in food. If you are unsure about whether ginger is safe for you to use, consult with a healthcare professional or a licensed herbalist.

Cultivation:
- Native to: Southeast Asia
- Zones: 9-12
- Soil (pH and type of soil): Ginger prefers well-drained, fertile soil with a pH between 6.0 and 7.0.
- Propagation: Ginger is propagated by planting rhizomes in the spring or summer.
- Growing information and garden care: Ginger prefers warm, humid conditions and should be grown in a partially shaded area. It should be watered regularly and fertilized with a balanced fertilizer.
- Insects and disease: Ginger is relatively pest-resistant, but it can be affected by some insect pests and diseases. Here are some of the most common pests and diseases that can affect ginger:

> Root-knot nematodes: These microscopic worms can cause galls on the roots of ginger plants, which can affect the growth and yield of the plant.
> Ginger rhizome rot: This fungal disease can cause rotting of the ginger rhizomes, leading to reduced yield and quality.
> Redback spider mites: These tiny spider mites can feed on the leaves of ginger plants, causing yellowing and browning of the leaves and reducing the plant's ability to photosynthesize.
> Aphids: These small insects can feed on the leaves of ginger plants, causing stunted growth and reduced yield.
> Armyworms: These caterpillars can feed on the leaves of ginger plants, causing defoliation and reduced yield.

To prevent these pests and diseases, it is important to practice good crop management practices, such as crop rotation, proper irrigation, and soil fertility management. Insect pests can be controlled through the use of natural predators, such as ladybugs and lacewings, or through the use of insecticides. Fungal diseases can be controlled through the use of fungicides and proper plant hygiene, such as removing and destroying infected plant material. • Harvesting and preparations: Ginger can be harvested after 8-10 months of growth. The rhizomes can be cleaned, peeled, and sliced for use in cooking or medicine.

What medicines are made with this herb:

Ginger is a widely used herb in traditional medicine systems, and is used to make a variety of medicines, including:

- Digestive aids: Ginger is commonly used to alleviate digestive issues such as nausea, bloating, and flatulence. It is often consumed as a tea, or in capsule or tablet form.
- Anti-inflammatory agents: Ginger contains compounds such as gingerols and shogaols that have anti-inflammatory properties, and is used to alleviate pain and inflammation associated with conditions such as osteoarthritis, rheumatoid arthritis, and other inflammatory conditions.
- Cold and flu remedies: Ginger is often used to alleviate symptoms of colds and flu, such as coughing, congestion, and sore throat. It is often consumed as a tea, or in combination with other herbs such as honey and lemon.
- Menstrual cramp relief: Ginger has been traditionally used to alleviate menstrual cramps, and has been shown in some studies to be effective at reducing pain associated with menstrual cramps.
- Motion sickness and vertigo relief: Ginger has been shown to be effective at alleviating symptoms of motion sickness and vertigo, and is often consumed in capsule or tablet form before traveling.

These are just some of the many medicinal uses of ginger. It is important to note that while ginger is generally considered safe, it is always a good idea to consult with a healthcare professional or licensed herbalist before using ginger as a medicinal herb.

What medicines this herb counteracts:

Ginger is generally considered safe for most people, but it may interact with certain medications. Here are some medications that ginger may interact with:

- Blood-thinning medications: Ginger may increase the risk of bleeding when taken with blood-thinning medications such as warfarin (Coumadin) or aspirin.
- Diabetes medications: Ginger may lower blood sugar levels, so it may interact with medications used to treat diabetes, such as insulin or oral hypoglycemic agents.
- High blood pressure medications: Ginger may lower blood pressure, so it may interact with medications used to treat high blood pressure.
- Anticoagulant and antiplatelet medications: Ginger may interact with medications such as clopidogrel (Plavix) or aspirin, which are used to prevent blood clots.
- Gallbladder medications: Ginger may increase the production of bile, so it may interact with medications used to treat gallbladder conditions.

It is always a good idea to consult with a healthcare professional or licensed herbalist before using ginger as a medicinal herb, especially if you are taking any medications or have any underlying health conditions.

Ginkgo Biloba

Herbal Identification:
- Common name: Ginkgo biloba
- Latin binomial: Ginkgo biloba
- Other common names: Maidenhair tree, Japanese silver apricot
- Plant family: Ginkgoaceae
- Botanical description: Ginkgo biloba is a deciduous tree that can grow up to 35 meters tall and has a spreading crown with fan-shaped leaves. The tree is dioecious, meaning that it has separate male and female trees. The leaves are typically two-lobed and can range from 5-15 centimeters in length. The leaves turn a bright yellow color in the fall before dropping.

The tree has a gray-brown bark that is deeply furrowed and can become quite thick with age. The tree is also known for its distinctive odor, which some people find unpleasant.

Ginkgo biloba is native to China, but it is now grown in many parts of the world, including North America and Europe. The tree is often planted in parks and gardens because of its attractive foliage and its tolerance to pollution.

The tree produces fruit that contains a single seed that is edible but has a strong odor that many people find unpleasant. The seeds are also used in traditional Chinese medicine.

Overall, Ginkgo biloba is a unique and interesting tree that is valued for both its aesthetic and medicinal properties.

Medicinal Properties:
- Parts used: Leaves
- Taste: Bitter
- Actions: Vasodilator, antioxidant, anti-inflammatory, neuroprotective, antiplatelet, circulatory stimulant
- Energetics: Neutral
- Specific indications: Ginkgo biloba is commonly used as a dietary supplement and has been traditionally used in Chinese medicine for a variety of purposes. Some of the specific indications for Ginkgo biloba include:

- Memory and cognitive function: Ginkgo biloba has been shown to improve memory and cognitive function in both healthy individuals and those with cognitive impairment.
- Tinnitus: Ginkgo biloba has been used to improve symptoms of tinnitus (ringing in the ears).
- Peripheral artery disease: Ginkgo biloba can improve symptoms of peripheral artery disease, such as leg pain and cramping during exercise.
- Vision: Ginkgo biloba may improve vision in people with glaucoma and age-related macular degeneration.
- Anxiety and depression: Some studies suggest that Ginkgo biloba may have a beneficial effect on symptoms of anxiety and depression.

It is important to note that while Ginkgo biloba may be helpful for some of these conditions, more research is needed to fully understand its potential benefits and risks.

As with any supplement or medication, it is important to talk to a healthcare provider before taking Ginkgo biloba. • Medicinal preparations: Capsules, tablets, tinctures, teas, and extracts

• Ratio and dosage information: The recommended daily dosage of ginkgo biloba extract is typically between 120-240 mg per day, divided into two or three doses.

• Medicinal uses: Ginkgo biloba has been traditionally used in Chinese medicine for thousands of years, and more recently, it has been studied for its potential medicinal uses. Some of the medicinal uses of Ginkgo biloba are:
- Improving cognitive function: Ginkgo biloba is commonly used to improve memory, attention, and other cognitive functions in healthy individuals and those with cognitive impairment. It may also help to slow down the progression of Alzheimer's disease and other forms of dementia.
- Reducing anxiety and depression: Ginkgo biloba has been shown to have anxiolytic and antidepressant effects in some studies. It may help to reduce symptoms of anxiety and depression by increasing the levels of neurotransmitters such as serotonin and dopamine in the brain.
- Managing symptoms of peripheral artery disease (PAD): Ginkgo biloba has been shown to improve blood flow in people with PAD, which can help to reduce symptoms such as leg pain, cramping, and fatigue.
- Reducing inflammation: Ginkgo biloba has anti-inflammatory properties, which may help to reduce inflammation in the body and improve symptoms of conditions such as arthritis, asthma, and irritable bowel syndrome (IBS).

- Managing symptoms of tinnitus: Ginkgo biloba may help to reduce the severity of tinnitus (ringing in the ears) by improving blood flow to the ears and reducing inflammation.

It is important to note that while Ginkgo biloba may be beneficial for some of these conditions, more research is needed to fully understand its potential benefits and risks. As with any supplement or medication, it is important to talk to a healthcare provider before taking Ginkgo biloba.

• Precautions and contradictions: While Ginkgo biloba is generally considered safe for most people when used as directed, there are some precautions and contraindications to be aware of. These include:
- Blood thinning: Ginkgo biloba may act as a blood thinner, which can increase the risk of bleeding or interfere with blood clotting in people taking blood-thinning medications such as aspirin, warfarin, or heparin. It is important to talk to a healthcare provider before taking Ginkgo biloba if you are taking any blood-thinning medications.
- Seizures: Ginkgo biloba may lower the seizure threshold in some people, which can increase the risk of seizures in people with epilepsy or other seizure disorders. It is important to talk to a healthcare provider before taking Ginkgo biloba if you have a history of seizures.
- Allergies: Some people may be allergic to Ginkgo biloba, and may experience symptoms such as itching, hives, or difficulty breathing. If you experience any allergic reactions after taking Ginkgo biloba, stop taking it immediately and seek medical attention.
- Pregnancy and breastfeeding: There is not enough information available about the safety of Ginkgo biloba during pregnancy or breastfeeding. It is recommended to avoid its use during these times.
- Surgery: Ginkgo biloba may increase the risk of bleeding during and after surgery. It is recommended to stop taking Ginkgo biloba at least two weeks before any scheduled surgery.

As with any supplement or medication, it is important to talk to a healthcare provider before taking Ginkgo biloba to determine if it is safe and appropriate for you.

Cultivation:
- Native to: China
- Zones: Hardy in zones 4-9
- Soil: Ginkgo biloba prefers well-draining soil that is slightly acidic and moist.
- Propagation: Ginkgo biloba can be propagated by seed, although it can take up to 20 years for the trees to produce viable seeds. It can also be propagated by cuttings, but this method is more difficult.
- Growing information and garden care: Ginkgo biloba trees prefer full sun to partial shade and can tolerate a wide range of temperatures. They are relatively low maintenance and do not require frequent pruning.
- Insects and disease: Ginkgo biloba is generally considered to be a hardy and low-maintenance tree, but like all trees, it is susceptible to certain insects and diseases. Some of the insects and diseases that can affect Ginkgo biloba include:
  - Ginkgo leaf miner: This insect can cause damage to the leaves of Ginkgo biloba, leading to defoliation and reduced tree vigor. The damage caused by the leaf miner is primarily cosmetic and does not usually have a significant impact on the overall health of the tree.
  - Ginkgo gall midge: This insect can cause galls to form on the leaves of Ginkgo biloba, which can lead to distorted growth and reduced tree vigor. Like the leaf miner, the damage caused by the gall midge is usually cosmetic.
  - Verticillium wilt: This fungal disease can cause the leaves of Ginkgo biloba to wilt and turn brown, and can eventually lead to the death of the tree. The fungus infects the vascular tissue of the tree, which can make it difficult to control.
  - Canker diseases: Several different types of canker diseases can affect Ginkgo biloba, causing damage to the bark and wood of the tree. The symptoms of canker diseases can include sunken lesions on the bark, wilting or dieback of branches, and reduced tree vigor.
  - Scale insects: Scale insects can feed on the sap of Ginkgo biloba, causing damage to the leaves and twigs of the tree. Heavy infestations can lead to defoliation and reduced tree vigor.

Proper maintenance and care can help to prevent or control insect and disease problems in Ginkgo biloba trees. Regular pruning, fertilization, and watering can help to keep the tree healthy and resilient. If insect or disease problems do occur, it is important to consult with a professional arborist or horticulturist to determine the best course of action.
- Harvesting and preparations: Ginkgo biloba leaves and seeds are the parts of the plant that are most commonly used for their medicinal properties. Here is some information on harvesting and preparation of these parts:

- Leaves: Ginkgo biloba leaves are typically harvested in the late summer or early fall, when they have turned yellow and begun to fall from the tree. They can be dried and used to make tea, or processed to extract the active ingredients. To make tea, use 1-2 teaspoons of dried Ginkgo biloba leaves per cup of boiling water, steep for 10-15 minutes, and strain before drinking. It is important to note that fresh Ginkgo biloba leaves contain toxic compounds that can cause skin irritation and other health problems, so they should not be consumed.
- Seeds: Ginkgo biloba seeds are harvested in the late fall or early winter, when they have fallen from the tree and the fleshy outer layer has begun to rot away. The seeds are typically dried, shelled, and processed to extract the active ingredients. It is important to note that Ginkgo biloba seeds contain toxic compounds that can cause skin irritation and other health problems, so they should not be consumed raw. They should be cooked or processed before use.
- Supplements: Ginkgo biloba supplements are widely available in various forms, including capsules, tablets, and extracts. These supplements are typically made from standardized extracts of the plant, which contain specific amounts of the active ingredients. It is important to follow the dosage instructions on the product label, and to talk to a healthcare provider before taking any supplements.
- Other preparations: Ginkgo biloba leaves and seeds can also be used in various other preparations, such as tinctures, creams, and ointments. These preparations should be used according to the instructions on the product label, and it is important to talk to a healthcare provider before using them.

Medicines made with this herb:

Ginkgo biloba is a plant that has been used for medicinal purposes for centuries, and its leaves and seeds have been used to make a variety of herbal medicines.

Here are some examples of medicines that are made with Ginkgo biloba:
- Ginkgo biloba extract: This is a standardized extract of the plant that is commonly used to improve cognitive function and memory, as well as to treat conditions such as vertigo and tinnitus.
- Ginkgo biloba tea: Dried Ginkgo biloba leaves can be brewed to make a tea that is used to improve circulation, boost memory, and reduce anxiety.
- Ginkgo biloba capsules: Capsules containing Ginkgo biloba extract are commonly used to treat conditions such as Alzheimer's disease, dementia, and peripheral artery disease.

- Ginkgo biloba tincture: A tincture is an alcohol-based extract of the plant that is used to treat a variety of conditions, including anxiety, depression, and circulatory disorders.
- Ginkgo biloba cream: A cream containing Ginkgo biloba extract is often used topically to improve circulation and reduce inflammation in the skin.

It is important to note that while Ginkgo biloba is generally considered safe when used as directed, it can interact with certain medications and may not be suitable for everyone. It is important to talk to a healthcare provider before using Ginkgo biloba or any other herbal medicines.

Medicines this herb counteracts:

Ginkgo biloba may interact with certain medications, and it is important to talk to a healthcare provider before using it if you are taking any prescription or over-the-counter medications.

Here are some examples of medications that may interact with Ginkgo biloba:
- Blood thinners: Ginkgo biloba may increase the risk of bleeding when taken with blood-thinning medications, such as warfarin, heparin, and aspirin.
- Antidepressants: Ginkgo biloba may interact with certain antidepressants, such as selective serotonin reuptake inhibitors (SSRIs), tricyclic antidepressants, and monoamine oxidase inhibitors (MAOIs).
- Anti-seizure medications: Ginkgo biloba may interact with medications used to treat seizures, such as carbamazepine, phenytoin, and valproic acid.
- Diabetes medications: Ginkgo biloba may interfere with the action of medications used to treat diabetes, such as insulin and oral hypoglycemic agents.
- Certain herbal supplements: Ginkgo biloba may interact with other herbal supplements, such as garlic, ginger, and ginseng.

It is important to note that this list is not exhaustive, and other medications may also interact with Ginkgo biloba. It is always best to talk to a healthcare provider before using Ginkgo biloba or any other herbal medicines.

Ginseng

Herbal Identification:
- Common Name: Ginseng
- Latin Binomial: Panax ginseng
- Other Common Names: Asian ginseng, Chinese ginseng, Korean ginseng, Red ginseng
- Plant Family: Araliaceae
- Botanical Description: Ginseng is a slow-growing perennial plant with fleshy roots and a single stem that grows to a height of 30 to 50 cm. The leaves are compound with 3 to 5 leaflets, and the flowers are yellow-green and grow in an umbrella-shaped cluster. The plant produces red berries that contain 2 seeds.

Ginseng belongs to the family Araliaceae, which also includes other medicinal plants like angelica and ivy. The genus Panax includes several species of ginseng, including Panax ginseng (Asian ginseng), Panax quinquefolius (American ginseng), and Panax notoginseng (Chinese ginseng). These species are similar in appearance, with slight variations in leaf shape and flower size.

Ginseng is typically cultivated in shaded, forested areas with well-drained soil. It is native to East Asia and North America, where it grows wild in mountainous regions. The plant has been extensively cultivated in China, Korea, and other Asian countries for thousands of years, and is now also grown in other parts of the world, including Canada and the United States.

Medicinal Properties:
- Recommended Cultivars: There are various cultivars of ginseng, including Korean ginseng, Chinese ginseng, and American ginseng. The Korean and Chinese varieties are considered to be more stimulating, while the American variety is considered to be more relaxing.
- Parts Used: The root is the primary part used medicinally.
- Taste: Bitter and slightly sweet
- Actions: Adaptogen, stimulant, immune modulator, anti-inflammatory, anti-cancer, anti-fatigue
- Energetics: Warm and slightly dry
- Specific Indications: Ginseng has been traditionally used for a variety of medicinal purposes. Some of the specific indications for which ginseng may be used include:

- Energy and Stamina: Ginseng is commonly used to improve physical and mental energy and increase stamina. It may help to reduce fatigue and improve endurance during physical activity.
- Immune System Support: Ginseng may help to strengthen the immune system and improve overall immune function. It may also help to reduce the severity and duration of infections.
- Cognitive Function: Ginseng has been shown to have a positive effect on cognitive function, including improving memory, concentration, and mental clarity. It may also help to reduce the risk of age-related cognitive decline.
- Stress and Anxiety: Ginseng may have a calming effect on the nervous system and help to reduce stress and anxiety. It may also improve mood and promote a sense of well-being.
- Diabetes: Ginseng may help to regulate blood sugar levels and improve insulin sensitivity. It may also help to reduce the risk of complications associated with diabetes.
- Erectile Dysfunction: Ginseng may help to improve sexual function in men with erectile dysfunction. It may also help to increase libido and improve overall sexual performance.

It is important to note that the use of ginseng for these specific indications is based on traditional use and anecdotal evidence, and more scientific research is needed to fully understand the potential benefits of ginseng for these conditions.

Medicinal Preparations:
- Ginseng can be prepared in a variety of ways to extract its medicinal properties. Some common medicinal preparations of ginseng include:
- Capsules and Tablets: Ginseng is available in capsule and tablet form, which can be taken orally as a dietary supplement.
- Tea: Ginseng can be prepared as a tea by steeping sliced or grated ginseng root in hot water for several minutes.
- Tincture: A ginseng tincture can be made by steeping ginseng root in alcohol for several weeks. The resulting liquid can be taken orally, diluted in water or juice.
- Powder: Ginseng root can be ground into a powder and added to food or drinks, or taken directly.
- Topical Applications: Ginseng can also be used topically in the form of creams or ointments to help relieve skin irritation or reduce inflammation.

It is important to note that the appropriate dosage and method of administration of ginseng may vary depending on the specific indication and individual needs. It is always recommended to consult with a healthcare provider before taking ginseng or any other herbal supplement.

Medicinal Uses:
Ginseng has been traditionally used for a variety of medicinal purposes. Some of the medicinal uses of ginseng include:
- Boosting Energy and Stamina: Ginseng is commonly used to improve physical and mental energy and increase stamina. It may help to reduce fatigue and improve endurance during physical activity.
- Immune System Support: Ginseng may help to strengthen the immune system and improve overall immune function. It may also help to reduce the severity and duration of infections.
- Cognitive Function: Ginseng has been shown to have a positive effect on cognitive function, including improving memory, concentration, and mental clarity. It may also help to reduce the risk of age-related cognitive decline.
- Stress and Anxiety: Ginseng may have a calming effect on the nervous system and help to reduce stress and anxiety. It may also improve mood and promote a sense of well-being.
- Diabetes: Ginseng may help to regulate blood sugar levels and improve insulin sensitivity. It may also help to reduce the risk of complications associated with diabetes.
- Erectile Dysfunction: Ginseng may help to improve sexual function in men with erectile dysfunction. It may also help to increase libido and improve overall sexual performance.

Again, it is important to note that the use of ginseng for these medicinal purposes is based on traditional use and anecdotal evidence, and more scientific research is needed to fully understand the potential benefits of ginseng for these conditions.

- Precautions and Contraindications: Ginseng should not be used during pregnancy or breastfeeding, and may interact with certain medications, including blood thinners and insulin. It can also cause insomnia, nervousness, and gastrointestinal upset if taken in excessive doses.

Cultivation:
- Native to: Ginseng is native to East Asia, including China, Korea, and Russia.
- Zones: Ginseng grows in USDA zones 3-8.
- Soil: Ginseng prefers a slightly acidic soil with a pH of 5.5 to 6.5. It requires well-draining soil that is rich in organic matter, such as leaf mold or compost.
- Propagation: Ginseng is typically grown from seed, which should be planted in the fall. The seeds require a cold stratification period of several months before germinating.

- Growing Information and Garden Care: Ginseng requires a shady, forested environment with consistent moisture. The plants should be protected from direct sunlight and wind, and the soil should be kept consistently moist. The plants require a period of dormancy during the winter months.
- Insects and Disease: Ginseng is susceptible to a variety of insect pests and diseases that can affect its growth and yield. Some common pests that can infest ginseng include:
  - Aphids: Aphids are small insects that feed on the sap of ginseng plants and can cause stunted growth and deformation of leaves.
  - Spider Mites: Spider mites are tiny insects that can cause yellowing and browning of leaves, as well as webbing on the plant.
  - Root Maggots: Root maggots are the larvae of flies that can burrow into the roots of ginseng plants and cause damage.
  - Leafhoppers: Leafhoppers are small insects that can cause damage to leaves and stunt growth.

To control these pests, it is important to practice good garden hygiene and remove any debris or weeds that may harbor insect pests. It may also be necessary to use insecticides or other pest control measures to prevent infestations.

In addition to insect pests, ginseng is also susceptible to a variety of diseases that can affect its growth and yield. Some common diseases that can affect ginseng include:
- Phytophthora Root Rot: Phytophthora root rot is a fungal disease that can cause rotting of the roots and stems of ginseng plants.
- Alternaria Blight: Alternaria blight is a fungal disease that can cause leaf spots, stem cankers, and other damage to ginseng plants.
- Bacterial Leaf Spot: Bacterial leaf spot is a bacterial disease that can cause spotting and blighting of leaves on ginseng plants.

To prevent these diseases, it is important to practice good garden hygiene, including proper crop rotation and soil management. It may also be necessary to use fungicides or other disease control measures to prevent the spread of disease.

- Harvesting and Preparations: Harvesting ginseng requires patience, as the plant takes several years to mature and develop a sufficient amount of root. The roots of ginseng are usually harvested in the fall after the leaves have turned yellow and begun to drop. To harvest the roots, the soil around the plant must be carefully loosened with a garden fork or similar tool to avoid damaging the roots. The roots can then be carefully dug up and washed clean of any dirt or debris.

Once harvested, ginseng roots can be prepared for use in a variety of ways. Some common preparations include:

- Drying: Ginseng roots can be dried in a cool, dry place and then stored for later use. Dried ginseng root can be used to make tea, tinctures, or other herbal preparations.
- Tinctures: Ginseng roots can be chopped or grated and then soaked in alcohol or glycerin to make a tincture. Tinctures can be taken orally and are a convenient way to use ginseng for medicinal purposes.
- Tea: Dried ginseng root can be brewed into a tea by steeping it in hot water for several minutes. Ginseng tea can be consumed daily as a tonic to support overall health and wellness.
- Capsules: Ginseng root can be ground into a fine powder and then encapsulated for easy consumption. Capsules can be a convenient way to take ginseng as a dietary supplement.

It is important to follow dosage recommendations and consult with a healthcare professional before using ginseng for medicinal purposes. Overuse or misuse of ginseng can lead to adverse effects.

Medicines made with this herb:

Ginseng is a widely used herb that is used in various medicines, including:

- Dietary supplements: Ginseng supplements are commonly used to support overall health and wellness, boost energy levels, and enhance mental clarity and focus.
- Traditional medicines: Ginseng has been used for centuries in traditional Chinese medicine and is still commonly used in Asia for a wide range of health conditions, including fatigue, stress, and immune system support.
- Herbal remedies: Ginseng is used in many herbal remedies, including tonics, teas, and tinctures, to support a variety of health conditions.
- Functional beverages: Ginseng is also used as an ingredient in many energy drinks and other functional beverages due to its reputation as an energy-boosting herb.

Overall, ginseng is a versatile herb that is used in a wide range of medicinal products, and its popularity continues to grow as more people seek out natural remedies for their health concerns.

Medicines this herb counteracts:

Ginseng may interact with certain medications, including:
- Blood thinners: Ginseng may increase the risk of bleeding when taken with blood-thinning medications such as warfarin.
- Insulin and other diabetes medications: Ginseng may lower blood sugar levels and may interact with medications used to treat diabetes, leading to hypoglycemia or low blood sugar levels.
- Immunosuppressants: Ginseng may interfere with medications used to suppress the immune system, leading to decreased effectiveness of the medication.
- Stimulants: Ginseng may increase the effects of stimulant medications such as caffeine or amphetamines, leading to jitteriness, insomnia, or other side effects.

It is important to talk to a healthcare professional before using ginseng if you are taking any medications or have any health conditions, as it may interact with other substances or have adverse effects if used inappropriately.

Holy Basil

Herbal Identification:
- Common name: Holy basil
- Latin binomial: Ocimum sanctum
- Other common names: Tulsi, sacred basil
- Plant family: Lamiaceae (mint family)
- Botanical description: Holy basil (Ocimum sanctum) is an aromatic perennial herb that grows up to 1 meter tall. It has green, fragrant leaves that are oval-shaped and slightly toothed. The plant produces small, white to purple flowers in late summer. The stems of the plant are square-shaped and green. Holy basil belongs to the

Lamiaceae family (mint family) and is closely related to other culinary herbs like basil, thyme, and oregano. The plant has a warm and pungent aroma, and the leaves have a slightly bitter taste. There are several cultivars of holy basil, including the Krishna and Rama varieties.

Medicinal Properties:
- Recommended cultivars: Krishna and Rama
- Parts used: Leaves, stems, and seeds
- Taste: Pungent and bitter
- Actions: Adaptogen, antibacterial, antifungal, antioxidant, immunomodulatory, nervine, and carminative
- Energetics: Warming and drying
- Specific indications: Holy basil has a long history of use in Ayurvedic medicine and is considered a sacred herb in India. It is believed to have a wide range of medicinal properties, and some of its specific indications include:
  - Adaptogenic: Holy basil is considered an adaptogen, meaning it can help the body adapt to stress and promote a sense of balance and well-being.
  - Respiratory issues: Holy basil may be helpful in relieving respiratory issues, such as asthma, bronchitis, and congestion.
  - Digestive issues: Holy basil may help with digestive issues, such as bloating, gas, and nausea.
  - Mental health: Holy basil may have a calming effect on the mind and be helpful for anxiety, depression, and insomnia.
  - Immune support: Holy basil may support the immune system and help the body fight off infections.

- It's important to note that the specific indications of holy basil have not been extensively studied, and further research is needed to better understand its potential health benefits.

Medicinal preparations:
Holy basil can be used in a variety of medicinal preparations, including:
- Tea: One of the simplest ways to use holy basil is by making a tea from the leaves. Simply steep a handful of fresh or dried leaves in hot water for 5-10 minutes, strain, and drink.
- Tincture: A tincture is an alcohol-based extraction of the herb. Holy basil tincture can be taken orally by adding it to water or another beverage.
- Capsules: Holy basil is available in capsule form, which can be taken orally as a supplement.
- Essential oil: Holy basil essential oil can be used topically or in a diffuser to promote relaxation and support respiratory and immune health.

It's important to note that the appropriate dosage and form of holy basil may vary depending on the specific indication and individual health needs. It's always best to consult with a qualified healthcare provider before using any herbal remedies.

- Ratio and dosage information: 1-2 teaspoons of dried herb per cup of water for tea, 2-4 mL of tincture three times a day, and 300-600 mg of standardized extract per day.

Medicinal uses:
Holy basil is a medicinal herb that has been traditionally used for a wide range of health issues. Some of its medicinal uses include:
- Anti-inflammatory: Holy basil contains compounds with anti-inflammatory properties that may help reduce inflammation in the body and alleviate conditions like arthritis and inflammatory bowel disease.
- Antioxidant: Holy basil is a rich source of antioxidants, which may help protect the body against damage from free radicals and reduce the risk of chronic diseases like heart disease, diabetes, and cancer.
- Anti-microbial: Holy basil has been traditionally used as an antimicrobial agent and may be effective against a variety of bacteria, viruses, and fungi.
- Anti-stress: Holy basil is considered an adaptogen, which means it may help the body cope with stress and anxiety.
- Cardiovascular health: Holy basil may help improve cardiovascular health by reducing blood pressure and cholesterol levels.

> Respiratory health: Holy basil may be helpful in relieving respiratory issues, such as asthma, bronchitis, and congestion.

It's important to note that the scientific evidence supporting the medicinal uses of holy basil is limited, and further research is needed to fully understand its potential health benefits. Holy basil should not be used as a replacement for conventional medical treatment without consulting a qualified healthcare provider.

• Precautions and contradictions: Holy basil is generally considered safe when used in culinary amounts or in medicinal preparations, but there are some precautions and contraindications to be aware of:
> Pregnancy and breastfeeding: Holy basil may stimulate uterine contractions and should be avoided during pregnancy and breastfeeding.
> Surgery: Holy basil may increase the risk of bleeding, so it should be avoided at least two weeks before surgery.
> Diabetes: Holy basil may lower blood sugar levels and may interfere with diabetes medications, so it should be used with caution by individuals with diabetes.
> Blood thinning medications: Holy basil may increase the risk of bleeding and should be used with caution by individuals taking blood thinning medications, such as warfarin.
> Allergic reactions: Some individuals may experience an allergic reaction to holy basil, especially if they are allergic to other members of the mint family.

It's always best to consult with a qualified healthcare provider before using holy basil or any other herbal remedies, especially if you have a pre-existing medical condition or are taking medication.

Cultivation:

• Native to: India and Southeast Asia
• Zones: Hardy in USDA zones 10-11, but can be grown as an annual in colder zones.
• Soil: Well-drained soil with a pH of 6.0-7.5
• Propagation: Seed or stem cuttings
• Growing information and garden care: Holy basil prefers full sun and moderate watering. It is a tender perennial in warm climates and can be grown as an annual in colder zones. It can be grown in containers or in the garden.
• Insects and disease: Holy basil is generally a hardy plant that is relatively resistant to pests and diseases. However, some common issues that may affect holy basil include:

- Aphids: Aphids are small, soft-bodied insects that can suck the sap from the leaves of holy basil. They can be controlled with insecticidal soap or neem oil.
- Whiteflies: Whiteflies are small, white, moth-like insects that can also feed on the sap of holy basil. They can be controlled with insecticidal soap or neem oil.
- Fusarium wilt: Fusarium wilt is a fungal disease that can affect the roots and stems of holy basil, causing wilting and yellowing of the leaves. It can be prevented by planting in well-draining soil and avoiding over-watering.
- Downy mildew: Downy mildew is a fungal disease that can cause yellowing and curling of the leaves of holy basil. It can be controlled with a copper-based fungicide and by avoiding over-watering.

Regular inspection and prompt treatment of any pest or disease problems can help keep holy basil healthy and productive.

- Harvesting and preparations: Harvesting and preparation of holy basil can vary depending on the intended use. Here are some general guidelines:
  - Harvesting: Holy basil can be harvested throughout the growing season, but the best time to harvest is when the plant has produced enough leaves for use. When harvesting, cut the stems just above a leaf node to encourage bushy growth. Avoid harvesting more than one-third of the plant at a time to avoid stressing it.
  - Culinary uses: Holy basil is commonly used in Indian and Southeast Asian cuisines. The fresh leaves can be added to salads, soups, curries, stir-fries, and other dishes. The leaves have a spicy, peppery flavor with a slightly sweet undertone.

Medicinal uses:

Holy basil is used in Ayurvedic medicine to treat a wide range of conditions. The leaves can be used fresh or dried to make teas, tinctures, and other preparations. Holy basil is known for its adaptogenic and anti-inflammatory properties, and may help reduce stress, improve immune function, and support cardiovascular health.

- Drying: To dry holy basil for later use, tie small bundles of stems together and hang them upside down in a warm, dry, well-ventilated area. Once the leaves are dry and brittle, strip them from the stems and store them in an airtight container in a cool, dark place.
- Infusions and decoctions: To make an infusion or tea with holy basil, steep 1-2 teaspoons of dried leaves in a cup of hot water for 5-10 minutes. For a stronger preparation, use more herb or steep for a longer period of time. To

make a decoction, simmer the herb in water for 20-30 minutes before straining and consuming.
- Tinctures: To make a tincture, combine 1 part fresh or dried holy basil with 5 parts high-proof alcohol, such as vodka or brandy. Let the mixture steep for 4-6 weeks, shaking it periodically, before straining and bottling. Tinctures can be taken by adding a few drops to water or juice.

Always follow dosage guidelines and precautions when using holy basil for medicinal purposes, and consult a qualified healthcare provider if you have any questions or concerns.

Medicines made with this herb:

Holy basil is used in traditional medicine systems like Ayurveda and Siddha, and is a common ingredient in many herbal remedies. Some of the medicines made with holy basil include:
- Herbal teas and infusions: Holy basil leaves are steeped in hot water to make a soothing tea that is used to relieve stress, anxiety, and promote relaxation.
- Tinctures: Holy basil is extracted in alcohol to make a tincture, which is a concentrated liquid that is used for medicinal purposes. Holy basil tincture is often used to treat respiratory conditions, digestive issues, and skin problems.
- Essential oils: Holy basil essential oil is used in aromatherapy to promote relaxation and relieve stress. It is also used topically to treat skin infections and inflammations.
- Capsules and tablets: Holy basil extracts are often encapsulated or pressed into tablets to make it easier to consume. These forms of holy basil are used to treat a variety of conditions, including high blood sugar, high cholesterol, and arthritis.

It is important to note that the production and sale of herbal medicines can be unregulated, and it is important to obtain herbal medicines from reputable sources to ensure quality and safety. Additionally, it is important to consult a qualified healthcare provider before using any herbal medicines, especially if you have a pre-existing medical condition or are taking prescription medications.

Medicines this herb counteracts:

There is no specific medicine that holy basil (Ocimum tenuiflorum) is known to counteract. However, as with any herbal medicine, it is important to be aware of potential interactions with other medications or supplements that you may be taking.

Holy basil has been shown to have blood-thinning effects and may interact with other blood-thinning medications such as warfarin or aspirin. It may also interact with medications for high blood pressure, diabetes, and cholesterol-lowering drugs. Additionally, holy basil may enhance the effects of sedative medications, such as benzodiazepines or barbiturates, so it is important to consult with a healthcare provider before using holy basil if you are taking any prescription medications.

It is also important to note that while holy basil is generally considered safe when used in moderation, there have been some reports of allergic reactions, gastrointestinal upset, and interference with fertility in animal studies. As with any herbal medicine, it is important to use caution and consult a qualified healthcare provider before using holy basil if you have any medical conditions or concerns.

Hops

Herbal Identification:
- Common name: Hops
- Latin binomial: Humulus lupulus
- Other common names: Hop, common hop
- Plant family: Cannabaceae
- Botanical description: Hops, or Humulus lupulus, are a species of flowering plant in the family Cannabaceae.

They are a perennial vine that grows up to 25 feet tall, with long, twining stems that wrap around supports such as trellises or poles. The leaves are palmately lobed, with serrated edges, and are arranged in an alternate pattern along the stem.

The female hop plant produces cone-like structures called strobiles, which are used primarily in the brewing industry to impart bitterness, flavor, and aroma to beer. The strobiles are made up of a papery outer layer, called the bract, which surrounds a central cone-like structure, called the lupulin gland. The lupulin gland contains the resins and oils that give hops their distinctive flavor and aroma.

Hops are dioecious, meaning that male and female flowers are produced on separate plants. Only the female plants are used for brewing, as the male plants do not produce the desired strobiles. Hops are typically grown in regions with cool, moist climates, such as the Pacific Northwest in the United States and parts of Europe, and require well-draining soil and plenty of sunlight.

Medicinal Properties:
- Parts used: Strobiles (the female flower cones)
- Taste: Bitter
- Actions: Sedative, nervine, anodyne, tonic, diuretic
- Energetics: Cooling and drying
- Specific indications: Hops have several specific indications, including:
  - Sedative: Hops have a mild sedative effect and are often used to promote relaxation and help with sleep disorders, such as insomnia.
  - Anxiety: Hops may help to reduce anxiety and have a calming effect on the nervous system.
  - Digestive issues: Hops have been used traditionally to aid digestion, reduce bloating and flatulence, and relieve stomach cramps.

- Menopause symptoms: Hops may help to alleviate symptoms associated with menopause, such as hot flashes, night sweats, and anxiety.
- Anti-inflammatory: Hops have anti-inflammatory properties and may help to reduce inflammation in the body.
- Pain relief: Hops may help to reduce pain and are often used to alleviate headaches and menstrual cramps.
- Appetite stimulant: Hops may help to stimulate the appetite and are sometimes used to treat anorexia nervosa.

It's important to note that hops should be used under the guidance of a healthcare professional, as they may interact with certain medications and have potential side effects.

Medicinal preparations:
Hops can be prepared in several ways for medicinal use, including:
- Tea: Hops can be brewed into a tea by steeping the dried strobiles in hot water. This can be consumed to help with sleep disorders, anxiety, and digestive issues.
- Tincture: Hops can be prepared as a tincture by steeping the dried strobiles in alcohol or glycerin. This can be taken orally to help with sleep disorders and anxiety.
- Capsules: Hops can be purchased in capsule form, which are often used to promote relaxation and aid sleep.
- Essential oil: Hops essential oil can be used in aromatherapy to help with relaxation, anxiety, and stress.
- Compress: A hop compress can be made by soaking a cloth in a tea made from hops and applying it to the affected area. This can be helpful for relieving pain and inflammation.

It's important to note that the dosage and method of preparation for hops may vary depending on the intended use, and it's important to consult with a healthcare professional before using hops for medicinal purposes.

• Ratio and dosage information: The usual dosage for hops is 1-2 grams of dried strobiles per day.

Medicinal uses:
Hops have several medicinal uses, including:
- Sleep disorders: Hops are commonly used to promote relaxation and aid in sleep. They may help to reduce anxiety and promote feelings of calmness, making them a helpful natural remedy for insomnia.

- Anxiety: Hops may help to reduce anxiety and have a calming effect on the nervous system. This can be helpful for people with generalized anxiety disorder, social anxiety disorder, and other anxiety-related conditions.
- Menopause symptoms: Hops may help to alleviate symptoms associated with menopause, such as hot flashes, night sweats, and anxiety. They may also help to improve sleep quality in menopausal women.
- Digestive issues: Hops have been used traditionally to aid digestion, reduce bloating and flatulence, and relieve stomach cramps. They may help to promote the production of digestive enzymes and reduce inflammation in the digestive tract.
- Pain relief: Hops may help to reduce pain and inflammation in the body, making them a potential natural remedy for conditions such as headaches and menstrual cramps.
- Anti-inflammatory: Hops have anti-inflammatory properties and may help to reduce inflammation in the body. This may be helpful for people with conditions such as arthritis, asthma, and inflammatory bowel disease.

It's important to note that while hops may be helpful for these conditions, they should be used under the guidance of a healthcare professional, as they may interact with certain medications and have potential side effects.

• Precautions and contradictions: Hops are generally safe when used in moderation, but there are some precautions and contraindications to be aware of. These include:

- Pregnancy and breastfeeding: Hops are not recommended for use during pregnancy or breastfeeding, as they may have estrogenic effects that could interfere with hormone levels.
- Sedation: Hops have a mild sedative effect and can cause drowsiness. They should not be used in conjunction with other sedative medications or alcohol, as this can increase the risk of excessive sedation.
- Depression: Hops may exacerbate symptoms of depression and should be used with caution in people with this condition.
- Hormone-sensitive conditions: Hops may have estrogenic effects and should be used with caution in people with hormone-sensitive conditions such as breast cancer or endometriosis.
- Allergies: Some people may be allergic to hops and should avoid using them.
- Interactions with medications: Hops may interact with certain medications, including sedatives, antidepressants, and hormone replacement therapy. It's important to talk to a healthcare professional before using hops if you are taking any medications.
- Liver disease: Hops may exacerbate liver disease and should be used with caution in people with this condition.

Overall, it's important to use hops under the guidance of a healthcare professional and to avoid excessive consumption.

Cultivation:
- Native to: Europe and western Asia
- Zones: 4-8
- Soil: Hops prefer well-drained, fertile soil with a pH between 6.0-8.0.
- Propagation: Hops can be propagated by rhizome or cutting.
- Growing information and garden care: Hops are typically grown on trellises or other supports. They require plenty of sunlight and water, and should be fertilized regularly. They are susceptible to a number of diseases and pests, including downy mildew, spider mites, and aphids.
- Insects and disease: Hops are susceptible to several insects and diseases, which can impact the health and yield of the plant. Some common insects that may affect hops include:
  - Aphids: These small, pear-shaped insects can suck the sap from the leaves, causing them to wilt and turn yellow.
  - Spider mites: These tiny insects can cause discoloration and stippling on the leaves, as well as webbing.
  - Hop flea beetle: This beetle can cause damage to the leaves and buds of the hop plant.
  - Japanese beetle: This beetle can cause damage to the foliage and flowers of the hop plant.

In addition to insects, hops are also susceptible to several diseases, including:
- Downy mildew: This fungal disease can cause yellowing and wilting of the leaves.
- Powdery mildew: This fungal disease can cause a white, powdery coating on the leaves and flowers.
- Verticillium wilt: This fungal disease can cause wilting, yellowing, and stunting of the plant.
- Fusarium wilt: This fungal disease can cause yellowing and wilting of the leaves and stunting of the plant.

To prevent and manage insect and disease problems in hops, it's important to practice good crop management techniques, such as crop rotation, timely harvesting, and the use of disease-resistant varieties. Additionally, insecticides and fungicides may be used, but should be used judiciously and with care to minimize environmental impact.

- Harvesting and preparations: Hops are typically harvested in the late summer or early fall, when the cones are mature and ready for picking. The cones should be picked when they are dry, papery, and slightly sticky to the touch.

Once the hops are harvested, they can be prepared for use in a variety of ways. Here are some common methods of preparation:
- Drying: Hops should be dried as soon as possible after harvesting to prevent spoilage. This can be done by spreading the cones out on a screen or tray in a warm, dry place until they are fully dry.
- Pelletizing: Hops can be processed into pellets by grinding the dried cones and compressing them into small, uniform pellets. Pellets are convenient for storage and transport and are often used in commercial brewing.
- Whole cone: Hops can be used whole by adding them directly to a brewing vessel. This method is often used in home brewing and can provide a more complex flavor profile than pelletized hops.
- Fresh hopping: Some brewers prefer to use fresh, undried hops in their brewing process. This method can provide a unique flavor profile but requires the hops to be used quickly after harvesting.
- Tincture: Hops can be used to make a tincture by steeping the dried cones in alcohol or glycerin. This can be used to add hop flavor to beer or for medicinal purposes.

It's important to store hops properly to maintain their quality and freshness. Hops should be stored in a cool, dry place away from light and oxygen to prevent spoilage. Pelletized hops can be stored in airtight containers in the freezer for long-term storage.

Medicines made with this herb:
Hops are used in a variety of medicinal preparations, including:
- Herbal teas: Hops can be brewed into a tea and consumed for its sedative and calming effects.
- Tinctures: Hops can be used to make a tincture, which can be taken orally for its calming and sleep-promoting effects.
- Essential oil: Hops essential oil can be used topically or in aromatherapy for its sedative and calming effects.
- Capsules: Hops can be encapsulated and taken orally as a dietary supplement for its calming and sleep-promoting effects.

- Combinations: Hops is often combined with other herbs, such as valerian root, passionflower, or chamomile, for its calming and sleep-promoting effects.

It's important to note that while hops can be effective for certain conditions, it should always be used under the guidance of a healthcare professional and in conjunction with other lifestyle modifications as needed.

Medicines this herb counteracts:
There is limited information on specific medicines that hops may counteract, but there are some general precautions to keep in mind when using hops as a medicinal herb.
- Central nervous system depressants: Hops may enhance the effects of sedative medications or other central nervous system depressants, such as benzodiazepines, barbiturates, or opioids. It is important to avoid using hops with these medications without the guidance of a healthcare professional.
- Hormonal therapies: Hops contain compounds called phytoestrogens, which may interact with hormonal therapies, such as hormone replacement therapy or oral contraceptives. If you are using any hormonal therapies, it's important to speak with a healthcare professional before using hops.
- Alcohol: Hops may enhance the effects of alcohol, so it's important to avoid consuming alcohol while taking hops supplements or medications.
- Diabetes medications: Some animal studies suggest that hops may lower blood sugar levels, which may interact with diabetes medications. It's important to monitor blood sugar levels closely if using hops supplements or medications with diabetes medications.

As always, it is important to speak with a healthcare professional before using hops as a medicinal herb to ensure its safety and appropriate use.

Hyssop

Herbal Identification:
- Common name: Hyssop
- Latin binomial: Hyssopus officinalis
- Other common names: Holy herb, Herb of the cross, Za'atar
- Plant family: Lamiaceae
- Botanical description: Hyssop (Hyssopus officinalis) is a small perennial herb that grows up to 2 feet tall. It has woody stems, small leaves, and produces spikes of small, bluish-purple flowers. The leaves and stems have a strong, aromatic scent. The plant belongs to the Lamiaceae family, which includes other culinary herbs such as mint and oregano. Hyssop is native to southern Europe and the Mediterranean region, but is now widely cultivated in many parts of the world. It prefers full sun and well-draining, sandy or loamy soil with a pH of 6.5-7.5. The leaves and flowers of hyssop are used medicinally and can be harvested in the morning after the dew has dried.

Medicinal Properties:
- Recommended cultivars: Hyssop officinalis is the most commonly used cultivar.
- Parts used: The leaves and flowers are used medicinally.
- Taste: Hyssop has a slightly bitter and pungent taste.
- Actions: Hyssop is a carminative, expectorant, and diaphoretic.
- Energetics: Hyssop is warming and drying.
- Specific indications: Hyssop has been traditionally used for a variety of medicinal purposes, including respiratory and digestive issues. Some specific indications for its use include:
  - Coughs, bronchitis, and other respiratory infections
  - Asthma and other breathing difficulties
  - Digestive complaints, such as bloating, gas, and indigestion
  - Loss of appetite
  - Anxiety, nervous tension, and insomnia
  - Menstrual cramps and other menstrual issues

However, it is important to note that there is limited scientific evidence to support these uses, and hyssop should not be used as a substitute for conventional medical treatment. It is always best to consult with a healthcare professional before using hyssop or any other herbal remedy.

Medicinal preparations:
Hyssop can be prepared and used in various ways to provide its medicinal benefits. Some common medicinal preparations of hyssop include:
- Infusions or teas: Dried hyssop leaves and flowers can be steeped in hot water to make a tea that can be drunk up to 3 times per day.
- Tinctures: Hyssop can also be prepared as a tincture by steeping the herb in alcohol for several weeks. Tinctures can be taken in small doses several times per day.
- Essential oil: Hyssop essential oil can be used topically or inhaled through steam inhalation to help relieve respiratory issues and support the immune system. However, it should be used with caution and under the guidance of a qualified aromatherapist, as it can be toxic in high doses.
- Poultices: Hyssop can be used in poultices or compresses to help relieve skin irritations, bruises, and other external issues.

It is important to note that different preparations may require different ratios and dosages, and should be used according to the instructions of a qualified healthcare professional.
- Ratio and dosage information: For teas, use 1-2 teaspoons of dried hyssop per cup of water. Drink 1-3 cups per day. Tincture dosage varies depending on the strength of the tincture.

Medicinal uses:
Hyssop has been used for its medicinal properties for centuries. Some of its traditional medicinal uses include:
- Respiratory health: Hyssop has been used to relieve coughs, colds, bronchitis, and other respiratory infections. It is thought to have expectorant and antispasmodic properties that can help to loosen phlegm and relieve chest congestion.
- Digestive health: Hyssop has been used to treat digestive complaints such as bloating, gas, indigestion, and loss of appetite. It is thought to stimulate digestion and improve the production of digestive juices.
- Immune system support: Hyssop has been used to support the immune system and protect against infections. It is thought to have antimicrobial and antiviral properties that can help to fight off pathogens.
- Menstrual issues: Hyssop has been used to relieve menstrual cramps and regulate menstruation. It is thought to have a calming effect on the uterus and help to balance hormones.

- Anxiety and stress: Hyssop has been used to relieve anxiety, nervous tension, and insomnia. It is thought to have a calming effect on the nervous system and promote relaxation.

It is important to note that scientific evidence for these traditional uses is limited, and hyssop should not be used as a substitute for conventional medical treatment. It is always best to consult with a healthcare professional before using hyssop or any other herbal remedy.

- Precautions and contradictions: While hyssop has been used for its medicinal properties for centuries, it is important to take precautions when using this herb. Some precautions and contradictions to be aware of include:
  - Pregnancy and breastfeeding: Hyssop should be avoided during pregnancy and breastfeeding, as there is insufficient evidence regarding its safety in these situations.
  - Epilepsy: Hyssop should not be used by individuals with epilepsy or other seizure disorders, as it may increase the risk of seizures.
  - Allergies: Individuals who are allergic to plants in the mint family, such as basil, oregano, or thyme, may also be allergic to hyssop.
  - Drug interactions: Hyssop may interact with certain medications, including sedatives, thyroid hormones, and antiviral medications. It is important to speak with a healthcare professional before using hyssop if you are taking any medications.
  - Toxicity: High doses of hyssop can be toxic and may cause seizures, convulsions, and other serious side effects. It is important to use hyssop only under the guidance of a qualified healthcare professional.

It is always best to speak with a healthcare professional before using hyssop or any other herbal remedy, particularly if you have any underlying health conditions or are taking medications.

Cultivation:

- Native to: Southern Europe and the Mediterranean region.
- Zones: Hyssop grows best in USDA zones 4-9.
- Soil: Hyssop prefers well-draining, sandy or loamy soil with a pH of 6.5-7.5.
- Propagation: Hyssop can be propagated by seed, division, or stem cuttings.
- Growing information and garden care: Hyssop prefers full sun and can tolerate dry soil conditions. It should be watered regularly during the growing season. Prune back the plants in the spring to promote bushier growth.
  - Insects and disease: Hyssop is generally a hardy plant that is relatively resistant to pests and diseases. However, there are a few issues to watch out for:

- Powdery mildew: This fungal disease can affect hyssop, causing a white or gray powdery coating to appear on the leaves. To prevent powdery mildew, avoid overwatering and provide good air circulation around the plant. If powdery mildew does appear, it can be treated with a fungicide or by removing the affected leaves.
- Aphids: These small, soft-bodied insects can suck the sap from hyssop leaves, causing them to curl and distort. To prevent aphids, keep the area around the plant clean and free of debris, and use insecticidal soap or neem oil to treat any infestations.
- Spider mites: These tiny pests can also attack hyssop, causing the leaves to turn yellow and the plant to become stunted. To prevent spider mites, keep the plant well-watered and misted, and use a miticide to treat any infestations.

Overall, hyssop is a relatively low-maintenance plant that can thrive in a variety of growing conditions. With proper care, it can be a beautiful addition to any garden.

• Harvesting and preparations: Hyssop can be harvested and prepared in a variety of ways for medicinal use. Here are some tips on harvesting and preparing hyssop:
- Harvesting: Hyssop leaves and flowers can be harvested throughout the growing season. The best time to harvest is in the morning, after the dew has evaporated, but before the sun is too hot. Cut the stems just above a leaf node, leaving at least two sets of leaves on the plant.
- Drying: To dry hyssop, tie the stems in small bunches and hang them upside down in a cool, dry place with good air circulation. Once the leaves are dry and brittle, remove them from the stems and store in an airtight container.
- Infusion: To make an infusion (herbal tea) with hyssop, steep 1-2 teaspoons of dried hyssop leaves or flowers in 1 cup of hot water for 5-10 minutes. Strain and drink up to three times per day.
- Tincture: Hyssop can also be prepared as a tincture, which involves steeping the plant in alcohol or another solvent to extract its active compounds. Follow instructions for making a tincture, and take as directed.
- Inhalation: Hyssop can be used as an inhalation for respiratory complaints. Add a few drops of hyssop essential oil to a bowl of hot water, and inhale the steam.

Always consult with a qualified healthcare professional before using hyssop or any other herbal remedy, particularly if you have any underlying health conditions or are taking medications.

What medicines are made with this herb:

Hyssop has been traditionally used in a variety of medicinal preparations, including:

- Hyssop tea or infusion: Used to soothe respiratory complaints, such as coughs, bronchitis, and asthma.
- Hyssop tincture: Used as an expectorant and to ease digestive issues, such as indigestion and bloating.
- Hyssop essential oil: Used in aromatherapy to relieve anxiety and stress, as well as for its antiviral and antibacterial properties.
- Hyssop poultice: Used topically to soothe skin irritations and wounds.
- Hyssop salve: Used topically to relieve muscle pain and joint stiffness.

Hyssop is also used as a flavoring agent in some foods and beverages, such as liqueurs and herbal teas.

It's important to note that while hyssop has been traditionally used for medicinal purposes, there is limited scientific evidence to support its effectiveness for many of these uses. Always consult with a qualified healthcare professional before using hyssop or any other herbal remedy.

What medicines this herb counteracts:

There is limited information on specific medications that hyssop may counteract. However, hyssop should be used with caution or avoided altogether in certain circumstances:

- Hyssop contains compounds called ketones, which can be toxic in high doses. Do not exceed recommended dosages of hyssop.
- Hyssop may stimulate the uterus and should be avoided by pregnant women.
- Hyssop may lower blood sugar levels, which could be a concern for people with diabetes who are taking medications to lower blood sugar.
- Hyssop may interfere with certain medications, including drugs metabolized by the liver and medications that slow blood clotting. Always consult with a qualified healthcare professional before using hyssop or any other herbal remedy, particularly if you are taking medications.

Juniper Berries

Herbal Identification:
- Common name: Juniper berries
- Latin binomial: Juniperus communis
- Other common names: Common juniper, gin berry, cedar berry
- Plant family: Cupressaceae
- Botanical description: JJuniper berries are a type of fruit that comes from several species of juniper plants in the genus Juniperus. They are small, round, and typically range from dark blue to purple-black in color. Juniper berries are actually a type of cone, with fleshy scales that give them their distinctive appearance.

The berries grow on small trees or shrubs that are typically found in dry, rocky areas. Juniper plants have needle-like leaves that are usually green or blue-green in color. The berries themselves are rich in essential oils, giving them a strong, woody aroma that is often used in cooking and perfumery.

In terms of flavor, juniper berries are highly aromatic and slightly sweet, with a resinous and slightly bitter taste. They are commonly used as a spice in a variety of dishes, particularly in European cuisine. Juniper berries are also a key ingredient in the production of gin, where they provide a distinctive pine-like flavor.

In traditional medicine, juniper berries are sometimes used to treat digestive problems, urinary tract infections, and respiratory conditions. However, they can be toxic in large amounts and should only be used under the guidance of a qualified healthcare professional.

Medicinal Properties:
- Parts used: Berries
- Taste: Bitter, pungent
- Actions: Diuretic, carminative, antiseptic, antirheumatic
- Energetics: Warming, drying
- Specific indications: Urinary tract infections, digestive complaints, arthritis, gout
- Medicinal preparations: Juniper berries have been used for medicinal purposes for centuries. They contain a variety of compounds with potential

health benefits, including essential oils, flavonoids, and terpenes. Some of the most common medicinal preparations of juniper berries include:

- Tea: Juniper berry tea is made by steeping crushed or whole berries in hot water. It is believed to have diuretic properties and is sometimes used to treat urinary tract infections.
- Tincture: A tincture is a concentrated liquid extract made by soaking juniper berries in alcohol. It can be taken orally or applied topically to treat a variety of conditions, including joint pain, skin irritations, and respiratory infections.
- Essential oil: Juniper berry essential oil is steam distilled from the berries and is used in aromatherapy to promote relaxation, ease stress, and improve respiratory function.
- Capsules: Juniper berry capsules are made by grinding the berries into a powder and placing them into a gelatin or vegetarian capsule. They may be taken orally to support urinary tract health, aid digestion, and reduce inflammation.

It is important to note that juniper berries can be toxic in high doses, and should only be used under the guidance of a qualified healthcare professional. Pregnant women, children, and individuals with kidney disease or other medical conditions should avoid using juniper berries.

• Ratio and dosage information: Infusion - 1-2 teaspoons of crushed berries per cup of boiling water, steeped for 10-15 minutes. Tincture - 2-4 ml, 3 times per day. Essential oil - 1-2 drops in a carrier oil for topical use or in a diffuser for aromatherapy.

Medicinal uses:
Juniper berries have a long history of medicinal use, and are believed to have a variety of health benefits. Some of the most common medicinal uses of juniper berries include:

- Urinary tract infections: Juniper berries have diuretic properties, which means they can increase urine production and help flush out bacteria from the urinary tract. They are sometimes used to treat urinary tract infections (UTIs), although it is important to seek medical advice if you suspect you have a UTI.
- Digestive problems: Juniper berries have been traditionally used to aid digestion and relieve bloating, gas, and indigestion. They are thought to stimulate the production of digestive enzymes and increase the flow of bile.
- Respiratory infections: Juniper berries have antimicrobial properties and are sometimes used to treat respiratory infections such as bronchitis and

pneumonia. They may help reduce inflammation and promote healing in the respiratory tract.
- Arthritis and joint pain: Juniper berries have anti-inflammatory properties and may help reduce joint pain and inflammation associated with conditions such as arthritis.
- Skin conditions: Juniper berries have antiseptic and astringent properties, and may be used topically to treat skin irritations, acne, and eczema.

It is important to note that juniper berries can be toxic in high doses, and should only be used under the guidance of a qualified healthcare professional. Pregnant women, children, and individuals with kidney disease or other medical conditions should avoid using juniper berries.

- Precautions and contradictions: While juniper berries have many potential health benefits, there are also some precautions and contraindications to be aware of. Some of the most important ones include:
  - Pregnancy and breastfeeding: Juniper berries should be avoided during pregnancy and breastfeeding, as they can stimulate uterine contractions and may be harmful to the developing fetus.
  - Kidney disease: Juniper berries can be toxic to the kidneys in high doses, and should be avoided by individuals with kidney disease or other kidney-related problems.
  - Allergies: Individuals who are allergic to juniper berries or other members of the Juniperus genus should avoid using juniper berries.
  - Medications: Juniper berries can interact with certain medications, including diuretics, lithium, and some diabetes medications. If you are taking any medications, it is important to consult with your healthcare provider before using juniper berries.
  - High doses: Consuming large amounts of juniper berries can be toxic and may cause adverse effects such as kidney damage, gastrointestinal irritation, and respiratory problems.

Overall, it is important to use juniper berries only under the guidance of a qualified healthcare professional, and to follow recommended dosages and precautions.

Cultivation:
- Native to: Europe, Asia, North America
- Zones: 2-8
- Soil: Well-drained, sandy soil with a pH of 6.0-7.5
- Propagation: By seed, cuttings, or layering

- Growing information and garden care: Juniper prefers full sun and is drought-tolerant once established. It can be susceptible to root rot in wet soil conditions. Pruning can be done in late winter to early spring to shape the plant.
- Insects and disease: Juniper berries are relatively resistant to insect pests and diseases, but they can still be affected by certain issues. Some of the most common insect pests that can affect juniper plants include spider mites, scale insects, and juniper berry moths. These pests can cause damage to the leaves and fruit of the plant, and may reduce the yield of berries.

In terms of diseases, juniper plants can be susceptible to several fungal pathogens, including cedar-apple rust, twig blight, and Phomopsis blight. These diseases can cause damage to the leaves, twigs, and berries of the plant, and may reduce the overall health and vigor of the plant.

To prevent insect pests and diseases, it is important to maintain good cultural practices, such as proper irrigation, fertilization, and pruning. Insecticides and fungicides may also be used to control pests and diseases, but it is important to follow all label instructions and safety precautions when using these chemicals.
- Harvesting and preparations: Juniper berries are typically harvested in the fall, when they are fully ripe and have turned a bluish-purple color. The berries are handpicked from the plant and can be used fresh or dried for later use. Here are some tips for harvesting and preparing juniper berries:
  - Harvesting: When harvesting juniper berries, it is important to wear gloves to protect your hands from the prickly foliage. Select berries that are fully ripe and have a blue-purple color. Gently pull the berries off the plant, being careful not to damage the branches or leaves.
  - Cleaning: Rinse the harvested berries under cool running water to remove any dirt or debris. Spread them out on a clean towel and gently pat dry.
  - Drying: If you plan to store the berries for later use, you can dry them by spreading them out in a single layer on a clean, dry surface. Place the berries in a warm, well-ventilated area out of direct sunlight. Stir the berries occasionally to ensure they dry evenly. They should be fully dried in 2-3 weeks.
  - Storage: Store the dried berries in an airtight container in a cool, dry place. They should keep for up to 1 year.
  - Preparation: Juniper berries can be used in a variety of culinary and medicinal preparations. They can be crushed or ground to make tea, tinctures, and capsules, or used whole to flavor gin, meat dishes, and pickles.

When using juniper berries, it is important to follow recommended dosages and precautions, as they can be toxic in high doses. It is also important to source the berries from a reputable supplier to ensure they are free from pesticides and other contaminants.

What medicines are made with this herb:

Juniper berries have been traditionally used in various medicinal preparations for their potential health benefits. Some of the medicinal preparations made with juniper berries include:

- Juniper berry essential oil: The essential oil of juniper berries is used in aromatherapy to promote relaxation and relieve stress. It is also used topically to help relieve muscle and joint pain.
- Herbal teas and tinctures: Juniper berry teas and tinctures have been used for their diuretic and detoxifying properties. They are believed to help flush toxins from the body and support kidney function.
- Capsules and tablets: Juniper berry capsules and tablets are used as a dietary supplement to support digestive health, improve immune function, and reduce inflammation.
- Gin: Juniper berries are a key ingredient in gin, a popular alcoholic beverage. Gin is believed to have some medicinal properties, and has been used historically to treat various ailments such as malaria and dyspepsia.
- Herbal poultices: Juniper berries can be crushed and used in herbal poultices to help relieve pain and inflammation.

It is important to note that while juniper berries have many potential health benefits, they can be toxic in high doses and may interact with certain medications. It is important to use juniper berries only under the guidance of a qualified healthcare professional.

What medicines this herb counteracts:

Juniper berries can potentially interact with certain medications, and may counteract their effects or cause unwanted side effects. Some medications that may be counteracted by juniper berries include:

- Diuretics: Juniper berries have diuretic properties and may enhance the effects of diuretic medications, which can increase the risk of dehydration and electrolyte imbalances.

- Diabetes medications: Juniper berries may lower blood sugar levels and may interfere with the effectiveness of diabetes medications, potentially leading to hypoglycemia (low blood sugar).
- Lithium: Juniper berries may increase the levels of lithium in the body, which can be toxic and may cause side effects such as tremors, confusion, and kidney damage.
- Blood pressure medications: Juniper berries may lower blood pressure and may enhance the effects of blood pressure medications, potentially causing hypotension (low blood pressure).
- Anticoagulants and antiplatelet medications: Juniper berries may have anticoagulant and antiplatelet properties, and may interact with medications such as aspirin and warfarin, potentially increasing the risk of bleeding.

It is important to consult with a qualified healthcare professional before using juniper berries, particularly if you are taking any medications or have any underlying health conditions. They can help determine whether juniper berries are safe and appropriate for you to use, and can advise you on any necessary precautions or monitoring.

Kava Kava

Herbal Identification:
- Common name: Kava Kava
- Latin binomial: Piper methysticum
- Other common names: Kava, Ava, Yaqona, Sakau
- Plant family: Piperaceae
- Botanical description: Kava kava (Piper methysticum) is a plant native to the South Pacific islands. It is a member of the pepper family (Piperaceae) and is known for its psychoactive and sedative effects.

Kava kava typically grows to a height of 6-10 feet and has broad, heart-shaped leaves that are green in color. The plant produces small flowers that are typically white or yellow in color and grow in clusters. The root of the kava plant is the part that is typically harvested and used for medicinal purposes.

The kava root is characterized by its brown, woody exterior and white interior, which is typically ground up into a fine powder or used to make a traditional kava drink. The active compounds in kava root are known as kavalactones, which are responsible for its psychoactive and anxiolytic effects.

Kava kava is typically grown in tropical environments and requires well-drained soil and plenty of moisture to thrive. It is often used for medicinal purposes, particularly in traditional South Pacific cultures, where it is used to alleviate anxiety and promote relaxation. However, it is important to note that kava kava can have potential side effects and should be used with caution under the guidance of a qualified healthcare professional.

Medicinal Properties:
- Recommended cultivars: There are different cultivars of Kava Kava, but the most commonly used for medicinal purposes is the noble kava variety.
- Parts used: The roots of the Kava Kava plant are used for medicinal purposes.
- Taste: Kava Kava has a bitter and slightly numbing taste.
- Actions: Kava Kava is a sedative, anxiolytic, muscle relaxant, and antispasmodic.
- Energetics: Kava Kava has a warming and drying energy.
- Specific indications: Kava kava (Piper methysticum) has been traditionally used for various indications, including anxiety, stress, insomnia, and as a muscle relaxant.

- Anxiety: Kava kava has been shown to have anxiolytic effects and may be useful for the treatment of generalized anxiety disorder (GAD). It may also be beneficial for social anxiety disorder (SAD) and other anxiety-related conditions.
- Stress: Kava kava has been traditionally used to reduce stress and promote relaxation. It may be helpful for stress-related conditions, such as tension headaches, nervousness, and restlessness.
- Insomnia: Kava kava has been used to promote sleep and may be helpful for insomnia. However, it is important to note that long-term use of kava kava may have negative effects on sleep quality and should be used with caution.
- Muscle relaxant: Kava kava has been traditionally used as a muscle relaxant and may be helpful for conditions such as muscle spasms and tension.

It is important to note that kava kava should be used with caution and under the guidance of a qualified healthcare professional, as it may have potential side effects and interact with other medications.

Medicinal preparations:
Kava kava (Piper methysticum) is typically prepared and consumed in traditional South Pacific cultures as a beverage made from the root of the plant. However, it is also available in other medicinal preparations for ease of use and standardized dosing.

Here are some common medicinal preparations of kava kava:
- Capsules or tablets: Kava kava can be found in capsule or tablet form, typically containing standardized doses of kavalactones. These can be convenient for those who prefer not to drink the traditional kava beverage.
- Tinctures: Kava kava tinctures are liquid extracts made from the root of the plant. They can be added to water or juice for easy consumption.
- Tea: Kava kava tea can be made by steeping the root of the plant in hot water for 5-10 minutes. However, it is important to note that kava tea may have a strong and bitter taste, which may not be suitable for everyone.
- Topical creams: Kava kava can also be found in topical creams, which can be applied to the skin for its analgesic and anti-inflammatory effects.

It is important to note that kava kava should be used with caution and under the guidance of a qualified healthcare professional, as it may have potential side effects and interact with other medications.
- Ratio and dosage information: The recommended dosage of Kava Kava varies depending on the preparation used and the specific indication. In general,

it is recommended to start with a low dose and gradually increase as needed. The root powder may be consumed in doses of 150-300mg up to three times per day. Kava Kava teas or tinctures are typically consumed in doses of 30-60 drops or 2-4 grams of dried root up to three times per day.

Medicinal uses:
Kava kava (Piper methysticum) has been traditionally used for a variety of medicinal purposes, primarily for its anxiolytic and sedative effects. Here are some of the medicinal uses of kava kava:
- Anxiety: Kava kava has been shown to have anxiolytic effects and may be useful for the treatment of generalized anxiety disorder (GAD) and social anxiety disorder (SAD). It may help to reduce symptoms of anxiety, such as nervousness, restlessness, and insomnia.
- Sleep disorders: Kava kava may be helpful for the treatment of sleep disorders, such as insomnia. It may help to improve sleep quality and duration.
- Muscle relaxation: Kava kava has been traditionally used as a muscle relaxant and may be helpful for conditions such as muscle spasms and tension.
- Pain relief: Kava kava may have analgesic effects and may be useful for the treatment of pain, such as headache and menstrual cramps.
- Withdrawal symptoms: Kava kava may be helpful for reducing withdrawal symptoms associated with alcohol, benzodiazepine, and opioid use.

It is important to note that kava kava should be used with caution and under the guidance of a qualified healthcare professional, as it may have potential side effects and interact with other medications.

• Precautions and contradictions: Kava kava (Piper methysticum) is generally considered safe when used in appropriate doses for short periods of time. However, it may have potential side effects and interact with other medications. Here are some precautions and contraindications for kava kava:
- Liver toxicity: Kava kava has been associated with rare cases of liver toxicity, particularly when used in high doses or for prolonged periods of time. Therefore, it is important to use kava kava under the guidance of a qualified healthcare professional and to avoid using it with other medications that may affect liver function.
- Pregnancy and breastfeeding: There is limited research on the safety of kava kava during pregnancy and breastfeeding, and it is not recommended for use during these periods.

- Interactions with medications: Kava kava may interact with certain medications, including benzodiazepines, antipsychotics, and alcohol. It is important to talk to a healthcare professional before using kava kava if you are taking any medications.
- Allergic reactions: Kava kava may cause allergic reactions in some people, particularly those who are allergic to plants in the pepper family (Piperaceae).
- Mental health conditions: Kava kava should be used with caution in individuals with mental health conditions, such as depression or bipolar disorder, as it may worsen symptoms.

It is important to use kava kava under the guidance of a qualified healthcare professional, and to follow recommended dosages and durations of use. If you experience any adverse effects or symptoms, stop using kava kava and seek medical attention.

Cultivation:
- Native to: Pacific Islands
- Zones: USDA Zones 11-12
- Soil: Kava Kava prefers well-draining, sandy soil with a pH between 6.0 and 7.5.
- Propagation: Kava Kava is typically propagated from stem cuttings.
- Growing information and garden care: Kava Kava requires warm temperatures and consistent moisture. It is typically grown in tropical regions and can be difficult to cultivate in other climates.
- Insects and disease: Kava kava (Piper methysticum) is relatively resistant to insects and disease, and is considered a hardy and low-maintenance plant. However, like all plants, it may be susceptible to certain pests and diseases under certain conditions.

Some of the pests that may affect kava kava include mealybugs, spider mites, and scale insects. These pests can damage the leaves and stems of the plant, and may reduce the yield and quality of the kava root. Proper pest management techniques, such as regular inspection, removal of infested plants, and the use of natural insecticides, can help to control these pests.

Kava kava is also susceptible to certain fungal and bacterial diseases, such as root rot and leaf spot. These diseases can be caused by poor soil drainage, excessive moisture, and poor air circulation. Proper cultural practices, such as planting in well-drained soil, regular pruning, and proper watering, can help to prevent these diseases. Additionally, the use of fungicides may be necessary in severe cases.

Overall, kava kava is a relatively low-maintenance plant, and with proper care and maintenance, it can be grown successfully with minimal insect and disease problems.
- Harvesting and preparations: Kava kava (Piper methysticum) is typically harvested for its root, which contains the active compounds that have medicinal properties. Here are some general guidelines for harvesting and preparing kava kava:
  - Harvesting: Kava kava is typically harvested when the plant is between three to five years old. The root is dug up, cleaned, and peeled to remove the outer layer of bark.
  - Drying: The peeled kava root is then cut into small pieces and dried in the sun or in a dehydrator. The dried root can then be stored for later use.
  - Preparation: To prepare kava kava for consumption, the dried root is ground into a fine powder. The powder is then mixed with water or another liquid, such as coconut milk, to create a drink. The drink is traditionally prepared by placing the kava powder in a cloth bag, adding water, and then squeezing the bag to extract the liquid.
  - Consumption: Kava kava is typically consumed as a drink, and is often used for its relaxing and sedative effects. It is important to use caution when consuming kava kava, as it may have potential side effects and interact with other medications. It is recommended to use kava kava under the guidance of a qualified healthcare professional.
  - Dosage: The appropriate dosage of kava kava can vary depending on the individual and the specific use. It is important to follow recommended dosages and to avoid using excessive amounts of kava kava, as this may increase the risk of side effects.

Overall, kava kava can be harvested and prepared for consumption with relative ease, but it is important to use caution and to follow recommended dosages to ensure safety and effectiveness.

What medicines are made with this herb:
Kava kava (Piper methysticum) is used in a variety of traditional and modern medicine preparations. Here are some examples:
- Herbal supplements: Kava kava is commonly used as a dietary supplement to promote relaxation and reduce anxiety.

- Traditional medicines: Kava kava has been used in traditional medicine practices in the South Pacific for centuries, and is often used to treat conditions such as pain, inflammation, and urinary tract infections.
- Topical preparations: Kava kava is sometimes used in topical creams or lotions for its anti-inflammatory properties, and may be used to relieve pain and swelling.
- Sleep aids: Kava kava may be used as a natural sleep aid, as it has sedative and hypnotic effects.
- Anxiolytics: Kava kava has been used as an anxiolytic to reduce anxiety and stress, and is sometimes used as an alternative to prescription medications such as benzodiazepines.
- Alcoholic beverages: Kava kava is traditionally consumed as a drink in the South Pacific, and is sometimes used in modern alcoholic beverages for its calming and relaxing effects.

It is important to use kava kava under the guidance of a qualified healthcare professional, and to follow recommended dosages and durations of use to ensure safety and effectiveness.

What medicines this herb counteracts:

Kava kava (Piper methysticum) may interact with certain medications and can counteract their effects. Here are some examples:

- Sedatives and tranquilizers: Kava kava has sedative and anxiolytic effects, and may interact with other sedative or tranquilizing medications, increasing their effects and potentially causing excessive drowsiness or sedation.
- Anti-convulsants: Kava kava may interact with anti-convulsant medications, reducing their effectiveness and potentially increasing the risk of seizures.
- Antidepressants: Kava kava may interact with certain antidepressant medications, such as selective serotonin reuptake inhibitors (SSRIs), increasing the risk of serotonin syndrome, a potentially life-threatening condition characterized by agitation, confusion, fever, and rapid heart rate.
- Alcohol: Kava kava is traditionally consumed as a drink in the South Pacific, and may interact with alcohol, increasing its sedative effects and potentially causing excessive drowsiness or impairment.

It is important to talk to a healthcare professional before using kava kava, especially if you are taking any medications or have any underlying health conditions, to avoid potential interactions or adverse effects.

Additionally, it is recommended to avoid using kava kava during pregnancy or breastfeeding, or if you have liver disease or a history of liver problems, as kava kava may cause liver damage.

Lady's Mantle

Herbal Identification:
- Common Name: Lady's Mantle
- Latin Binomial: Alchemilla vulgaris
- Other Common Names: Lion's Foot, Nine Hooks
- Plant Family: Rosaceae
- Botanical Description: Lady's Mantle is a perennial herb that grows up to 60cm tall. The leaves are deeply lobed and can range from 2-7cm in diameter. They are covered in fine hairs that collect dew and raindrops, giving them a distinctive appearance. The flowers are small and yellow-green, and appear in clusters from late spring to mid-summer. Lady's Mantle has a shallow root system and spreads easily through self-seeding. The plant is hardy and can grow in a variety of soil types, but prefers well-drained soil that is slightly acidic to neutral.

Lady's Mantle is closely related to other members of the Rosaceae family, including roses, strawberries, and apples.

Medicinal Properties:
- Recommended Cultivars: There are no specific recommended cultivars for Lady's Mantle.
- Parts Used: The aerial parts of the plant, including leaves and flowering tops, are used for medicinal purposes.
- Taste: Lady's Mantle has a slightly astringent taste.
- Actions: Lady's Mantle has astringent, anti-inflammatory, and antimicrobial properties.
- Energetics: Lady's Mantle is considered cooling and drying.
- Specific Indications: Lady's Mantle has astringent and anti-inflammatory properties, which make it useful for a variety of conditions. Some specific indications for using Lady's Mantle include:
  - Excessive menstrual bleeding: Lady's Mantle can help reduce heavy bleeding during menstruation and is often used to regulate the menstrual cycle.
  - Wounds and skin conditions: Lady's Mantle can be used topically to help heal wounds, reduce inflammation, and improve the appearance of the skin.
  - Digestive issues: Lady's Mantle can help soothe digestive upset, including diarrhea and indigestion.

- Urinary tract infections: Lady's Mantle has diuretic properties and may be useful in treating urinary tract infections.
- Menopause: Lady's Mantle may be helpful in relieving symptoms of menopause, such as hot flashes and night sweats.

Medicinal Preparations:
Lady's Mantle can be prepared and used in a variety of ways, including:
- Infusion: A tea made from Lady's Mantle leaves can be consumed to help with menstrual irregularities, digestive upset, and urinary tract infections. To make an infusion, steep 1-2 teaspoons of dried Lady's Mantle leaves in 8 ounces of hot water for 10-15 minutes, then strain and drink.
- Tincture: Lady's Mantle can also be prepared as a tincture, which is an alcohol-based extract of the herb. Tinctures are often used for their concentrated medicinal properties and can be taken directly or diluted in water. The typical dosage for a Lady's Mantle tincture is 30-60 drops, 2-3 times per day.
- Poultice: A poultice made from Lady's Mantle leaves can be applied topically to help with wounds, skin conditions, and inflammation. To make a poultice, crush fresh or dried Lady's Mantle leaves and apply directly to the affected area. Cover with a bandage or cloth and leave on for 20-30 minutes.
- Salve or ointment: Lady's Mantle can be infused into oil and used to make a salve or ointment for topical use. This can be helpful for wound healing, reducing inflammation, and improving skin health. Apply the salve or ointment to the affected area as needed.

It's important to consult with a healthcare provider before using any new herbal remedy, including Lady's Mantle, especially if you have any underlying medical conditions or are taking medications.

- Ratio and Dosage Information: The typical dosage for Lady's Mantle tea is 1-2 teaspoons of dried herb per cup of water, steeped for 10-15 minutes. Tincture dosage can vary depending on the preparation and the condition being treated.

Medicinal Uses:
Lady's Mantle has been traditionally used for a variety of medicinal purposes, including:
- Menstrual irregularities: Lady's Mantle can help reduce heavy menstrual bleeding and regulate the menstrual cycle.
- Wound healing: Lady's Mantle has astringent properties that can help reduce bleeding and promote healing of wounds.

- Skin health: Lady's Mantle can be applied topically to improve the appearance of the skin, reduce inflammation, and soothe irritated skin.
- Digestive health: Lady's Mantle can help soothe digestive upset, including diarrhea and indigestion.
- Urinary tract infections: Lady's Mantle has diuretic properties and may be useful in treating urinary tract infections.
- Menopause: Lady's Mantle may be helpful in relieving symptoms of menopause, such as hot flashes and night sweats.

While Lady's Mantle has been traditionally used for these purposes, it's important to note that more research is needed to fully understand its medicinal properties and potential uses. It's always a good idea to consult with a healthcare provider before using any herbal remedy for medicinal purposes.

• Precautions and Contradictions: Lady's Mantle is generally considered safe when used in recommended amounts. However, there are a few precautions and contradictions to be aware of:

- Pregnancy and breastfeeding: There is not enough scientific evidence to determine the safety of using Lady's Mantle during pregnancy and breastfeeding. It's best to avoid using Lady's Mantle during these times unless under the supervision of a healthcare provider.
- Allergies: Some people may be allergic to Lady's Mantle. If you experience symptoms such as rash, hives, or difficulty breathing after using Lady's Mantle, discontinue use and seek medical attention.
- Drug interactions: There is not enough information to determine the potential interactions between Lady's Mantle and prescription medications or other herbs. It's always a good idea to consult with a healthcare provider before using any herbal remedy, especially if you are taking medications.
- Heavy menstrual bleeding: While Lady's Mantle is traditionally used to help reduce heavy menstrual bleeding, it may also have blood-thinning effects. If you have a bleeding disorder or are taking medications that affect blood clotting, it's best to avoid using Lady's Mantle.

As with any herbal remedy, it's important to use Lady's Mantle with caution and under the guidance of a healthcare provider.

Cultivation:
• Native to: Lady's Mantle is native to Europe and western Asia.
• Zones: Lady's Mantle can be grown in USDA zones 3-8.
• Soil: Lady's Mantle prefers well-drained soil that is slightly acidic to neutral.
• Propagation: Lady's Mantle can be propagated by seed or by dividing established plants.

- Growing Information and Garden Care: Lady's Mantle prefers partial shade to full sun and can be grown in a variety of soil types. It is a low-maintenance plant that requires regular watering and occasional fertilization.
- Insects and Disease: Lady's Mantle is generally a hardy and disease-resistant plant. However, there are a few insects and diseases that can affect it:
  - Powdery mildew: This fungal disease can affect the leaves and stems of Lady's Mantle, causing a white powdery coating on the foliage. To prevent powdery mildew, make sure the plant is well-ventilated and not overcrowded. If powdery mildew is present, remove the affected foliage and treat with a fungicide if necessary.
  - Aphids: These small insects can suck the sap from Lady's Mantle, causing distorted growth and yellowing foliage. To control aphids, you can use insecticidal soap or neem oil.
  - Slugs and snails: These pests can eat holes in the foliage and damage the plant. To control slugs and snails, you can use baits or physical barriers such as copper tape or eggshells around the base of the plant.

Overall, Lady's Mantle is a relatively low-maintenance plant that is not prone to many pests or diseases. Proper care and maintenance can help keep the plant healthy and prevent issues from arising.

- Harvesting and Preparations: The leaves and aerial parts of Lady's Mantle can be harvested for medicinal purposes. Here are some guidelines for harvesting and preparations:
  - Harvesting: The best time to harvest Lady's Mantle is when it is in full bloom, usually in the summer months. You can harvest the aerial parts of the plant (leaves and stems) by cutting them off with sharp scissors or pruning shears. It's best to harvest in the morning when the dew has dried but before the sugets too hot.
  - • Drying: Once you have harvested the plant, you can dry it for later use. To do this, spread the leaves and stems out in a single layer on a clean, dry surface. You can use a dehydrator, an oven set to a low temperature, or simply air dry them. Once the plant material is completely dry and crispy, store it in an airtight container in a cool, dry place.
  - Medicinal preparations: Lady's Mantle can be prepared in a variety of ways, including teas, tinctures, and capsules. Here are some common preparations:
  - Tea: To make a tea, steep 1-2 teaspoons of dried Lady's Mantle in a cup of hot water for 10-15 minutes. Strain and drink up to three cups per day.
  - Tincture: A tincture is a concentrated liquid extract made by steeping the plant in alcohol or glycerin. You can take 30-60 drops of Lady's Mantle tincture up to three times per day.

> Capsules: You can find Lady's Mantle capsules at health food stores and online retailers. Follow the manufacturer's instructions for dosage.

• Ratio and dosage information: The appropriate ratio and dosage of Lady's Mantle will depend on the specific preparation and individual factors such as age, health status, and weight. It's best to consult with a healthcare provider or herbalist for personalized guidance.

Overall, Lady's Mantle is a versatile and easy-to-use herb with a range of medicinal benefits. By following proper harvesting and preparation techniques, you can enjoy the many benefits of this plant.

What medicines are made with this herb:
Lady's Mantle is commonly used in herbal medicine to treat various health conditions, and it is included in many traditional remedies. While it is not typically used in conventional medicine, it can be found in some over-the-counter herbal supplements and tinctures.

Here are a few examples of medicines that may contain Lady's Mantle:
> Menstrual support supplements: Lady's Mantle is often used to regulate menstrual cycles and reduce menstrual pain. It may be included in herbal supplements designed to support menstrual health.
> Digestive aids: Lady's Mantle has astringent properties, which means it can help to tighten and tone tissues. This makes it useful for treating digestive issues such as diarrhea, colitis, and gastritis. It may be included in digestive aids or remedies.
> Skin care products: Lady's Mantle is known for its anti-inflammatory and antioxidant properties, which make it useful for treating skin conditions such as eczema, acne, and rosacea. It may be included in creams, lotions, and other topical preparations.

Keep in mind that the quality and efficacy of herbal supplements can vary widely, and it's important to choose products from reputable manufacturers. It's also important to talk to your healthcare provider before taking any new supplements or medications, especially if you have a pre-existing medical condition or are taking prescription medications.

What medicines this herb counteracts:
There are no known medications or herbs that Lady's Mantle specifically counteracts or interacts with. However, as with any herbal supplement, it's important to talk to your healthcare provider before taking Lady's Mantle if you

are currently taking prescription medications or have a pre-existing medical condition.

This is because Lady's Mantle may interact with certain medications or affect certain medical conditions, particularly if taken in large doses or for an extended period of time. Additionally, some individuals may be allergic to Lady's Mantle or experience side effects such as stomach upset or skin irritation. If you experience any negative side effects while taking Lady's Mantle, stop use immediately and consult with your healthcare provider.

Lavender

Herbal Identification:
- Common name: Lavender
- Latin binomial: Lavandula angustifolia
- Other common names: English lavender, True lavender, Garden lavender
- Plant family: Lamiaceae (mint family)
- Botanical description: Lavender is a perennial shrub that belongs to the Lamiaceae family. It typically grows to a height of 30-60cm, although some cultivars can grow up to 1-2 meters. The leaves are narrow, linear, and silvery-grey in color, and are arranged in opposing pairs along the stems. The leaves are also highly aromatic and contain essential oils. The flowers are arranged in dense, spike-like clusters on long, slender stems that rise above the foliage. The flowers are usually shades of purple or blue, although some cultivars may have pink or white flowers. The individual flowers have a tubular shape and are surrounded by small bracts. Lavender blooms from mid to late summer, depending on the cultivar and climate. The plant has a woody stem and can live for several years if properly cared for.

Medicinal Properties:
- Recommended cultivars: Lavandula angustifolia 'Munstead' and 'Hidcote' are commonly used in herbal medicine.
- Parts used: The flowers and occasionally the leaves.
- Taste: Aromatic, slightly bitter, and pungent.
- Actions: Nervine, carminative, anti-spasmodic, anti-inflammatory, analgesic, sedative, and antidepressant.
- Energetics: Cooling and drying.
- Specific indications: Lavender has a variety of medicinal properties and has been used traditionally to treat a range of ailments. Some of its specific indications include:
  - Anxiety and stress: Lavender is commonly used to promote relaxation and relieve feelings of anxiety and stress. It has a calming effect on the nervous system and can help to reduce feelings of restlessness and irritability.
  - Insomnia: Lavender can be used to promote restful sleep and relieve insomnia. It can be taken as a tea or used in aromatherapy to create a calming environment conducive to sleep.
  - Headaches and migraines: Lavender has been used to relieve headaches and migraines, particularly those caused by tension and stress.

- Digestive issues: Lavender can be used to relieve digestive issues such as bloating, flatulence, and abdominal cramps. It can also be used to stimulate appetite and aid in digestion.
- Respiratory issues: Lavender can help to relieve respiratory issues such as coughs, colds, and bronchitis. It has expectorant properties, which help to loosen and expel phlegm from the respiratory tract.
- Skin conditions: Lavender has antiseptic and anti-inflammatory properties, which make it useful for treating skin conditions such as eczema, acne, and psoriasis. It can also be used to soothe insect bites and minor burns.
- Menstrual cramps: Lavender can help to relieve menstrual cramps and other symptoms of premenstrual syndrome (PMS). It has antispasmodic properties, which help to relax the muscles of the uterus and relieve cramping.

It is important to note that while lavender is generally considered safe, it may not be appropriate for everyone. As with all herbal remedies, it is important to consult with a healthcare professional before using lavender to treat any medical condition.

Medicinal preparations:
Lavender can be used in a variety of medicinal preparations, including:
- Tea: Lavender flowers can be brewed as a tea and consumed to promote relaxation, relieve anxiety, aid in digestion, and promote restful sleep.
- Essential oil: Lavender essential oil is widely used in aromatherapy to promote relaxation and relieve anxiety. It can also be applied topically to the skin to relieve minor burns, insect bites, and other skin irritations.
- Tincture: A lavender tincture can be made by soaking the dried flowers in alcohol or glycerin. This preparation can be used to relieve headaches, anxiety, and other conditions.
- Salve: A lavender salve can be made by combining the essential oil with a carrier oil, such as coconut or olive oil, and beeswax. This preparation can be applied topically to the skin to relieve minor burns, insect bites, and other skin irritations.
- Inhalation: Lavender essential oil can be added to a diffuser or humidifier to create a calming environment. It can also be added to a bowl of hot water and inhaled to relieve respiratory issues.

The appropriate dosage and method of preparation will depend on the specific condition being treated and the individual's age, weight, and overall health. It is important to consult with a healthcare professional or licensed herbalist before using lavender or any other herbal remedy.

- Ratio and dosage information: Infusion: 1-2 teaspoons of dried flowers per cup of water, 1-2 cups daily. Tincture: 1-2 ml, three times daily. Essential oil: 2-3 drops diluted in a carrier oil, applied topically or added to bathwater. Herbal pillows: Place dried flowers in a muslin bag and place under pillow. Bath salts: Mix 1 cup of Epsom salt with 10 drops of lavender essential oil and add to bathwater.

Medicinal uses:
Lavender has a wide range of medicinal uses, some of which include:
- Promoting relaxation: Lavender is commonly used to promote relaxation and relieve stress and anxiety. It can be consumed as a tea or used in aromatherapy to create a calming environment.
- Relieving headaches and migraines: Lavender can be used to relieve tension headaches and migraines, which are often caused by stress and anxiety.
- Improving sleep: Lavender is often used to improve sleep quality and promote restful sleep. It can be consumed as a tea or used in aromatherapy to create a relaxing environment.
- Relieving digestive issues: Lavender can help to relieve digestive issues such as bloating, flatulence, and abdominal cramps. It can also stimulate appetite and aid in digestion.
- Relieving respiratory issues: Lavender has expectorant properties and can help to relieve coughs, colds, and bronchitis.
- Treating skin conditions: Lavender has antiseptic and anti-inflammatory properties and can be used to treat skin conditions such as eczema, acne, and psoriasis. It can also be used to soothe insect bites and minor burns.
- Relieving menstrual cramps: Lavender has antispasmodic properties and can help to relax the muscles of the uterus, relieving menstrual cramps and other symptoms of PMS.

It is important to note that while lavender is generally considered safe, it may not be appropriate for everyone. As with all herbal remedies, it is important to consult with a healthcare professional before using lavender to treat any medical condition.

- Precautions and contradictions: Lavender is generally considered safe when used appropriately. However, there are a few precautions and contraindications to keep in mind:
- Allergic reactions: Some people may experience an allergic reaction to lavender. If you have a known allergy to plants in the Lamiaceae family

(which includes mint, rosemary, and sage), you may also be allergic to lavender.
- ➢ Drug interactions: Lavender may interact with certain medications, particularly sedatives and CNS depressants. It is important to consult with a healthcare professional before using lavender if you are taking any medications.
- ➢ Skin irritation: Lavender essential oil can cause skin irritation in some people, particularly if it is not diluted properly. It is important to perform a patch test before using lavender essential oil topically.
- ➢ Hormone disruption: Some studies suggest that lavender may have estrogenic effects and could potentially disrupt hormone balance. It is important to avoid using lavender in high doses or for extended periods of time if you have a history of hormone-related conditions.
- ➢ Internal use: While lavender is generally considered safe when used externally or consumed in small amounts as a tea, consuming large amounts of lavender oil or tincture can be toxic and lead to nausea, vomiting, and other symptoms.

As with all herbal remedies, it is important to consult with a healthcare professional or licensed herbalist before using lavender or any other herbal remedy.

Cultivation:
- Native to: The Mediterranean region, particularly the mountainous areas of the western Mediterranean.
- Zones: 5-9
- Soil: Well-draining, alkaline soil with a pH of 6.5-7.5.
- Propagation: Lavender can be propagated from cuttings, layering, or seeds.
- Growing information and garden care: Lavender prefers full sun and moderate watering. It can be grown in pots or in the ground, and benefits from annual pruning.
- Insects and disease: Lavender is generally a hardy and disease-resistant plant, but it can still be affected by a few pests and diseases. Some common insects that can infest lavender include:
- ➢ Aphids: These small, soft-bodied insects can suck sap from the plant and cause yellowing and stunted growth.
- ➢ Spider mites: These tiny pests can cause yellowing and stippling on the leaves of the plant.
- ➢ Thrips: These small, slender insects can cause silvery patches on the leaves and flowers of the plant.

To prevent insect infestations, it is important to maintain good hygiene in your lavender garden, such as removing dead or diseased plant material and avoiding overcrowding.

Lavender is also susceptible to a few diseases, including:
- Root rot: This fungal disease can cause the plant to wilt and eventually die. It is often caused by overwatering or poor drainage.
- Gray mold: This fungal disease can cause gray, fuzzy growth on the leaves and flowers of the plant. It is often caused by high humidity and poor air circulation.

To prevent fungal diseases, it is important to avoid overwatering and provide good air circulation around the plant. If you notice any signs of disease, it is important to remove and dispose of the affected plant material to prevent the spread of the disease.

- Harvesting and preparations: Harvesting lavender is best done when the plant has just started to bloom, which is typically in midsummer. The flowers should be harvested in the morning after the dew has evaporated but before the sun is too hot. The flowers can be harvested by cutting the stems with a sharp knife or pruning shears.

Once harvested, the flowers can be used fresh or dried for later use. To dry the flowers, they should be hung upside down in a cool, dark, well-ventilated area. Once the flowers are dry, they can be stored in airtight containers.

Lavender can be used in a variety of preparations, including teas, tinctures, oils, and balms. To make a lavender tea, steep 1-2 teaspoons of dried flowers in 1 cup of hot water for 5-10 minutes. Lavender essential oil can be used topically or in aromatherapy, but should always be diluted properly in a carrier oil before use.

To make a lavender-infused oil or balm, the dried flowers can be infused in a carrier oil such as olive oil or coconut oil for several weeks. The resulting oil can be used topically for a variety of purposes, including massage, skin care, and aromatherapy.

It is important to note that while lavender is generally considered safe for most people, it is always important to consult with a healthcare professional or licensed herbalist before using lavender or any other herbal remedy.

What medicines are made with this herb:

Lavender is a versatile herb that can be used in a variety of medicinal and cosmetic products. Here are some examples of medicines and products that can be made with lavender:

- Essential oil: Lavender essential oil is a popular ingredient in aromatherapy and is used to promote relaxation and reduce stress. It can also be used topically to soothe skin irritation and promote wound healing.
- Tea: Lavender tea can be used to help calm the mind and promote relaxation. It can also be used to relieve headaches and improve digestion.
- Tincture: Lavender tincture can be used as a natural remedy for anxiety, depression, and insomnia.
- Massage oil: Lavender-infused massage oil can be used to promote relaxation and relieve muscle tension.
- Skin care products: Lavender is a popular ingredient in skin care products, as it has anti-inflammatory and antimicrobial properties that can help soothe and heal the skin. It can be found in products such as lotions, creams, and soaps.
- Hair care products: Lavender can also be found in hair care products, as it can help soothe the scalp and promote healthy hair growth.
- Culinary uses: Lavender can also be used in culinary applications, such as in baking or as a garnish for drinks.

It is important to note that while lavender is generally considered safe for most people, it is always important to consult with a healthcare professional or licensed herbalist before using lavender or any other herbal remedy.

What medicines this herb counteract:

Lavender does not counteract any specific medicines, but it may interact with sedative medications and increase their effects. Therefore, it is important to consult with a healthcare professional before taking any new herbal remedies, particularly if you are taking other medications.

Lemon Balm

Herbal Identification:
- Common Name: Lemon Balm
- Latin Binomial: Melissa officinalis
- Other Common Names: Bee balm, Cure-all, Dropsy plant, Garden balm, Melissa, Sweet balm
- Plant Family: Lamiaceae (mint family)
- Botanical Description: Lemon Balm (Melissa officinalis) is a perennial herb that belongs to the mint family (Lamiaceae). It can grow up to 2 feet (60 cm) tall and has a square, hairy stem that is branched near the top. The leaves of lemon balm are opposite, ovate or heart-shaped, and have a deeply veined surface with a wrinkled appearance. They are light green in color and have a slightly toothed margin. When crushed, the leaves emit a strong, pleasant lemon scent.

The flowers of lemon balm are small and white or pale pink, and grow in clusters at the leaf axils. They are tubular and bilaterally symmetrical, with two lips and four stamens. The fruit of lemon balm is a small, brown, nut-like achene that contains a single seed.

Lemon balm can be distinguished from other members of the mint family by its lemony scent and the shape of its leaves. It is closely related to other mint family members such as peppermint (Mentha x piperita) and spearmint (Mentha spicata). Lemon balm is commonly grown as an ornamental herb in gardens and can also be found growing wild in Europe and Asia.

Medicinal Properties:
- Recommended Cultivars: None specific, but it is recommended to grow from reputable seed sources to ensure quality.
- Parts Used: Leaves and stems
- Taste: Lemon balm has a pleasant, lemony taste.
- Actions: Nervine, carminative, antispasmodic, diaphoretic, sedative, antiviral, antioxidant
- Energetics: Cooling, drying
- Specific Indications: Lemon balm has been used for various medicinal purposes for centuries. Some of the specific indications for which it may be helpful include:
  - Anxiety: Lemon balm has a calming effect on the nervous system and can help to reduce feelings of anxiety and stress.

- Insomnia: Lemon balm has sedative properties that can help to promote relaxation and improve sleep quality.
- Digestive issues: Lemon balm can be useful in treating digestive issues such as bloating, gas, and indigestion.
- Cold sores: Lemon balm has antiviral properties that can help to reduce the frequency and severity of cold sores.
- Menstrual cramps: Lemon balm can help to reduce menstrual cramps and other symptoms associated with menstruation.
- Cognitive function: Lemon balm may improve cognitive function, including memory and attention, and may be useful in the treatment of Alzheimer's disease.
- Thyroid health: Lemon balm may help to regulate an overactive thyroid and reduce symptoms of hyperthyroidism.
- Herpes simplex virus: Lemon balm has antiviral properties that may be helpful in the treatment of herpes simplex virus infections.

It is important to note that these indications are based on traditional uses of lemon balm and may not be supported by clinical research. As with any herb or supplement, it is important to consult with a healthcare practitioner before using lemon balm for medicinal purposes.

Medicinal Preparations:
Lemon balm can be prepared and used in various ways for medicinal purposes. Some of the most common medicinal preparations of lemon balm include:
- Tea: Lemon balm tea can be made by steeping fresh or dried leaves in hot water for 5-10 minutes. This can be consumed 1-3 times daily for its calming and digestive properties.
- Tincture: Lemon balm tincture is a concentrated liquid extract made by steeping fresh or dried leaves in alcohol. It can be taken orally and may be more effective than tea for certain indications.
- Essential oil: Lemon balm essential oil can be used topically or inhaled for its calming and antiviral properties. It should be diluted before use and should not be ingested.
- Capsules: Lemon balm capsules are available in health food stores and can be taken orally for anxiety, insomnia, and other indications.
- Salve: Lemon balm salve can be applied topically to cold sores or other skin irritations for its antiviral and soothing properties.

The appropriate preparation and dosage of lemon balm will depend on the specific indication and individual circumstances. It is important to consult with a healthcare practitioner before using lemon balm for medicinal purposes and to follow dosage instructions carefully.

• Ratio and Dosage Information: For tea, use 1-2 teaspoons of dried lemon balm leaves per cup of water, steeped for 10-15 minutes. For tincture, take 2-4 ml up to three times per day. For infused oil, use 1-2 cups of fresh lemon balm leaves per cup of oil and steep for several weeks before straining.

Medicinal Uses:
Lemon balm has been used for various medicinal purposes for centuries, and is known for its calming and soothing properties. Some of the most common medicinal uses of lemon balm include:
- Anxiety: Lemon balm has a calming effect on the nervous system and can help to reduce feelings of anxiety and stress.
- Insomnia: Lemon balm has sedative properties that can help to promote relaxation and improve sleep quality.
- Digestive issues: Lemon balm can be useful in treating digestive issues such as bloating, gas, and indigestion.
- Cold sores: Lemon balm has antiviral properties that can help to reduce the frequency and severity of cold sores.
- Menstrual cramps: Lemon balm can help to reduce menstrual cramps and other symptoms associated with menstruation.
- Cognitive function: Lemon balm may improve cognitive function, including memory and attention, and may be useful in the treatment of Alzheimer's disease.
- Thyroid health: Lemon balm may help to regulate an overactive thyroid and reduce symptoms of hyperthyroidism.
- Herpes simplex virus: Lemon balm has antiviral properties that may be helpful in the treatment of herpes simplex virus infections.

Lemon balm may also have anti-inflammatory, antioxidant, and immune-modulating effects, and may be useful in the treatment of other conditions such as high blood pressure and diabetes. However, further research is needed to determine its effectiveness for these indications.

It is important to note that lemon balm should not be used as a replacement for conventional medical treatment, and it is important to consult with a healthcare practitioner before using lemon balm for medicinal purposes.

• Precautions and Contradictions: Lemon balm is generally considered safe when used appropriately, but there are some precautions and contraindications to be aware of:

- Pregnancy and breastfeeding: Lemon balm is generally considered safe for pregnant and breastfeeding women when used in small amounts as a flavoring agent in food. However, medicinal doses should be avoided, as there is not enough research on its safety in these populations.
- Children: Lemon balm is considered safe for children when used in appropriate doses, but it is important to consult with a healthcare practitioner before using it in children.
- 3 Thyroid conditions: Lemon balm can interact with thyroid medications, so people with thyroid conditions should consult a healthcare practitioner before using lemon balm.
- Sedative medications: Lemon balm can enhance the effects of sedative medications, so it should not be used in combination with these medications without the supervision of a healthcare practitioner.
- 5 Allergies: Some people may be allergic to lemon balm, and should avoid using it.
- 6 Sun sensitivity: Lemon balm may cause sun sensitivity in some people, so it is important to use sunscreen and protective clothing when using lemon balm topically.

It is important to consult with a healthcare practitioner before using lemon balm for medicinal purposes, especially if you have any underlying medical conditions or are taking medications.

Cultivation:
- Native to: Southern Europe and the Mediterranean
- Zones: Lemon balm grows best in zones 4-9.
- Soil: Lemon balm prefers well-drained, moist soil with a pH of 6.0-7.5.
- Propagation: Lemon balm can be propagated by seed or division.
- Growing Information and Garden Care: Lemon balm is a hardy perennial that prefers full sun to part shade. It can be grown in pots or in the ground. Lemon balm requires regular watering and benefits from occasional fertilization with a balanced fertilizer.
- Insects and Disease: Lemon balm is generally a hardy and disease-resistant plant, but it can be susceptible to some pests and diseases. Some of the common insects that can affect lemon balm include:
  - Aphids: These small, soft-bodied insects can suck the sap from the leaves and stems, causing damage to the plant.
  - Spider mites: These tiny insects can cause yellowing and stippling of the leaves, and can reduce the overall vigor of the plant.
  - Whiteflies: These small, moth-like insects can suck the sap from the leaves, causing yellowing and stunted growth.

To control these insects, you can use insecticidal soap, neem oil, or other natural insecticides. In some cases, pruning the affected areas may also be necessary.

Lemon balm can also be susceptible to some diseases, such as powdery mildew and leaf spot. These diseases can cause yellowing and wilting of the leaves, and can reduce the overall vigor of the plant. To prevent these diseases, it is important to keep the plant well-watered, but not over-watered, and to provide good air circulation around the plant. In some cases, fungicides may also be necessary to control these diseases.

Overall, with proper care and maintenance, lemon balm can be a healthy and productive plant in the garden.
- Harvesting and Preparations: Lemon balm can be harvested throughout the growing season, but the best time to harvest is just before the plant begins to flower, when the essential oils are most concentrated. To harvest, simply cut the stems of the plant just above a set of leaves, leaving enough of the plant for it to continue growing.

Once harvested, lemon balm can be used fresh or dried. To dry lemon balm, tie the stems in small bundles and hang them upside down in a well-ventilated area out of direct sunlight. Once the leaves are dry and brittle, remove them from the stems and store in an airtight container in a cool, dark place.

Lemon balm can be used in a variety of ways, including:
- Tea: Lemon balm tea can be made by steeping fresh or dried leaves in hot water for 5-10 minutes. The tea can be sweetened with honey or other natural sweeteners, and can be enjoyed hot or iced.
- Tincture: Lemon balm tincture can be made by steeping fresh or dried leaves in alcohol, such as vodka or brandy, for several weeks. The resulting tincture can be taken orally in small doses.
- 3 Essential oil: Lemon balm essential oil can be extracted from the plant using steam distillation. The oil can be used in aromatherapy, massage, or added to bathwater.
- 4 Culinary use: Lemon balm can be used to flavor a variety of dishes, including soups, salads, and desserts. The leaves can be used fresh or dried, and can be chopped finely or left whole.

It is important to follow dosage guidelines and use caution when using lemon balm for medicinal purposes. Always consult with a healthcare practitioner before using lemon balm if you have any underlying medical conditions or are taking medications.

What medicines are made with this herb:

Lemon balm is a versatile herb that is used in a variety of medicinal and cosmetic preparations. Some of the medicines and products that can be made with lemon balm include:

- Herbal tea blends: Lemon balm is often combined with other herbs, such as chamomile, lavender, or valerian, to create relaxing and calming tea blends.
- Tinctures: Lemon balm tinctures can be made by steeping fresh or dried leaves in alcohol, and are often used to help relieve anxiety, insomnia, and di=-gestive issues.
- 3 Essential oil: Lemon balm essential oil is extracted from the leaves and can be used in aromatherapy, massage, or added to bathwater.
- 4 Salves and balms: Lemon balm can be infused in oil and used to make healing salves and balms for the skin.
- 5 Cosmetics: Lemon balm is often used in natural cosmetics, such as soaps, lotions, and facial cleansers, due to its soothing and calming properties.
- 6 Culinary use: Lemon balm can also be used in cooking and baking, adding a lemony flavor to dishes and desserts.

Lemon balm is a safe and gentle herb, but it is important to use caution and follow dosage guidelines when using it for medicinal purposes. Always consult with a healthcare practitioner before using lemon balm if you have any underlying medical conditions or are taking medications.

What medicines this herb counteract:

There is no specific information on which medicines lemon balm counteracts. However, it can interact with thyroid medications, so people with thyroid conditions should consult a healthcare practitioner before using lemon balm. Additionally, lemon balm may have a sedative effect and may interact with medications that have sedative properties, such as benzodiazepines, barbiturates, and certain antidepressants. As always, it is important to consult with a healthcare practitioner before using any herbal remedies if you have underlying medical conditions or are taking medications.

Licorice

Herbal Identification:
- Common Name: Licorice
- Latin Binomial: Glycyrrhiza glabra
- Other Common Names: Sweet root, gan zao (Chinese)
- Plant Family: Fabaceae (Legume family)
- Botanical Description: Licorice (Glycyrrhiza glabra) is a perennial herbaceous plant that belongs to the Fabaceae or pea family. It is native to the Mediterranean region and southwestern Asia and is widely cultivated in many parts of the world.

The plant can grow up to 1 meter tall and has a woody root system that can reach up to 4 meters in length. The leaves of the licorice plant are pinnately compound, with 9 to 17 leaflets that are elliptic in shape and 2 to 4 cm long. The plant produces small, purplish-blue flowers that grow in spikes on long stems.

The root of the licorice plant is the most commonly used part in traditional medicine and has a sweet, earthy flavor. The root is woody and can be up to 2.5 cm in diameter. When dried, the licorice root is dark brown on the outside and yellow on the inside.

Licorice is often confused with wild licorice (Astragalus glycyphyllos) and Spanish licorice (Amorpha fruticosa), which are both members of the pea family and have similar-looking roots. However, they do not have the same sweet flavor or medicinal properties as Glycyrrhiza glabra.

Medicinal Properties:
- Recommended cultivars: Glycyrrhiza glabra var. typica, Glycyrrhiza glabra var. glandulifera
- Parts used: The roots are the part used medicinally
- Taste: Sweet
- Actions: Demulcent, expectorant, anti-inflammatory, antispasmodic, adrenal tonic, immune modulator, hepatoprotective, anti-ulcer, anti-viral
- Energetics: Cooling and moistening
- Specific Indications: Licorice root has a variety of medicinal properties and can be used to treat a wide range of conditions. Some specific indications for licorice root include:

- Respiratory infections: Licorice root has expectorant and anti-inflammatory properties, making it useful for treating respiratory infections such as bronchitis, colds, and flu.
- Digestive issues: Licorice root can be used to treat digestive complaints such as acid reflux, stomach ulcers, and constipation. It has demulcent and soothing properties that help to protect the mucous membranes of the digestive tract.
- Adrenal support: Licorice root is known to support adrenal function and can be used to treat adrenal fatigue and other conditions related to stress.
- Hormonal balance: Licorice root contains compounds that can help to regulate hormone levels in the body, making it useful for treating conditions such as polycystic ovary syndrome (PCOS) and menopause.
- Skin conditions: Licorice root has anti-inflammatory and antimicrobial properties that make it useful for treating skin conditions such as eczema, psoriasis, and acne.

It is important to note that licorice root should be used under the guidance of a healthcare professional, as it can interact with certain medications and can cause side effects in some people.

Medicinal Preparations:
Licorice root can be prepared in a variety of ways for medicinal use. Some common medicinal preparations of licorice root include:
- Licorice tea: Steep 1-2 teaspoons of dried licorice root in a cup of hot water for 5-10 minutes. Licorice tea can be consumed 2-3 times per day to treat respiratory and digestive complaints.
- Licorice tincture: Licorice root can be extracted in alcohol to make a tincture. The recommended dosage for licorice tincture is 1-5 mL, taken up to three times per day.
- Licorice capsules: Licorice root can be purchased in capsule form, with a recommended dosage of 200-400 mg, taken up to three times per day.
- Licorice syrup: Licorice root can be simmered in water with other herbs and sweeteners to make a syrup. Licorice syrup can be taken to soothe sore throats and coughs.

It is important to note that licorice root should not be used long-term or in high doses, as it can cause side effects such as high blood pressure, low potassium levels, and fluid retention. Licorice should not be used by individuals with high blood pressure, kidney disease, or heart disease, and it should not be used during pregnancy or breastfeeding. It is important to consult a healthcare provider before using licorice root or any other herbal supplement. • Ratio and Dosage

Information: 1-4 grams of licorice root per day (dried herb equivalent), or as directed by a healthcare provider.

Medicinal Uses:
Licorice root has a long history of use in traditional medicine and has been used to treat a variety of conditions. Some medicinal uses of licorice root include:
- Respiratory infections: Licorice root has expectorant and anti-inflammatory properties, making it useful for treating respiratory infections such as bronchitis, colds, and flu.
- Digestive issues: Licorice root can be used to treat digestive complaints such as acid reflux, stomach ulcers, and constipation. It has demulcent and soothing properties that help to protect the mucous membranes of the digestive tract.
- Adrenal support: Licorice root is known to support adrenal function and can be used to treat adrenal fatigue and other conditions related to stress.
- Hormonal balance: Licorice root contains compounds that can help to regulate hormone levels in the body, making it useful for treating conditions such as polycystic ovary syndrome (PCOS) and menopause.
- Skin conditions: Licorice root has anti-inflammatory and antimicrobial properties that make it useful for treating skin conditions such as eczema, psoriasis, and acne.
- Sore throat and cough: Licorice root can be used to soothe sore throats and coughs. It can be consumed as a tea or taken in syrup form.
- Immune system support: Licorice root has immune-modulating properties that can help to support the immune system.

It is important to note that licorice root should be used under the guidance of a healthcare professional, as it can interact with certain medications and can cause side effects in some people.
- Precautions and Contradictions: Licorice root should be used with caution and under the guidance of a healthcare professional, as it can interact with certain medications and can cause side effects in some people. Some precautions and contraindications of licorice root include:
  - High blood pressure: Licorice root can cause an increase in blood pressure and should be avoided by individuals with high blood pressure.
  - Low potassium levels: Licorice root can cause a decrease in potassium levels in the body, which can be dangerous for individuals with certain medical conditions.

- Hormonal imbalances: Licorice root can affect hormone levels in the body and should be avoided by individuals with hormone-sensitive conditions, such as breast cancer.
- Kidney disease: Licorice root can worsen kidney disease and should be avoided by individuals with this condition.
- Pregnancy and breastfeeding: Licorice root should be avoided during pregnancy and breastfeeding, as it can have negative effects on fetal development and lactation.
- Medication interactions: Licorice root can interact with certain medications, such as blood thinners, diuretics, and corticosteroids, and should be avoided or used with caution by individuals taking these medications.

It is important to speak with a healthcare professional before using licorice root or any other herbal supplement, especially if you have a medical condition or are taking medication.

Cultivation:
- Native to: Licorice is native to the Mediterranean region and parts of Asia, including China and India.
- Zones: Licorice can be grown in zones 6-9.
- Soil (pH and type of soil): Licorice prefers well-drained sandy loam soil with a pH between 6.0-8.0.
- Propagation: Licorice can be propagated by seed or root division.
- Growing information and garden care: Licorice prefers full sun to partial shade and requires regular watering. The plants should be spaced 1 meter apart. Licorice can be harvested in the fall of the second or third year of growth.
- Insects and disease: Licorice plants can be susceptible to certain insects and diseases. Some common pests that can affect licorice plants include:
  - Aphids: These small insects can suck the sap from the leaves and stems of the plant, causing stunted growth and yellowing of the leaves.
  - Spider mites: These tiny insects can cause webbing on the leaves and can damage the plant's ability to photosynthesize.
  - Whiteflies: These small, winged insects can cause yellowing of the leaves and can transmit viral diseases to the plant.

Some common diseases that can affect licorice plants include:
- Root rot: This fungal disease can cause the roots to rot and can result in stunted growth, wilting, and eventual death of the plant.
- Leaf spot: This fungal disease can cause brown or black spots on the leaves of the plant and can eventually lead to defoliation.

➢ Powdery mildew: This fungal disease can cause a white, powdery coating on the leaves of the plant, which can eventually lead to stunted growth and defoliation.

To prevent insect and disease problems, it is important to plant licorice in well-drained soil and to avoid overwatering. It is also important to practice crop rotation and to remove any infected plant material to prevent the spread of disease. If insect or disease problems are severe, it may be necessary to use an insecticide or fungicide, but this should be done only as a last resort and with caution, as these chemicals can have negative effects on the environment and on beneficial insects.

• Harvesting and preparations: The roots of the licorice plant are typically harvested in the fall of the second or third year of growth, after the plant has had a chance to establish a strong root system. The roots should be dug up carefully, taking care not to damage them, and then washed and dried in a warm, dry location.

Licorice root can be prepared in a variety of ways for medicinal use, including:
➢ Tea: Licorice root can be made into a tea by steeping 1-2 teaspoons of dried root in a cup of boiling water for 5-10 minutes. This tea can be drunk up to three times per day.
➢ Tincture: Licorice root can be made into a tincture by soaking the dried root in alcohol for several weeks, then straining the liquid and bottling it for use. This tincture can be taken in doses of 10-30 drops, up to three times per day.
➢ Powder: Licorice root can be ground into a powder and then encapsulated or mixed with water or juice for consumption. The recommended dosage for powdered licorice root is 1-2 grams, up to three times per day.

Licorice root can also be used topically as a poultice or in a bath for skin conditions, such as eczema and psoriasis. However, licorice root should not be applied topically to open wounds, as it can delay the healing process.

It is important to speak with a healthcare professional before using licorice root or any other herbal supplement, especially if you have a medical condition or are taking medication.

What medicines are made with this herb:

Licorice root has a long history of use in traditional medicine, and is still used today in a variety of herbal remedies and over-the-counter medications. Some medicines and products that contain licorice root include:

- Herbal supplements: Licorice root is commonly sold as a dietary supplement, either on its own or in combination with other herbs, for a variety of purposes, including digestive health, respiratory health, and immune support.
- Cough syrups and lozenges: Licorice root is a common ingredient in cough syrups and throat lozenges, as it is believed to soothe sore throats and calm coughs.
- Topical creams and ointments: Licorice root is sometimes used in topical preparations for skin conditions such as eczema and psoriasis, as it is believed to have anti-inflammatory and soothing properties.
- Traditional Chinese medicine: Licorice root is a common ingredient in many traditional Chinese herbal formulas, where it is used to tonify the spleen, harmonize the digestive system, and nourish the lungs.
- Ayurvedic medicine: In Ayurvedic medicine, licorice root is used to balance the doshas, or constitutional types, and is believed to have a cooling and soothing effect on the body.

It is important to note that licorice root can interact with certain medications, and should be used with caution in people with certain medical conditions, such as high blood pressure and kidney disease. It is always a good idea to consult with a healthcare professional before using any herbal supplement or medication.

What medicines this herb counteracts:

Licorice root can interact with certain medications and may counteract the effects of certain drugs, particularly those that are broken down in the liver. Licorice root may also interact with certain herbs and supplements, and should be used with caution in people with certain medical conditions, such as high blood pressure and kidney disease. Some of the medications that licorice root may counteract include:

- Diuretics: Licorice root can interfere with the effectiveness of diuretics, which are used to increase urine production and treat conditions such as high blood pressure and edema.
- Corticosteroids: Licorice root can increase the effects of corticosteroids, which are used to reduce inflammation and treat conditions such as asthma and rheumatoid arthritis.

- Hormone replacement therapy (HRT): Licorice root can interfere with the effectiveness of HRT, which is used to alleviate symptoms of menopause and osteoporosis.
- Blood thinners: Licorice root can increase the risk of bleeding in people taking blood thinners, such as warfarin and aspirin.
- Blood pressure medications: Licorice root can increase blood pressure and counteract the effects of blood pressure medications, such as beta-blockers and ACE inhibitors.

It is important to speak with a healthcare professional before using licorice root or any other herbal supplement, especially if you have a medical condition or are taking medication.

Maca

Herbal Identification:
- Common name: Maca
- Latin binomial: Lepidium meyenii
- Other common names: Peruvian ginseng, maino, ayak chichira, ayak willku
- Plant family: Brassicaceae
- Botanical description: Maca (Lepidium meyenii) is a biennial herbaceous plant that belongs to the Brassicaceae family. It has a fleshy taproot that is typically harvested for medicinal and culinary purposes. The plant can grow up to 20 centimeters in height and has oval-shaped leaves that form a rosette at the base of the plant. The flowers of maca are small, off-white, and grow in clusters. The plant is similar in appearance to a turnip or radish, with a large taproot that can range in color from white to black. The taproot is typically harvested after 8-12 months of growth, washed, dried, and then either powdered or used to make tinctures or other preparations.

Medicinal Properties:
- Recommended cultivars: There are several different cultivars of maca available, each with slightly different properties. Some of the most popular include black maca, red maca, and yellow maca.
- Parts used: The root of the maca plant is the part used for medicinal purposes.
- Taste: Maca has a slightly sweet, nutty taste.
- Actions: Adaptogen, tonic, aphrodisiac.
- Energetics: Warming.
- Specific indications: Maca (Lepidium meyenii) is traditionally used to support energy, stamina, and sexual function. It is also sometimes used to help balance hormones and alleviate symptoms of menopause. Some specific indications for maca include:
  - Low libido or sexual dysfunction
  - Fatigue and low energy
  - Poor concentration and memory
  - Hormonal imbalances, including menopause and menstrual irregularities
  - Mood imbalances, including anxiety and depression
  - Poor athletic performance or recovery after exercise

It is important to note that while maca has been traditionally used for these purposes, there is limited scientific evidence to support its effectiveness in these areas. If you are experiencing any of these symptoms, it is important to speak with a healthcare provider before using maca or any other herbal supplement.

Medicinal preparations:
Maca (Lepidium meyenii) can be consumed in a variety of forms, including:
- Powder: Maca root is dried and ground into a fine powder, which can be added to smoothies, juices, or other foods.
- Capsules: Maca root is ground into a powder and then encapsulated for easy consumption.
- Tincture: Maca root can be steeped in alcohol or another solvent to create a concentrated liquid extract.
- Tea: Maca root can be steeped in hot water to create a tea.

The appropriate preparation and dosage of maca will depend on the specific health concern being addressed and the individual's overall health status. It is important to follow the manufacturer's instructions and consult with a healthcare provider before using maca or any other herbal supplement.
• Ratio and dosage information: Dosage recommendations for maca vary depending on the preparation used and the specific health concern being addressed. In general, it is recommended to start with a low dose and gradually increase as tolerated.

Medicinal uses:
Maca (Lepidium meyenii) has been traditionally used for a variety of medicinal purposes. Some of the most common medicinal uses of maca include:
- Boosting energy and stamina: Maca is often used to improve energy levels and increase stamina, making it a popular supplement among athletes and those with physically demanding jobs.
- Enhancing sexual function: Maca is sometimes used to improve libido and sexual function in both men and women. Some studies have suggested that maca may have a beneficial effect on sexual desire, but more research is needed in this area.
- Supporting hormonal balance: Maca is sometimes used to help balance hormones, particularly in women experiencing menopause or menstrual irregularities. Some research has suggested that maca may help to alleviate symptoms such as hot flashes and night sweats, but more research is needed to confirm these findings.
- Improving mood and mental clarity: Maca is sometimes used to improve mood, reduce anxiety, and improve mental clarity. Some research has

suggested that maca may have a beneficial effect on mood, but more research is needed in this area.
- Supporting overall health and wellness: Maca is sometimes used as a general health tonic to support overall wellness and vitality.

It is important to note that while maca has been traditionally used for these purposes, there is limited scientific evidence to support its effectiveness in these areas. If you are considering using maca for a specific health concern, it is important to speak with a healthcare provider to determine whether it is a safe and appropriate treatment option.

• Precautions and contradictions: Maca (Lepidium meyenii) is generally considered safe for most people when used as directed. However, there are a few precautions and contraindications to be aware of:
- Hormone-sensitive conditions: Maca may have estrogen-like effects, so people with hormone-sensitive conditions such as breast cancer, uterine cancer, ovarian cancer, endometriosis, or uterine fibroids should use caution when using maca. It is recommended that these individuals avoid maca or consult with a healthcare provider before use.
- Thyroid conditions: Maca may interfere with thyroid function, so people with thyroid conditions should use caution when using maca. It is recommended that these individuals avoid maca or consult with a healthcare provider before use.
- Pregnancy and breastfeeding: There is not enough research to determine whether maca is safe for use during pregnancy or breastfeeding. It is recommended that women who are pregnant or breastfeeding avoid maca or consult with a healthcare provider before use.
- Allergic reactions: Some people may be allergic to maca, particularly those who are allergic to other plants in the Brassicaceae family. If you experience any symptoms of an allergic reaction, such as rash, itching, or difficulty breathing, discontinue use and seek medical attention immediately.

As with any herbal supplement, it is important to use caution and consult with a healthcare provider before using maca, particularly if you have any underlying health conditions or are taking medication.

Cultivation:
• Native to: Peru
• Zones: Maca is typically grown in zones 8-11.
• Soil: Maca prefers well-draining, slightly acidic soil.
• Propagation: Maca is typically propagated through seed or division of the root.

- Growing information and garden care: Maca is a hardy plant that is relatively easy to grow. It prefers cool temperatures and moderate rainfall. It can be grown in full sun or partial shade.
  - Insects and disease: Maca (Lepidium meyenii) is generally a hardy and disease-resistant plant, but it may be susceptible to some pests and diseases. Some common pests that may affect maca include:
  - Aphids: Aphids are small, soft-bodied insects that feed on the sap of plants. They can cause stunted growth and yellowing leaves. Aphids can be controlled by spraying the plant with a strong stream of water or with insecticidal soap.
  - Root-knot nematodes: Root-knot nematodes are microscopic worms that infect the roots of plants. They can cause stunted growth, wilting, and poor yields. There is no cure for nematode infestations, but they can be managed by rotating crops and using nematode-resistant cultivars.
  - Whiteflies: Whiteflies are small, winged insects that feed on the sap of plants. They can cause yellowing leaves and stunted growth. Whiteflies can be controlled by spraying the plant with insecticidal soap or neem oil.

Maca may also be susceptible to fungal diseases such as root rot and leaf spot. These diseases can be controlled by improving drainage, avoiding overwatering, and removing infected plant material. It is also important to practice good crop rotation and maintain healthy soil to help prevent disease.

- Harvesting and preparations: Maca (Lepidium meyenii) is typically harvested once the plant has reached maturity, which usually occurs after 7-9 months of growth. The roots are the most commonly used part of the plant, and they can be harvested by carefully digging up the entire plant and removing the roots. The roots can then be washed, sliced, and dried in the sun or in a dehydrator.

Once the roots are dry, they can be ground into a fine powder and used in a variety of culinary and medicinal preparations. Some common ways to use maca powder include:
- Adding it to smoothies or juices
- Mixing it into oatmeal or yogurt
- Using it as a natural sweetener in baked goods
- Brewing it as a tea or tincture

Maca powder can also be encapsulated for convenience.

It is important to note that while maca is generally considered safe for most people, there is limited scientific research on its safety and efficacy. If you are considering using maca for a specific health concern, it is important to speak with a healthcare provider to determine whether it is a safe and appropriate treatment option.

What medicines are made with this herb:

Maca (Lepidium meyenii) is primarily used as a dietary supplement and is often sold in the form of capsules, tablets, powders, and extracts. It is not typically used to make conventional medicines.

However, in traditional Andean medicine, maca has been used for a variety of medicinal purposes, including as a remedy for fatigue, fertility issues, and hormonal imbalances. It has also been used to improve mood, enhance energy levels, and support overall health and wellbeing.

Today, maca is sometimes used in herbal formulations and supplements that are marketed for specific health concerns such as menopause symptoms, sexual dysfunction, and fertility issues. However, it is important to note that the safety and efficacy of these products have not been extensively studied. If you are considering using maca for a specific health concern, it is important to speak with a healthcare provider to determine whether it is a safe and appropriate treatment option.

What medicines this herb counteracts:

Maca (Lepidium meyenii) is generally considered safe and does not have any known significant interactions with other medications or herbs. However, it is always important to talk to your healthcare provider before using any new supplement or herb, especially if you are taking medications or have a medical condition.

Additionally, while maca is generally considered safe for most people, it may not be appropriate for everyone. Some people may experience mild side effects such as digestive upset or insomnia when using maca, and it may not be appropriate for people with certain conditions such as thyroid disorders. It is also important to note that the safety and efficacy of maca supplements have not been extensively studied, so it is important to use them with caution and under the guidance of a healthcare provider.

Maitake Mushroom

Herbal Identification:
- Common Name: Maitake mushroom
- Latin Binomial: Grifola frondosa
- Other Common Names: Hen of the Woods, Ram's Head, Sheep's Head
- Plant Family: Meripilaceae
- Botanical Description: The Maitake mushroom, scientifically known as Grifola frondosa, is a polypore fungus with a fruiting body that typically grows in clusters at the base of trees, particularly oak trees. The fruiting body is fan-shaped, with a brownish-gray cap that is often ruffled or curled at the edges. The underside of the cap has multiple pores that release spores. The stem is thick, white, and often has a woolly texture. The Maitake mushroom can grow up to 50 pounds in the wild, but cultivated specimens are typically smaller. The fruiting body is the part of the mushroom that is used for culinary and medicinal purposes.

Medicinal Properties:
- Recommended Cultivars: There are no recommended cultivars for Maitake mushrooms.
- Parts Used: The fruiting body of the mushroom is used for medicinal purposes.
- Taste: Maitake mushrooms have a mild, earthy taste.
- Actions: Adaptogen, immune modulating, antiviral, antioxidant, hypoglycemic, hepatoprotective.
- Energetics: Neutral to slightly warm.
- Specific Indications: Maitake mushrooms have been traditionally used for a variety of medicinal purposes, and research suggests that they may offer several health benefits. Specific indications for Maitake mushrooms as a medicinal herb may include:
  - Immune system support: Maitake mushrooms are believed to stimulate the immune system, which may help to prevent and treat infections and diseases.
  - Blood sugar regulation: Maitake mushrooms may help to regulate blood sugar levels, making them potentially useful for individuals with type 2 diabetes.
  - Cancer support: Maitake mushrooms contain compounds that may have anti-cancer properties and may help to prevent or treat certain types of cancer.

- Cardiovascular health: Maitake mushrooms may help to lower blood pressure and cholesterol levels, which can improve cardiovascular health.
- Anti-inflammatory effects: Maitake mushrooms contain compounds that may have anti-inflammatory effects, which may be useful for reducing inflammation and pain in the body.

It is important to note that more research is needed to fully understand the medicinal properties of Maitake mushrooms and their potential uses. Additionally, Maitake mushrooms should not be used as a replacement for conventional medical treatment without the guidance of a healthcare provider.

Medicinal Preparations:
Maitake mushrooms can be prepared in several ways for medicinal use, including:
- Fresh or dried: The fruiting body of the Maitake mushroom can be consumed fresh or dried and used to make teas, soups, and broths.
- Extracts: Maitake mushroom extracts can be made by soaking the dried fruiting body in alcohol or hot water to extract the active compounds. The resulting liquid can be used as a tincture or added to other preparations.
- Capsules: Maitake mushroom supplements are available in capsule form, which can provide a convenient and standardized dosage.

Dosages for Maitake mushroom supplements can vary depending on the product and the condition being treated. It is important to follow the manufacturer's instructions and to consult with a healthcare provider before using Maitake mushrooms as a medicinal herb.
- Ratio and Dosage Information: There is no standard dosage for Maitake mushrooms, but typical doses range from 1-3 grams per day.

Medicinal Uses:
Maitake mushrooms have been used for various medicinal purposes, and research suggests that they may offer several health benefits. Some medicinal uses of Maitake mushrooms may include:
- Supporting the immune system: Maitake mushrooms may stimulate the immune system, which can help to prevent and treat infections and diseases.
- Regulating blood sugar: Maitake mushrooms may help to regulate blood sugar levels, making them potentially useful for individuals with type 2 diabetes.
- Supporting cancer treatment: Maitake mushrooms may have anti-cancer properties and may help to prevent or treat certain types of cancer.

- Improving cardiovascular health: Maitake mushrooms may help to lower blood pressure and cholesterol levels, which can improve cardiovascular health.
- Reducing inflammation and pain: Maitake mushrooms may have anti-inflammatory effects, which may be useful for reducing inflammation and pain in the body.

It is important to note that more research is needed to fully understand the medicinal properties of Maitake mushrooms and their potential uses. Additionally, Maitake mushrooms should not be used as a replacement for conventional medical treatment without the guidance of a healthcare provider.

• Precautions and Contradictions: Maitake mushrooms are generally considered safe when consumed as food or taken as a dietary supplement, but there are some precautions and contraindications to keep in mind:
- Blood thinners: Maitake mushrooms may have blood-thinning properties, so individuals taking blood-thinning medications, such as warfarin, should use Maitake mushrooms with caution and under the supervision of a healthcare provider.
- Immunosuppressants: Maitake mushrooms may stimulate the immune system, so individuals taking immunosuppressant medications should use Maitake mushrooms with caution and under the supervision of a healthcare provider.
- Allergic reactions: Some individuals may be allergic to Maitake mushrooms or other mushrooms. It is important to discontinue use if an allergic reaction occurs.
- Digestive issues: Maitake mushrooms may cause digestive issues, such as diarrhea or stomach discomfort, in some individuals.
- Pregnancy and breastfeeding: There is limited research on the safety of Maitake mushrooms during pregnancy and breastfeeding, so it is best to avoid their use or consult with a healthcare provider before use.

As with any medicinal herb or dietary supplement, it is important to consult with a healthcare provider before using Maitake mushrooms, especially if you have any underlying medical conditions or are taking medications.

Cultivation:
• Native to: Japan, North America, and Europe.
• Zones: Maitake mushrooms can be grown in USDA zones 3-9.
• Soil: Maitake mushrooms prefer well-drained soil that is rich in organic matter. The pH of the soil should be between 5.5 and 7.5.

- Propagation: Maitake mushrooms can be propagated by spores or by using mycelium plugs or spawn to inoculate logs or sawdust blocks.
- Growing Information and Garden Care: Maitake mushrooms require shade and high humidity to grow. They can be grown outdoors on logs or in sawdust blocks, or indoors on supplemented substrates. The growing environment should be kept moist and the temperature should be between 60-70°F. Harvest the mushrooms when they are young and the edges of the caps are still curled.
- Insects and Disease: Maitake mushrooms are generally considered to be relatively resistant to pests and diseases, although they may be susceptible to certain issues under certain conditions. Some common pests and diseases that may affect Maitake mushrooms include:
  - Verticillium wilt: This is a fungal disease that can cause wilting, yellowing, and stunting of the mushroom caps. It can be prevented by maintaining proper humidity levels and providing good air circulation.
  - Mite infestations: Spider mites can infest Maitake mushroom beds and cause damage to the mycelium. They can be controlled with insecticidal soap or neem oil.
  - Contamination: Maitake mushrooms can be contaminated by other fungi or bacteria, which can cause off-flavors or spoilage. It is important to maintain proper sanitation practices and to avoid introducing contaminants into the growing environment.

To prevent these issues, it is important to maintain proper growing conditions for Maitake mushrooms, including providing proper air circulation, humidity levels, and temperature. Additionally, maintaining good sanitation practices can help to prevent contamination and disease.

- Harvesting and Preparations: Harvesting Maitake mushrooms can be done by cutting the stem of the mushroom at the base of the fruiting body. Maitake mushrooms can be harvested at various stages of growth, but the flavor and texture can vary depending on the age of the mushroom. Younger mushrooms may have a more delicate flavor and texture, while older mushrooms may be denser and have a stronger flavor.

Maitake mushrooms can be consumed raw or cooked, and can be prepared in a variety of ways, including sautéing, roasting, grilling, or adding to soups and stews. They have a rich, earthy flavor and a meaty texture, making them a popular meat substitute in vegetarian and vegan dishes.

As a dietary supplement, Maitake mushrooms are commonly available in supplement form, including capsules, powders, and extracts. They can also be found as an ingredient in various dietary supplements and functional foods.

It is important to follow dosage and preparation instructions carefully when using Maitake mushrooms as a dietary supplement. Always consult with a healthcare provider before adding Maitake mushrooms to your diet or supplement regimen.

What Medicines Are Made with This Herb:
Maitake mushrooms are primarily used as a dietary supplement and are not typically made into standardized medicinal products. However, some natural health practitioners may use Maitake mushrooms as a component in herbal formulas for various health conditions. Maitake mushrooms are also sometimes included in medicinal mushroom blends or extracts, which may be used to support the immune system, improve cardiovascular health, or promote overall wellness.

Maitake mushrooms have also been studied for their potential anti-cancer properties. Some researchers have investigated the use of Maitake mushroom extracts in cancer treatment and prevention, although more research is needed to fully understand the potential benefits and risks.

It is important to note that Maitake mushrooms are not a substitute for conventional medical treatment, and should not be used to self-treat or manage any medical condition without the guidance of a healthcare professional.

What Medicines This Herb Counteracts:
There is no evidence to suggest that Maitake mushrooms counteract any specific medications or herbs. However, if you are taking any medications or supplements, it is always a good idea to speak with a healthcare professional before adding Maitake mushrooms to your diet or supplement regimen, as they may interact with certain medications or supplements.

Maitake mushrooms may have blood sugar-lowering effects, so people taking medications for diabetes should use caution when consuming Maitake mushrooms or Maitake mushroom supplements. Additionally, Maitake mushrooms may have blood-thinning effects, so people taking medications for blood thinning should use caution when consuming Maitake mushrooms or Maitake mushroom supplements.

Marshmallow Root

Herbal Identification:
- Common name: Marshmallow Root
- Latin binomial: Althaea officinalis
- Other common names: Althaea root, white mallow, mortification root
- Plant family: Malvaceae (mallow family)
- Botanical description: Marshmallow (Althaea officinalis) is a perennial herbaceous plant that belongs to the mallow family (Malvaceae). It is native to Europe, Western Asia, and North Africa, but has been widely naturalized in other parts of the world.

Marshmallow typically grows to a height of 3 to 4 feet (90 to 120 cm) and has a woody base with many upright stems that are covered in soft, velvety hairs. The leaves are heart-shaped and toothed, with long petioles, and can grow up to 4 inches (10 cm) in length.

The flowers of the marshmallow plant are typically pale pink or white and are borne in clusters in the leaf axils. They have five petals that are fused at the base and a characteristic column of stamens that surround the central pistil. The flowers bloom from July to September.

The plant's roots are thick and fleshy and contain high levels of mucilage, a gel-like substance that swells in water. This mucilage has been used for centuries as a natural remedy for sore throats, coughs, and other respiratory problems. In addition to its medicinal properties, marshmallow is also a popular ornamental plant and is commonly grown in gardens and borders.

Medicinal Properties:
- Recommended cultivars: No specific cultivars are recommended.
- Parts used: The root and leaves are used medicinally.
- Taste: The root is bland and slightly sweet.
- Actions: Demulcent, expectorant, anti-inflammatory, mucilaginous.
- Energetics: Cooling and moistening.
- Specific indications: Marshmallow root (Althaea officinalis radix) has been used for centuries as a natural remedy for a variety of ailments. It is particularly valued for its soothing and anti-inflammatory properties, which make it useful

for treating conditions that involve irritation and inflammation of the mucous membranes.

Some specific indications for marshmallow root include:
- Sore throat and cough: Marshmallow root is commonly used to treat sore throats and coughs due to its soothing properties. It can help to reduce inflammation and irritation in the throat and respiratory tract, and may also help to loosen and expel phlegm.
- Digestive problems: Marshmallow root is also used to treat digestive problems such as irritable bowel syndrome (IBS), constipation, and ulcers. It can help to soothe and protect the digestive tract, reducing inflammation and promoting healing.
- Skin conditions: Marshmallow root can be applied topically to treat a variety of skin conditions, including eczema, psoriasis, and burns. Its anti-inflammatory and soothing properties can help to reduce itching and irritation and promote healing.
- Urinary tract infections (UTIs): Marshmallow root may also be useful for treating UTIs due to its ability to soothe and protect the urinary tract. It can help to reduce inflammation and irritation and may also have antibacterial properties.

It is important to note that while marshmallow root is generally considered safe, it may interact with certain medications and should not be used in place of medical treatment for serious conditions. As with any herbal remedy, it is always best to consult with a healthcare provider before using marshmallow root for medicinal purposes.

Medicinal preparations:
Marshmallow root (Althaea officinalis radix) can be used to prepare a variety of medicinal preparations, including teas, tinctures, capsules, and topical applications. Here are some common ways to use marshmallow root for medicinal purposes:
- Tea: Marshmallow root tea is a popular way to take this herb. To make the tea, add 1 to 2 teaspoons of dried marshmallow root to a cup of hot water and let steep for 10 to 15 minutes. You can drink up to three cups of marshmallow root tea per day to help soothe and protect the mucous membranes.
- Tincture: Marshmallow root tincture is a concentrated liquid extract that can be taken orally or applied topically. To make a tincture, combine dried marshmallow root with alcohol or glycerin and let steep for several weeks.

You can take 1 to 2 droppersful of marshmallow root tincture up to three times per day.
- Capsules: Marshmallow root capsules are another convenient way to take this herb. Capsules are typically available in doses of 500 to 1000 mg, and you can take up to 6 grams per day divided into several doses.
- Topical applications: Marshmallow root can also be applied topically to soothe and protect the skin. You can make a poultice by mixing powdered marshmallow root with water to form a paste, and then applying it to the affected area. You can also make a soothing marshmallow root salve by mixing melted beeswax with marshmallow root-infused oil.

It is important to note that while marshmallow root is generally considered safe, it may interact with certain medications and should not be used in place of medical treatment for serious conditions. As with any herbal remedy, it is always best to consult with a healthcare provider before using marshmallow root for medicinal purposes.

- Ratio and dosage information: Dosage will vary depending on the preparation and the individual, but a common recommendation is 1-2 teaspoons of dried root per cup of water, steeped for 10-15 minutes, taken up to 3 times per day.

Medicinal uses:

Marshmallow root (Althaea officinalis radix) has been used for centuries for its medicinal properties. Here are some common medicinal uses of marshmallow root:

- Soothing sore throats and coughs: Marshmallow root contains high levels of mucilage, a gel-like substance that can help to soothe and coat the throat and respiratory tract, reducing inflammation and irritation. This makes it useful for treating sore throats, coughs, and other respiratory problems.
- Reducing digestive inflammation: Marshmallow root can help to reduce inflammation in the digestive tract, making it useful for treating conditions such as irritable bowel syndrome (IBS), colitis, and gastritis. It can also help to soothe and protect the stomach and intestines, reducing symptoms such as pain, cramping, and diarrhea.
- Healing skin conditions: Marshmallow root can be applied topically to treat a variety of skin conditions, including eczema, psoriasis, and burns. Its anti-inflammatory and soothing properties can help to reduce itching and irritation and promote healing.
- Reducing urinary tract inflammation: Marshmallow root can help to soothe and protect the urinary tract, reducing inflammation and irritation. This makes it useful for treating conditions such as urinary tract infections (UTIs), bladder infections, and kidney stones.

- Supporting overall immune function: Marshmallow root contains a variety of antioxidants and other compounds that can help to support overall immune function, reducing the risk of infections and other illnesses.

It is important to note that while marshmallow root is generally considered safe, it may interact with certain medications and should not be used in place of medical treatment for serious conditions. As with any herbal remedy, it is always best to consult with a healthcare provider before using marshmallow root for medicinal purposes.

• Precautions and contradictions: While marshmallow root (Althaea officinalis radix) is generally considered safe, there are some precautions and contraindications to be aware of:
- Allergic reactions: People who are allergic to other plants in the mallow family (such as hibiscus or okra) may also be allergic to marshmallow root. If you experience symptoms such as rash, itching, or difficulty breathing after using marshmallow root, stop using it immediately and seek medical attention.
- Blood sugar: Marshmallow root may lower blood sugar levels, so people with diabetes or hypoglycemia should use it with caution and monitor their blood sugar levels closely.
- Pregnancy and breastfeeding: There is not enough information available about the safety of marshmallow root during pregnancy and breastfeeding, so it is best to avoid using it during these times.
- Medication interactions: Marshmallow root may interact with certain medications, including blood thinners, diabetes medications, and medications that are broken down by the liver. If you are taking any medications, it is important to talk to your healthcare provider before using marshmallow root.
- Surgery: Marshmallow root may affect blood sugar levels and increase the risk of bleeding, so it is important to stop using it at least two weeks before any scheduled surgery.

It is always best to consult with a healthcare provider before using any herbal remedy, including marshmallow root, especially if you have a medical condition or are taking medications.

Cultivation:
- Native to: Europe, Western Asia, and North Africa
- Zones: Marshmallow root is hardy in zones 3-9.
- Soil: Marshmallow root prefers moist, fertile soil with a pH of 6.0-8.0.

- Propagation: Marshmallow root can be propagated by seed or by dividing the root in the spring or fall.
- Growing information and garden care: Marshmallow root prefers full sun to partial shade and should be watered regularly. It may require staking as it grows taller.
- Insects and disease: Marshmallow root (Althaea officinalis radix) is susceptible to a variety of insects and diseases. Here are some common pests and diseases that can affect marshmallow plants:
  - Aphids: These small insects feed on the sap of marshmallow plants, causing leaves to curl and distort. They can also transmit plant viruses. To control aphids, you can use insecticidal soap or neem oil, or introduce natural predators such as ladybugs or lacewings.
  - Spider mites: These tiny pests can suck the sap out of leaves, causing them to turn yellow and brown. They can also produce fine webs on the plant. To control spider mites, you can use insecticidal soap or neem oil, or introduce natural predators such as predatory mites.
  - Rust: This fungal disease causes orange or brown spots on the leaves of marshmallow plants. It can also affect the stems and flowers. To control rust, you can remove infected plant parts and apply a fungicide if necessary.
  - Powdery mildew: This fungal disease causes a white, powdery coating on the leaves of marshmallow plants, which can eventually cause them to yellow and drop off. To control powdery mildew, you can remove infected plant parts and apply a fungicide if necessary.
  - Root rot: This fungal disease can affect the roots of marshmallow plants, causing them to turn brown and mushy. It can be caused by overwatering or poor drainage. To prevent root rot, make sure your marshmallow plants are grown in well-draining soil and water them only when the top inch of soil is dry.

To keep your marshmallow plants healthy and prevent insect and disease problems, it is important to provide them with proper care, including regular watering, fertilization, and pruning. You can also use organic pest control methods, such as introducing natural predators or using homemade insecticidal sprays, to avoid the use of harmful chemicals.

- Harvesting and preparations: Marshmallow root (Althaea officinalis radix) is usually harvested in the fall, after the plant has completed its growing cycle and the leaves have died back. Here are some steps to follow for harvesting and preparing marshmallow root:
  - Dig up the plant: Use a spade or garden fork to dig up the marshmallow plant, being careful not to damage the roots.
  - Clean the roots: Use a soft brush or cloth to remove any dirt or debris from the roots. Rinse the roots with water to remove any remaining dirt.

- Cut the roots: Use a sharp knife or scissors to cut the roots into small pieces, about 1-2 inches long.
- Dry the roots: Spread the roots out in a single layer on a clean, dry surface such as a screen or paper towel. Allow them to dry completely, either in a well-ventilated room or in a dehydrator set to a low temperature (around 100-110°F).
- Store the roots: Once the roots are dry, store them in an airtight container in a cool, dry place. They will keep for up to a year.

To prepare marshmallow root for use, you can make a tea by simmering the dried root in water for about 20-30 minutes. You can also use marshmallow root in tinctures, capsules, or as a poultice for topical use. It is always best to consult with a healthcare provider or a qualified herbalist for guidance on the appropriate use and dosage of marshmallow root.

What medicines are made with this herb:
Marshmallow root (Althaea officinalis radix) is used in various herbal preparations and medicines due to its mucilaginous and anti-inflammatory properties. Here are some examples of medicines that are made with marshmallow root:
- Cough and cold remedies: Marshmallow root is often used in cough and cold remedies due to its soothing and expectorant properties. It can be used in teas, syrups, or lozenges to help relieve coughs and sore throats.
- Digestive aids: Marshmallow root can help soothe and protect the digestive tract, making it useful for conditions such as gastritis, irritable bowel syndrome (IBS), and ulcers. It can be used in teas, capsules, or tinctures to help reduce inflammation and promote healing.
- Skin remedies: Marshmallow root can be used topically to help soothe and heal skin conditions such as eczema, psoriasis, and sunburn. It can be used in poultices, salves, or creams to help reduce inflammation and promote healing.
- Anti-inflammatory agents: Marshmallow root can help reduce inflammation throughout the body, making it useful for conditions such as arthritis and respiratory infections. It can be used in teas, capsules, or tinctures to help reduce inflammation and promote healing.
- Wound healing aids: Marshmallow root can be used topically to help promote wound healing and reduce the risk of infection. It can be used in poultices or salves to help protect and soothe the skin.

It is important to note that while marshmallow root is generally considered safe, it is always best to consult with a healthcare provider or a qualified herbalist before using it as a medicine, especially if you have a medical condition or are taking medications.

What medicines this herb counteracts:

Marshmallow root (Althaea officinalis radix) is generally considered safe and has no known major contraindications or interactions with medications. However, it is always best to consult with a healthcare provider or a qualified herbalist before using marshmallow root as a medicine, especially if you have a medical condition or are taking medications.

There is a possibility that marshmallow root could interfere with the absorption of other medications if taken at the same time. Therefore, it is recommended to take marshmallow root supplements at least 2 hours before or after taking any other medications. Additionally, if you are pregnant or breastfeeding, it is important to consult with a healthcare provider before using marshmallow root as a medicine.

Milk Thistle

Herbal Identification:
- Common name: Milk thistle
- Latin binomial: Silybum marianum
- Other common names: St. Mary's thistle, holy thistle, lady's thistle
- Plant family: Asteraceae (daisy family)
- Botanical description: Milk thistle, also known as Silybum marianum, is a tall, spiny plant that belongs to the Asteraceae family. It can grow up to 10 feet in height and has large, glossy, green leaves that are deeply lobed and have white veins running through them. The plant produces beautiful pink-purple flowers with spiky bracts around the base.

The fruit of the milk thistle plant is a hard, round, spiky capsule that contains small black seeds with white, feathery pappus. The seeds are the part of the plant that is commonly used for medicinal purposes.

The milk thistle plant is native to the Mediterranean region and has been naturalized in many parts of the world. It grows well in dry, rocky soil and can often be found along roadsides and in fields. The plant is known for its ability to thrive in harsh conditions and is considered a noxious weed in some areas.

Milk thistle is a popular herb in traditional medicine and is believed to have many health benefits, particularly for the liver. It contains a group of compounds called silymarin, which are antioxidants that can help protect liver cells from damage caused by toxins and other harmful substances.

Medicinal Properties:
- Parts used: The seeds of milk thistle are used for medicinal purposes.
- Taste: Bitter
- Actions: Hepatoprotective, antioxidant, anti-inflammatory, cholagogue, choleretic
- Energetics: Cooling and drying
- Specific indications: Milk thistle is primarily used for its hepatoprotective properties, which means it helps protect and support the liver. It is commonly used to treat liver diseases such as cirrhosis, hepatitis, and fatty liver disease. Here are some specific indications for milk thistle:
  - Liver diseases: Milk thistle is known to improve liver function and may help reduce inflammation and liver damage caused by alcohol, toxins, or viral

- infections like hepatitis. It may also help prevent liver damage caused by certain medications.
- Gallbladder disorders: Milk thistle may help relieve symptoms of gallbladder disorders such as gallstones, cholecystitis, and bile duct inflammation.
- High cholesterol levels: Some studies suggest that milk thistle may help lower LDL ("bad") cholesterol levels and improve overall lipid profiles.
- Type 2 diabetes: Milk thistle may help improve insulin resistance and blood sugar control in people with type 2 diabetes.
- Skin health: Milk thistle is believed to have antioxidant and anti-inflammatory properties that may help improve skin health and reduce the risk of skin damage and aging.

It is important to note that milk thistle should not be used as a substitute for medical treatment for liver diseases or other medical conditions. If you are considering using milk thistle for any of the above indications, it is best to consult with a healthcare professional first.

Medicinal preparations:
Milk thistle is available in various medicinal preparations, including:
- Capsules and tablets: Milk thistle is available in the form of capsules and tablets, which are easy to take and convenient for daily use. These preparations usually contain standardized extracts of milk thistle seed.
- Tinctures: Milk thistle tinctures are liquid extracts made by soaking the plant in alcohol or another solvent. They are often used to make teas, but can also be taken directly or added to water or juice.
- Tea: Milk thistle tea can be made by steeping the dried herb in hot water for several minutes. It has a slightly bitter taste but can be sweetened with honey or other natural sweeteners.
- Topical preparations: Milk thistle extract is sometimes used in topical preparations for skin conditions such as eczema and psoriasis.

When using milk thistle as a medicinal herb, it is important to follow the recommended dosage and talk to a healthcare professional if you have any concerns or are taking medications that may interact with milk thistle.

• Ratio and dosage information: The standard dosage for milk thistle is 20-150 mg of a standardized extract, taken 1-3 times per day. Consult a healthcare provider or qualified herbalist for specific dosing instructions.

Medicinal uses:

Milk thistle has been used for centuries as a traditional herbal medicine for various health conditions. Here are some of the most common medicinal uses of milk thistle:

- Liver support: Milk thistle is well-known for its hepatoprotective properties, which means it helps protect and support the liver. It has been shown to improve liver function and may help reduce inflammation and liver damage caused by alcohol, toxins, or viral infections like hepatitis.
- Gallbladder disorders: Milk thistle may help relieve symptoms of gallbladder disorders such as gallstones, cholecystitis, and bile duct inflammation.
- High cholesterol levels: Some studies suggest that milk thistle may help lower LDL ("bad") cholesterol levels and improve overall lipid profiles.
- Type 2 diabetes: Milk thistle may help improve insulin resistance and blood sugar control in people with type 2 diabetes.
- Skin health: Milk thistle is believed to have antioxidant and anti-inflammatory properties that may help improve skin health and reduce the risk of skin damage and aging.
- Cancer: Some studies suggest that milk thistle may have anti-cancer properties and may help prevent the growth and spread of certain types of cancer cells.
- Hangover relief: Milk thistle is sometimes used as a natural remedy to help alleviate the symptoms of hangovers, as it may help protect the liver from the harmful effects of alcohol.

It is important to note that more research is needed to fully understand the medicinal uses and potential benefits of milk thistle. If you are considering using milk thistle for any of the above indications, it is best to consult with a healthcare professional first.

- Precautions and contradictions: Milk thistle is generally considered safe for most people when used as directed. However, there are some precautions and contraindications to be aware of:

- Allergies: Some people may be allergic to milk thistle or other plants in the Asteraceae family.
- Pregnancy and breastfeeding: The safety of milk thistle during pregnancy and breastfeeding is not well established, and therefore it is not recommended for use in these populations.
- Medication interactions: Milk thistle may interact with certain medications, including statins, antipsychotics, and immunosuppressive drugs. It is important to talk to a healthcare professional before taking milk thistle if you are currently taking any medications.
- Surgery: Milk thistle may increase the risk of bleeding during surgery, so it should be stopped at least two weeks before any scheduled surgery.

- Digestive issues: In some cases, milk thistle may cause mild digestive issues such as diarrhea, bloating, or gas.
- Blood sugar: Milk thistle may lower blood sugar levels, so people with diabetes or hypoglycemia should monitor their blood sugar levels closely when using milk thistle.
- Hormone-sensitive conditions: Milk thistle may have estrogenic effects and may not be recommended for people with hormone-sensitive conditions such as breast cancer, uterine fibroids, or endometriosis.

It is always a good idea to talk to a healthcare professional before using any herbal supplements or natural remedies, including milk thistle.

Cultivation:
- Native to: Southern Europe, North Africa, and the Middle East
- Zones: Milk thistle is a hardy biennial or annual that can grow in zones 4-9.
- Soil: Milk thistle prefers well-drained soil with a pH between 6.0 and 7.0. It can grow in poor or rocky soil, but requires full sun.
- Propagation: Milk thistle is typically grown from seed, which can be sown directly in the garden in early spring or fall. Seeds can also be started indoors and transplanted outdoors after the last frost.
- Growing information and garden care: Milk thistle requires full sun and moderate watering. It can grow up to 6 feet tall and may require staking to prevent toppling. Milk thistle can be grown as an annual or biennial, depending on your climate.
- Insects and disease: Milk thistle is relatively resistant to pests and diseases. However, there are some insects and diseases that may affect milk thistle plants:
  - Aphids: Aphids are small insects that can suck the sap out of the plant and cause it to wilt or yellow. They can be controlled with insecticidal soap or by spraying the plant with a strong stream of water.
  - Whiteflies: Whiteflies are small, winged insects that can cause leaves to yellow and drop off. They can be controlled with insecticidal soap or by introducing natural predators such as ladybugs or lacewings.
  - Powdery mildew: Powdery mildew is a fungal disease that can affect milk thistle plants, causing a white powdery coating on the leaves. It can be controlled with fungicides or by improving air circulation around the plants.
  - Verticillium wilt: Verticillium wilt is a soil-borne fungal disease that can cause yellowing, wilting, and death of the plant. There is no cure for verticillium wilt, but it can be prevented by planting resistant varieties and by practicing good sanitation in the garden.

Overall, milk thistle is a relatively low-maintenance plant that is easy to grow and care for. Regular watering and fertilization, as well as proper pest and disease control, can help ensure healthy and productive milk thistle plants.

- Harvesting and preparations: The seeds of milk thistle are typically used for medicinal purposes, and they can be harvested when the flower heads begin to dry out and turn brown. Here are the steps for harvesting and preparing milk thistle seeds:
  - Wait until the flower heads of the milk thistle plant begin to dry out and turn brown.
  - Cut the flower heads off the plant using pruning shears or scissors.
  - Place the flower heads in a paper bag and hang them upside down in a dry, well-ventilated area for several weeks until the seeds are fully dried.
  - Once the seeds are dry, shake the flower heads to release the seeds into the bag.
  - Store the seeds in an airtight container in a cool, dry place until ready to use.

Milk thistle seeds can be used to make tea, tinctures, capsules, or extracts. To make milk thistle tea, simply steep 1-2 teaspoons of crushed milk thistle seeds in boiling water for 10-15 minutes, then strain and drink. For tinctures or extracts, follow the manufacturer's instructions or consult with a healthcare professional for dosage recommendations.

What medicines are made with this herb:

Milk thistle is used in a variety of medicinal preparations, including:
- Milk thistle extract: Milk thistle extract is a concentrated form of the plant's active ingredients, including silymarin. It is commonly used to support liver health and protect against liver damage.
- Milk thistle tea: Milk thistle tea is made by steeping milk thistle seeds in hot water. It is often used as a gentle liver tonic and digestive aid.
- Milk thistle capsules: Milk thistle capsules contain a standardized extract of the plant and are commonly used to support liver health and detoxification.
- Milk thistle tincture: Milk thistle tincture is a concentrated liquid extract of the plant that is typically taken orally. It is often used to support liver health and promote detoxification.
- Milk thistle oil: Milk thistle oil is made by cold-pressing the seeds of the plant. It is often used in skincare products due to its anti-inflammatory and antioxidant properties.

Milk thistle is also sometimes used in combination with other herbs or nutrients to support overall liver health and function. It is important to talk to a healthcare professional before using milk thistle or any other natural remedy, especially if you have a medical condition or are taking medication.

What medicines this herb counteracts:

Milk thistle is generally considered safe and well-tolerated, and there are no known interactions with conventional medications. However, there are a few potential interactions that should be noted:

- Blood-thinning medications: Milk thistle may have mild blood-thinning effects, so it may interact with blood-thinning medications like warfarin (Coumadin) or aspirin. It is recommended to talk to a healthcare professional before using milk thistle if you are taking these types of medications.
- Diabetes medications: Milk thistle may lower blood sugar levels, so it may interact with diabetes medications such as insulin or oral hypoglycemic agents. It is recommended to monitor blood sugar levels closely and talk to a healthcare professional before using milk thistle if you have diabetes or are taking these types of medications.
- Allergy medications: Milk thistle may interact with allergy medications, such as antihistamines or corticosteroids, by potentially reducing their effectiveness. It is recommended to talk to a healthcare professional before using milk thistle if you are taking these types of medications.

It is important to note that these potential interactions are not well-established, and more research is needed to fully understand how milk thistle may interact with conventional medications. As always, it is recommended to talk to a healthcare professional before using milk thistle or any other natural remedy, especially if you have a medical condition or are taking medication.

Mint

Herbal Identification:
- Common name: Mint
- Latin binomial: Mentha spicata (spearmint), Mentha piperita (peppermint)
- Other common names: Lamb mint, mackerel mint, menthol mint, brandy mint, green mint, English spearmint, American spearmint
- Plant family: Lamiaceae (mint family)
- Botanical description: Mint is a perennial herb belonging to the family Lamiaceae. It has a square stem that grows up to 1 meter tall, with opposite leaves that are 2-6 cm long and 1-4 cm wide. The leaves are typically a bright green color and are slightly hairy or fuzzy to the touch.

Mint flowers are small and white or purple, arranged in dense spikes that are 2-9 cm long. The flowers bloom in the summer months and attract bees and other pollinators.

Mint has a characteristic strong and refreshing aroma due to the presence of essential oils in its leaves and stems, which are used in various culinary and medicinal applications. The plant has a creeping root system that spreads quickly, and can become invasive if not managed properly.

There are many varieties of mint, including peppermint, spearmint, and chocolate mint, each with its own unique flavor and aroma. Mint is widely cultivated and can be found in many regions of the world, including North America, Europe, and Asia.

Medicinal Properties:
- Recommended cultivars: Peppermint and spearmint are the most commonly used medicinal varieties of mint.
- Parts used: The leaves and essential oil are used medicinally.
- Taste: Mint has a refreshing, cooling taste.
- Actions: Mint is a carminative, diaphoretic, and anti-inflammatory herb that can help to soothe digestive issues, reduce fevers, and alleviate headaches.
- Energetics: Mint is cooling and drying, and it has an affinity for the digestive system.

• Specific indications: Mint has a wide range of uses and is commonly used for both culinary and medicinal purposes. Some specific indications for the use of mint include:
    ➢ Digestive issues: Mint is known to have a calming effect on the stomach, making it useful for treating digestive problems such as indigestion, bloating, and nausea.
    ➢ Bad breath: The essential oils in mint have a strong and refreshing aroma that can help mask bad breath and freshen the breath.
    ➢ Headaches: Mint has a cooling and soothing effect that can help alleviate headaches and migraines.
    ➢ Respiratory problems: Mint has been used traditionally to treat respiratory problems such as congestion, coughs, and colds due to its expectorant properties.
    ➢ Skin irritation: Mint has anti-inflammatory properties and can be used topically to soothe skin irritation and inflammation.
    ➢ Mental clarity: Mint has been shown to have a stimulating effect on the brain, promoting mental clarity and improving concentration.

Overall, mint is a versatile herb that can be used in various forms such as tea, essential oils, or fresh leaves, to provide relief for various health issues. However, it is important to consult with a healthcare professional before using mint for medicinal purposes, especially if you have any pre-existing medical conditions or are taking medication.

Medicinal preparations:
Mint can be used in various medicinal preparations, including:
    ➢ Mint tea: Fresh or dried mint leaves can be used to make tea, which can help with digestion, soothe the stomach, and promote relaxation.
    ➢ Mint essential oil: The essential oil of mint can be extracted from the leaves and used topically or inhaled to treat respiratory problems, headaches, and muscle pain.
    ➢ Mint capsules or tablets: Mint supplements are available in the form of capsules or tablets, which can be used to promote digestive health, relieve headaches, and improve mental clarity.
    ➢ Mint mouthwash: Mint essential oil is a common ingredient in mouthwash due to its ability to freshen eath and kill bacteria that cause bad breath.
    ➢ 5 Mint ointment or cream: Mint can be used topically in the form of ointments or creams to soothe skin irritation, reduce inflammation, and relieve muscle pain.

It is important to note that while mint is generally considered safe, some people may be allergic to it or experience side effects such as heartburn,

headaches, or skin irritation. It is always advisable to consult with a healthcare professional before using mint for medicinal purposes, especially if you have any pre-existing medical conditions or are taking medication.
- Ratio and dosage information: The recommended dosage of mint depends on the specific preparation being used. Consult with a healthcare professional for dosage recommendations.

Medicinal uses:
Mint has been used for centuries for its medicinal properties, and modern research has shown that it can be effective in treating various health conditions. Some of the medicinal uses of mint include:
- Digestive problems: Mint is a natural digestive aid that can help relieve bloating, gas, and indigestion. It has a calming effect on the stomach and can help ease nausea and vomiting.
- Headaches and migraines: Mint has a cooling and soothing effect that can help alleviate headaches and migraines. It can be used topically or inhaled through the use of essential oils.
- Respiratory problems: Mint is a natural decongestant and can help relieve coughs and congestion. It can also be used to treat asthma and other respiratory conditions.
- Skin irritation: Mint has anti-inflammatory properties and can be used topically to soothe skin irritation, reduce inflammation, and relieve itching.
- Mental clarity: Mint has been shown to have a stimulating effect on the brain, improving mental clarity and concentration. It can be used to combat fatigue and improve cognitive function.
- Bad breath: Mint has a refreshing and pleasant aroma that can help mask bad breath and improve oral hygiene. It is a common ingredient in mouthwash and toothpaste.

Overall, mint is a versatile herb that can be used to treat a variety of health conditions. However, it is important to consult with a healthcare professional before using mint for medicinal purposes, especially if you have any pre-existing medical conditions or are taking medication.
- Precautions and contradictions: While mint is generally considered safe, there are some precautions and contraindications to keep in mind. These include:
- Allergic reactions: Some people may be allergic to mint, and can experience symptoms such as rash, hives, or difficulty breathing.
- Gastroesophageal reflux disease (GERD): Mint can exacerbate symptoms of GERD, including heartburn and acid reflux.
- Gallstones: Mint can cause the gallbladder to contract, which can be painful for those with gallstones.

- Medication interactions: Mint can interact with certain medications, including blood thinners, antacids, and diabetes medications.
- Pregnancy and breastfeeding: While mint is generally considered safe during pregnancy and breastfeeding, it is advisable to consult with a healthcare professional before using it in medicinal amounts.
- Children: Mint essential oil should not be used on children under the age of 6, as it can cause respiratory distress or other adverse reactions.

It is always advisable to consult with a healthcare professional before using mint for medicinal purposes, especially if you have any pre-existing medical conditions or are taking medication. It is also important to use caution when using mint essential oil, as it is highly concentrated and can be toxic if ingested in large amounts.

Cultivation:

- Native to: Mint is native to Europe, but it is widely cultivated in many other regions of the world.
- Zones: Mint is hardy in USDA zones 3-11.
- Soil: Mint prefers moist, well-drained soil with a pH of 6.0-7.0.
- Propagation: Mint can be propagated by seed, division, or cuttings.
- Growing information and garden care: Mint is a hardy and easy-to-grow herb that prefers full sun to partial shade. It is a vigorous grower and can be invasive, so it is often grown in containers or confined to a specific area of the garden. It benefits from regular watering and occasional fertilization.
- Insects and disease: Mint is known for its insect-repellent properties and can help deter a variety of pests. Some common insects that mint can repel include ants, mosquitoes, moths, and flies.

In addition to its insect-repellent properties, mint also has antibacterial and antifungal properties that can help prevent and treat various diseases. Some studies have shown that mint essential oil can be effective against bacteria such as E. coli and Staphylococcus aureus, as well as fungi such as Candida albicans.

However, it is important to note that while mint can help repel insects and prevent certain diseases, it is not a substitute for proper hygiene and sanitation practices. In addition, it is important to use caution when using mint essential oil, as it can be toxic if ingested in large amounts or applied directly to the skin without dilution.

Overall, mint can be a useful natural tool for repelling insects and preventing certain diseases, but it is important to use it safely and in conjunction with other preventive measures.

- Harvesting and preparations: Mint is a hardy and easy-to-grow herb that can be harvested throughout the growing season. Here are some tips on how to harvest and prepare mint:
  - Harvesting: The best time to harvest mint is in the morning, after the dew has dried but before the sun is too hot. You can either harvest the entire plant or cut off individual stems or leaves. Be sure to leave at least 1/3 of the plant intact to ensure healthy regrowth.
  - Cleaning: Rinse the mint leaves thoroughly in cold water to remove any dirt or debris.
  - Drying: You can dry mint leaves by hanging them upside down in a cool, dry place with good air circulation. Alternatively, you can use a dehydrator or oven to dry the leaves at a low temperature.
  - Storing: Once the mint leaves are dry, store them in an airtight container in a cool, dark place. Alternatively, you can freeze the leaves by placing them in a freezer-safe bag or container.
  - Preparing: Mint can be used fresh or dried in a variety of dishes and preparations, including tea, salads, sauces, and marinades. To release the full flavor and aroma of mint, bruise the leaves slightly by rubbing them between your fingers or chopping them finely.

Overall, harvesting and preparing mint is relatively easy and straightforward. By following these tips, you can enjoy the fresh, invigorating taste and aroma of mint all year round.

What medicines are made with this herb:

Mint is used in a variety of medicinal preparations, including:
- Mint tea: Mint tea is made by steeping fresh or dried mint leaves in hot water. It is commonly used to soothe digestive issues, reduce fevers, and alleviate headaches.
- Mint tincture: Mint tincture is a concentrated liquid extract of the herb that is typically taken orally. It is often used to support digestive health and relieve symptoms such as bloating, gas, and indigestion. It can also be used as a natural remedy for headaches and other minor pain.

Ratio and dosage information for mint tincture may vary depending on the individual and the specific product, but generally, the recommended dose is 1-2 ml (20-40 drops) taken 2-3 times daily. It can be added to water or other beverages or taken directly under the tongue.

Mint tincture is also commonly used in topical preparations for its cooling and soothing properties. It can be added to creams, lotions, and balms to help relieve minor skin irritations and inflammation.

Some precautions and contradictions of mint tincture include avoiding use during pregnancy and breastfeeding, as well as potential interactions with certain medications, such as those used to treat diabetes, high blood pressure, and acid reflux. It is always recommended to consult with a healthcare provider before adding any new herbal supplement to your routine.

Some medicines that may be made with mint include cough syrups, lozenges, and teas for respiratory symptoms, as well as topical creams and balms for skin irritations and inflammation. Mint is also a common flavoring agent in various food and beverage products, such as toothpaste, gum, and candy. There are no known medicines that specifically counteract mint.

What medicines this herb counter act:
There are no known medicines that mint counteracts. However, it is important to note that mint may interact with certain medications, such as those used to treat diabetes, high blood pressure, and acid reflux. It is always recommended to consult with a healthcare provider before adding any new herbal supplement to your routine, especially if you are currently taking prescription medication.

Mugwort

Herbal Identification:
- Common name: Mugwort
- Latin binomial: Artemisia vulgaris
- Other common names: Common wormwood, wild wormwood, felon herb, sailor's tobacco
- Plant family: Asteraceae (daisy family)
- Botanical description: Mugwort (Artemisia vulgaris) is a perennial herbaceous plant that belongs to the family Asteraceae. It grows to a height of 1-2 meters and has a woody, reddish-brown stem with multiple branches. The leaves are green, lance-shaped, and have a deeply toothed margin. They are covered with fine hairs and have a slightly bitter taste and aromatic odor when crushed.

Mugwort produces small, insignificant flowers that bloom from July to October. The flowers are arranged in clusters at the end of the stem and are yellowish-green in color. The plant is known for its ability to grow in a wide range of soils and conditions, and it can often be found growing in waste places, along roadsides, and in disturbed areas.

Mugwort has a long history of use in traditional medicine and is believed to have a variety of health benefits. It contains several bioactive compounds, including essential oils, flavonoids, and sesquiterpene lactones, which are thought to contribute to its medicinal properties. Mugwort is commonly used in traditional Chinese medicine, as well as in European folk medicine, to treat a range of conditions such as digestive disorders, menstrual cramps, and anxiety. Additionally, mugwort has been used as a flavoring agent in food and beverages, as well as a natural insect repellent.

Medicinal Properties:
- Recommended cultivars: There are no specific recommended cultivars for mugwort.
- Parts used: The aerial parts of the plant (leaves, stems, and flowers) are used for medicinal purposes.
- Taste: Mugwort has a bitter, aromatic taste.
- Actions: Mugwort is considered a nervine, digestive stimulant, emmenagogue, and mild sedative.
- Energetics: Mugwort is considered to be warming and drying.

• Specific indications: Mugwort (Artemisia vulgaris) is a plant with a long history of use in traditional medicine. It has been used for a variety of purposes, including:
- Digestive issues: Mugwort is believed to have properties that can help with digestive problems such as bloating, gas, and indigestion. It is often used as a tea or tincture to alleviate these symptoms.
- Menstrual cramps: Mugwort has been traditionally used to ease menstrual cramps and regulate menstruation. It is often consumed as a tea or used topically as a compress or poultice.
- Anxiety and stress: Mugwort is believed to have calming properties that can help reduce anxiety and stress. It is often used as a tea or tincture to promote relaxation.
- Insomnia: Mugwort is believed to have sedative properties that can help improve sleep quality and duration. It can be consumed as a tea or taken as a tincture before bed.
- Skin conditions: Mugwort has been traditionally used to treat skin conditions such as eczema and psoriasis. It can be applied topically as a poultice or used in a bath to soothe irritated skin.

It is important to note that mugwort should not be used by pregnant women or individuals with allergies to plants in the Asteraceae family, as it may cause adverse reactions. Additionally, mugwort should always be used under the guidance of a healthcare professional.

Medicinal preparations:
Mugwort (Artemisia vulgaris) can be prepared and consumed in a variety of forms for its medicinal properties. Some common preparations include:
- Tea: Mugwort tea is made by steeping the dried leaves and/or flowers in hot water for several minutes. This is the most common way to consume mugwort medicinally.
- Tincture: A tincture is a concentrated liquid extract made by soaking the plant material in alcohol or vinegar. Mugwort tincture can be taken orally or used topically.
- Essential oil: Mugwort essential oil can be inhaled or used topically to promote relaxation and relieve stress.
- Compress: A compress can be made by soaking a cloth in a mugwort infusion and applying it to the affected area to alleviate pain or inflammation.
- Bath: Mugwort can be added to a bath to soothe skin irritations, promote relaxation, and improve sleep.

It is important to note that mugwort should always be used under the guidance of a healthcare professional, as it can cause adverse reactions in some individuals.

Additionally, it should not be used by pregnant women or individuals with allergies to plants in the Asteraceae family.
- Ratio and dosage information: For a standard infusion, use 1 to 2 teaspoons of dried mugwort per cup of boiling water. Steep for 10 to 15 minutes, then strain and drink up to 3 cups per day. Tincture dosage is typically 1 to 2 mL taken up to 3 times per day.

Medicinal uses:
Mugwort (Artemisia vulgaris) has been used in traditional medicine for a variety of medicinal purposes. Some of its most common medicinal uses include:
- Digestive issues: Mugwort has been used to alleviate digestive issues such as bloating, gas, and indigestion. It is believed to have properties that stimulate the production of digestive enzymes and improve overall digestive function.
- Menstrual cramps: Mugwort has been used traditionally to ease menstrual cramps and regulate menstruation. It is believed to have properties that help to stimulate blood flow to the uterus and alleviate pain and discomfort.
- Anxiety and stress: Mugwort has been traditionally used to promote relaxation and reduce anxiety and stress. It is believed to have properties that can help to calm the nervous system and promote a sense of wellbeing.
- Insomnia: Mugwort has been used to improve sleep quality and duration. It is believed to have sedative properties that can help to promote relaxation and improve sleep.
- Skin conditions: Mugwort has been used to treat a variety of skin conditions such as eczema, psoriasis, and dermatitis. It is believed to have properties that help to soothe irritated skin and reduce inflammation.

It is important to note that mugwort should be used under the guidance of a healthcare professional, as it can cause adverse reactions in some individuals. Additionally, it should not be used by pregnant women or individuals with allergies to plants in the Asteraceae family.
- Precautions and contradictions: Mugwort (Artemisia vulgaris) should be used with caution, as it may cause adverse reactions in some individuals. Here are some precautions and contraindications to consider:
- Allergies: Mugwort is a member of the Asteraceae family and may cause allergic reactions in individuals with allergies to this family of plants. If you have a known allergy to ragweed, chrysanthemums, marigolds, or other plants in the Asteraceae family, you should avoid using mugwort.
- Pregnancy and breastfeeding: Mugwort should not be used by pregnant or breastfeeding women, as it may cause uterine contractions and other adverse effects.

- Medication interactions: Mugwort may interact with certain medications, including blood thinners and sedatives. If you are taking any medications, you should consult with a healthcare professional before using mugwort.
- Neurological conditions: Mugwort may worsen symptoms in individuals with neurological conditions such as epilepsy.
- Liver disease: Mugwort may be harmful to individuals with liver disease, as it can cause liver damage in high doses.
- Children: Mugwort should not be used in children, as its safety and efficacy have not been well-studied in this population.

If you are considering using mugwort for medicinal purposes, it is important to consult with a healthcare professional to determine whether it is safe and appropriate for you to use. Additionally, you should always follow the recommended dosage and preparation methods, as excessive use of mugwort may cause adverse reactions.

Cultivation:

- Native to: Eurasia and northern Africa, but has naturalized in North America and other parts of the world.
- Zones: Mugwort is hardy in USDA zones 3-9.
- Soil: Mugwort prefers well-drained soil with a pH of 6.0-7.0.
- Propagation: Mugwort can be propagated by seed or division.
- Growing information and garden care: Mugwort prefers full sun to partial shade and can tolerate a range of soil types. It is a hardy plant that can be invasive, so it should be grown in a contained area or with other aggressive plants. Mugwort can be cut back to promote bushier growth and prevent flowering.
- Insects and disease: Mugwort (Artemisia vulgaris) is relatively resistant to pests and diseases, but it can still be affected by some insects and diseases. Here are some common issues to watch out for:
  - Powdery mildew: Mugwort can be susceptible to powdery mildew, a fungal disease that appears as a white or gray powdery coating on the leaves. To prevent powdery mildew, avoid overwatering and ensure good air circulation around the plant.
  - Aphids: Aphids are small, soft-bodied insects that can infest mugwort and cause stunted growth, yellowing leaves, and distorted plant growth. To control aphids, use an insecticidal soap or spray the plant with a strong stream of water.
  - Spider mites: Spider mites are tiny, spider-like pests that can infest mugwort and cause yellow or brown spots on the leaves. To control spider mites,

spray the plant with a mixture of water and dish soap, or use a horticultural oil.
- Root rot: Mugwort can be susceptible to root rot if it is grown in soil that is too wet or poorly drained. To prevent root rot, ensure that the soil is well-draining and avoid overwatering the plant.

It is important to monitor mugwort regularly for signs of pests or diseases, and to take appropriate measures to control and prevent these issues. Additionally, avoid using chemical pesticides or fungicides on mugwort, as these may be harmful to beneficial insects and may contaminate the plant.

- Harvesting and preparations: Mugwort (Artemisia vulgaris) can be harvested and prepared for various medicinal uses. Here are some guidelines for harvesting and preparation:
  - Harvesting: Mugwort can be harvested in the summer when the plant is in full bloom. Choose healthy plants and cut the stems just above the ground.
  - Drying: Once harvested, mugwort can be dried by hanging the stems upside down in a well-ventilated area. Alternatively, the leaves can be spread out on a clean, dry surface and left to air dry.
  - Tea: Mugwort can be brewed into a tea by steeping 1-2 teaspoons of dried leaves in a cup of hot water for 10-15 minutes. Strain the tea and drink up to three times per day.
  - Tincture: Mugwort can be prepared as a tincture by soaking the dried leaves in alcohol for several weeks. Strain the mixture and take 1-2 dropperfuls up to three times per day.
  - Essential oil: Mugwort essential oil can be extracted from the leaves and used in aromatherapy or applied topically. However, it should be used with caution and under the guidance of a healthcare professional, as it can be toxic in high doses.

When harvesting and preparing mugwort, it is important to follow appropriate safety precautions and to avoid overharvesting or damaging the plant. Additionally, mugwort should be used under the guidance of a healthcare professional, as it can cause adverse reactions in some individuals.

Medicines made with this herb:

Mugwort (Artemisia vulgaris) has been used in traditional medicine for a variety of purposes. Here are some medicines made with this herb:
- Digestive aid: Mugwort has been used as a digestive aid to stimulate appetite, relieve indigestion, and ease stomach cramps.
- Menstrual cramps: Mugwort has been used to alleviate menstrual cramps and regulate the menstrual cycle.

- Insomnia: Mugwort has been used as a sleep aid to promote relaxation and alleviate insomnia.
- Anxiety and stress: Mugwort has been used to relieve anxiety and stress and promote relaxation.
- Pain relief: Mugwort has been used to relieve pain associated with rheumatism, arthritis, and other conditions.
- Skin conditions: Mugwort has been used topically to relieve skin conditions such as eczema, psoriasis, and acne.
- Parasites: Mugwort has been used to expel intestinal parasites.

Mugwort can be prepared as a tea, tincture, essential oil, or applied topically for various medicinal uses. However, it is important to use mugwort under the guidance of a healthcare professional, as it can cause adverse reactions in some individuals. Additionally, mugwort should not be used during pregnancy or breastfeeding.

Medicines this herb counteracts:

There is currently no evidence suggesting that mugwort (Artemisia vulgaris) counteracts any specific medicines. However, it is important to note that mugwort can interact with certain medications and medical conditions, so it should be used under the guidance of a healthcare professional.

Mugwort can increase the effects of sedatives and should not be used in conjunction with other sedatives or tranquilizers. It may also interact with anticoagulant medications and should be used with caution by individuals with bleeding disorders or who are taking blood-thinning medications.

Additionally, mugwort may cause an allergic reaction in some individuals, particularly those who are sensitive to plants in the Asteraceae family, such as ragweed, daisies, and chrysanthemums.

If you are taking any medications or have any medical conditions, it is important to consult with a healthcare professional before using mugwort or any other herbal remedy.

Muira Puama

Herbal Identification:
- Common name: Muira puama
- Latin binomial: Ptychopetalum olacoides
- Other common names: Marapuama, potency wood
- Plant family: Olacaceae
- Botanical description: Muira puama is a small tree that can grow up to 15 feet in height, and it belongs to the Olacaceae family. It has a straight, cylindrical trunk and a bushy crown. The bark is light brown and smooth, and the wood is white and hard. The leaves are compound and alternate, with 5-7 leaflets, and they are dark green and glossy. The tree produces small white flowers that are arranged in clusters, and they have a sweet, jasmine-like fragrance. The fruit is small, round, and brown, and it contains a single seed. The bark and roots are used for medicinal purposes, and they have a bitter taste and astringent properties.

Medicinal Properties:
- Parts used: Bark and roots
- Taste: Bitter, astringent
- Actions: Nervine, aphrodisiac, stimulant
- Energetics: Warming, drying
- Specific indications: Muira puama has been traditionally used for a variety of indications, including:
  - Erectile dysfunction and low libido: Muira puama is commonly used as an aphrodisiac and to improve sexual function in both men and women.
  - Nervous system disorders: Muira puama is often used to alleviate symptoms of nervous system disorders, such as depression, anxiety, and stress. It is also believed to improve memory and cognitive function.
  - Fatigue and exhaustion: Muira puama is used to increase energy levels and combat fatigue and exhaustion.
  - Joint pain and rheumatism: Muira puama is used to relieve joint pain and inflammation, as well as symptoms of rheumatism.
  - Menstrual cramps: Muira puama is sometimes used to alleviate menstrual cramps and other menstrual-related symptoms.

It is important to note that while muira puama has been traditionally used for these indications, more research is needed to fully understand its effectiveness and safety.

Medicinal preparations:
Muira puama is prepared for medicinal use by using the bark and roots of the tree. Some common preparations include:
- Infusion: The dried bark and/or roots can be boiled in water to make a tea, which can be consumed daily.
- Tincture: Muira puama can be prepared as a tincture by soaking the bark and/or roots in alcohol for several weeks, and then straining out the plant material. This can be taken in small doses daily.
- Capsules: Muira puama is available in capsule form, which can be taken orally as directed by a healthcare practitioner.

It is important to note that muira puama may interact with certain medications, so it is important to consult with a healthcare practitioner before using this herb medicinally. Additionally, dosage recommendations may vary depending on the preparation and the individual's health status, so it is important to follow a healthcare practitioner's recommendations.

• Ratio and dosage information: 1-2 grams of dried bark or root per day; 1:2 tincture, 2-4 ml, up to three times per day

Medicinal uses:
Muira puama has been traditionally used for a variety of medicinal purposes, including:
- Sexual dysfunction: Muira puama is commonly used to improve sexual function in both men and women, including erectile dysfunction and low libido.
- Nervous system disorders: Muira puama is often used to alleviate symptoms of nervous system disorders, such as depression, anxiety, and stress. It is also believed to improve memory and cognitive function.
- Fatigue and exhaustion: Muira puama is used to increase energy levels and combat fatigue and exhaustion.
- Joint pain and rheumatism: Muira puama is used to relieve joint pain and inflammation, as well as symptoms of rheumatism.
- Digestive disorders: Muira puama is sometimes used to alleviate digestive disorders, such as diarrhea and colic.
- Headaches: Muira puama is used to alleviate headaches and migraines.

It is important to note that while muira puama has been traditionally used for these indications, more research is needed to fully understand its effectiveness and safety.

• Precautions and contradictions: Muira puama is generally considered safe when used in recommended doses, but it may interact with certain medications

and has some potential side effects. Here are some precautions and contraindications to keep in mind:
- Pregnancy and breastfeeding: There is not enough evidence to determine the safety of muira puama during pregnancy and breastfeeding, so it should be avoided during these times.
- Surgery: Muira puama may interact with anesthesia and increase the risk of bleeding during surgery, so it should be avoided at least two weeks before a scheduled surgery.
- Bleeding disorders: Muira puama may increase the risk of bleeding in people with bleeding disorders or who are taking blood-thinning medications.
- High blood pressure: Muira puama may increase blood pressure in some people, so it should be used with caution in people with high blood pressure.
- Interactions with medications: Muira puama may interact with certain medications, including blood-thinning medications, anticoagulants, and some antidepressants. It is important to consult with a healthcare practitioner before using muira puama if you are taking any medications.

As with any herbal remedy, it is important to consult with a healthcare practitioner before using muira puama, especially if you have any underlying health conditions or are taking medications.

Cultivation:
- Native to: Brazil, Peru
- Zones: 9-11
- Soil (ph and type of soil): Muira puama prefers well-draining, fertile soil with a pH of 5.5-7.5.
- Propagation: Muira puama can be propagated from seeds or cuttings.
- Growing information and garden care: Muira puama is a tropical plant that requires warm temperatures and high humidity. It prefers partial shade and should be watered regularly.
- Insects and disease: There is limited information available on insects and diseases that affect muira puama, as it is primarily grown and harvested in the Amazon rainforest. However, like any plant, muira puama can be susceptible to insect infestations and fungal diseases. Some common pests that may affect muira puama include spider mites, aphids, and mealybugs. In terms of diseases, muira puama may be susceptible to root rot, which can be caused by overwatering or poor soil drainage. It is important to maintain proper growing conditions and monitor plants for any signs of pest or disease problems.
- Harvesting and preparations: Muira puama is typically harvested from wild trees in the Amazon rainforest, and the roots and bark are the parts of the plant

used for medicinal purposes. The bark is usually harvested in small pieces and then dried and powdered for use in medicinal preparations.

Here are some common preparations of muira puama:
- Powdered bark: The dried and powdered bark can be used to make teas, tinctures, and capsules.
- Tincture: A tincture can be made by soaking the dried bark in alcohol for several weeks and then straining out the solids. The resulting liquid can be used as a concentrated extract.
- Tea: Muira puama tea can be made by steeping the dried bark in hot water for several minutes. The tea can be sweetened with honey or other natural sweeteners to improve the taste.
- Capsules: Muira puama is also available in capsule form, which can be taken orally with water.

It is important to follow dosage instructions carefully and consult with a healthcare practitioner before using muira puama, especially if you have any underlying health conditions or are taking medications.

What medicines are made with this herb:

Muira puama is primarily used as an herbal remedy and is not commonly used in mainstream pharmaceuticals. However, it is a popular ingredient in some dietary supplements and natural health products marketed for its potential medicinal properties. Some common products that may contain muira puama include:
- Herbal supplements: Muira puama is often sold as a standalone supplement or combined with other herbs to support sexual function, energy, and overall vitality.
- Natural aphrodisiacs: Muira puama is sometimes marketed as a natural aphrodisiac and is often found in sexual enhancement products for men and women.
- Energy supplements: Some energy supplements contain muira puama as an ingredient, claiming to boost stamina, endurance, and mental alertness.
- Topical creams and oils: Muira puama is sometimes added to topical creams and oils for its potential benefits on skin and hair health.

It is important to note that the effectiveness and safety of these products may vary, and it is important to consult with a healthcare practitioner before using any dietary supplement or natural health product containing muira puama.

What medicines this herb counteracts:

There is no information to suggest that muira puama counteracts any specific medicine. However, as with any herbal supplement, it is important to consult with a healthcare practitioner before using muira puama if you are taking any medications or have any underlying health conditions, as it may interact with certain medications or have contraindications. Additionally, muira puama may not be safe for everyone, and caution should be exercised in pregnant or breastfeeding women, children, and those with certain medical conditions such as high blood pressure or heart disease.

Nettle

Herbal Identification:
- Common name: Nettle
- Latin binomial: Urtica dioica
- Other common names: Stinging nettle, common nettle, nettle leaf, European nettle
- Plant family: Urticaceae
- Botanical description: Nettle (Urtica dioica) is a perennial herb that belongs to the family Urticaceae. It can grow up to 1-2 meters in height and has a fibrous root system. The plant produces green, serrated leaves that are heart-shaped and covered with fine hairs that can cause a stinging sensation when touched. The stem of the plant is square-shaped and also covered in fine hairs. Nettle produces small green flowers that are arranged in clusters, which bloom from June to September. The plant is known for its medicinal properties and is used to support various health conditions. Nettle is native to Europe, Asia, and North Africa and is now widely cultivated throughout the world.

Medicinal Properties:
- Recommended cultivars: There are several cultivars of nettle, including 'Dwarf Siberian', 'Goldfinch', and 'Green Twister'. However, the medicinal properties of these cultivars are similar to the standard Urtica dioica.
- Parts used: The aerial parts of the plant, including the leaves and stems, are used for medicinal purposes.
- Taste: Nettle has a slightly bitter and earthy taste.
- Actions: Nettle is considered to be a nutritive, tonic, diuretic, astringent, and anti-inflammatory herb.
- Energetics: Nettle is considered to be a cooling and drying herb.
- Specific indications: Nettle (Urtica dioica) has several specific indications and is used to support various health conditions. Some of the specific indications for nettle include:
  - Allergies: Nettle may help alleviate symptoms of seasonal allergies, such as sneezing, runny nose, and itchy eyes. It is believed to work by reducing inflammation and inhibiting the release of histamine, a compound that causes allergy symptoms.
  - Arthritis: Nettle has anti-inflammatory properties that may help reduce pain and stiffness associated with arthritis.

- Benign prostatic hyperplasia (BPH): Nettle may help relieve symptoms of BPH, such as frequent urination and difficulty urinating. It is believed to work by reducing inflammation and inhibiting the growth of prostate cells.
- Urinary tract infections (UTIs): Nettle may help prevent and treat UTIs by reducing inflammation and fighting bacteria that cause infections.
- Anemia: Nettle is rich in iron, which may help prevent and treat anemia, a condition characterized by low levels of red blood cells.
- Skin conditions: Nettle may help relieve symptoms of skin conditions, such as eczema and acne. It is believed to work by reducing inflammation and promoting healthy skin.

It is important to note that more research is needed to fully understand the specific indications and mechanisms of action of nettle. It is always important to consult with a healthcare provider before using any herbal medicine, especially if you have a medical condition or are taking other medications.

Medicinal preparations:
Nettle (Urtica dioica) can be prepared in various forms for medicinal use. Some of the common medicinal preparations of nettle include:
- Tea: Nettle tea can be made by steeping 1-2 teaspoons of dried nettle leaves in hot water for 10-15 minutes. The tea can be consumed 2-3 times a day to support various health conditions.
- Tincture: Nettle tincture can be made by soaking nettle leaves in alcohol for several weeks. The tincture can be taken 2-3 times a day in doses of 30-60 drops to support various health conditions.
- Capsules: Nettle capsules can be made by drying and grinding nettle leaves and filling them into capsules. The capsules can be taken 2-3 times a day in doses of 300-600 mg to support various health conditions.
- Topical preparations: Nettle can also be used topically to relieve symptoms of skin conditions, such as eczema and psoriasis. Topical preparations include creams, lotions, and salves that contain nettle extract.

The appropriate preparation and dosage of nettle may vary depending on the specific health condition being treated and the individual's age, weight, and overall health. It is always important to consult with a healthcare provider before using any herbal medicine, especially if you have a medical condition or are taking other medications.

• Ratio and dosage information: The ratio and dosage of nettle will depend on the specific preparation and condition being treated. As a general guideline, a standard infusion can be made by steeping 1-2 teaspoons of dried nettle leaves in a cup of boiling water for 10-15 minutes. This can be consumed up to three times per day.

Medicinal uses:
Nettle (Urtica dioica) has several medicinal uses and is used to support various health conditions. Some of the common medicinal uses of nettle include:
- Allergies: Nettle may help alleviate symptoms of seasonal allergies, such as sneezing, runny nose, and itchy eyes.
- Arthritis: Nettle has anti-inflammatory properties that may help reduce pain and stiffness associated with arthritis.
- Benign prostatic hyperplasia (BPH): Nettle may help relieve symptoms of BPH, such as frequent urination and difficulty urinating.
- Urinary tract infections (UTIs): Nettle may help prevent and treat UTIs by reducing inflammation and fighting bacteria that cause infections.
- Anemia: Nettle is rich in iron, which may help prevent and treat anemia, a condition characterized by low levels of red blood cells.
- Skin conditions: Nettle may help relieve symptoms of skin conditions, such as eczema and acne.
- Digestive health: Nettle may help improve digestion and alleviate symptoms of gastrointestinal disorders, such as constipation and diarrhea.
- Blood sugar control: Nettle may help lower blood sugar levels and improve insulin sensitivity.

It is important to note that more research is needed to fully understand the medicinal uses and mechanisms of action of nettle. It is always important to consult with a healthcare provider before using any herbal medicine, especially if you have a medical condition or are taking other medications.

• Precautions and contradictions: Nettle (Urtica dioica) is generally considered safe when used appropriately. However, there are some precautions and contraindications that should be considered before using nettle:
- Allergic reactions: Some individuals may be allergic to nettle, especially if they are allergic to plants in the Urticaceae family. Symptoms of an allergic reaction may include rash, hives, and difficulty breathing.
- Medication interactions: Nettle may interact with certain medications, such as blood thinners, diuretics, and medications for diabetes. It is important to talk to a healthcare provider before using nettle if you are taking any medications.
- Pregnancy and breastfeeding: There is limited information on the safety of nettle during pregnancy and breastfeeding. It is recommended to avoid nettle during pregnancy and breastfeeding.
- Low blood pressure: Nettle may lower blood pressure, and individuals with low blood pressure should use nettle with caution.
- Kidney disorders: Nettle may have diuretic effects and may worsen kidney disorders. Individuals with kidney disorders should use nettle with caution.

> Oxalate sensitivity: Nettle contains high levels of oxalates, which may exacerbate oxalate sensitivity or kidney stone formation.

It is always important to consult with a healthcare provider before using any herbal medicine, especially if you have a medical condition or are taking other medications.

Cultivation:
- Native to: Europe, Asia, and North Africa
- Zones: 3-10
- Soil: Nettle prefers rich, moist soil that is high in nitrogen. It can grow in a wide range of soil types, but prefers a pH between 5.5-7.5.
- Propagation: Nettle can be propagated by seeds or by division of the root ball in early spring or autumn.
- Growing information and garden care: Nettle can be grown in full sun to partial shade and requires regular watering to keep the soil moist. It can be invasive, so it is recommended to plant it in a container or in an area where it can be contained.
- Insects and disease: Nettle (Urtica dioica) is a hardy plant that is generally not affected by many pests or diseases. However, there are some insects and diseases that may affect nettle plants:

> Aphids: Aphids are small, sap-sucking insects that may infest nettle plants. They can be controlled with insecticidal soap or neem oil.

> Spider mites: Spider mites are tiny insects that may infest nettle plants, causing yellowing of the leaves. They can be controlled with insecticidal soap or neem oil.

> Rust: Rust is a fungal disease that may affect nettle plants, causing yellow-orange spots on the leaves. It can be controlled with copper fungicides.

> Powdery mildew: Powdery mildew is a fungal disease that may affect nettle plants, causing white, powdery growth on the leaves. It can be controlled with fungicides.

> Root rot: Root rot is a fungal disease that may affect nettle plants, causing wilting and yellowing of the leaves. It can be prevented by planting nettle in well-drained soil.

It is important to maintain good plant hygiene and provide adequate growing conditions to prevent insect and disease infestations in nettle plants.

- Harvesting and preparations: Nettle (Urtica dioica) is a perennial plant that can be harvested for its leaves, stems, and roots. Here are some tips for harvesting and preparing nettle:

> Harvesting: Nettle can be harvested in the spring or early summer when the plants are young and tender. Wear gloves and long sleeves when harvesting

nettle to avoid getting stung by the fine hairs on the leaves and stems. Cut the top 6-8 inches of the plant, including the leaves and stems.
- Drying: Once harvested, nettle can be dried for later use. Spread the leaves and stems out on a drying rack or hang them upside down in a well-ventilated area. Once the leaves and stems are completely dry, store them in an airtight container.
- Infusions: Nettle can be used to make an infusion by steeping the dried leaves and stems in hot water for 10-15 minutes. This can be used as a tea or as a base for other preparations.
- Tinctures: Nettle can also be used to make a tincture by steeping the dried roots in alcohol or vinegar for several weeks. The tincture can be used in small doses as needed.
- Cooking: Nettle leaves can be blanched and used in soups, stews, and other dishes. They can also be sautéed or stir-fried with other vegetables. The young shoots of nettle can be cooked and eaten like asparagus.

It is important to consult with a healthcare provider before using any herbal medicine, especially if you have a medical condition or are taking other medications.

Medicines made with this herb

Nettle (Urtica dioica) has a long history of use as a medicinal herb and is still used in modern herbal medicine. Here are some examples of medicines made with nettle:
- Nettle tea: Nettle tea is made by steeping dried nettle leaves and stems in hot water. It is commonly used as a diuretic and to relieve symptoms of allergies and arthritis.
- Nettle tincture: Nettle tincture is made by steeping dried nettle roots in alcohol or vinegar for several weeks. It is commonly used as a natural remedy for urinary tract infections and to support the immune system.
- Nettle capsules: Nettle capsules are made from dried nettle leaves and are commonly used to relieve symptoms of allergies, arthritis, and prostate enlargement.
- Nettle extract: Nettle extract is made from the root of the nettle plant and is commonly used to relieve symptoms of benign prostatic hyperplasia (BPH).
- Nettle oil: Nettle oil is made by infusing nettle leaves and stems in a carrier oil, such as olive oil or coconut oil. It is commonly used in massage to relieve joint and muscle pain.
- Nettle hair rinse: Nettle hair rinse is made by steeping nettle leaves in water and using the resulting infusion as a hair rinse. It is said to promote hair growth and reduce dandruff.

It is important to consult with a healthcare provider before using any herbal medicine, especially if you have a medical condition or are taking other medications.

Medicines this herb counteracts:

Nettle (Urtica dioica) is generally considered safe and does not counteract any specific medications. However, it is always important to consult with a healthcare provider before using any herbal medicine, especially if you have a medical condition or are taking other medications. Nettle may interact with certain medications, such as blood thinners and diuretics, and may not be appropriate for everyone. Additionally, some individuals may experience allergic reactions to nettle, particularly those with a history of allergies to plants in the Urticaceae family. If you experience any adverse reactions to nettle, stop using it immediately and seek medical attention.

Oregon Grape Root

Herbal Identification:
- Common name: Oregon grape root
- Latin binomial: Mahonia aquifolium (previously Berberis aquifolium)
- Other common names: Mountain grape, holly-leaved barberry, trailing mahonia
- Plant family: Berberidaceae
- Botanical description: Oregon grape root (Mahonia aquifolium) is a perennial shrub native to western North America, including the Pacific Northwest region of the United States. It is also known by other common names such as mountain grape, holly-leaved barberry, and tall Oregon grape.

The plant typically grows to a height of 3 to 6 feet and has a spreading habit. It has glossy, holly-like leaves that are green in the summer and turn reddish-purple in the fall. The leaves are pinnate, with 5-9 leaflets that are sharply toothed and have spiny tips.

The shrub produces bright yellow flowers in early spring, which are arranged in clusters and have a sweet, honey-like fragrance. The flowers are followed by small, bluish-purple berries that are edible but tart.

The roots of the Oregon grape are woody and yellowish-brown in color, with a distinct, bitter taste. They contain a number of alkaloids, including berberine, which give the plant its medicinal properties. The root is often used in herbal medicine to treat a variety of ailments, including digestive issues, skin conditions, and infections.

Medicinal Properties:
- Parts used: The roots and bark of the stem and root are used in herbal medicine.
- Taste: Bitter
- Actions: Alterative, cholagogue, antimicrobial, astringent, hepatic, laxative
- Energetics: Cooling and drying
- Specific indications: Oregon grape root has been used in herbal medicine for a variety of conditions, and some of its specific indications include:
  - Digestive issues: Oregon grape root has a long history of use for digestive issues such as indigestion, constipation, and liver congestion. It stimulates

bile production, which aids in the digestion of fats and can help relieve bloating and abdominal discomfort.
- Skin conditions: Oregon grape root has anti-inflammatory and antimicrobial properties that make it useful for treating skin conditions such as psoriasis, eczema, and acne. It can also help soothe skin irritation and itching.
- Urinary tract infections: Oregon grape root has been shown to have antimicrobial properties that make it effective against bacteria that can cause urinary tract infections. It can also help reduce inflammation in the urinary tract.
- Respiratory infections: Oregon grape root has antimicrobial and anti-inflammatory properties that can help fight respiratory infections such as bronchitis and sinusitis. It can also help relieve congestion and coughing.
- Immune system support: Oregon grape root contains compounds that have been shown to stimulate the immune system, making it useful for preventing and fighting infections.

It is important to note that while Oregon grape root has been used traditionally for these conditions, more research is needed to determine its safety and efficacy for each specific use. As with any herbal remedy, it is best to consult with a healthcare provider before using Oregon grape root to treat any health condition.

Medicinal preparations:
Oregon grape root can be prepared in various forms for medicinal use. Some of the most common preparations include:
- Tincture: Oregon grape root can be prepared as a tincture by soaking the root in alcohol or glycerin for several weeks. This extract can be taken orally in small doses and is often used for digestive issues and skin conditions.
- Tea: Oregon grape root can be made into a tea by steeping the dried or fresh root in boiling water for 10-15 minutes. This can be consumed as a beverage or used topically as a wash for skin conditions.
- Capsules: Oregon grape root is also available in capsule form, which can be taken orally. This is a convenient way to take the herb, especially for those who do not like the taste of the tea or tincture.
- Topical preparations: Oregon grape root can be used topically in creams, lotions, and salves for skin conditions such as psoriasis and eczema. These preparations can be applied directly to the affected area.

It is important to note that Oregon grape root should be used under the guidance of a healthcare professional, as it can interact with certain medications and may not be safe for everyone.

• Ratio and dosage information: Dosage depends on the preparation used and the individual's needs. Consult with a healthcare provider or a qualified herbalist for specific dosage information.

Medicinal uses:
Oregon grape root has a long history of use in herbal medicine and has been used for a variety of medicinal purposes. Some of the most common uses include:
- Digestive issues: Oregon grape root has been traditionally used to treat digestive issues such as constipation, indigestion, and diarrhea. It is believed to stimulate the liver and gallbladder, which can improve digestion and relieve symptoms.
- Skin conditions: Oregon grape root has anti-inflammatory and antimicrobial properties that make it useful for treating skin conditions such as psoriasis, eczema, and acne. It can help reduce inflammation and soothe irritation.
- Urinary tract infections: Oregon grape root contains compounds that have been shown to have antimicrobial properties and can be effective against bacteria that cause urinary tract infections. It can also help reduce inflammation in the urinary tract.
- Respiratory infections: Oregon grape root has been used to treat respiratory infections such as bronchitis and sinusitis. It has antimicrobial and anti-inflammatory properties that can help fight the infection and reduce symptoms such as congestion and coughing.
- Immune system support: Oregon grape root contains compounds that have been shown to stimulate the immune system and may help prevent and fight infections.

It is important to note that while Oregon grape root has been used traditionally for these conditions, more research is needed to determine its safety and efficacy for each specific use. As with any herbal remedy, it is best to consult with a healthcare provider before using Oregon grape root to treat any health condition.

• Precautions and contradictions: While Oregon grape root is generally considered safe for most people, there are some precautions and contraindications to be aware of. These include:
- Pregnancy and breastfeeding: There is not enough research on the safety of Oregon grape root during pregnancy and breastfeeding, so it is best to avoid using it during these times.
- Children: Oregon grape root should not be used in children under 6 years of age.
- Liver disease: Oregon grape root can stimulate the liver, so it should not be used by people with liver disease.

- Medication interactions: Oregon grape root can interact with certain medications, including blood thinners, heart medications, and antidepressants. It can increase the effects of these medications and may cause unwanted side effects.
- Allergies: Some people may be allergic to Oregon grape root. Symptoms of an allergic reaction can include rash, itching, and difficulty breathing.
- High doses: Taking high doses of Oregon grape root can cause stomach upset, diarrhea, and other digestive issues.

It is important to talk to a healthcare provider before using Oregon grape root, especially if you are taking any medications or have a medical condition. They can help determine if it is safe and appropriate for you to use.

Cultivation:
- Native to: Western North America
- Zones: 4-8
- Soil: Well-draining soil with a pH between 5.0-7.0
- Propagation: Oregon grape root can be propagated from seeds or cuttings.
- Growing information and garden care: Oregon grape root prefers partial shade and moist soil. It is a slow-growing plant that can take several years to reach maturity.
- Insects and disease: Oregon grape root is generally resistant to most diseases and insect pests. However, like any plant, it can still be affected by some issues. Here are some of the potential insect and disease problems that may affect Oregon grape root:
- Rust: Rust is a fungal disease that can cause yellow or brown spots on the leaves of Oregon grape root. It can be treated with a fungicide, but prevention is the best approach. Good cultural practices such as keeping the area clean and free of debris, proper watering, and proper spacing of plants can help prevent rust.
- Root rot: Root rot is a fungal disease that can be caused by overwatering or poorly drained soil. Symptoms include wilting, yellowing, and stunted growth. The best way to prevent root rot is to provide proper drainage and avoid overwatering.
- Aphids: Aphids are small insects that can cause damage to the leaves of Oregon grape root by sucking sap from the plant. They can be controlled with insecticidal soap or neem oil.
- Leaf miners: Leaf miners are insects that tunnel through the leaves of Oregon grape root, leaving white trails on the surface. They can be controlled with insecticides or by removing and destroying affected leaves.

- Scale insects: Scale insects are small, immobile insects that attach themselves to the leaves and stems of plants, causing yellowing and stunted growth. They can be controlled with insecticidal soap or neem oil.

Regular monitoring of Oregon grape root plants can help detect and address any issues before they become serious problems. Proper care and maintenance can also help prevent insect and disease issues.

• Harvesting and preparations: Oregon grape root can be harvested in the fall or spring when the plant is dormant. The root should be dug up carefully to avoid damaging it, and any attached soil should be removed. The root can then be washed and dried in a warm, dry place until it is completely dry.

Once the root is dried, it can be prepared for use in a variety of ways, including:

- Tea: Oregon grape root can be brewed into a tea by steeping 1-2 teaspoons of dried root in hot water for 10-15 minutes. The tea can be sweetened with honey or another sweetener if desired.
- Tincture: Oregon grape root can be made into a tincture by soaking the dried root in alcohol for several weeks. The resulting liquid can be used as a concentrated herbal extract.
- Capsules: Oregon grape root can be ground into a powder and placed into capsules for easy use.
- Salve: Oregon grape root can be made into a salve by combining it with a carrier oil and beeswax. The resulting salve can be applied topically to the skin to treat a variety of conditions.

It is important to follow proper dosage instructions and consult with a healthcare provider before using Oregon grape root in any form. Pregnant and breastfeeding women, as well as children under 6 years of age, should avoid using Oregon grape root.

Medicines made with this herb:

Oregon grape root is used in various herbal remedies and supplements. Here are some examples of medicines made with this herb:

- Digestive aids: Oregon grape root is commonly used to support digestion and may be included in digestive supplements or teas.
- Immune support: Oregon grape root is believed to have immune-boosting properties and may be included in immune support supplements or teas.
- Skin treatments: Oregon grape root is often used in skin treatments due to its antibacterial and anti-inflammatory properties. It may be included in creams, ointments, or salves for conditions such as eczema, psoriasis, and acne.

- Liver support: Oregon grape root is known to stimulate the liver and may be included in supplements or teas designed to support liver health.
- Anti-inflammatory: Oregon grape root has anti-inflammatory properties and may be included in supplements or teas to reduce inflammation in the body.
- Antimicrobial: Oregon grape root has antimicrobial properties and may be included in supplements or teas to help fight bacterial, viral, or fungal infections.

It is important to note that the safety and effectiveness of herbal medicines can vary depending on the individual and the specific product. Always consult with a healthcare provider before using any herbal supplement or remedy, especially if you have a medical condition or are taking any medications.

Medicines this herb counteracts:

Oregon grape root may interact with certain medications due to its potential effects on liver enzymes. Here are some medications that may be affected by Oregon grape root:

- Blood thinners: Oregon grape root may increase the effects of blood-thinning medications such as warfarin, leading to an increased risk of bleeding.
- Immunosuppressants: Oregon grape root may reduce the effectiveness of medications used to suppress the immune system, such as cyclosporine and tacrolimus.
- Antidepressants: Oregon grape root may interact with certain antidepressant medications, such as fluoxetine and sertraline, leading to increased side effects.
- Antiarrhythmic medications: Oregon grape root may interact with medications used to regulate heart rhythm, such as amiodarone and quinidine.
- Antihistamines: Oregon grape root may interact with certain antihistamines, such as fexofenadine and loratadine, reducing their effectiveness.

It is important to talk to a healthcare provider before using Oregon grape root or any herbal supplement, especially if you are taking any medications or have a medical condition.

Parsley

Herbal Identification:
- Common name: Parsley
- Latin binomial: Petroselinum crispum
- Other common names: Garden parsley, curly parsley, flat leaf parsley, Italian parsley
- Plant family: Apiaceae (carrot family)
- Botanical description: Parsley is a biennial herb that can grow up to 1-2 feet tall. It has bright green leaves that are divided into three sections, with toothed edges, and a pointed tip. The leaves are arranged in a rosette at the base of the plant and along the stems. The stem is also green and slightly hairy. Small, white or yellow flowers grow in umbrella-shaped clusters called umbels. The fruits are small, oval, and brownish in color. There are two main types of parsley: curly leaf and flat leaf. Curly leaf parsley has tightly curled leaves, while flat leaf parsley has flat, more open leaves. Parsley belongs to the Apiaceae (carrot family) and is related to other plants such as celery, fennel, and carrot.

Medicinal Properties:
- Parts used: Leaves, stems, and seeds
- Taste: Pungent, bitter, slightly sweet
- Actions: Diuretic, carminative, expectorant, emmenagogue, anti-inflammatory, antioxidant, antimicrobial
- Energetics: Warming, drying
- Specific indications: Parsley has a wide range of specific indications, some of which include:
  - Urinary tract infections and inflammation
  - Kidney stones and kidney disease
  - Digestive disorders such as bloating, gas, and constipation
  - Bad breath and other oral health issues
  - Menstrual irregularities and pain
  - Anemia and iron deficiency
  - High blood pressure
  - Inflammation and swelling
  - Rheumatoid arthritis

Please note that these indications are based on traditional use and anecdotal evidence, and further research is needed to confirm their effectiveness.

- Ratio and dosage information: Tea: 1-2 teaspoons of dried herb per cup of water, steeped for 10-15 minutes; Tincture: 2-4 ml up to three times per day; Capsules: 400-600 mg up to three times per day

Medicinal uses:
Parsley has a long history of medicinal use and is valued for its various therapeutic properties. Some of the medicinal uses of parsley include:
- Diuretic: Parsley has a diuretic effect, which means it can increase urine production and help to flush out excess fluid from the body. This makes it useful for conditions such as edema, kidney stones, and urinary tract infections.
- Anti-inflammatory: Parsley contains compounds that have anti-inflammatory properties, which can help to reduce inflammation and swelling in the body. This makes it useful for conditions such as arthritis and other inflammatory conditions.
- Digestive aid: Parsley can help to stimulate digestion and relieve digestive issues such as bloating, gas, and constipation. It may also help to improve appetite and promote overall digestive health.
- Antioxidant: Parsley is rich in antioxidants, which can help to protect the body against damage from free radicals. This may help to reduce the risk of chronic diseases such as cancer and heart disease.
- Oral health: Parsley has been used traditionally to freshen breath and improve oral health. It may also help to reduce inflammation and infection in the mouth.
- Menstrual irregularities: Parsley may help to regulate menstrual cycles and relieve menstrual pain and cramps.

It is important to note that while parsley has many potential medicinal uses, further research is needed to confirm its effectiveness and safety. As with any herbal remedy, it is important to speak with a healthcare provider before using parsley for medicinal purposes.

- Precautions and contradictions: While parsley is generally considered safe when used in food amounts, there are some precautions and contraindications to be aware of when using it medicinally. Some of these include:
  - Allergic reactions: Parsley can cause allergic reactions in some people, especially those who are allergic to other plants in the same family, such as celery, fennel, or carrot.
  - Kidney disease: Because parsley is a diuretic, it can increase urine production and potentially worsen kidney disease in people with impaired kidney function.

- Bleeding disorders: Parsley contains compounds that may increase the risk of bleeding, so it should be avoided by people with bleeding disorders or those taking blood-thinning medications.
- Pregnancy and breastfeeding: Parsley is not recommended for use in pregnant or breastfeeding women, as it may stimulate uterine contractions and cause a miscarriage.

• Interaction with medications: Parsley may interact with certain medications, including lithium, diuretics, and blood thinners. If you are taking medication, speak with your healthcare provider before using parsley medicinally.

It is important to use parsley only under the guidance of a qualified healthcare provider, especially if you have any underlying medical conditions or are taking medications.

Cultivation:
- Native to: Mediterranean region
- Zones: 5-9
- Soil: Well-draining soil with a pH of 6.0-7.0
- Propagation: Seeds or cuttings
- Growing information and garden care: Parsley can be grown in full sun or partial shade and prefers cooler temperatures. It should be watered regularly and fertilized with a balanced fertilizer. Parsley can be grown in containers or in the ground and may need to be protected from frost in colder climates.
- Insects and disease: Parsley can be susceptible to certain insects and diseases. Some common pests that may affect parsley include aphids, spider mites, and whiteflies, which can cause damage to the leaves and stems of the plant. Parsley may also be susceptible to diseases such as powdery mildew and root rot, especially in humid or damp conditions.

To prevent insect infestations, it is important to keep the parsley plant healthy and well-maintained. This includes providing proper sunlight, water, and fertilization, as well as regularly inspecting the plant for signs of pest damage. Insecticidal soaps or horticultural oils may also be used to control infestations.

To prevent disease, it is important to plant parsley in well-draining soil and avoid overwatering. Good air circulation can also help to prevent fungal infections such as powdery mildew. If disease does occur, infected plant parts should be removed and destroyed to prevent further spread.

It is also important to practice crop rotation and avoid planting parsley in the same spot year after year, as this can increase the risk of disease. By following these practices, you can help to keep your parsley plant healthy and free from pests and disease.

• Harvesting and preparations: Parsley leaves can be harvested as soon as the plant has developed several sets of true leaves, which typically occurs about 70-90 days after planting.

The leaves can be harvested as needed throughout the growing season, but it is best to avoid harvesting more than one-third of the plant at a time to allow it to recover and continue growing.

To harvest parsley, simply cut off the stems at the base of the plant, or pluck individual leaves as needed. The leaves can be used fresh or dried for later use.

Parsley leaves can be used in a variety of culinary dishes, including soups, stews, sauces, and salads. The roots of the plant can also be harvested and used in cooking or for medicinal purposes, but they are less commonly used than the leaves.

Parsley can also be prepared as a medicinal tea, tincture, or infusion. To make a tea, simply steep a handful of fresh parsley leaves in hot water for several minutes. To make a tincture or infusion, the leaves can be dried and then soaked in alcohol or vinegar for several weeks to extract the medicinal compounds.

When preparing parsley for culinary or medicinal use, it is important to wash the leaves thoroughly to remove any dirt or debris. It is also important to use only fresh or properly dried parsley, as wilted or spoiled parsley can be harmful to health.

What medicines are made with this herb:
Parsley is not typically used to make medicines in modern Western herbalism, but it has been used traditionally for a variety of medicinal purposes. In some traditional systems of medicine, such as Ayurveda, parsley is considered to have medicinal properties and is used to treat a variety of ailments.

In traditional herbal medicine, parsley has been used to treat digestive disorders such as bloating, indigestion, and gas. It has also been used as a diuretic to help eliminate excess fluids from the body, and to support urinary tract health.

Additionally, parsley has been used as a natural breath freshener and to help treat bad breath.

Parsley may also have anti-inflammatory and antioxidant properties, and some research has suggested that it may have potential as a natural cancer-fighting agent. However, more research is needed to fully understand the potential medicinal benefits of parsley and its active compounds.

Overall, while parsley is not typically used to make specific medicines, it is a versatile herb with a long history of use in traditional herbal medicine.

What medicines this herb counteract:
Parsley is generally considered safe and is not known to counteract any specific medicines. However, it is important to note that parsley may interact with certain medications or supplements, particularly those that affect blood clotting or blood sugar levels.

Parsley contains compounds that may have mild blood-thinning effects, so it is possible that it could interact with anticoagulant medications such as warfarin or aspirin. Additionally, parsley may have hypoglycemic effects and may interact with diabetes medications or supplements.

If you are taking any medications or supplements and are considering using parsley for medicinal purposes, it is important to talk to your healthcare provider first to ensure that it is safe and appropriate for you to do so. They can advise you on any potential interactions or contraindications based on your individual health history and medication regimen.

Passionflower

Herbal Identification:
- Common Name: Passionflower
- Latin Binomial: Passiflora incarnata
- Other Common Names: Maypop, purple passionflower, wild apricot
- Plant Family: Passifloraceae
- Botanical Description: Passionflower, also known as Passiflora, is a genus of flowering plants that includes over 500 species. The plant is known for its striking flowers, which typically have five petals and come in a range of colors, including white, pink, red, purple, and blue.

Passionflowers are typically vines or climbing plants, but some species can also grow as shrubs or trees. They have a woody stem and alternate, palmately-lobed leaves that can be up to 10 inches long. The leaves are usually green, but some species have variegated or purple-tinged foliage.

The flowers of the passionflower are complex and ornate, with a central column of stamens and pistils surrounded by a ring of colorful petals. The flowers are typically 2 to 3 inches wide and have a distinctive, almost alien-like appearance.

After flowering, passionflowers produce small, egg-shaped fruit that are edible in some species. The fruit is typically green or yellow when unripe and turns orange or purple when ripe. The fruit contains numerous seeds that can be used for propagation.

Passionflowers are native to tropical and subtropical regions of the Americas, and they are commonly grown as ornamental plants in gardens and greenhouses around the world. They are also used in traditional medicine to treat a range of ailments, including anxiety, insomnia, and high blood pressure.

Medicinal Properties:
- Parts Used: Aerial parts, including the leaves, stems, and flowers
- Taste: Slightly bitter, astringent
- Actions: Sedative, anxiolytic, antispasmodic, nervine, hypnotic, analgesic, hypotensive
- Energetics: Cooling, moistening

- **Specific Indications:** Passionflower has been used in traditional medicine to treat various conditions, and some research studies have suggested that it may have certain therapeutic effects. Some of the specific indications for passionflower include:
  - Anxiety: Passionflower has been traditionally used as a natural remedy for anxiety and stress. Some studies have found that passionflower may have anxiolytic effects and may be effective in reducing symptoms of anxiety.
  - Insomnia: Passionflower has sedative properties and may help improve sleep quality. It has been used in traditional medicine to treat insomnia and other sleep disorders.
  - Hypertension: Passionflower may have antihypertensive effects and may help lower blood pressure. It has been traditionally used to treat hypertension and other cardiovascular conditions.
  - Menopausal symptoms: Passionflower has been traditionally used to treat symptoms of menopause, such as hot flashes and insomnia.
  - Pain relief: Passionflower may have analgesic properties and may help relieve pain and inflammation.

It's important to note that while passionflower may have potential therapeutic benefits, more research is needed to fully understand its effects and determine appropriate dosages and safety considerations. It's always best to consult with a healthcare provider before using any herbal supplement or natural remedy.

Medicinal Preparations:

Passionflower can be used to prepare a variety of medicinal preparations. Here are some of the most common ways to use passionflower:
- Tea: Passionflower tea can be made by steeping 1 to 2 teaspoons of dried passionflower in a cup of hot water for 10 to 15 minutes. This can be consumed 2 to 3 times a day.
- Tincture: Passionflower tincture can be made by soaking the plant material in a mixture of alcohol and water for several weeks. The resulting liquid can be taken orally, usually diluted in water or juice.
- Capsules or tablets: Passionflower supplements are available in the form of capsules or tablets. These can be taken according to the manufacturer's instructions.
- Topical ointment: Passionflower ointment can be applied topically to the skin to help with skin inflammation and irritation.

It's important to note that while passionflower is generally considered safe, it can interact with certain medications and may not be suitable for everyone. It's always best to consult with a healthcare provider before using any herbal

supplement or natural remedy, especially if you have any underlying health conditions or are taking medications.
- Ratio and Dosage Information: Infusion: 1-2 teaspoons of dried herb per cup of water; steep for 10-15 minutes, 3 times per day. Tincture: 2-4 ml, 3 times per day. Capsules: 400-500 mg, 2-3 times per day.

Medicinal Uses:
Passionflower has been used for various medicinal purposes for centuries. Here are some of the most common medicinal uses of passionflower:
- Anxiety and stress: Passionflower has been traditionally used as a natural remedy for anxiety and stress. Some studies have suggested that it may help reduce symptoms of anxiety, such as restlessness, irritability, and insomnia.
- Insomnia and sleep disorders: Passionflower has sedative properties and may help improve sleep quality. It has been used in traditional medicine to treat insomnia and other sleep disorders.
- Hypertension: Passionflower may help lower blood pressure and improve cardiovascular health. It has been traditionally used to treat hypertension and other cardiovascular conditions.
- Menopausal symptoms: Passionflower has been used to alleviate symptoms of menopause, such as hot flashes and insomnia.
- Pain relief: Passionflower may have analgesic properties and may help relieve pain and inflammation.
- Digestive problems: Passionflower has been used to treat digestive issues such as irritable bowel syndrome (IBS) and gastrointestinal spasms.
- Respiratory problems: Passionflower has been used to treat respiratory conditions such as asthma and bronchitis.
- Skin inflammation: Passionflower ointment can be applied topically to the skin to help with skin inflammation and irritation.

It's important to note that while passionflower may have potential therapeutic benefits, more research is needed to fully understand its effects and determine appropriate dosages and safety considerations. It's always best to consult with a healthcare provider before using any herbal supplement or natural remedy.
- Precautions and Contraindications: While passionflower is generally considered safe when used appropriately, there are some precautions and contraindications to be aware of. Here are some important considerations:
- Pregnancy and breastfeeding: Passionflower may not be safe for use during pregnancy and breastfeeding, as there is not enough research to determine its safety in these populations.

- Sedative effects: Passionflower has sedative properties and may cause drowsiness or sleepiness. It should not be taken before driving or operating heavy machinery.
- Interaction with medications: Passionflower may interact with certain medications, including sedatives, anti-anxiety drugs, and blood thinners. It's important to talk to a healthcare provider before taking passionflower if you are taking any medications.
- Allergic reaction: Some people may have an allergic reaction to passionflower, especially if they are allergic to other plants in the same family.
- Liver toxicity: There have been a few reports of liver toxicity associated with passionflower use, although it is rare. People with liver disease or a history of liver problems should consult with a healthcare provider before using passionflower.
- Children: Passionflower should not be used in children without the guidance of a healthcare provider.

As with any herbal supplement or natural remedy, it's important to talk to a healthcare provider before using passionflower, especially if you have any underlying health conditions or are taking medications.

Cultivation:
- Native to: Southeastern United States and Central and South America
- Zones: 6-10
- Soil: Well-draining, fertile soil with a pH of 6.0-7.0
- Propagation: Seed, stem cuttings
- Growing Information and Garden Care: Passionflower prefers full sun to partial shade and can be grown on a trellis or support structure. It is a hardy plant that can withstand drought and poor soil conditions, but may benefit from occasional fertilization and pruning to promote healthy growth.
- Insects and Disease: Passionflower Passionflower can be affected by a number of insects and diseases. Here are some of the most common issues:

Insects:
- Passionflower vine borer: This is a moth whose larvae tunnel into the stems of the plant, causing wilt and death of the vine.
- Passionflower butterfly: This is a common pest that feeds on the leaves of the plant. While it can cause significant damage, it is also an important pollinator for the plant.
- Spider mites: These tiny insects can infest the plant and cause damage to the leaves, including yellowing and drying out.

Diseases:

- Fusarium wilt: This fungal disease causes yellowing and wilting of the leaves, and can eventually lead to the death of the plant.
- Powdery mildew: This fungal disease appears as a white, powdery coating on the leaves and stems of the plant. It can be caused by high humidity and poor air circulation.
- Leaf spot: This fungal disease causes circular spots on the leaves, which can eventually lead to the death of the plant if left untreated.

To prevent and manage these issues, it's important to maintain good plant health through proper watering, fertilization, and pruning practices. Insect pests can be managed with insecticidal soaps or other natural remedies, while fungal diseases may require the use of fungicides.

It's always important to read and follow label instructions when using any chemical treatments on plants.

• Harvesting and Preparations: Passionflower can be harvested and prepared for use in a variety of ways. Here are some guidelines:

Harvesting:
- Timing: Passionflower can be harvested when the plant is in full bloom, typically in late summer or early fall.
- Look for mature flowers: Look for flowers that have fully opened and have a bright, vibrant color.
- Harvest in the morning: It's best to harvest passionflower in the morning when the flowers are fresh and have not yet been exposed to the sun for too long.

Preparations:
- Tea: Passionflower tea can be made by steeping 1-2 teaspoons of dried passionflower in hot water for 5-10 minutes. It can be consumed up to three times per day.
- Tincture: A tincture can be made by soaking the dried passionflower in alcohol or glycerin for several weeks. The resulting liquid can then be strained and used as needed.
- Capsules: Passionflower supplements are available in capsule form. It's important to follow the recommended dosage on the label.
- Ointment: A passionflower ointment can be made by blending the dried plant material with a carrier oil, such as coconut oil or olive oil. The mixture can then be applied topically to the skin.

It's important to note that passionflower is not a substitute for medical treatment, and it's always best to consult with a healthcare provider before using any herbal supplement or natural remedy.

What medicines are made with this herb:
Passionflower is used in a variety of medicinal products, including:
- Herbal supplements: Passionflower is available in capsule, tablet, and liquid form as an herbal supplement.
- Teas: Passionflower is used to make herbal teas that are commonly used to promote relaxation and alleviate anxiety.
- Tinctures: Passionflower is used to make tinctures that are used to treat anxiety, insomnia, and other conditions.
- Topical ointments: Passionflower is sometimes used in topical ointments and creams for its anti-inflammatory and pain-relieving properties.
- Homeopathic remedies: Passionflower is sometimes used in homeopathic remedies to treat anxiety, nervousness, and insomnia.

It's important to note that passionflower should be used under the guidance of a healthcare provider and should not be used as a substitute for medical treatment. Additionally, passionflower may interact with certain medications, so it's important to talk to a healthcare provider before using passionflower if you are taking any medications.

What medicines this herb counteracts:
Passionflower is generally considered safe and does not have any known counteractions with specific medications. However, it's important to note that it may interact with certain medications, including:
- Sedatives: Passionflower has mild sedative properties and may increase the effects of sedative medications, including benzodiazepines, barbiturates, and sleeping pills. It's important to talk to a healthcare provider before using passionflower if you are taking any sedative medications.
- Anti-anxiety medications: Passionflower may increase the effects of anti-anxiety medications, including benzodiazepines and selective serotonin reuptake inhibitors (SSRIs). It's important to talk to a healthcare provider before using passionflower if you are taking any anti-anxiety medications.
- Blood thinners: There is some evidence to suggest that passionflower may have a mild blood-thinning effect. It's important to talk to a healthcare provider before using passionflower if you are taking any blood-thinning medications, such as warfarin or aspirin.
- MAO inhibitors: Passionflower may interact with monoamine oxidase (MAO) inhibitors, which are a type of medication used to treat depression.

It's important to talk to a healthcare provider before using passionflower if you are taking any MAO inhibitors.

As with any herbal supplement or natural remedy, it's important to talk to a healthcare provider before using passionflower if you are taking any medications or have any underlying medical conditions.

Peppermint

Herbal Identification:
- Common name: Peppermint
- Latin binomial: Mentha x piperita
- Other common names: Brandy mint, balm mint, lamb mint
- Plant family: Lamiaceae (mint family)
- Botanical description: Peppermint is a hybrid plant that is a cross between spearmint and watermint. It has square stems that are green or purplish in color, opposite leaves that are dark green and slightly hairy, and produces small, pinkish-purple flowers in summer. Peppermint grows up to 3 feet tall and has a spreading habit. It has a strong minty aroma and flavor, and its leaves are slightly rough to the touch.

Medicinal Properties:
- Recommended cultivars: Black Mitcham, Todd's Mitcham, and Native
- Parts used: Leaves and essential oil
- Taste: Aromatic, pungent, cooling
- Actions: Carminative, anti-spasmodic, anti-inflammatory, analgesic, diaphoretic, and expectorant
- Energetics: Cooling and drying
- Specific indications: Peppermint has a variety of medicinal properties and can be used for the following specific indications:
  - Digestive issues: Peppermint is known for its ability to soothe digestive issues such as indigestion, bloating, and gas.
  - Headaches: Peppermint can help to alleviate tension headaches and migraines.
  - Respiratory issues: Peppermint can help to relieve congestion and soothe coughs.
  - Nausea: Peppermint can help to reduce nausea and vomiting.
  - Muscle pain: Peppermint can help to alleviate muscle pain and soreness.
  - Menstrual cramps: Peppermint can help to relieve menstrual cramps.
  - Anxiety and stress: Peppermint can help to calm the nerves and reduce anxiety and stress.

Medicinal preparations:
Peppermint can be used in a variety of medicinal preparations, including:

- Tea: Peppermint tea can be made by steeping 1-2 teaspoons of dried peppermint leaves in a cup of hot water for 10-15 minutes. This can be consumed up to three times per day.
- Tincture: A peppermint tincture can be made by steeping peppermint leaves in alcohol for several weeks. This can be taken by adding a few drops to water or juice.
- Essential oil: Peppermint essential oil can be used topically by diluting it with a carrier oil and applying it to the skin. It can also be used aromatically by adding a few drops to a diffuser.
- Capsules: Peppermint capsules can be taken orally to alleviate digestive issues and other conditions. Follow the manufacturer's instructions for dosage.

It's important to note that peppermint oil and capsules should be used with caution in individuals with acid reflux or gastroesophageal reflux disease (GERD) as they can worsen symptoms.

- Ratio and dosage information: 1-2 tsp of dried leaves in 1 cup of hot water, 2-4 mL of tincture three times a day, 1-2 drops of essential oil diluted in a carrier oil, 1-2 capsules up to three times per day

Medicinal uses:

Peppermint has a variety of medicinal uses, including:
- Digestive issues: Peppermint can help to soothe digestive issues such as indigestion, bloating, and gas. It can also improve digestion and stimulate the production of bile.
- Headaches: Peppermint can help to alleviate tension headaches and migraines by relaxing the muscles in the head and neck.
- Respiratory issues: Peppermint can help to relieve congestion and soothe coughs by acting as a natural decongestant and expectorant.
- Nausea: Peppermint can help to reduce nausea and vomiting by relaxing the muscles in the digestive tract.
- Muscle pain: Peppermint can help to alleviate muscle pain and soreness by acting as a natural analgesic and anti-inflammatory agent.
- Menstrual cramps: Peppermint can help to relieve menstrual cramps by relaxing the muscles in the uterus and reducing inflammation.
- Anxiety and stress: Peppermint can help to calm the nerves and reduce anxiety and stress by acting as a natural sedative.

Peppermint can also be used topically to soothe skin irritation and promote wound healing.

- Precautions and contraindications: While peppermint is generally considered safe, there are some precautions and contraindications to be aware of:
  - Peppermint oil and capsules should be used with caution in individuals with acid reflux or gastroesophageal reflux disease (GERD) as they can worsen symptoms.
  - Peppermint oil should not be applied directly to the skin as it can cause irritation and allergic reactions. It should always be diluted with a carrier oil.
  - Peppermint oil should not be used on infants and young children as it can cause breathing difficulties.
  - Peppermint can interact with certain medications, including those for diabetes, high blood pressure, and acid reflux. Consult with a healthcare provider before using peppermint if you are taking any medications.
  - Peppermint should be avoided during pregnancy as it can stimulate menstruation and potentially cause miscarriage.
  - Peppermint can also cause side effects such as heartburn, nausea, and allergic reactions in some individuals.

Cultivation:
- Native to: Europe and the Middle East
- Zones: 3-11
- Soil: Well-draining soil with a pH between 6.0 and 7.0
- Propagation: Peppermint can be propagated by dividing the root ball or from stem cuttings. It can also be grown from seed.
- Growing information and garden care: Peppermint prefers full sun to partial shade and regular watering. It can be invasive, so it's best to plant it in a container or in an area where it can be contained.
- Insects and disease: Peppermint is generally resistant to insects and diseases. However, there are a few pests and diseases that may affect peppermint plants:
  - Spider mites: These small pests can infest the leaves of peppermint plants, causing them to turn yellow and die. Spider mites can be controlled with insecticidal soap or neem oil.
  - Mint root borer: This insect can burrow into the roots of peppermint plants, causing them to wilt and die. Infected plants should be removed and destroyed to prevent the spread of the pest.
  - Peppermint rust: This fungal disease appears as yellow-orange spots on the leaves of peppermint plants. It can be controlled with fungicides and by practicing good sanitation in the garden.

Proper garden care and maintenance can help to prevent pest and disease issues in peppermint plants. This includes planting peppermint in well-draining soil, providing adequate water and sunlight, and avoiding overcrowding.

- Harvesting and preparations: Peppermint leaves can be harvested throughout the growing season, but they are most potent just before the plant blooms. Here are some tips for harvesting and preparing peppermint:
- Harvest the leaves in the morning when the oils are most concentrated.
- Cut the stems just above a set of leaves, leaving some foliage on the plant so it can continue to grow.
- Rinse the leaves with cold water and pat them dry.
- Peppermint can be used fresh or dried for later use. To dry, tie small bunches of peppermint and hang them upside down in a well-ventilated area until they are completely dry.
- To make peppermint tea, steep 1-2 teaspoons of dried peppermint leaves in a cup of boiling water for 5-10 minutes.
- Peppermint can also be used in culinary dishes, such as desserts, drinks, and savory dishes, to add a refreshing minty flavor.

Peppermint oil can also be extracted from the leaves through steam distillation. However, this should only be done by experienced individuals as it can be dangerous if not done properly.

What medicines are made with this herb:

Peppermint is used in a variety of medicinal preparations, including:
- Peppermint tea: Peppermint tea is a popular herbal infusion that can help soothe digestive issues, relieve nausea, and promote relaxation.
- Peppermint essential oil: Peppermint oil is a highly concentrated extract of the peppermint plant that is used in aromatherapy, as well as in topical applications for pain relief, headaches, and respiratory issues.
- Peppermint capsules: Peppermint capsules are used to treat digestive issues such as irritable bowel syndrome (IBS), indigestion, and bloating.
- Peppermint tincture: Peppermint tincture is an alcohol-based extract of peppermint that can be taken orally for digestive issues or used topically for headaches or muscle pain.
- Peppermint lozenges: Peppermint lozenges can help soothe sore throats and coughs, as well as freshen breath.

Peppermint is also used in many over-the-counter products, including toothpaste, mouthwash, and cough drops.

What medicines this herb counteract:

Peppermint is generally considered safe for most people and does not typically counteract any medications. However, it is always important to consult with a healthcare professional before using any herbal supplement, especially if you are taking any prescription medications. Peppermint may interact with certain medications, such as those that are broken down by the liver, so it is important to discuss any potential interactions with your doctor or pharmacist. Additionally, peppermint may worsen symptoms of gastroesophageal reflux disease (GERD) in some people, so it may not be appropriate for individuals with this condition.

Red Clover

Herbal Identification:
- Common name: Red Clover
- Latin binomial: Trifolium pratense
- Other common names: Beebread, Cow Clover, Meadow Clover, Purple Clover
- Plant family: Fabaceae (Leguminosae)
- Botanical description: Red clover is a herbaceous, short-lived perennial plant that grows up to 60 cm tall. It has a hairy stem and leaves composed of three leaflets, each up to 15 mm long. The leaflets are ovate and have a pale, V-shaped mark in the center. The flowers are pink to reddish-purple and are arranged in a dense, globular head or inflorescence. Each flower is about 1 cm long and has a characteristic shape that resembles a tiny upside-down V. The plant has a sweet, mild fragrance.

Red clover belongs to the Fabaceae (Leguminosae) family and is closely related to other clover species such as white clover (Trifolium repens) and alsike clover (Trifolium hybridum).

Medicinal Properties:
- Recommended cultivars: Dutch white, Kenland, and S100
- Parts used: Flowers, leaves
- Taste: Sweet
- Actions: Alterative, expectorant, antispasmodic, lymphatic, tonic
- Energetics: Cooling, moistening
- Specific indications: Red clover has been traditionally used for various specific indications, including:
  - Skin conditions: Red clover is often used to help with skin conditions such as eczema, psoriasis, and acne. It is believed to help purify the blood, which in turn can help to improve the appearance of the skin.
  - Respiratory infections: Red clover has been used as a respiratory tonic and expectorant to help with respiratory infections such as bronchitis and whooping cough.
  - Menopausal symptoms: Red clover is believed to contain phytoestrogens, which are plant compounds that can mimic the effects of estrogen in the body. This has led to its use in easing menopausal symptoms such as hot flashes, night sweats, and mood swings.

- Cancer prevention: Red clover is high in isoflavones, which are compounds that have been shown to have anticancer properties. It is believed that red clover may help to prevent certain types of cancer, including breast and prostate cancer.
- Osteoporosis: Red clover is believed to help prevent osteoporosis by increasing bone density and preventing the loss of bone mass.
- Infertility: Red clover has been used as a fertility herb for women, as it is believed to help regulate the menstrual cycle and promote ovulation. It may also help to improve the quality of cervical mucus, which can aid in fertilization.

Medicinal preparations:
Red clover can be prepared and consumed in various forms for medicinal purposes, including:
- Infusion: An infusion, also known as a tea, is made by steeping dried or fresh red clover flowers and leaves in hot water for 10-15 minutes. This is the most common preparation for using red clover internally.
- Tincture: A tincture is made by steeping dried or fresh red clover flowers and leaves in alcohol for several weeks. The resulting liquid is then strained and consumed in small doses.
- Capsules: Red clover supplements are available in capsule form, which can be taken orally.
- Creams: Red clover creams and ointments are used topically for skin conditions such as eczema and psoriasis.
- Poultices: Poultices can be made by crushing fresh or dried red clover flowers and leaves and applying them directly to the affected area. This is often used for skin conditions and wounds.

It is important to note that the ratio and dosage information for each preparation will vary depending on the specific product and intended use. It is always best to consult with a healthcare provider or qualified herbalist for personalized advice on how to use red clover safely and effectively.

- Ratio and dosage information: 1-2 teaspoons of dried herb per cup of water for tea, 1:2 45-60% tincture, 3-4 ml three times per day

Medicinal uses:
Red clover has a long history of use in traditional medicine for various medicinal purposes, including:
- Blood purification: Red clover is believed to have a cleansing effect on the blood, and is often used as a detoxifying agent to help eliminate toxins from the body.
- Respiratory health: Red clover has been used as a respiratory tonic and expectorant to help with respiratory infections such as bronchitis and whooping cough.
- Menopausal symptoms: Red clover is believed to contain phytoestrogens, which can help to ease menopausal symptoms such as hot flashes, night sweats, and mood swings.
- Cancer prevention: Red clover is high in isoflavones, which have been shown to have anticancer properties. It is believed that red clover may help to prevent certain types of cancer, including breast and prostate cancer.
- Osteoporosis: Red clover is believed to help prevent osteoporosis by increasing bone density and preventing the loss of bone mass.
- Fertility: Red clover has been used as a fertility herb for women, as it is believed to help regulate the menstrual cycle and promote ovulation. It may also help to improve the quality of cervical mucus, which can aid in fertilization.
- Skin conditions: Red clover is often used topically for skin conditions such as eczema and psoriasis. It may help to soothe inflammation and promote healing.

It is important to note that while red clover is generally considered safe for most people, there may be potential interactions with certain medications and it should not be used by individuals who are pregnant or breastfeeding.

As with any herbal remedy, it is always best to consult with a healthcare provider or qualified herbalist before using red clover for medicinal purposes.

• Precautions and contradictions: While red clover is generally considered safe for most people, there are some precautions and contraindications to be aware of, including:
- Pregnancy and breastfeeding: Red clover should not be used by women who are pregnant or breastfeeding due to its potential effects on hormones.
- Blood clotting disorders: Red clover may have blood-thinning effects, and should not be used by individuals with blood clotting disorders or those taking blood-thinning medications.
- Hormone-sensitive conditions: Red clover contains isoflavones, which may have estrogen-like effects in the body. As such, it should be used with

caution by individuals with hormone-sensitive conditions such as breast cancer, ovarian cancer, or endometriosis.
- Interactions with medications: Red clover may interact with certain medications, including blood-thinning medications, hormone replacement therapy, and birth control pills. Individuals taking these medications should consult with a healthcare provider before using red clover.
- Allergies: Individuals who are allergic to plants in the legume family (such as peanuts or soybeans) may also be allergic to red clover.

It is always important to consult with a healthcare provider or qualified herbalist before using red clover or any other herbal remedy, especially if you have any underlying health conditions or are taking medications.

Cultivation:
- Native to: Europe, Western Asia, and Northwest Africa
- Zones: 4-8
- Soil: Well-drained soil with a pH range of 6.0-7.0
- Propagation: Seed or division
- Growing information and garden care: Red clover prefers full sun to partial shade and moist, well-drained soil. It can be grown as a cover crop or forage crop. It is a legume and fixes nitrogen in the soil.
- Insects and disease: Red clover is generally a hardy plant that is resistant to many common insects and diseases. However, there are a few issues that can affect its growth and health:
  - Aphids: Aphids can occasionally infest red clover plants and cause damage to the leaves and stems. Regular monitoring and the use of insecticidal soap or neem oil can help to control aphids.
  - Clover root curculio: This is a beetle that can cause damage to the roots of red clover plants, resulting in stunted growth and reduced yields. Crop rotation and the use of insecticides can help to control clover root curculio.
  - Leaf spot: This is a fungal disease that can cause brown or black spots on the leaves of red clover plants. Planting in well-draining soil and avoiding overhead watering can help to prevent leaf spot.
  - Powdery mildew: Powdery mildew is a fungal disease that can cause a white or grayish coating on the leaves of red clover plants. Proper plant spacing and the use of fungicides can help to control powdery mildew.
  - Crown rot: Crown rot is a fungal disease that can cause wilting and death of the plant. Planting in well-draining soil and avoiding overwatering can help to prevent crown rot.

Overall, proper plant care and maintenance can help to prevent insect and disease issues with red clover plants.

• Harvesting and preparations: The timing of harvesting and preparation of red clover depends on the intended use of the plant. Here are some general guidelines:
  - Harvesting: Red clover flowers should be harvested when they are in full bloom, typically in early to mid-summer. The flowers can be harvested by hand or with a sickle, and should be dried as soon as possible to prevent spoilage.
  - Drying: Red clover flowers can be dried by hanging them in a well-ventilated area out of direct sunlight. Once they are completely dry, the flowers can be stored in an airtight container in a cool, dry place.
  - Tea: Red clover flowers can be used to make a medicinal tea. To make the tea, steep 1-2 teaspoons of dried flowers in a cup of boiling water for 10-15 minutes. The tea can be consumed up to three times per day.
  - Tincture: Red clover flowers can also be used to make a tincture. To make the tincture, combine 1 part dried flowers with 5 parts 80-proof alcohol (such as vodka) in a glass jar. Shake the jar daily for 2-4 weeks, then strain out the solids and store the tincture in a dark glass bottle.
  - Topical use: Red clover flowers can also be used topically to soothe skin irritations and promote healing. To make a topical application, steep 2-3 teaspoons of dried flowers in 1 cup of boiling water for 10-15 minutes. Once the mixture has cooled, strain out the solids and apply the liquid to the affected area with a clean cloth or cotton ball.

As always, it is important to consult with a healthcare provider or qualified herbalist before using red clover or any other herbal remedy.

What medicines are made with this herb:
Red clover is a versatile herb that is used in various medicinal preparations. Some of the common medicines made with red clover include:
  - Red clover tea: Red clover flowers can be used to make a medicinal tea that is often used to treat respiratory issues, skin problems, and menopausal symptoms.
  - Red clover tincture: Red clover flowers can also be used to make a tincture, which is an alcohol-based herbal extract. Red clover tincture is commonly used to treat menopausal symptoms, improve blood flow, and as a general health tonic.
  - Red clover salve: Red clover flowers can be infused into oil to make a salve, which can be applied topically to soothe skin irritations, such as eczema and psoriasis.

- Red clover capsules: Red clover extract can be encapsulated and taken as a dietary supplement. Red clover capsules are commonly used to alleviate menopausal symptoms, such as hot flashes and night sweats.
- Red clover oil: Red clover flowers can be infused into oil to make an oil extract, which can be used topically to soothe skin irritations and promote healing.

It is important to note that while red clover is generally considered safe, it may interact with certain medications and should be used with caution in people with hormone-sensitive conditions. It is always best to consult with a healthcare provider or qualified herbalist before using red clover or any other herbal remedy.

What medicines this herb counter act:

There are no known medications that red clover specifically counteracts. However, red clover may interact with certain medications, particularly those that are metabolized by the liver or have hormonal effects.

Some medications that may interact with red clover include:
- Estrogen-based medications: Red clover has estrogen-like effects and may interact with medications that contain estrogen, such as birth control pills or hormone replacement therapy.
- Blood thinners: Red clover may have blood-thinning effects and may interact with medications that also thin the blood, such as warfarin or aspirin.
- Chemotherapy drugs: Red clover may interact with chemotherapy drugs and may interfere with their effectiveness.
- Liver-metabolized medications: Red clover may interact with medications that are metabolized by the liver, such as statins or antifungal drugs.

As always, it is important to consult with a healthcare provider or qualified herbalist before using red clover or any other herbal remedy, especially if you are taking any medications or have a medical condition.

Reishi Mushroom

Herbal Identification:
- Common name: Reishi Mushroom
- Latin binomial: Ganoderma lucidum
- Other common names: Lingzhi, ling chih, ling chi, "mushroom of immortality"
- Plant family: Ganodermataceae
- Botanical description: Reishi mushrooms (Ganoderma lucidum) are a type of medicinal mushroom that grow in various parts of the world, including Asia, North America, and Europe. They are commonly known as lingzhi in China, and are highly valued in traditional Chinese medicine for their health benefits.

The fruiting body of the Reishi mushroom is shaped like a fan or a kidney, with a distinctive reddish-brown color and a glossy, lacquered appearance. The cap can reach up to 30 centimeters (12 inches) in diameter and is often kidney-shaped or circular.

The top of the cap is typically marked with a series of concentric rings, while the underside is covered with small, white, porous pores. The stem of the mushroom is short and stubby, and may or may not be present depending on the growth conditions.

Reishi
mushrooms are typically found growing on dead or dying hardwood trees, and may also be cultivated on sawdust or other organic substrates. They are slow-growing and can take up to 5 years to mature.

Reishi mushrooms have a bitter, woody flavor and are typically consumed in the form of supplements or tea for their health benefits. They are rich in antioxidants and have been shown to have anti-inflammatory, anti-tumor, and immune-modulating properties.

Medicinal Properties:
- Parts used: The fruiting body of the mushroom is used medicinally.
- Taste: Bitter
- Actions: Adaptogen, immunomodulator, anti-inflammatory, hepatoprotective, antioxidant, anti-cancer, anti-allergy, anti-viral
- Energetics: Sweet, slightly warm, and nourishing to the spirit

- Specific indications: Reishi mushrooms have a wide range of health benefits, and are commonly used in traditional Chinese medicine to support overall health and wellness. Some of the specific indications for Reishi mushrooms include:
  - Immune system support: Reishi mushrooms have been shown to have immune-modulating properties, which may help to support the immune system and reduce the risk of infections and other immune-related disorders.
  - Anti-inflammatory activity: Reishi mushrooms contain compounds that have anti-inflammatory properties, which may help to reduce inflammation in the body and alleviate symptoms of inflammatory conditions such as arthritis, asthma, and eczema.
  - Cardiovascular health: Reishi mushrooms may help to reduce high blood pressure and cholesterol levels, which can improve overall cardiovascular health and reduce the risk of heart disease.
  - Anti-tumor activity: Reishi mushrooms contain compounds that have been shown to have anti-tumor activity, and may help to reduce the risk of certain types of cancer.
  - Liver support: Reishi mushrooms may help to support liver health and improve liver function, which can be beneficial for people with liver disease or liver damage.
  - Stress and anxiety relief: Reishi mushrooms may help to reduce stress and anxiety levels, and improve overall mood and well-being.

It's important to note that while Reishi mushrooms have been shown to have health benefits, they should not be used as a substitute for medical treatment. If you have any health concerns or medical conditions, it's important to speak with your healthcare provider before using Reishi mushrooms or any other dietary supplements.

Medicinal preparations:
Reishi mushrooms can be prepared and consumed in various ways, including:
- Capsules and tablets: Reishi mushroom extract is often available in capsule or tablet form, which makes it easy to consume and provides a standardized dose.
- Tea: Reishi mushroom tea is made by steeping dried or powdered Reishi mushrooms in hot water. The tea has a slightly bitter taste, and may be sweetened with honey or another natural sweetener.
- Tincture: Reishi mushroom tincture is a liquid extract of the mushroom, which is typically mixed with alcohol or glycerin. It can be added to drinks or taken directly by mouth.

- Powder: Reishi mushroom powder is made by grinding dried Reishi mushrooms into a fine powder. It can be added to smoothies, soups, or other foods for a nutritional boost.
- Topical applications: Reishi mushroom extracts can be added to skincare products, such as creams and lotions, for their anti-inflammatory and antioxidant properties.

When purchasing Reishi mushroom products, it's important to choose a reputable brand that uses high-quality ingredients and has undergone third-party testing for purity and potency. It's also important to follow dosage instructions carefully and speak with a healthcare provider before using Reishi mushrooms or any other dietary supplement.

- Ratio and dosage information: Dosage and preparation depend on the specific product and intended use. Follow the instructions on the label or consult with a qualified herbalist or healthcare provider.

Medicinal uses:
Reishi mushrooms (Ganoderma lucidum) have been used for centuries in traditional medicine systems, and have gained popularity in recent years for their potential health benefits. Some of the medicinal uses of Reishi mushrooms include:

- Immune system support: Reishi mushrooms contain beta-glucans, polysaccharides, and other compounds that have been shown to stimulate and support the immune system. They may help to reduce the risk of infections, improve immune function, and reduce inflammation.
- Cardiovascular health: Reishi mushrooms may help to reduce high blood pressure and cholesterol levels, which can improve overall cardiovascular health and reduce the risk of heart disease.
- Anti-tumor activity: Reishi mushrooms contain compounds that have been shown to have anti-tumor activity, and may help to reduce the risk of certain types of cancer.
- Liver support: Reishi mushrooms may help to support liver health and improve liver function, which can be beneficial for people with liver disease or liver damage.
- Anti-inflammatory activity: Reishi mushrooms contain compounds that have anti-inflammatory properties, which may help to reduce inflammation in the body and alleviate symptoms of inflammatory conditions such as arthritis, asthma, and eczema.
- Stress and anxiety relief: Reishi mushrooms may help to reduce stress and anxiety levels, and improve overall mood and well-being.

It's important to note that while Reishi mushrooms have been shown to have health benefits, they should not be used as a substitute for medical treatment. If you have any health concerns or medical conditions, it's important to speak with your healthcare provider before using Reishi mushrooms or any other dietary supplements.

• Precautions and contradictions: Reishi mushrooms are generally considered safe when used appropriately, but there are some precautions and contraindications to be aware of:
- Blood-thinning medications: Reishi mushrooms may have a mild blood-thinning effect, so they should be used with caution in people taking blood-thinning medications such as warfarin or aspirin.
- Surgery: Due to their potential blood-thinning effect, Reishi mushrooms should be stopped at least 2 weeks before any scheduled surgery.
- Autoimmune diseases: Reishi mushrooms may stimulate the immune system, so they should be used with caution in people with autoimmune diseases such as lupus, multiple sclerosis, or rheumatoid arthritis.
- Allergies: Reishi mushrooms may cause allergic reactions in some people, particularly those who are allergic to other types of mushrooms.
- Pregnancy and breastfeeding: There is not enough research to determine the safety of Reishi mushrooms during pregnancy or breastfeeding, so they should be avoided during these times.
- Interactions with medications: Reishi mushrooms may interact with some medications, including immunosuppressant drugs, anticoagulants, and chemotherapy drugs. It's important to speak with a healthcare provider before using Reishi mushrooms or any other dietary supplements if you are taking medications.

As with any dietary supplement, it's important to choose a reputable brand that uses high-quality ingredients and has undergone third-party testing for purity and potency. It's also important to follow dosage instructions carefully and speak with a healthcare provider before using Reishi mushrooms or any other dietary supplement.

Cultivation:
• Native to: Asia, including China, Japan, and Korea
• Zones: Reishi mushrooms grow in temperate and tropical regions and are commonly cultivated in Asia, Europe, and North America.
• Soil: Reishi mushrooms grow on hardwood trees, particularly oak and maple trees. They prefer well-drained soil with a pH of 6.0 to 7.5.

- Propagation: Reishi mushrooms are typically cultivated on logs, sawdust, or other substrates that have been inoculated with the mushroom's spores. They can also be grown indoors in bags or trays.
- Growing information and garden care: Reishi mushrooms require a warm and humid environment and should be protected from direct sunlight. They are typically grown in a controlled environment such as a greenhouse or indoors.
- Insects and disease: Reishi mushrooms (Ganoderma lucidum) are susceptible to various insects and diseases that can affect their growth and yield. Some common pests and diseases that can affect Reishi mushrooms include:
  - Green mold: Green mold is a fungal disease that can affect Reishi mushrooms and cause discoloration, softening, and decay. It's typically caused by poor growing conditions or contaminated substrate.
  - Drying and cracking: Reishi mushrooms are prone to drying and cracking, which can be caused by inadequate moisture levels, low humidity, or changes in temperature.
  - Mites: Mites can infest Reishi mushroom crops and cause damage to the mycelium, which can result in stunted growth and reduced yields.
  - Trichoderma: Trichoderma is a fungal disease that can affect Reishi mushrooms and cause yellowing and softening of the fruiting bodies. It's typically caused by poor growing conditions or contaminated substrate.
  - Contamination: Reishi mushrooms are vulnerable to contamination from bacteria and other microorganisms, which can result in poor growth and yield.

To prevent these issues, it's important to follow proper growing practices and maintain optimal growing conditions, including temperature, humidity, and air circulation. It's also important to use high-quality substrate and take steps to prevent contamination from bacteria and other microorganisms. Insecticides and fungicides may be used to control pests and diseases, but care should be taken to use only products that are safe for use on Reishi mushrooms and follow the manufacturer's instructions carefully.ices can help prevent these problems.

- Harvesting and preparations: Reishi mushrooms (Ganoderma lucidum) are typically harvested when they are mature and fully grown. The fruiting body of the mushroom can be harvested by cutting it off at the base with a sharp knife or scissors. It's important to handle the mushrooms gently to avoid damaging the delicate fruiting body.

Once harvested, Reishi mushrooms can be prepared and consumed in various ways. Here are some common preparations:
  - Tea: Reishi mushroom tea is a popular way to consume Reishi mushrooms. To make Reishi tea, simply steep dried Reishi mushroom slices or powder in hot water for several minutes.

- Powder: Reishi mushroom powder can be added to smoothies, soups, or other recipes to provide a nutritional boost.
- Tincture: Reishi mushroom tinctures are made by steeping the mushrooms in alcohol or glycerin for several weeks to extract the medicinal compounds. The resulting liquid can be taken orally or added to recipes.
- Capsules: Reishi mushroom capsules are a convenient way to take Reishi mushrooms. They contain powdered Reishi mushrooms in a capsule form, and can be taken orally with water.

When purchasing Reishi mushrooms or Reishi mushroom products, it's important to choose a reputable supplier that uses high-quality ingredients and has undergone third-party testing for purity and potency. It's also important to follow dosage instructions carefully and speak with a healthcare provider before using Reishi mushrooms or any other dietary supplement.

What medicines are made with this herb:

Reishi mushrooms (Ganoderma lucidum) are used to make various medicines and supplements due to their medicinal properties. Some of the medicinal preparations made with Reishi mushrooms include:
- Capsules and tablets: Reishi mushroom capsules and tablets are a convenient way to take Reishi mushrooms. They may contain powdered Reishi mushroom extract, which is concentrated to provide a higher dose of the active compounds.
- Tinctures: Reishi mushroom tinctures are made by steeping the mushrooms in alcohol or glycerin for several weeks to extract the medicinal compounds. The resulting liquid can be taken orally or added to recipes.
- Tea: Reishi mushroom tea is a popular way to consume Reishi mushrooms. To make Reishi tea, dried Reishi mushroom slices or powder are steeped in hot water for several minutes.
- Extracts: Reishi mushroom extracts are concentrated forms of the mushroom's active compounds, typically made by boiling the mushroom in water or alcohol to extract the beneficial compounds. The resulting liquid is then dried and powdered to make an extract that can be used in capsules, tablets, or other preparations.
- Topical creams and lotions: Reishi mushrooms are sometimes used in topical creams and lotions to treat skin conditions such as eczema and psoriasis.

Reishi mushrooms are believed to have a range of health benefits, including boosting the immune system, reducing inflammation, and supporting heart health. However, more research is needed to fully understand the potential benefits and risks of using Reishi mushrooms for medicinal purposes. It's important to speak with a healthcare provider before using Reishi mushrooms or any other dietary supplement.

What medicines this herb counteract:

Reishi mushrooms (Ganoderma lucidum) are generally considered safe for most people when taken in recommended doses. However, there are some medications that Reishi mushrooms may interact with.

Here are some medications that may be affected by the use of Reishi mushrooms:
- Blood-thinning medications: Reishi mushrooms may increase the risk of bleeding when taken with blood-thinning medications, such as warfarin or aspirin.
- Immunosuppressant medications: Reishi mushrooms may increase the activity of the immune system, which could potentially reduce the effectiveness of immunosuppressant medications used to prevent rejection after organ transplantation.
- Antidiabetic medications: Reishi mushrooms may lower blood sugar levels, so they should be used with caution in people taking antidiabetic medications, as it may increase the risk of hypoglycemia.
- Blood pressure medications: Reishi mushrooms may lower blood pressure, so they should be used with caution in people taking blood pressure medications, as it may increase the risk of hypotension.
- 5edatives: Reishi mushrooms may have a mild sedative effect, so they should be used with caution in people taking sedative medications, as it may increase the risk of drowsiness and dizziness.

It's important to speak with a healthcare provider before using Reishi mushrooms or any other dietary supplement, especially if you are taking prescription medications or have underlying health conditions. Your healthcare provider can advise you on potential interactions and help determine whether Reishi mushrooms are safe and appropriate for you.

Rose Hips

Herbal Identification:
- Common name: Rose hips
- Latin binomial: Rosa canina
- Other common names: Dog Rose, Wild Rose
- Plant family: Rosaceae
- Botanical description: RRose hips are the fruit of the rose plant, which typically develop after the petals have fallen off. They are small, round, and usually red or orange in color, though some species of roses may produce hips that are yellow or black. Rose hips are typically 1-2 cm in diameter, though some varieties can be smaller or larger.

The outer layer of the rose hip is typically firm and slightly fleshy, with a texture similar to that of a cranberry or cherry. Inside the fruit, there are numerous small seeds that are embedded in a fibrous matrix.

Rose hips are rich in vitamin C and other nutrients, and are often used to make teas, jams, and other food products. They are also used in traditional medicine to treat a variety of ailments, including arthritis, indigestion, and the common cold.

Medicinal Properties:
- Recommended cultivars: Rosa rugosa, Rosa gallica, and Rosa rubiginosa are commonly used for medicinal purposes.
- Parts used: The fruit (hips) is the most commonly used part of the plant for medicinal purposes, although the petals and leaves can also be used.
- Taste: Rose hips are sour and slightly astringent.
- Actions: Anti-inflammatory, antioxidant, immune stimulant, astringent, diuretic, and laxative.
- Energetics: Cooling and drying.
- Specific indications: Rose hips have several specific indications and benefits, including:
  - Boosting the immune system: Rose hips are a rich source of vitamin C, which is an essential nutrient for the immune system. Regular consumption of rose hips can help boost the body's defenses against infections and diseases.

- Reducing inflammation: The antioxidants found in rose hips have anti-inflammatory properties, which can help reduce inflammation throughout the body. This makes rose hips a popular natural remedy for conditions such as arthritis and other inflammatory conditions.
- Supporting skin health: The vitamin C and other antioxidants found in rose hips can help support healthy skin by promoting collagen synthesis and reducing oxidative stress.
- Improving digestion: Rose hips have been used traditionally to treat digestive ailments such as constipation, diarrhea, and indigestion. The fruit's high fiber content may help promote regularity and improve gut health.
- Managing diabetes: Some research suggests that the polyphenols and other compounds found in rose hips may help improve insulin sensitivity and blood sugar control in people with diabetes.

It is important to note that while rose hips are generally considered safe for most people, individuals who are pregnant or have certain medical conditions should consult with their healthcare provider before using rose hips or any other natural remedy.

Medicinal preparations:
Rose hips can be prepared in several ways to make medicinal preparations, including:
- Tea: Rose hip tea is a popular way to consume this fruit. To make rose hip tea, simply steep 1-2 teaspoons of dried rose hips in a cup of hot water for 10-15 minutes. The tea can be sweetened with honey or other natural sweeteners to taste.
- Syrup: Rose hip syrup is a sweet and tangy preparation that can be used to boost the immune system and treat colds and other respiratory ailments. To make rose hip syrup, simmer 1 cup of dried rose hips in 4 cups of water for 30-45 minutes. Strain the liquid, and then add 1 cup of honey or sugar to the liquid. Simmer the mixture for an additional 10-15 minutes, or until the syrup has thickened. Store the syrup in the refrigerator for up to a month.
- Oil: Rose hip oil is a popular natural remedy for improving skin health and reducing the appearance of scars and stretch marks. To make rose hip oil, simply infuse dried rose hips in a carrier oil such as jojoba or almond oil for several weeks. Strain the mixture, and then use the oil topically on the skin.
- Capsules: Rose hip capsules are a convenient way to consume this fruit as a dietary supplement. Capsules are typically available in health food stores and online retailers, and dosage instructions will vary based on the specific product.

It is important to follow recommended dosage instructions and consult with a healthcare provider before using any new herbal remedy, including rose hips.
- Ratio and dosage information: The recommended dosage varies depending on the form of preparation and the condition being treated. As a general guideline, a standard dose of rose hip extract is 500 mg taken two to three times daily.

Medicinal uses:
Rose hips have several medicinal uses, including:
- Boosting the immune system: Rose hips are a rich source of vitamin C, which is an essential nutrient for the immune system. Regular consumption of rose hips can help strengthen the body's defenses against infections and diseases.
- Reducing inflammation: The antioxidants found in rose hips have anti-inflammatory properties, which can help reduce inflammation throughout the body. This makes rose hips a popular natural remedy for conditions such as arthritis and other inflammatory conditions.
- Supporting skin health: The vitamin C and other antioxidants found in rose hips can help support healthy skin by promoting collagen synthesis and reducing oxidative stress. Rose hip oil is a popular natural remedy for improving skin health and reducing the appearance of scars and stretch marks.
- Improving digestion: Rose hips have been used traditionally to treat digestive ailments such as constipation, diarrhea, and indigestion. The fruit's high fiber content may help promote regularity and improve gut health.
- Managing diabetes: Some research suggests that the polyphenols and other compounds found in rose hips may help improve insulin sensitivity and blood sugar control in people with diabetes.
- Supporting cardiovascular health: The antioxidants found in rose hips may help improve cardiovascular health by reducing oxidative stress and inflammation. Some studies suggest that rose hips may help lower blood pressure and cholesterol levels, which can reduce the risk of heart disease.
- Relieving menstrual cramps: Rose hips may help relieve menstrual cramps and other menstrual-related symptoms, thanks to their anti-inflammatory and pain-relieving properties.

It is important to note that while rose hips are generally considered safe for most people, individuals who are pregnant or have certain medical conditions should consult with their healthcare provider before using rose hips or any other natural remedy.
- Precautions and contradictions: While rose hips are generally considered safe for most people, there are some precautions and contraindications to be aware of:

- Allergic reactions: Some individuals may be allergic to roses or other plants in the Rosaceae family, and may experience allergic reactions after consuming rose hips or using rose hip products. Symptoms of an allergic reaction may include hives, itching, swelling, and difficulty breathing. If you experience any of these symptoms after consuming or using rose hips, seek medical attention immediately.
- Interactions with medications: Rose hips may interact with certain medications, including blood thinners, diuretics, and medications for high blood pressure. If you are taking any medications, consult with your healthcare provider before using rose hips or any other natural remedy.
- Pregnancy and breastfeeding: While there is limited research on the safety of rose hips during pregnancy and breastfeeding, it is generally recommended that pregnant and breastfeeding women avoid using rose hip supplements or high doses of rose hip products.
- Gastrointestinal upset: Consuming large amounts of rose hips may cause gastrointestinal upset, including diarrhea, nausea, and abdominal pain. It is important to follow recommended dosage instructions and start with small amounts of rose hips to see how your body reacts.
- Kidney stones: Some sources suggest that consuming large amounts of rose hips may increase the risk of kidney stones in some individuals. If you have a history of kidney stones or are at risk for developing them, consult with your healthcare provider before using rose hips or any other natural remedy.

As always, it is important to consult with a healthcare provider before using any new herbal remedy, including rose hips, especially if you have any underlying medical conditions or are taking any medications.

Cultivation:
- Native to: Europe, North Africa, and Asia
- Zones: Rose hips can be grown in zones 3-9.
- Soil: Rose hips prefer well-drained soil that is slightly acidic (pH 6-6.5). They can tolerate a range of soil types.
- Propagation: Rose hips can be propagated by seed or by cuttings.
- Growing information and garden care: Rose hips prefer full sun and require regular watering. They can be pruned in late winter or early spring to promote growth and flowering.
- Insects and disease: Rose hips are generally hardy and resistant to many pests and diseases, but they can be susceptible to some common issues:
  - Insects: Rose hips may be susceptible to a variety of insect pests, including aphids, spider mites, and Japanese beetles. Insecticidal soaps or oils may be

effective in controlling infestations, and using beneficial insects such as ladybugs can also help keep populations in check.
- Fungal diseases: Some fungal diseases, such as black spot and powdery mildew, can affect rose hips. These diseases can cause leaf yellowing and leaf drop, and may lead to defoliation and reduced fruit production. Fungicides may be effective in controlling these diseases, but it is important to practice good cultural practices, such as keeping the area around the rose bushes free of debris and pruning to improve air circulation.
- Rose hips gall wasp: This pest is a common problem in rose hips and causes abnormal growths or galls to form on the stems and branches of the plant. Infected plants should be pruned to remove the galls and prevent further damage.

To prevent and manage pest and disease problems in rose hips, it is important to practice good cultural practices, such as proper watering and fertilization, pruning to promote air circulation, and maintaining a clean garden environment. Regular monitoring of the plants for signs of infestation or disease can help catch and treat problems early before they become more severe.

• Harvesting and preparations: Rose hips are typically harvested in the fall after the first frost, when they have reached their peak ripeness. Here are some tips on how to harvest and prepare rose hips:
- Harvesting: Use garden shears or scissors to cut the rose hips from the stem, making sure to leave a short stem attached to the fruit. Choose firm, plump rose hips that are free from blemishes and insect damage.
- Cleaning: Rinse the rose hips under cold water to remove any dirt or debris. You can also remove the blossom and stem ends of the rose hips, although this is not necessary.
- Drying: To dry rose hips, spread them out on a clean, dry surface and allow them to air dry completely. Alternatively, you can use a dehydrator set at a low temperature to dry the rose hips.
- Storage: Once the rose hips are completely dry, store them in an airtight container in a cool, dry place. They can be stored whole or ground into a powder.
- Preparations: There are many ways to use rose hips, including making tea, syrup, jam, or using them as a supplement. To make rose hip tea, steep 1-2 teaspoons of dried rose hips in hot water for 10-15 minutes. To make rose hip syrup, simmer rose hips in water until they soften, then strain and add sugar to the liquid to make a sweet syrup.

It is important to note that while rose hips are generally safe for consumption, it is recommended to consult with a healthcare provider before using them as a supplement, especially if you are taking any medications or have any underlying medical conditions.

What medicines are made with this herb:
Rose hips are used to make various medicines and supplements due to their high vitamin C content and other beneficial compounds. Some of the medicinal preparations made with rose hips include:
- Capsules and tablets: Rose hip capsules and tablets are a convenient way to take rose hips. They may contain powdered rose hip extract, which is concentrated to provide a higher dose of the active compounds.
- Syrups: Rose hip syrup is a popular way to consume rose hips. It is typically made by simmering fresh or dried rose hips with water and sugar to create a sweet and sour syrup that can be taken by the spoonful.
- Tea: Rose hip tea is a traditional remedy for colds and flu, as it is rich in vitamin C and other beneficial compounds. To make rose hip tea, dried rose hips are infused in hot water for several minutes.
- Tinctures: Rose hip tinctures are made by steeping rose hips in alcohol for several weeks. They are a concentrated form of rose hips and are typically taken in small doses.

What medicines this herb counteract:
Rose hips may interact with certain medications, including blood thinners, diuretics, and medications for high blood pressure. If you are taking any medications, it is recommended to consult with your healthcare provider before using rose hips or any other natural remedy to avoid any potential interactions.

Rose hips are rich in vitamin C, which can enhance the absorption of iron and other minerals. Therefore, consuming large amounts of rose hips may increase the risk of iron toxicity in individuals who have an iron overload condition, such as hemochromatosis. If you have a history of iron overload or are at risk for developing it, it is recommended to consult with your healthcare provider before using rose hips or any other vitamin C supplement.

It is always important to talk to your healthcare provider before taking any herbal remedies, especially if you are taking any medications or have any underlying medical conditions. Your healthcare provider can help you determine if rose hips are safe for you to use and whether they may interact with any medications you are currently taking.

Rosemary

Herbal Identification:
- Common name: Rosemary
- Latin binomial: Rosmarinus officinalis
- Other common names: Polar plant, compass plant, garden rosemary, old man, sea dew, anthos, rosemarine.
- Plant family: Lamiaceae (mint family)
- Botanical description: Rosemary (Rosmarinus officinalis) is an evergreen shrub that can grow up to 6 feet tall. It has needle-like leaves that are green on top and silver on the bottom, and small blue or purple flowers that bloom in the summer. The plant has a woody stem and is highly aromatic, with a distinctive pine-like fragrance. The leaves are arranged opposite each other on the stem and are about 1-2 inches long. The plant can be propagated by seed or by taking stem cuttings, and prefers well-drained soil and full sun. It is native to the Mediterranean region and is hardy in zones 7-10. Rosemary is a member of the Lamiaceae family, which also includes mint, basil, and thyme.

Medicinal Properties:
- Recommended cultivars: There are several cultivars of rosemary that are recommended for medicinal use, including 'Tuscan Blue', 'Arp', and 'Madalene Hill'.
- Parts used: The leaves and flowering tops of the plant are used medicinally.
- Taste: Rosemary has a bitter and pungent taste.
- Actions: Rosemary is a stimulating herb that is considered to be a carminative, digestive, diaphoretic, expectorant, nervine, and tonic.
- Energetics: Rosemary is considered to be warming and drying.
- Specific indications: Rosemary has a long history of medicinal use and is believed to have a number of beneficial properties. Some of its specific indications include:
  - Improving digestion: Rosemary is believed to stimulate the production of digestive juices and may help to relieve symptoms of indigestion, bloating, and stomach cramps.
  - Enhancing memory and concentration: Rosemary has been shown to improve cognitive function and may help to enhance memory and concentration.
  - Reducing inflammation: Rosemary has anti-inflammatory properties and may be beneficial for reducing inflammation in conditions such as arthritis, asthma, and eczema.

- Boosting the immune system: Rosemary contains antioxidants and may help to boost the immune system, making it useful for preventing and treating colds and flu.
- Relieving stress and anxiety: Rosemary is believed to have a calming effect on the nervous system and may be helpful for relieving stress and anxiety.
- Improving circulation: Rosemary may help to improve circulation and can be useful for conditions such as varicose veins and poor circulation in the extremities.

Medicinal preparations:

Rosemary can be used in a variety of medicinal preparations, including:
- Infusions or teas: Add 1-2 teaspoons of dried rosemary leaves to 1 cup of boiling water, steep for 10-15 minutes, and strain. This can be taken up to 3 times per day.
- Tinctures: Rosemary tinctures can be purchased or made by steeping fresh or dried rosemary in alcohol for several weeks. Dosage will vary depending on the strength of the tincture, but typically 30-60 drops can be taken up to 3 times per day.
- Essential oil: Rosemary essential oil can be used topically or in aromatherapy. It should be diluted in a carrier oil before use and should not be taken internally.
- Capsules: Rosemary capsules can be purchased or made by grinding dried rosemary leaves and placing them into empty capsules. Dosage will vary depending on the strength of the capsules, but typically 500-1000 mg can be taken up to 3 times per day.
- Culinary use: Rosemary can also be used in cooking and is a flavorful addition to many dishes.

It is important to follow dosage instructions carefully and to speak with a healthcare provider before using rosemary medicinally.

• Ratio and dosage information: The recommended dosage for rosemary is 2-4 grams of dried herb or 4-6 milliliters of tincture three times per day.

Medicinal uses:

Rosemary has been traditionally used for a wide range of medicinal purposes, and some of its most common uses include:
- Digestive issues: Rosemary has been used to relieve indigestion, flatulence, bloating, and stomach cramps. It is believed to stimulate the production of digestive juices and improve digestion.

- Memory and concentration: Rosemary has been shown to improve cognitive function and may be helpful for enhancing memory and concentration.
- Respiratory conditions: Rosemary may help to relieve respiratory symptoms such as coughs, colds, and bronchitis. It is believed to have expectorant and antimicrobial properties.
- Inflammatory conditions: Rosemary has anti-inflammatory properties and may be useful for reducing inflammation in conditions such as arthritis, asthma, and eczema.
- Immune system support: Rosemary contains antioxidants and may help to boost the immune system, making it useful for preventing and treating colds and flu.
- Stress and anxiety: Rosemary is believed to have a calming effect on the nervous system and may be helpful for relieving stress and anxiety.
- Circulation issues: Rosemary may help to improve circulation and can be useful for conditions such as varicose veins and poor circulation in the extremities.

It is important to note that while rosemary has a long history of traditional use, more research is needed to confirm its effectiveness for these and other health conditions. It is also important to speak with a healthcare provider before using rosemary medicinally.

• Precautions and contradictions: While rosemary is generally considered safe when used in moderate amounts, there are some precautions and contraindications to be aware of:

- Pregnancy and breastfeeding: Rosemary should be avoided during pregnancy and breastfeeding, as it may stimulate menstruation and cause miscarriage.
- Seizure disorders: There have been reports of rosemary causing seizures in individuals with epilepsy and other seizure disorders. If you have a history of seizures, speak with a healthcare provider before using rosemary.
- Allergies: Some individuals may be allergic to rosemary, and may experience symptoms such as rash, itching, and difficulty breathing.
- Drug interactions: Rosemary may interact with certain medications, including blood thinners, diuretics, and lithium. Speak with a healthcare provider before using rosemary if you are taking any medications.
- Topical use: Rosemary essential oil should be diluted in a carrier oil before use on the skin, as it can be irritating and may cause skin reactions in some individuals.

It is always important to speak with a healthcare provider before using any herbal remedies, including rosemary. They can help you determine the appropriate dosage and potential interactions or contraindications.

Cultivation:
- Native to: The Mediterranean region.
- Zones: Rosemary is hardy in zones 7-10.
- Soil: Rosemary prefers well-drained soil with a pH between 6.0 and 7.0.
- Propagation: Rosemary can be propagated by seed or by taking stem cuttings.
- Growing information and garden care: Rosemary requires full sun and moderate watering. It is a slow-growing plant that can be pruned to maintain its shape and size. It can be grown in containers or in the ground, and should be protected from frost in colder climates.
- Insects and disease: Rosemary is generally a hardy plant that is relatively resistant to pests and diseases. However, there are a few issues that can affect rosemary plants:
  - Spider mites: These tiny pests can infest rosemary plants and cause leaves to become speckled and discolored. They can be controlled with regular misting and by keeping the plant well-watered.
  - Aphids: Aphids can also infest rosemary plants, causing leaves to become distorted and yellowed. They can be controlled with insecticidal soap or by attracting beneficial insects such as ladybugs.
  - Root rot: Rosemary plants are susceptible to root rot if they are over-watered or planted in poorly draining soil. To prevent root rot, make sure the soil is well-draining and allow it to dry out between waterings.
  - Powdery mildew: This fungal disease can affect rosemary plants, causing leaves to become coated in a white, powdery substance. It can be controlled with a fungicide or by improving air circulation around the plant.

Regular pruning and good garden hygiene can also help prevent pest and disease issues in rosemary plants.
- Harvesting and preparations: Rosemary can be harvested throughout the growing season, although it is best to wait until the plant has reached at least 6-8 inches in height before taking cuttings. The plant can be harvested by snipping off small sprigs of leaves, or by cutting larger branches with a pair of garden shears.

Fresh rosemary can be used in a variety of culinary and medicinal preparations, while dried rosemary is commonly used in spice blends and herbal remedies. To dry rosemary, simply hang the cuttings upside down in a cool, dry place with good air circulation, and allow them to dry completely. Once dried, the leaves can be removed from the stems and stored in an airtight container for later use.

Rosemary can also be prepared as an herbal tea or infusion by steeping fresh or dried leaves in hot water for several minutes. Rosemary essential oil can also be used topically in dilution with a carrier oil for its aromatic and therapeutic properties.

When using rosemary medicinally, it is important to consult with a healthcare provider or qualified herbalist to determine the appropriate dosage and preparation method for your needs.

What medicines are made with this herb:
Rosemary is used in a variety of herbal medicines, including:
- Digestive remedies: Rosemary is used to stimulate digestion, ease indigestion, and relieve gas and bloating.
- Respiratory remedies: Rosemary is used to soothe sore throats, relieve coughs, and promote respiratory health.
- Cognitive support: Rosemary has been traditionally used to enhance memory and concentration, and is sometimes used in supplements marketed for cognitive support.
- Topical remedies: Rosemary essential oil is used in aromatherapy and topically to promote relaxation, ease muscle tension, and relieve pain.
- Hair and skin care: Rosemary is used in natural hair and skin care products to promote healthy hair growth, soothe irritated skin, and support overall skin health.

It is important to note that while rosemary has been traditionally used for these purposes, more research is needed to confirm its efficacy and safety for various conditions. It is always recommended to consult with a healthcare provider or qualified herbalist before using rosemary or any herbal remedy for medicinal purposes.

What medicines this herb counteract:
Rosemary is generally considered safe when used in appropriate doses, but it may interact with certain medications.

Rosemary may interact with blood-thinning medications, such as warfarin, and increase the risk of bleeding. It may also interfere with the absorption of iron, so individuals taking iron supplements should separate their doses of rosemary and iron by at least two hours.

Additionally, individuals with high blood pressure should use caution when taking rosemary as it may cause blood pressure to rise in some people.

It is always important to consult with a healthcare provider before using rosemary or any herbal remedy, especially if you are taking medication or have a pre-existing medical condition.

Sage

Herbal Identification:
- Common name: Sage
- Latin binomial: Salvia officinalis
- Other common names: Garden sage, true sage, common sage
- Plant family: Lamiaceae (mint family)
- Botanical description: SSage, or Salvia officinalis, is a perennial woody herb native to the Mediterranean region, but now widely cultivated in many parts of the world. It belongs to the family Lamiaceae, which also includes other aromatic herbs such as rosemary, thyme, and mint.

Sage grows up to 60 cm (24 inches) tall and has square stems that are covered with fine hairs. The leaves are 2-3 cm (0.8-1.2 inches) long, oval-shaped, and grayish-green in color with a pebbled texture. They have a strong, slightly bitter, and slightly peppery flavor that makes them a popular culinary herb.

Sage produces small, bluish-purple flowers in the summer, arranged in whorls around the stem. The flowers are rich in nectar and attract many pollinators, such as bees, butterflies, and hummingbirds.

Sage is also known for its medicinal properties and has been used for centuries to treat a variety of ailments, including digestive problems, sore throat, and inflammation. Its essential oils are used in aromatherapy to promote relaxation and ease stress.

Medicinal Properties:
- Recommended cultivars: Common sage (Salvia officinalis) is the most widely used and studied variety, but there are many other cultivars available, including purple sage, golden sage, and tricolor sage.
- Parts used: The leaves are the most commonly used part of the plant for medicinal purposes.
- Taste: Sage has a strong, pungent, and slightly bitter taste.
- Actions: Sage has astringent, antimicrobial, anti-inflammatory, and antioxidant properties.
- Energetics: Sage is warming and drying.
- Specific indications: Sage has a variety of uses and specific indications, including:

- Digestive disorders: Sage has antispasmodic properties that can help relieve digestive problems such as indigestion, bloating, and flatulence.
- Sore throat and cough: Sage has antibacterial and anti-inflammatory properties that can help soothe a sore throat and alleviate coughing.
- Menopause symptoms: Sage is commonly used to alleviate menopause symptoms such as hot flashes, night sweats, and mood swings.
- Memory and cognitive function: Sage has been shown to improve memory and cognitive function, particularly in older adults.
- Inflammation: Sage has anti-inflammatory properties that can help reduce inflammation in the body and alleviate symptoms of conditions such as arthritis.
- Skin health: Sage has antiseptic and antioxidant properties that can help improve skin health and reduce the appearance of wrinkles and fine lines.

It is important to note that while sage has many potential health benefits, it should be used with caution and under the guidance of a healthcare professional, particularly for pregnant or breastfeeding women and individuals with certain medical conditions.

Medicinal preparations:

Sage can be used in various medicinal preparations, including:
- Infusions: Sage leaves can be steeped in hot water to make a tea, which can be consumed to help alleviate digestive problems, sore throat, and cough.
- Tinctures: Sage leaves can be infused in alcohol or glycerin to create a concentrated liquid extract that can be taken orally to help relieve menopause symptoms, improve memory, and reduce inflammation.
- Essential oils: Sage essential oil can be extracted from the leaves and used in aromatherapy to promote relaxation, ease stress, and improve mood.
- Topical applications: Sage can be applied topically as a poultice or in a cream or ointment to help soothe skin inflammation, reduce redness, and alleviate pain.

It is important to note that while sage is generally considered safe when used in culinary amounts, it can have side effects when used in medicinal amounts, particularly if used for extended periods or in high doses. It is recommended to consult with a healthcare professional before using sage in medicinal preparations.

- Ratio and dosage information: Dosage will vary depending on the specific preparation and intended use. It is recommended to consult with a healthcare provider or qualified herbalist for personalized dosage recommendations.

Medicinal uses:

Sage has a long history of use for medicinal purposes, and it has been used to treat a variety of conditions, including:

- Digestive disorders: Sage has antispasmodic properties that can help relieve digestive problems such as indigestion, bloating, and flatulence.
- Sore throat and cough: Sage has antibacterial and anti-inflammatory properties that can help soothe a sore throat and alleviate coughing.
- Menopause symptoms: Sage is commonly used to alleviate menopause symptoms such as hot flashes, night sweats, and mood swings.
- Memory and cognitive function: Sage has been shown to improve memory and cognitive function, particularly in older adults.
- Inflammation: Sage has anti-inflammatory properties that can help reduce inflammation in the body and alleviate symptoms of conditions such as arthritis.
- Skin health: Sage has antiseptic and antioxidant properties that can help improve skin health and reduce the appearance of wrinkles and fine lines.
- Depression and anxiety: Sage has been used traditionally to help alleviate symptoms of depression and anxiety.
- Diabetes: Some studies suggest that sage may help regulate blood sugar levels in people with diabetes.

It is important to note that while sage has many potential health benefits, it should be used with caution and under the guidance of a healthcare professional, particularly for pregnant or breastfeeding women and individuals with certain medical conditions.

• Precautions and contradictions: While sage is generally safe when used in culinary amounts, there are some precautions and contradictions to consider when using it for medicinal purposes, including:

- Pregnancy and breastfeeding: Sage should be used with caution during pregnancy and breastfeeding, as it may stimulate contractions in the uterus and reduce milk supply.
- Allergic reactions: Some people may be allergic to sage and may experience symptoms such as itching, swelling, and difficulty breathing.
- Seizures: Sage contains a compound called thujone, which can be toxic in large amounts and may trigger seizures in some individuals.
- Drug interactions: Sage may interact with certain medications, including blood thinners, diabetes medications, and anticonvulsants, so it is important to consult with a healthcare professional before using sage in medicinal amounts.
- Surgery: Sage may increase the risk of bleeding during and after surgery, so it is recommended to stop using it at least two weeks before a scheduled surgery.

> Children: Sage should not be given to children under the age of 2, as it may cause toxicity.

It is important to note that the above precautions and contradictions are not exhaustive, and it is recommended to consult with a healthcare professional before using sage in medicinal amounts, particularly if you have any underlying medical conditions or are taking any medications.

Cultivation:
- Native to: Mediterranean region
- Zones: 5-9
- Soil: Sage prefers well-draining soil with a pH between 6.0 and 7.0.
- Propagation: Sage can be propagated from seed or cuttings.
- Growing information and garden care: Sage prefers full sun and moderate watering. It can be grown in containers or in the ground.
- Insects and disease: Sage is generally resistant to most insect pests and diseases, making it a low-maintenance herb to grow in a garden or container. However, there are a few pests and diseases that can affect sage plants, including:

> Spider mites: These tiny pests can cause yellowing and wilting of sage leaves. To prevent spider mites, make sure to keep the plants well-watered and occasionally mist the leaves with water to increase humidity. You can also use insecticidal soap or neem oil to control an infestation.
> Aphids: These small insects can cause curling and distortion of sage leaves. To prevent aphids, make sure to keep the plants well-watered and regularly prune any infested leaves. You can also use insecticidal soap or neem oil to control an infestation.
> Powdery mildew: This fungal disease can cause a white, powdery coating on sage leaves. To prevent powdery mildew, make sure to plant sage in a well-drained location with good air circulation, and avoid overhead watering. You can also use a fungicide to control an infestation.
> Root rot: This fungal disease can cause the roots of sage plants to rot and the leaves to wilt. To prevent root rot, make sure to plant sage in well-drained soil and avoid over-watering. You can also use a fungicide to control an infestation.

Overall, sage is a hardy and resilient plant that can thrive in a variety of growing conditions. With proper care and maintenance, you can keep your sage plants healthy and free from pests and diseases.

- Harvesting and preparations: Sage is a perennial herb that can be harvested throughout the growing season. Here are some tips on how to harvest and prepare sage:

- Harvesting: Sage leaves can be harvested at any time during the growing season, but it is best to wait until the plant is mature and has developed enough leaves for harvesting. When harvesting sage, use a sharp pair of scissors or pruning shears to snip the leaves off the plant, leaving about 2-3 inches of stem attached to each leaf.
- Drying: To dry sage, tie the stems together in small bunches and hang them upside down in a well-ventilated, dry location. Once the leaves are dry and brittle, remove them from the stems and store them in an airtight container.
- Freezing: Sage leaves can also be frozen for later use. To freeze sage, wash and dry the leaves, then spread them out on a baking sheet and freeze them until they are solid. Once frozen, transfer the leaves to a freezer-safe container and store them in the freezer.
- Culinary uses: Sage is a popular herb used in a variety of culinary dishes, including stuffing, soups, stews, and sauces. Fresh or dried sage leaves can be added to dishes to add flavor and aroma.
- Medicinal uses: Sage can be used in various medicinal preparations, including teas, tinctures, essential oils, and topical applications. It is important to consult with a healthcare professional before using sage for medicinal purposes.

Overall, sage is a versatile herb that can be used in a variety of ways. Whether you are using it for culinary or medicinal purposes, harvesting and preparing sage is a simple process that can be done at home.

What medicines are made with this herb:

Sage is a versatile herb that has been used for medicinal purposes for centuries. Some common medicinal preparations made with sage include:

- Sage tea: Sage tea is a popular home remedy for sore throats, colds, and coughs. It is also used to improve digestion and reduce inflammation.
- Sage tincture: Sage tincture is made by soaking sage leaves in alcohol to extract the active compounds. It is often used to treat menopausal symptoms, including hot flashes and night sweats.
- Sage essential oil: Sage essential oil is used in aromatherapy to promote relaxation and reduce stress. It is also used topically to treat skin conditions like acne and eczema.
- Sage capsules: Sage capsules are often used as a natural remedy for cognitive function and memory support. They may also have anti-inflammatory and antimicrobial properties.
- Sage mouthwash: Sage mouthwash is used to soothe sore throats, mouth ulcers, and gum disease. It is also used as a natural breath freshener.

It is important to note that while sage is generally considered safe when used in culinary amounts, it is important to consult with a healthcare professional before using sage for medicinal purposes, as it may interact with certain medications and may not be appropriate for everyone.

What medicines this herb counteract:

Sage is generally considered safe when used in culinary amounts, but when used medicinally, it can interact with certain medications. Here are some medications that may be affected by the use of sage:

- Diabetes medications: Sage may lower blood sugar levels and can potentially interact with medications used to treat diabetes, such as insulin and metformin.
- Blood thinners: Sage contains compounds that can thin the blood and may increase the risk of bleeding when taken with medications like warfarin or aspirin.
- High blood pressure medications: Sage may lower blood pressure and can potentially interact with medications used to treat high blood pressure, such as ACE inhibitors and calcium channel blockers.
- Hormone replacement therapy: Sage has estrogenic properties and may interact with hormone replacement therapy or oral contraceptives.

It is important to talk to a healthcare professional before using sage medicinally, especially if you are taking any medications or have a medical condition. They can advise you on the appropriate dosage and potential interactions with other medications.

Self-Heal

Herbal Identification:
- Common Name: Self-Heal
- Latin Binomial: Prunella vulgaris
- Other Common Names: Heal-All, All-Heal, Woundwort, Heart-of-the-Earth, and Hercules Woundwort
- Plant Family: Lamiaceae (mint family)
- Botanical Description: Self-Heal (Prunella vulgaris) is a low-growing, creeping perennial herb that can grow up to 30 cm tall. It has square stems that are hairy or glandular, opposite leaves that are oval to lance-shaped, and spikes of tiny purple or blue flowers that bloom from June to September. The flowers are arranged in dense, cylindrical, and terminal spikes, which are 2-10 cm long. Each flower has a hood-like upper lip and a lower lip that is divided into three lobes. The leaves and stems of Self-Heal are also hairy or glandular. Self-Heal is native to Europe, but has naturalized throughout North America and other parts of the world. It is commonly found in lawns, meadows, and waste areas.

Medicinal Properties:
- Recommended Cultivars: None
- Parts Used: Leaves, flowers
- Taste: Bitter, astringent
- Actions: Antiviral, antibacterial, anti-inflammatory, immune-stimulating, vulnerary
- Energetics: Cooling, drying
- Specific Indications: Self-Heal has a variety of traditional medicinal uses, including:
  - Sore throat and mouth: Self-Heal has a soothing and anti-inflammatory effect on sore throats and mouth sores. It is commonly used as a gargle or mouthwash.
  - Wounds and skin irritations: Self-Heal has astringent, anti-inflammatory, and antimicrobial properties that can help promote healing of wounds and reduce inflammation and infection in skin irritations, such as eczema and acne.
  - Respiratory infections: Self-Heal has been traditionally used to treat respiratory infections, including bronchitis and colds, due to its expectorant and antimicrobial properties.
  - Digestive issues: Self-Heal has been used as a digestive aid to relieve symptoms such as diarrhea and stomach pain.

> Immune system support: Self-Heal has been traditionally used to boost the immune system and promote overall health.

It is important to note that there is limited scientific evidence to support the medicinal uses of Self-Heal, and it is recommended to consult with a healthcare practitioner before using Self-Heal for medicinal purposes.

Medicinal Preparations:
Self-Heal can be prepared and used in various medicinal forms, including:
> Infusion or tea: Steep 1-2 teaspoons of dried Self-Heal leaves or flowers in 1 cup of hot water for 10-15 minutes. Strain and drink up to three times per day.
> Tincture: Combine 1 part dried Self-Heal herb with 5 parts 80-proof vodka. Allow the mixture to steep for 2-4 weeks, shaking daily. Strain and take 2-4 ml up to three times per day.
> Poultice: Crush fresh or dried Self-Heal leaves or flowers and apply to wounds or skin irritations.
> Salve or ointment: Combine Self-Heal infused oil with beeswax and apply topically to wounds or skin irritations.
> Gargle or mouthwash: Prepare an infusion of Self-Heal and use as a gargle or mouthwash for sore throat and mouth sores.

It is recommended to consult with a healthcare practitioner for proper dosage and use of Self-Heal preparations.

• Ratio and Dosage Information: Tea - 1-2 tsp of dried herb per cup of boiling water, steeped for 10-15 minutes; Tincture - 2-4 mL, 3 times per day

Medicinal Uses:
Self-Heal has a long history of traditional medicinal use, and it is believed to have various health benefits, including:
> Wound healing: Self-Heal has been traditionally used to speed up the healing process of wounds and to prevent infections due to its antimicrobial and astringent properties.
> Anti-inflammatory: Self-Heal has been used to reduce inflammation in the body, including inflammation in the digestive tract, respiratory system, and skin.

- Immune system support: Self-Heal is believed to have immune-boosting properties, helping to support the body's natural defenses.
- Respiratory health: Self-Heal has been used to alleviate respiratory issues such as coughs, colds, and sore throats, due to its expectorant and antimicrobial properties.
- Digestive health: Self-Heal is believed to have digestive benefits and can be used to alleviate digestive symptoms such as diarrhea and stomach pain.

It is important to note that more research is needed to determine the efficacy and safety of Self-Heal for medicinal purposes, and it is recommended to consult with a healthcare practitioner before using Self-Heal for any health concerns.

• Precautions and Contradictions: Self-Heal is generally considered safe for most people when consumed in moderate amounts, but there are some precautions and contradictions to keep in mind:

- Allergic reactions: Some people may be allergic to Self-Heal, especially those who are allergic to other plants in the mint family.
- Pregnancy and breastfeeding: There is not enough reliable information available about the safety of Self-Heal during pregnancy and breastfeeding, so it is best to avoid using it during these times.
- Interactions with medications: Self-Heal may interact with certain medications, such as blood thinners, so it is recommended to consult with a healthcare practitioner before using Self-Heal if you are taking any medications.
- Dosage: It is important to follow recommended dosage instructions when using Self-Heal, as excessive amounts may cause adverse effects such as nausea and diarrhea.
- Toxicity: While there is no known toxicity associated with Self-Heal, it is recommended to avoid consuming large amounts of the plant as a precaution.

As with any herbal remedy, it is important to consult with a healthcare practitioner before using Self-Heal for any health concerns.

Cultivation:
• Native to: Europe, Asia, and North America
• Zones: 4-9
• Soil: Self-Heal prefers well-drained soil with a pH between 6.0 and 7.0. It can tolerate a variety of soil types, including sandy, loamy, or clay soils.
• Propagation: Self-Heal can be propagated by seeds, division, or stem cuttings.
• Growing Information and Garden Care: Self-Heal can be grown in full sun to partial shade and prefers moist soil. It is a low-maintenance plant that requires little care once established.

- Insects and Disease: Self-Heal is generally a hardy plant that is not prone to significant insect or disease problems. However, like any plant, it can occasionally be affected by pests and diseases.

Some common pests that may affect Self-Heal include aphids, spider mites, and leafhoppers. These pests can be controlled with insecticidal soap or by introducing natural predators such as ladybugs or lacewings.

Self-Heal is also susceptible to fungal diseases such as powdery mildew, which can be prevented by providing good air circulation around the plants and avoiding overhead watering. If powdery mildew does occur, it can be treated with a fungicidal spray.

Overall, Self-Heal is a relatively low-maintenance plant that is not typically plagued by significant insect or disease problems. Regular watering and proper care can help keep Self-Heal healthy and free of pests and diseases.
- Harvesting and Preparations: Self-Heal can be harvested throughout the growing season, but the aerial parts of the plant are typically harvested when the plant is in full bloom in midsummer.

To harvest Self-Heal, the aerial parts of the plant (stems, leaves, and flowers) are typically cut just above the ground with sharp scissors or pruners. The plant can be dried for later use by hanging it in a warm, dry, and well-ventilated area until it is fully dry.

Once dried, Self-Heal can be prepared in various ways for medicinal use, including:
- Infusion/tea: Steep 1-2 teaspoons of dried Self-Heal in a cup of hot water for 10-15 minutes. This can be consumed up to three times per day.
- Tincture: Place dried Self-Heal in a jar and cover with high-proof alcohol, such as vodka. Let the mixture sit for four to six weeks, shaking the jar daily. Strain and store the tincture in a dark, cool place. This can be taken in small doses as recommended by a healthcare practitioner.
- Poultice: Crush fresh Self-Heal leaves and apply them directly to the skin to soothe wounds or burns.

It is important to note that the dosage and preparation method of Self-Heal may vary depending on the specific health concern being treated, and it is recommended to consult with a healthcare practitioner before using Self-Heal for any medicinal purposes.

Medicines made with this herb:

Self-Heal has been used for medicinal purposes for centuries and is still commonly used today. Some of the medicines made with this herb include:
- Teas and infusions: Self-Heal can be made into a tea or infusion to help treat sore throats, coughs, and other respiratory issues, as well as to promote overall immune health.
- Tinctures: Self-Heal tinctures are often used to help treat digestive issues, such as upset stomachs and diarrhea, as well as to support liver and kidney health.
- Salves and ointments: Self-Heal salves and ointments are used to soothe minor skin irritations, such as cuts, burns, and insect bites.
- Mouthwashes and gargles: Self-Heal is often used in mouthwashes and gargles to help treat oral health issues, such as mouth sores and gingivitis.

It is important to note that while Self-Heal has been traditionally used for medicinal purposes, more research is needed to fully understand its effectiveness and potential side effects. As with any herbal remedy, it is recommended to consult with a healthcare practitioner before using Self-Heal for any medicinal purposes.

Medicines this herb counteracts:

There is limited information available on the potential interactions or counteractions that Self-Heal may have with other medicines. However, as with any herbal remedy, it is important to exercise caution and consult with a healthcare practitioner before using Self-Heal, especially if you are currently taking any prescription or over-the-counter medications. This is because Self-Heal may interact with certain medications, including blood-thinning drugs, immunosuppressants, and sedatives. It is also recommended to avoid using Self-Heal if you are pregnant or breastfeeding, or if you have any known allergies to plants in the mint family.

Shiitake Mushroom

Herbal Identification:
- Common name: Shiitake Mushroom
- Latin binomial: Lentinula edodes
- Other common names: Black Forest mushroom, Oakwood mushroom
- Plant family: Marasmiaceae
- Botanical description: Shiitake mushrooms, also known as Lentinula edodes, are a type of edible mushroom that are native to East Asia. They are popularly cultivated for their culinary and medicinal properties.

The caps of shiitake mushrooms are typically 5-10 cm in diameter and are a reddish-brown color. The caps are convex when young but flatten out as they mature. The caps are also covered with a velvety texture when young but become smooth as they mature. The gills on the underside of the cap are white or cream-colored and are spaced fairly far apart.

The stems of shiitake mushrooms are tough and woody and can be up to 10 cm in length. The stems are typically a lighter color than the cap and may have some fine scales or fibers on them.

Shiitake mushrooms grow naturally on decaying wood, particularly on oak trees, but are also cultivated on artificial logs made of sawdust and other materials. They are rich in nutrients and are believed to have various health benefits, such as boosting the immune system and reducing inflammation.

Medicinal Properties:
- Parts used: The entire mushroom is used for medicinal purposes.
- Taste: Umami, slightly sweet, and slightly bitter.
- Actions: Immune-modulating, anti-tumor, antioxidant, anti-inflammatory, hypoglycemic, and cholesterol-lowering.
- Energetics: Warming and moistening.
- Specific indications: Shiitake mushrooms have various health benefits and are used for different indications. Here are some specific indications for shiitake mushrooms:
  - Boosting the immune system: Shiitake mushrooms contain beta-glucans, which are believed to enhance the activity of immune cells and improve overall immunity.

- Reducing inflammation: Shiitake mushrooms contain compounds that have anti-inflammatory properties, which may help reduce inflammation in the body.
- Lowering cholesterol: Some studies suggest that consuming shiitake mushrooms may help lower LDL (bad) cholesterol levels in the blood.
- Fighting cancer: Shiitake mushrooms contain compounds that have been shown to have anti-cancer properties and may help prevent the growth and spread of cancer cells.
- Improving heart health: Shiitake mushrooms may help improve heart health by reducing inflammation, lowering cholesterol levels, and improving blood flow.
- Supporting liver health: Shiitake mushrooms have been shown to have hepatoprotective effects, which may help protect the liver from damage and improve liver function.
- Improving skin health: Shiitake mushrooms contain compounds that have been shown to have anti-aging and skin-protective properties, which may help improve skin health and prevent skin damage.

Medicinal preparations:
Shiitake mushrooms can be consumed fresh or dried, and there are different medicinal preparations that can be made with them. Here are some examples:
- Shiitake mushroom tea: Dried shiitake mushrooms can be brewed into a tea by steeping them in hot water for several minutes. This tea can be consumed regularly for its immune-boosting and anti-inflammatory properties.
- Shiitake mushroom extract: Shiitake mushroom extract is a concentrated form of the mushroom that is made by simmering the mushrooms in water for several hours and then straining out the liquid. The resulting liquid can be consumed as a tonic or added to soups or other dishes.
- Shiitake mushroom capsules: Shiitake mushroom capsules contain dried and powdered shiitake mushrooms in a convenient form for consumption. These capsules can be taken regularly as a dietary supplement for their various health benefits.
- Shiitake mushroom tincture: A tincture is a concentrated liquid extract made by soaking shiitake mushrooms in alcohol. This tincture can be added to water or other beverages and consumed regularly for its medicinal properties.
- Shiitake mushroom powder: Dried shiitake mushrooms can be ground into a fine powder and used as a seasoning or added to smoothies or other drinks for their nutritional and medicinal properties.
  - Ratio and dosage information: There is no established dosage for shiitake mushrooms, but typical dosages range from 1 to 3 grams per day.

Medicinal uses:
Shiitake mushrooms have been used for centuries in traditional Chinese medicine and are believed to have various medicinal properties. Here are some of the most common medicinal uses of shiitake mushrooms:
- Immune support: Shiitake mushrooms contain beta-glucans, which are believed to enhance the activity of immune cells and improve overall immunity. They are used to support the immune system and prevent infections.
- Anti-inflammatory: Shiitake mushrooms contain compounds that have anti-inflammatory properties and may help reduce inflammation in the body. They are used to treat conditions such as arthritis, asthma, and inflammatory bowel disease.
- Cholesterol-lowering: Some studies suggest that consuming shiitake mushrooms may help lower LDL (bad) cholesterol levels in the blood. They are used to prevent and treat high cholesterol.
- Anti-cancer: Shiitake mushrooms contain compounds that have been shown to have anti-cancer properties and may help prevent the growth and spread of cancer cells. They are used to support cancer treatment and prevent cancer recurrence.
- Cardiovascular health: Shiitake mushrooms may help improve heart health by reducing inflammation, lowering cholesterol levels, and improving blood flow. They are used to prevent and treat heart disease.
- Liver health: Shiitake mushrooms have been shown to have hepatoprotective effects, which may help protect the liver from damage and improve liver function. They are used to treat liver disease and support liver health.
- Skin health: Shiitake mushrooms contain compounds that have been shown to have anti-aging and skin-protective properties. They are used to improve skin health and prevent skin damage.

• Precautions and contradictions: While shiitake mushrooms are generally considered safe for consumption, there are some precautions and contraindications to be aware of:
- Allergies: Some people may be allergic to shiitake mushrooms, and consuming them can cause allergic reactions such as hives, itching, and difficulty breathing.
- Blood-thinning medications: Shiitake mushrooms contain a compound called lentinan, which may have blood-thinning properties. People taking blood-thinning medications such as warfarin or aspirin should consult their healthcare provider before consuming shiitake mushrooms.

- Autoimmune diseases: Shiitake mushrooms may stimulate the immune system, which could worsen autoimmune diseases such as multiple sclerosis, lupus, and rheumatoid arthritis. People with these conditions should consult their healthcare provider before consuming shiitake mushrooms.
- Digestive problems: Some people may experience digestive upset or diarrhea after consuming shiitake mushrooms. This may be due to the high fiber content or the presence of compounds that can irritate the digestive system.
- Interaction with medications: Shiitake mushrooms may interact with certain medications, including chemotherapy drugs and immunosuppressants. People taking these medications should consult their healthcare provider before consuming shiitake mushrooms.

As with any dietary supplement, it is important to consult with a healthcare provider before consuming shiitake mushrooms, especially if you have any underlying health conditions or are taking medications.

Cultivation:
- Native to: East Asia
- Zones: 6-8
- Soil: Shiitake mushrooms grow best on hardwood logs or sawdust, and prefer a slightly acidic soil with a pH range of 6.0 to 6.5.
- Propagation: Shiitake mushrooms are typically cultivated by inoculating hardwood logs or sawdust with shiitake spawn.
- Growing information and garden care: Shiitake mushrooms require a partially shaded area with good air circulation and consistent moisture. They can be grown outdoors on hardwood logs or indoors on sawdust or straw substrate.
- Insects and disease: Shiitake mushrooms can be affected by insects and diseases, which can impact their growth and quality. Here are some of the most common pests and diseases that affect shiitake mushrooms:
  - Insects: Shiitake mushrooms can be infested with various insects, including mites, flies, and beetles. These pests can damage the mushrooms and reduce their quality. To prevent infestations, shiitake mushroom growers often use insecticides or natural predators such as nematodes and predatory mites.
  - Fungi: Shiitake mushrooms are susceptible to various fungal diseases, including green mold, brown spot, and bacterial blight. These diseases can cause the mushrooms to rot and reduce their quality. To prevent fungal infections, shiitake mushroom growers often use fungicides and maintain proper ventilation and humidity levels in their growing environment.
  - Bacteria: Shiitake mushrooms can also be affected by bacterial infections, such as bacterial blight and soft rot. These diseases can cause the

mushrooms to rot and become discolored. To prevent bacterial infections, shiitake mushroom growers often practice good hygiene and sanitation practices and use antibiotics when necessary.
- Viruses: Shiitake mushrooms can be infected with various viruses, which can cause stunted growth, discolored caps, and reduced quality. To prevent viral infections, shiitake mushroom growers often use virus-free spawn and maintain proper hygiene and sanitation practices.

It is important for shiitake mushroom growers to monitor their crops for pests and diseases and take appropriate measures to prevent and treat any issues that arise. Proper hygiene, sanitation, and environmental conditions are key to maintaining healthy and high-quality shiitake mushrooms.

- Harvesting and preparations: Shiitake mushrooms are typically harvested when the caps have fully expanded and before the edges start to curl upwards. Here are some tips on harvesting and preparing shiitake mushrooms:
- Harvesting: To harvest shiitake mushrooms, gently twist the stem at the base of the cap until it comes loose. Avoid pulling or cutting the mushrooms, as this can damage the mycelium and reduce future yields. It is best to harvest shiitake mushrooms when they are still young and firm.
- Cleaning: To clean shiitake mushrooms, gently wipe them with a damp cloth or rinse them briefly under running water. Avoid soaking them in water, as this can cause them to become waterlogged and lose their flavor.
- Storage: Shiitake mushrooms can be stored in the refrigerator for up to a week in a paper bag or wrapped in a damp cloth. Do not store them in a plastic bag, as this can cause them to become slimy.
- Cooking: Shiitake mushrooms have a meaty texture and a rich, earthy flavor. They can be used in a variety of dishes, such as soups, stir-fries, and risottos. They are also commonly used in Asian cuisine and are a popular ingredient in vegetarian and vegan dishes.
- Drying: Shiitake mushrooms can also be dried for later use. To dry them, slice them thinly and lay them out on a drying rack or in a dehydrator. Once they are dry and brittle, store them in an airtight container. Dried shiitake mushrooms can be rehydrated by soaking them in warm water for about 30 minutes before using them in a recipe.

Shiitake mushrooms are a versatile and nutritious ingredient that can add flavor and texture to many dishes. Whether fresh or dried, they are a popular ingredient in many cuisines and are known for their medicinal properties as well.

What medicines are made with this herb:
Shiitake mushrooms are not typically used to make conventional medicines, but they are used as a dietary supplement and a functional food for their potential

health benefits. Some supplement manufacturers use shiitake mushrooms as an ingredient in immune-boosting supplements, as they contain a compound called lentinan, which has been shown to have immunomodulatory effects.

In traditional Chinese medicine, shiitake mushrooms have been used for centuries to treat a variety of ailments, including colds, flu, and digestive disorders. They are believed to have tonic properties that can help strengthen the body and support overall health. However, it is important to note that traditional use does not necessarily equate to proven medical efficacy, and more scientific research is needed to fully understand the potential health benefits of shiitake mushrooms.

Overall, shiitake mushrooms are mostly used as a food and dietary supplement rather than a conventional medicine. As with any dietary supplement, it is important to consult with a healthcare provider before consuming shiitake mushrooms, especially if you have any underlying health conditions or are taking medications.

What medicines this herb counteracts:
Shiitake mushrooms are generally considered safe and are not known to counteract any specific medications. However, as a dietary supplement, they can interact with certain medications and should be used with caution, especially if you are taking prescription medications or have any underlying health conditions.

Shiitake mushrooms contain a compound called eritadenine, which has been shown to lower cholesterol levels. If you are taking cholesterol-lowering medications, such as statins, taking shiitake mushroom supplements may enhance the effects of these medications, potentially leading to low cholesterol levels. Therefore, it is important to monitor your cholesterol levels closely if you are taking both shiitake mushrooms and cholesterol-lowering medications.

Shiitake mushrooms can also have a mild blood-thinning effect, and therefore should be used with caution if you are taking blood-thinning medications, such as warfarin or aspirin. If you are taking any medications or have any underlying health conditions, it is important to talk to your healthcare provider before taking shiitake mushroom supplements to avoid any potential interactions or adverse effects.

Siberian Ginseng

Herbal Identification:
- Common name: Siberian Ginseng
- Latin binomial: Eleutherococcus senticosus
- Other common names: Eleuthero, Ciwujia
- Plant family: Araliaceae
- Botanical description: Siberian Ginseng, also known as Eleuthero, is a deciduous shrub that belongs to the Araliaceae family. It is native to the Far East region of Siberia, northern China, Korea, and Japan. The plant typically grows up to 2-3 meters in height and has thorny stems with dark green leaves.

The leaves of the Siberian Ginseng plant are compound and consist of five leaflets that are sharply toothed. The flowers are small, yellow-green, and arranged in clusters. The fruit of the plant is a small, black, and round berry that contains several seeds.

The root of the Siberian Ginseng plant is the most commonly used part for medicinal purposes. The root is woody, cylindrical, and branched, and it is usually harvested in the fall when the plant is three to six years old. The root contains a variety of active compounds, including eleutherosides, polysaccharides, and lignans, which are believed to provide the plant's health benefits.

Siberian Ginseng is commonly used in traditional medicine to improve stamina, reduce fatigue, and enhance cognitive function. It is also used to boost the immune system, reduce inflammation, and improve athletic performance.

Medicinal Properties:
- Parts used: The root and stem bark are used medicinally.
- Taste: Bitter, slightly sweet
- Actions: Adaptogen, immune stimulant, tonic, anti-inflammatory, antioxidant, nervine
- Energetics: Warm, dry
- Specific indications: Siberian Ginseng, or Eleuthero, has been used for various health purposes in traditional medicine. Here are some specific indications for which it may be used:

- Improving physical performance: Siberian Ginseng is believed to enhance physical endurance, strength, and overall athletic performance by improving oxygen utilization, reducing fatigue, and increasing energy levels.
- Boosting immune function: The active compounds in Siberian Ginseng are thought to support the immune system by stimulating the production of white blood cells and enhancing their ability to fight infections.
- Reducing stress and anxiety: Siberian Ginseng has been shown to reduce stress and anxiety levels by regulating cortisol, the body's stress hormone. It may also improve mood and cognitive function.
- Supporting cardiovascular health: The active compounds in Siberian Ginseng may help lower blood pressure, improve circulation, and reduce the risk of heart disease by reducing inflammation and oxidative stress.
- Enhancing mental performance: Siberian Ginseng is believed to improve cognitive function, memory, and concentration by increasing blood flow to the brain and stimulating the production of neurotransmitters.

It is important to note that while Siberian Ginseng may offer these potential health benefits, it should not be used as a substitute for medical treatment. It is always recommended to consult with a healthcare professional before using any herbal supplement. • Medicinal preparations: Decoction, tincture, capsule, powder, tea

• Ratio and dosage information: 1:5 60%, 2-4 ml 3 times per day (tincture), 3-9 g per day (powder)

Medicinal uses:
Siberian Ginseng, or Eleuthero, has a long history of use in traditional medicine for various health purposes. Here are some of the medicinal uses of Siberian Ginseng:
- Immune system support: Siberian Ginseng is believed to support the immune system by stimulating the production of white blood cells and enhancing their ability to fight infections.
- Energy and stamina: Siberian Ginseng is commonly used to increase energy levels and reduce fatigue. It is believed to enhance physical endurance and improve athletic performance by improving oxygen utilization.
- Stress reduction: Siberian Ginseng has been shown to reduce stress and anxiety levels by regulating cortisol, the body's stress hormone. It may also improve mood and cognitive function.
- Cardiovascular health: Siberian Ginseng may help lower blood pressure, improve circulation, and reduce the risk of heart disease by reducing inflammation and oxidative stress.

- Mental performance: Siberian Ginseng is believed to improve cognitive function, memory, and concentration by increasing blood flow to the brain and stimulating the production of neurotransmitters.
- Anti-inflammatory and antioxidant effects: Siberian Ginseng contains compounds with anti-inflammatory and antioxidant properties that may help reduce inflammation and protect cells from damage caused by free radicals.

It is important to note that while Siberian Ginseng may offer these potential health benefits, it should not be used as a substitute for medical treatment. It is always recommended to consult with a healthcare professional before using any herbal supplement.

• Precautions and contradictions: While Siberian Ginseng is generally considered safe for most people when used as directed, there are some precautions and contraindications to consider:
- Pregnancy and breastfeeding: Pregnant and breastfeeding women should avoid using Siberian Ginseng as there is not enough information about its safety in these populations.
- Autoimmune diseases: Siberian Ginseng may stimulate the immune system, which can worsen autoimmune diseases such as multiple sclerosis, lupus, and rheumatoid arthritis.
- Blood pressure and diabetes medications: Siberian Ginseng may interact with medications for high blood pressure and diabetes, so it is important to speak with a healthcare provider before using it.
- Bleeding disorders: Siberian Ginseng may increase the risk of bleeding, so it should be avoided or used with caution in people with bleeding disorders or those taking blood-thinning medications.
- Allergic reactions: Some people may have an allergic reaction to Siberian Ginseng, especially if they are allergic to plants in the same family, such as celery, carrots, or ivy.

It is always recommended to consult with a healthcare professional before using any herbal supplement, especially if you have a pre-existing medical condition, are taking medications, or are pregnant or breastfeeding.

Cultivation:
- Native to: Northeast Asia
- Zones: 3-8
- Soil: Well-drained loamy soil, pH 5.5-7.0
- Propagation: Seeds or root cuttings

- Growing information and garden care: Siberian Ginseng is a hardy perennial that prefers partial shade and moist, well-drained soil. It can be propagated from seed or root cuttings, and can take several years to mature. It is a slow-growing plant and should not be harvested until it is at least 3-4 years old.
- Insects and disease: Siberian Ginseng, like all plants, is susceptible to certain insects and diseases. Here are some of the common ones that can affect this plant:
  - Insects: Siberian Ginseng can be attacked by various insects such as aphids, spider mites, and scale insects. These pests can cause leaf yellowing, leaf drop, and stunted growth.
  - Fungal diseases: Siberian Ginseng can be susceptible to various fungal diseases such as root rot, leaf spot, and powdery mildew. These diseases can cause leaf yellowing, leaf drop, and stem dieback.
  - Viral diseases: Siberian Ginseng can also be affected by various viral diseases, which can cause stunted growth, leaf mottling, and yellowing.
  - Bacterial diseases: Bacterial diseases such as crown gall and bacterial leaf spot can also affect Siberian Ginseng, causing wilting, leaf spotting, and stem cankers.

To prevent and control these issues, it is important to maintain good plant health by providing proper growing conditions, such as well-drained soil and adequate sunlight, and practicing good sanitation measures, such as removing infected plant debris. Insect pests can be controlled by using natural predators or insecticides, while diseases may require the use of fungicides or bactericides. It is always recommended to consult with a gardening expert for specific recommendations on preventing and treating these issues.

- Harvesting and preparations: Siberian Ginseng roots are the most commonly used part of the plant for medicinal purposes, although the leaves and stems can also be used. Here are some guidelines for harvesting and preparing Siberian Ginseng:
  - Harvesting: Siberian Ginseng roots are typically harvested in the fall, after the plant has gone dormant. The roots should be at least three years old before harvesting to ensure their potency. To harvest the roots, dig around the base of the plant with a shovel, being careful not to damage the roots.
  - Drying: After harvesting, the roots should be washed and dried. They can be air-dried in a cool, dry place or dried in a dehydrator at a low temperature. The roots are dry when they snap easily and are free of moisture.
  - Preparation: Once the roots are dry, they can be ground into a powder and used to make teas, tinctures, or capsules. To make a tea, steep 1-2 teaspoons of powdered root in hot water for 10-15 minutes. Tinctures can be made by soaking the powdered root in alcohol for several weeks, then straining and bottling the liquid. Capsules can be filled with powdered root and taken as a supplement.

It is important to note that while Siberian Ginseng may offer potential health benefits, it should not be used as a substitute for medical treatment. It is always recommended to consult with a healthcare professional before using any herbal supplement, especially if you have a pre-existing medical condition or are taking medications.

What medicines are made with this herb:
Siberian Ginseng is used as an herbal supplement and is not an ingredient in any FDA-approved medicines in the United States. However, it is used in traditional medicine systems in various forms for a wide range of health conditions.

In traditional Chinese medicine, Siberian Ginseng is used to strengthen the immune system, increase energy and stamina, and improve overall health. It is also used to treat conditions such as high blood pressure, diabetes, and respiratory infections.

In Ayurvedic medicine, Siberian Ginseng is used to improve mental function, reduce stress and anxiety, and enhance physical performance.

In Western herbal medicine, Siberian Ginseng is used as an adaptogen to help the body cope with stress and improve physical and mental performance. It is also used to support the immune system and improve circulation.

Siberian Ginseng is available in various forms, including capsules, tablets, tinctures, and teas. It is often used in combination with other herbs to enhance its effects. As with all herbal supplements, it is important to consult with a healthcare professional before using Siberian Ginseng, especially if you have a pre-existing medical condition, are taking medications, or are pregnant or breastfeeding.

What medicines this herb counteracts:
Siberian Ginseng may interact with certain medications, so it is important to talk to your healthcare provider before taking this herb if you are currently taking any prescription or over-the-counter medications. Here are some examples of medications that Siberian Ginseng may interact with:

- Immunosuppressant drugs: Siberian Ginseng may increase the effects of immunosuppressant drugs, such as cyclosporine and corticosteroids, which are used to suppress the immune system. Taking Siberian Ginseng with these medications may increase the risk of infection.

- Blood-thinning medications: Siberian Ginseng may increase the effects of blood-thinning medications, such as warfarin and aspirin. Taking Siberian Ginseng with these medications may increase the risk of bleeding.
- Stimulant medications: Siberian Ginseng has stimulant effects and may increase the effects of stimulant medications, such as caffeine, amphetamines, and ADHD medications. Taking Siberian Ginseng with these medications may increase the risk of side effects such as jitteriness, insomnia, and rapid heartbeat.
- Diabetes medications: Siberian Ginseng may lower blood sugar levels and may interact with diabetes medications, such as insulin and oral hypoglycemic agents. Taking Siberian Ginseng with these medications may increase the risk of hypoglycemia (low blood sugar).

It is important to note that these are not the only medications that Siberian Ginseng may interact with, and it is always recommended to consult with a healthcare professional before taking any herbal supplement.

Skullcap

Herbal Identification:
- Common name: Skullcap
- Latin binomial: Scutellaria lateriflora
- Other common names: Blue Skullcap, Mad Dog Skullcap, Hoodwort
- Plant family: Lamiaceae (mint family)
- Botanical description: Skullcap is a perennial herb that grows up to 60 cm tall. It has square stems with pairs of leaves that are oval or lance-shaped and toothed. The leaves and stem are covered in fine hairs. The flowers are small, blue or purple, and arranged in spikes at the top of the stem. Skullcap belongs to the mint family (Lamiaceae) and is native to eastern North America. It prefers partial shade to full sun and moist soil. Skullcap is generally pest-free and disease-resistant.

Medicinal Properties:
- Recommended cultivars: N/A
- Parts used: Aerial parts (leaves and stems)
- Taste: Bitter
- Actions: Nervine, sedative, antispasmodic, anxiolytic, febrifuge
- Energetics: Cooling and drying
- Specific indications: Skullcap is commonly used as a nervine tonic and is traditionally known to support the nervous system. It is often used to help with anxiety, stress, insomnia, and nervous tension. Skullcap is also known to have mild sedative properties, making it useful for promoting relaxation and sleep. It can be helpful in reducing muscle tension and headaches caused by stress and anxiety. Additionally, skullcap has been used to support the digestive system, specifically for digestive inflammation and discomfort. It may also have anti-inflammatory and antioxidant properties.

Medicinal preparations:
Skullcap can be prepared in a variety of ways, including:
- Infusion: The dried leaves and flowers of the plant can be steeped in hot water to make a tea. This is a gentle way to extract the medicinal properties of the herb.
- Tincture: The dried herb can be soaked in alcohol or vinegar to create a tincture. This is a more concentrated form of the herb and can be taken in small doses.

- Capsules: Skullcap is also available in capsule form. These capsules contain a powdered form of the herb and can be taken orally.
- Topical preparations: Skullcap can be used topically in the form of creams or ointments to help with skin irritation or inflammation.
- Herbal smoking blend: Dried skullcap leaves can also be used in smoking blends as a relaxing alternative to tobacco.

It is important to follow proper dosage guidelines and consult with a healthcare professional before using any herbal preparation.

• Ratio and dosage information: Infusion: 1-2 tsp of dried herb per cup of boiling water, steep for 10-15 minutes, drink 1-3 cups per day. Tincture: 2-4 ml, 3 times per day. Capsules/tablets: Follow the manufacturer's instructions.

Medicinal uses:
Skullcap has a wide range of medicinal uses, including:
- Anxiety and Stress: Skullcap is commonly used to help with anxiety and stress. It has a calming effect on the nervous system and can help to reduce feelings of anxiety and tension.
- Insomnia: Skullcap has mild sedative properties and can be useful in promoting relaxation and sleep. It is often used as a natural sleep aid.
- Headaches: Skullcap has muscle relaxant properties and may help to reduce tension headaches caused by stress and anxiety.
- Digestive Issues: Skullcap has been used to support the digestive system and may be helpful for digestive inflammation and discomfort.
- Anti-inflammatory and Antioxidant Properties: Skullcap may have anti-inflammatory and antioxidant properties, which can help to protect the body from oxidative stress and inflammation.
- Muscle Relaxant: Skullcap is also known to have muscle relaxant properties and can be useful in reducing muscle tension and spasms.
- Menstrual Cramps: Skullcap may help to alleviate menstrual cramps by reducing inflammation and promoting relaxation.

It is important to note that while skullcap can be helpful in supporting these conditions, it is not a substitute for professional medical advice and treatment. It is important to consult with a healthcare professional before using any herbal remedies.

• Precautions and contradictions: Skullcap is generally considered safe when used in recommended doses, but there are some precautions and contraindications to be aware of:
- Pregnancy and Breastfeeding: Skullcap is not recommended for use during pregnancy or breastfeeding as there is not enough information available on its safety.

- Sedative Medications: Skullcap has mild sedative properties and may interact with other sedative medications, including benzodiazepines and barbiturates.
- Liver Disease: There have been rare reports of liver damage associated with the use of skullcap. It is recommended that individuals with liver disease avoid using skullcap or consult with a healthcare professional before use.
- Allergic Reactions: Some individuals may experience allergic reactions to skullcap, particularly those with allergies to other plants in the mint family.

It is important to consult with a healthcare professional before using skullcap, especially if you have any pre-existing medical conditions or are taking any medications.

Cultivation:
- Native to: Eastern North America
- Zones: 3-8
- Soil: Well-drained, fertile soil with a pH of 6.0-7.0
- Propagation: Seeds, cuttings, division
- Growing information and garden care: Skullcap prefers partial shade to full sun and moist soil. It can be propagated by seeds, cuttings, or division. It may self-seed and spread quickly, so it is recommended to grow it in a container or in a designated area in the garden. Prune back after flowering to encourage bushier growth.
- Insects and disease: Skullcap is generally a hardy plant that is resistant to most pests and diseases. However, it can be susceptible to a few common issues:
  - Powdery Mildew: This is a fungal disease that can affect the leaves of the plant, causing a white, powdery coating. It can be prevented by ensuring good air circulation around the plant and avoiding overhead watering.
  - Root Rot: Skullcap can be susceptible to root rot if the soil is too wet or poorly drained. To prevent this, ensure that the soil is well-draining and that the plant is not overwatered.
  - Aphids: These small insects can sometimes infest skullcap, sucking sap from the leaves and causing distortion and damage. They can be controlled using insecticidal soap or by introducing natural predators such as ladybugs.
  - Spider Mites: These tiny insects can also infest skullcap, causing yellowing and bronzing of the leaves. They can be controlled using insecticidal soap or by introducing natural predators such as predatory mites.

Regular inspection and maintenance of the plant can help to prevent and control these issues.

- Harvesting and preparations: Skullcap can be harvested when the plant is in full bloom, usually in mid-summer. The aerial parts of the plant, including the leaves, stems, and flowers, are used for medicinal purposes.

To harvest, simply cut the aerial parts of the plant with a sharp, clean pair of scissors or shears. It is important to avoid damaging the plant or taking too much of it at once, as this can harm the plant's growth and sustainability.

Once harvested, the aerial parts of the plant can be dried in a cool, dark, and well-ventilated area. Once completely dry, the plant can be stored in an airtight container away from heat and moisture.

Skullcap can be prepared in a variety of ways for medicinal use, including:
- Tea: Infuse 1-2 teaspoons of dried skullcap in 1 cup of hot water for 10-15 minutes. Strain and drink up to 3 cups per day.
- Tincture: Combine 1 part dried skullcap with 5 parts alcohol (such as vodka or brandy) and let steep for several weeks. Strain and take 20-40 drops up to 3 times per day.
- Capsules: Capsules containing dried skullcap are available for purchase and can be taken according to the manufacturer's instructions.

It is important to follow recommended dosages and consult with a healthcare professional before using skullcap for medicinal purposes.

What medicines are made with this herb:

Skullcap is used in a variety of traditional and alternative medicines. Some examples of medicines made with this herb include:
- Dietary Supplements: Skullcap supplements are available in a variety of forms, including capsules, tablets, and tinctures. They are used to support a healthy mood, promote relaxation, and reduce anxiety and stress.
- Traditional Chinese Medicine: In traditional Chinese medicine, skullcap is used to support healthy liver function and promote relaxation.
- Native American Medicine: Native Americans have used skullcap for its sedative and relaxing properties, as well as for treating nervous system disorders.
- Homeopathy: Skullcap is used in homeopathy to treat nervous system disorders, anxiety, and insomnia.
- Topical Applications: Skullcap can be used topically in salves and creams to soothe irritated skin and promote wound healing.

It is important to note that herbal medicines are not regulated in the same way as pharmaceuticals, and the safety and efficacy of skullcap and other herbs have not been extensively studied. It is important to consult with a healthcare professional before using skullcap or any other herbal medicine.

What medicines this herb counteracts:

There are no known medications that skullcap specifically counteracts. However, skullcap can interact with certain medications, so it is important to consult with a healthcare professional before using skullcap if you are taking any prescription or over-the-counter medications.

Skullcap may have sedative properties and may enhance the effects of medications that also have sedative effects, such as benzodiazepines, barbiturates, and antidepressants. Skullcap may also interact with medications that are metabolized by the liver, as it may affect liver enzymes and the way that these medications are broken down in the body.

It is important to note that herbal medicines are not regulated in the same way as pharmaceuticals, and the safety and efficacy of skullcap and other herbs have not been extensively studied. It is important to consult with a healthcare professional before using skullcap or any other herbal medicine.

St. John's Wort

Herbal Identification:
- Common name: St. John's Wort
- Latin binomial: Hypericum perforatum
- Other common names: Tipton's weed, Klamath weed, chase-devil
- Plant family: Hypericaceae
- Botanical description: St. John's Wort (Hypericum perforatum) is a flowering plant that belongs to the Hypericaceae family. It is a herbaceous perennial that grows up to a height of one to three feet.

The leaves of St. John's Wort are opposite, simple, and oblong in shape, with no teeth or lobes. They are yellow-green in color and have translucent dots on the undersides of the leaves, which are visible when held up to the light.

The flowers of St. John's Wort are yellow in color and have five petals. They are arranged in clusters at the end of the branches, and each flower is about an inch in diameter. The flowers bloom in the summer months and have a distinct, pleasant smell.

St. John's Wort is known for its numerous medicinal properties, and the plant has been used for centuries to treat a variety of ailments. It contains a number of active compounds, including hypericin, hyperforin, and flavonoids, which are thought to be responsible for its therapeutic effects.

Overall, St. John's Wort is a hardy plant that thrives in sunny locations with well-drained soil. It is often used in landscaping as a ground cover, and its medicinal properties have made it a popular herbal supplement in many parts of the world.

Medicinal Properties:
- Parts used: The aerial parts of the plant, including the leaves, flowers, and stems, are used for medicinal purposes.
- Taste: St. John's Wort has a bitter and astringent taste.
- Actions: St. John's Wort is known for its antidepressant, antiviral, anti-inflammatory, and sedative properties.
- Energetics: St. John's Wort is considered to be warming and drying.
- Specific indications: St. John's Wort (Hypericum perforatum) has been traditionally used for a range of indications, and research has also found it to be

effective for several conditions. Some specific indications for which St. John's Wort may be useful include:
- Depression: St. John's Wort has been studied extensively for its antidepressant effects, and several clinical trials have found it to be as effective as standard antidepressant medications, with fewer side effects.
- Anxiety: St. John's Wort may also be helpful in reducing symptoms of anxiety, including nervousness, restlessness, and irritability.
- Seasonal Affective Disorder (SAD): This is a type of depression that occurs in the winter months, when there is less sunlight. St. John's Wort may be effective in reducing symptoms of SAD, as it is thought to help regulate the body's circadian rhythms.
- Nerve pain: St. John's Wort has been used traditionally to treat nerve pain, and research has found it to be effective in reducing symptoms of neuropathic pain.
- Menopausal symptoms: St. John's Wort may be useful in reducing symptoms of menopause, including hot flashes and mood swings.

It is important to note that St. John's Wort can interact with certain medications, including antidepressants, birth control pills, and blood thinners. As such, it is important to speak with a healthcare provider before using St. John's Wort as a supplement.

Medicinal preparations:
St. John's Wort (Hypericum perforatum) can be prepared in several ways for medicinal use, including:
- Capsules or tablets: St. John's Wort supplements are widely available in capsule or tablet form, and are commonly used for depression, anxiety, and other mood disorders. It is important to follow dosage instructions carefully, and to speak with a healthcare provider before using St. John's Wort if you are taking any other medications.
- Tincture: St. John's Wort tincture is made by soaking the plant in alcohol for several weeks. The resulting liquid can be taken orally, either alone or diluted in water or juice. Tinctures are often used for nerve pain, and may also be useful for mild to moderate depression.
- Tea: St. John's Wort tea can be made by steeping the dried herb in hot water for several minutes. It is commonly used for its calming and mood-stabilizing effects, and may be useful for mild to moderate depression.
- Oil: St. John's Wort oil is made by infusing the plant in an oil base, such as olive or almond oil, for several weeks. The resulting oil can be applied topically to treat burns, bruises, and other skin conditions.

It is important to note that St. John's Wort can interact with certain medications, including antidepressants, birth control pills, and blood thinners. As such, it is important to speak with a healthcare provider before using St. John's Wort as a supplement.

• Ratio and dosage information: The recommended dosage of St. John's Wort depends on the preparation and the specific condition being treated. It is important to consult with a healthcare professional for guidance on dosage and usage.

• Precautions and contradictions: While St. John's Wort (Hypericum perforatum) is generally considered safe when used appropriately, there are several precautions and contraindications to keep in mind. These include:

- Interactions with medications: St. John's Wort can interact with several medications, including antidepressants, birth control pills, and blood thinners. This can reduce the effectiveness of these medications or lead to harmful side effects. If you are taking any medications, it is important to speak with a healthcare provider before using St. John's Wort as a supplement.
- Photosensitivity: St. John's Wort can cause increased sensitivity to sunlight, which can lead to sunburn and other skin damage. If you are taking St. John's Wort, it is important to avoid excessive sun exposure and to wear protective clothing and sunscreen when outdoors.
- Pregnancy and breastfeeding: St. John's Wort has not been extensively studied in pregnant or breastfeeding women, and its safety in these populations is not well established. As such, it is generally recommended that pregnant or breastfeeding women avoid using St. John's Wort.
- Surgery: St. John's Wort may increase the risk of bleeding during surgery, and should be stopped at least two weeks before any scheduled surgical procedures.
- Bipolar disorder: St. John's Wort may worsen symptoms of bipolar disorder, and should be used with caution or avoided in individuals with this condition.

It is important to speak with a healthcare provider before using St. John's Wort as a supplement, particularly if you have any underlying health conditions or are taking any medications.

Cultivation:
- Native to: Europe, western Asia, and northern Africa
- Zones: St. John's Wort grows in zones 3-8.
- Soil: St. John's Wort prefers well-drained, slightly acidic soil.
- Propagation: St. John's Wort can be propagated by division or by seed.

- Growing information and garden care: St. John's Wort prefers full sun and can tolerate a variety of soil types. It is a hardy plant that does not require much care once established.
- Insects and disease: St. John's Wort (Hypericum perforatum) is generally resistant to most pests and diseases, which makes it a relatively low-maintenance plant. However, there are still a few insects and diseases that can affect St. John's Wort, including:
  - Aphids: These tiny insects feed on the sap of the plant, which can cause leaves to yellow and wilt. Aphids can be controlled with insecticidal soap or by introducing natural predators, such as ladybugs or lacewings.
  - Leaf spot: This fungal disease can cause dark, circular spots to appear on the leaves of the plant. Leaf spot can be controlled by removing infected leaves and applying a fungicide.
  - Rust: This fungal disease can cause orange or brown spots on the leaves of the plant, as well as stunted growth and premature leaf drop. Rust can be controlled by removing infected leaves and applying a fungicide.
  - Beetles: Certain types of beetles, such as the hypericum beetle, can feed on the leaves and flowers of St. John's Wort, causing significant damage. Beetles can be controlled with insecticidal soap or by handpicking them off the plant.

It is important to monitor St. John's Wort for signs of insect or disease infestation, and to take appropriate steps to control any problems that arise. Proper plant care, including regular watering and fertilization, can help keep St. John's Wort healthy and resistant to pests and diseases.

- Harvesting and preparations: St. John's Wort (Hypericum perforatum) can be harvested and prepared for medicinal use in several ways. Here are the general steps to follow:
  - Harvesting: The best time to harvest St. John's Wort is in mid-summer, when the plant is in full bloom. Use sharp scissors or shears to cut the flowering tops of the plant, leaving a few inches of stem attached.
  - Drying: Once harvested, the flowering tops of St. John's Wort should be dried immediately to prevent spoilage. Spread the plant material out on a clean, dry surface, such as a drying rack or a clean towel, and allow it to air dry for several days. Turn the plant material occasionally to ensure even drying.
  - Storage: Once the plant material is dry, store it in an airtight container, such as a glass jar with a tight-fitting lid. Store the container in a cool, dry place away from direct sunlight.
  - Preparation: There are several ways to prepare St. John's Wort for medicinal use, including making teas, tinctures, and oils. For tea, steep 1-2 teaspoons of dried St. John's Wort in hot water for several minutes, then strain and

drink. For tinctures, soak the dried plant material in alcohol for several weeks, then strain and use the resulting liquid as directed. For oils, infuse the dried plant material in an oil base, such as olive or almond oil, for several weeks, then strain and use the resulting oil topically.

It is important to follow dosage instructions carefully and to speak with a healthcare provider before using St. John's Wort as a supplement. Additionally, it is important to properly identify St. John's Wort and avoid harvesting or consuming any other plants that resemble it, as there are several toxic lookalike species.

What medicines are made with this herb:

St. John's Wort (Hypericum perforatum) has been used for medicinal purposes for centuries, and is commonly used today to treat mild to moderate depression and anxiety. It is also used for a range of other conditions, including insomnia, nerve pain, and skin disorders. Here are some of the medicines that are made with St. John's Wort:

- Antidepressants: St. John's Wort is commonly used as a natural alternative to prescription antidepressants. It is thought to work by increasing levels of serotonin and other neurotransmitters in the brain. However, it is important to note that St. John's Wort can interact with prescription antidepressants and other medications, and should only be used under the guidance of a healthcare provider.
- Topical creams and ointments: St. John's Wort is sometimes used topically to treat skin conditions such as burns, bruises, and wounds. It is thought to have anti-inflammatory and antibacterial properties that can help soothe and heal damaged skin.
- Herbal teas and supplements: St. John's Wort is often consumed as a tea or taken as a supplement in capsule form. These products are widely available in health food stores and online, and are used to treat a range of conditions, including depression, anxiety, and nerve pain.
- Homeopathic remedies: St. John's Wort is also used in some homeopathic remedies, which are believed to work by stimulating the body's natural healing processes.

It is important to speak with a healthcare provider before using St. John's Wort as a supplement or in any other form, particularly if you are taking any medications or have any underlying health conditions.

What medicines this herb counteracts:

St. John's Wort (Hypericum perforatum) can interact with a wide range of medications, and should not be taken with certain medications without the guidance of a healthcare provider. Some of the medications that St.

John's Wort can counteract include:
- Antidepressants: St. John's Wort can interact with prescription antidepressants, including selective serotonin reuptake inhibitors (SSRIs) and monoamine oxidase inhibitors (MAOIs), and can cause potentially serious side effects. Therefore, it should not be used in combination with these medications without the guidance of a healthcare provider.
- Blood thinners: St. John's Wort can interfere with the effectiveness of blood thinning medications, such as warfarin, and can increase the risk of blood clots. Therefore, it should not be used in combination with these medications without the guidance of a healthcare provider.
- Birth control pills: St. John's Wort can decrease the effectiveness of birth control pills, and may increase the risk of unintended pregnancy. Therefore, it should not be used in combination with birth control pills without the guidance of a healthcare provider.
- Immunosuppressants: St. John's Wort can reduce the effectiveness of immunosuppressant medications, which are used to prevent rejection of transplanted organs. Therefore, it should not be used in combination with these medications without the guidance of a healthcare provider.

It is important to speak with a healthcare provider before using St. John's Wort as a supplement or in any other form, particularly if you are taking any medications or have any underlying health conditions.

Thyme

Herbal Identification:
- Common Name: Thyme
- Latin Binomial: Thymus vulgaris
- Other Common Names: Common thyme, garden thyme
- Plant Family: Lamiaceae (mint family)
- Botanical Description: Thyme is a small, perennial shrub with woody stems and small, aromatic leaves that are greenish-gray in color. It produces clusters of pink or purple flowers in the summer. The plant typically grows to be around 15-30 cm in height and 30-40 cm in width. Thyme has a bushy growth habit and its stems may become woody with age. The leaves of thyme are small and oval-shaped, with smooth edges and a slightly fuzzy texture. The plant has a strong, pleasant aroma and a pungent, slightly bitter taste.

Medicinal Properties:
- Recommended Cultivars: 'Common' and 'English'
- Parts Used: Leaves, stems, and flowers
- Taste: Pungent, bitter
- Actions: Antimicrobial, antispasmodic, expectorant, carminative, diaphoretic
- Energetics: Warming, drying
- Specific Indications: Thyme has a variety of traditional uses and is known for its antimicrobial, antitussive, expectorant, and antispasmodic properties. It is often used to treat respiratory infections, such as bronchitis, whooping cough, and sore throat. Thyme is also known to have a stimulating effect on the digestive system, and can be used to relieve digestive complaints such as indigestion, flatulence, and bloating. Additionally, thyme has been used to treat menstrual cramps and as a natural remedy for insomnia. It is also thought to have antioxidant properties, and may help to boost the immune system.

Medicinal Preparations:
Thyme can be used in a variety of medicinal preparations, including:
- Infusion: A tea made by steeping fresh or dried thyme in boiling water can be used to treat respiratory infections, digestive complaints, and menstrual cramps.
- Tincture: Thyme can be prepared as a tincture by steeping the herb in alcohol for several weeks. This can be used to treat respiratory infections and as a digestive aid.

- Essential oil: The essential oil of thyme can be used in aromatherapy or diluted with a carrier oil for use in massage. It is thought to have antibacterial and antifungal properties and can be used to treat respiratory infections, as well as to relieve muscle tension and joint pain.
- Inhalation: Adding thyme essential oil to a bowl of hot water and inhaling the steam can help to relieve respiratory infections.
- Poultice: A poultice made by crushing fresh thyme leaves and applying them directly to the skin can be used to relieve joint pain and inflammation.

Dosage information and preparation methods can vary depending on the specific intended use, so it is important to consult a qualified healthcare practitioner for individualized recommendations.

- Ratio and Dosage Information: Infusion: 1-2 tsp of dried herb per cup of hot water, steep for 10-15 minutes; Tincture: 1:5, 40-60% alcohol, 2-4 mL, 3 times per day

Medicinal Uses:

Thyme has a variety of medicinal uses, including:
- Respiratory infections: Thyme has antimicrobial properties and can help to relieve respiratory infections, such as bronchitis, whooping cough, and sore throat. It can be used in the form of an infusion, tincture, essential oil, or inhalation.
- Digestive complaints: Thyme is known to have a stimulating effect on the digestive system and can be used to relieve digestive complaints such as indigestion, flatulence, and bloating. It can be used in the form of an infusion or tincture.
- Menstrual cramps: Thyme can be used to relieve menstrual cramps when taken in the form of an infusion.
- Insomnia: Thyme is believed to have a calming effect on the nervous system and can be used to promote relaxation and relieve insomnia. It can be used in the form of an infusion or essential oil.
- Immune system support: Thyme has antioxidant properties and can help to boost the immune system. It can be used in the form of an infusion, tincture, or essential oil.
- Topical applications: Thyme can be used topically in the form of a poultice or essential oil to relieve joint pain, inflammation, and muscle tension.

It is important to note that while thyme has many traditional uses and may be beneficial for certain health conditions, it is not a substitute for professional medical advice and treatment. It is important to consult a qualified healthcare practitioner for individualized recommendations.

- Precautions and Contradictions: Thyme is generally considered safe for most people when used in culinary amounts or as a medicinal herb. However, there are some precautions and contradictions to keep in mind:
  - Allergic reactions: Some people may be allergic to thyme, particularly if they are allergic to other plants in the Lamiaceae family, such as oregano, basil, or mint.
  - Pregnancy and breastfeeding: Thyme should be used with caution during pregnancy and breastfeeding, as there is limited research on its safety in these situations.
  - Blood clotting disorders: Thyme may increase the risk of bleeding in people with blood clotting disorders, or when used in combination with certain medications that have a blood-thinning effect.
  - Surgery: Thyme should be avoided for at least two weeks prior to surgery, as it may increase the risk of bleeding.
  - Medication interactions: Thyme may interact with certain medications, such as blood-thinning medications, and should be used with caution in people taking these medications.

As with any herbal remedy, it is important to consult with a qualified healthcare practitioner before using thyme as a medicinal herb, particularly if you have any underlying health conditions or are taking any medications.

Cultivation:
- Native to: Mediterranean region
- Zones: 5-9
- Soil: Well-drained, sandy or loamy soil, pH of 6.0-8.0
- Propagation: Seeds, cuttings, division
- Growing Information and Garden Care: Thyme prefers full sun and well-drained soil, and can be grown from seed or purchased as seedlings. It is drought-tolerant and can be harvested regularly to promote bushy growth. Thyme can be prone to powdery mildew and other fungal diseases, so it is important to avoid overhead watering and provide good air circulation.
- Insects and Disease: Thyme is generally a hardy plant that is not susceptible to many pests or diseases. However, some common issues that may affect thyme include:
  - Spider mites: These tiny insects can infest thyme and cause the leaves to turn yellow and die. Regular watering and misting can help to deter spider mites, as can using insecticidal soap.
  - Root rot: Thyme may be susceptible to root rot if the soil is too wet or if it is planted in poorly draining soil. To prevent root rot, ensure that the soil is well-draining and do not over-water the plant.

- Powdery mildew: This fungal disease can affect thyme and cause a white, powdery coating to appear on the leaves. Powdery mildew can be prevented by ensuring good air circulation around the plant and avoiding overhead watering.
- Leaf spot: This fungal disease can cause brown or black spots to appear on the leaves of thyme. It can be prevented by avoiding overhead watering and ensuring good air circulation around the plant.

Overall, thyme is a relatively low-maintenance plant that is not prone to many pests or diseases, particularly when grown in well-draining soil with good air circulation.

- Harvesting and Preparations: Thyme can be harvested and used fresh or dried for culinary or medicinal purposes. Here are some tips for harvesting and preparing thyme:
  - Harvesting: Thyme can be harvested throughout the growing season, but the leaves are most flavorful just before the plant flowers. Cut the stems about 4 to 6 inches long and snip off the leaves. Avoid cutting back more than one-third of the plant at a time.
  - Drying: To dry thyme, tie the stems in small bunches and hang them upside down in a warm, dry, and well-ventilated area. Once the leaves are dry and crispy, remove them from the stems and store them in an airtight container.
  - Culinary uses: Thyme is a popular culinary herb that can be used fresh or dried in a variety of dishes, including soups, stews, roasts, and marinades. It pairs well with meats, poultry, fish, vegetables, and beans.
  - Medicinal uses: Thyme is used medicinally for a variety of purposes, including as an antiseptic, expectorant, and digestive aid. It can be made into teas, tinctures, or infused oils.
  - Infused oil: To make thyme infused oil, fill a jar with fresh thyme leaves and cover with a carrier oil such as olive oil or coconut oil. Let the jar sit in a warm, sunny spot for 4-6 weeks, then strain out the thyme leaves and store the oil in a dark bottle. Thyme infused oil can be used topically for a variety of purposes, including as a muscle rub or wound healer.

Remember to always wash thyme thoroughly before using it, as it may contain dirt or small insects.

Medicines Made with Thyme:

Thyme is used in a variety of medicinal preparations, including:
- Thyme essential oil: Thyme essential oil is used in aromatherapy and is believed to have antibacterial, antifungal, and antiviral properties. It is also used topically for skin conditions, such as acne and eczema.

- Thyme tea: Thyme tea is used to treat respiratory infections, such as coughs and bronchitis. It is also used as a digestive aid and to help relieve menstrual cramps.
- Thyme tincture: Thyme tincture is made by steeping thyme leaves in alcohol and is used to treat respiratory infections and digestive issues.
- Thyme honey: Thyme honey is made by infusing thyme leaves in honey and is used to soothe sore throats and coughs.
- Thyme capsules: Thyme capsules are available as a dietary supplement and are used to boost the immune system and support respiratory health.

Overall, thyme is a versatile herb that is used in many different medicinal preparations. However, it is important to consult with a healthcare provider before using thyme for medicinal purposes, particularly if you are pregnant or have a medical condition.

What Medicines Thyme Counteracts:

Thyme is generally considered safe for most people, and it does not typically counteract any medications. However, if you are taking any medications or have a medical condition, it is important to consult with a healthcare provider before using thyme for medicinal purposes. Thyme may interact with certain medications, such as blood thinners, and may not be safe for individuals with certain medical conditions, such as liver or kidney disease. Additionally, thyme essential oil should be used with caution, as it can be irritating to the skin and should be diluted before use.

Turmeric

Herbal Identification:
- Common name: Turmeric
- Latin binomial: Curcuma longa
- Other common names: Indian saffron, yellow ginger
- Plant family: Zingiberaceae (ginger family)
- Botanical description: Turmeric (Curcuma longa) is a perennial plant in the ginger family (Zingiberaceae). It is native to Southeast Asia and is widely cultivated in tropical regions around the world. The plant grows up to 1 meter in height and has long, lance-shaped leaves that are green on top and pale green underneath. The flowers are small, yellow or white, and grow in dense spikes at the end of the stem. The root, which is the part of the plant used in cooking and medicine, is a thick, orange-yellow rhizome with a rough, scaly texture. Turmeric has a distinctive aroma and a warm, bitter taste.

Medicinal Properties:
- Parts used: Rhizome
- Taste: Bitter, pungent
- Actions: Anti-inflammatory, antioxidant, antimicrobial, antiviral, digestive, carminative, hepatic, cholagogue, alterative, anticancer
- Energetics: Warming, drying
- Specific indications: Turmeric has been traditionally used for a variety of health purposes and is known to have anti-inflammatory, antioxidant, and antimicrobial properties. Some of its specific indications are:
  - Digestive issues: Turmeric can help improve digestion and relieve symptoms of bloating, gas, and indigestion.
  - Arthritis and joint pain: Turmeric's anti-inflammatory properties can help reduce joint pain and stiffness in people with arthritis.
  - Skin health: Turmeric may help improve skin health by reducing inflammation, fighting acne, and promoting wound healing.
  - Brain health: Turmeric's antioxidant properties may protect against cognitive decline and improve brain function.
  - Heart health: Turmeric may help reduce the risk of heart disease by improving blood flow, reducing inflammation, and lowering cholesterol levels.
  - Cancer prevention: Some studies suggest that turmeric may have anti-cancer properties and may help prevent the growth and spread of cancer cells.

It is important to note that while turmeric has many potential health benefits, more research is needed to fully understand its effects and to determine the optimal dosage and duration of use. As with any supplement or medication, it is also important to talk to your healthcare provider before using turmeric, especially if you have any underlying medical conditions or are taking other medications.

Medicinal preparations:
Turmeric can be used in various medicinal preparations, including:
- Turmeric powder: Turmeric powder can be added to food or drinks as a spice or consumed as a supplement.
- Turmeric tea: Turmeric can be steeped in hot water to make a tea that can help with digestive issues and inflammation.
- Turmeric paste: A paste made from turmeric and water can be applied topically to the skin to reduce inflammation and promote wound healing.
- Turmeric capsules: Turmeric extract is available in capsule form and can be taken as a supplement.
- Turmeric oil: Turmeric oil can be used topically to relieve pain, reduce inflammation, and improve skin health.
- Turmeric tincture: Turmeric can be made into a tincture by soaking it in alcohol or glycerin. This preparation can be used as a supplement or added to food or drinks.

It is important to note that the dosage and duration of use of turmeric preparations may vary depending on the intended use and individual needs. It is always recommended to consult with a healthcare provider before starting any new supplement or medication.

- Ratio and dosage information: 500-2000 mg per day of standardized extract, or 1-3 teaspoons of powdered root per day

Medicinal uses:
Turmeric has been traditionally used for various medicinal purposes and has been studied extensively for its potential health benefits. Some of its medicinal uses include:
- Anti-inflammatory: Turmeric has potent anti-inflammatory properties and can help reduce inflammation in the body, which may help alleviate symptoms of conditions such as arthritis, inflammatory bowel disease, and asthma.
- Antioxidant: Turmeric is a potent antioxidant that can help protect cells from damage caused by free radicals, which may contribute to the development of chronic diseases such as cancer and heart disease.

- Pain relief: Turmeric may help relieve pain, particularly in people with arthritis, by reducing inflammation and improving joint function.
- Digestive health: Turmeric can help improve digestion and may alleviate symptoms of conditions such as indigestion, bloating, and gas.
- Skin health: Turmeric can help improve skin health by reducing inflammation, fighting acne, and promoting wound healing.
- Brain health: Turmeric may have neuroprotective effects and may help improve brain function and reduce the risk of cognitive decline.
- Heart health: Turmeric may help improve heart health by reducing inflammation, improving blood flow, and lowering cholesterol levels.
- Cancer prevention: Some studies suggest that turmeric may have anti-cancer properties and may help prevent the growth and spread of cancer cells.

It is important to note that while turmeric has many potential health benefits, more research is needed to fully understand its effects and to determine the optimal dosage and duration of use. As with any supplement or medication, it is also important to talk to your healthcare provider before using turmeric, especially if you have any underlying medical conditions or are taking other medications.

- Precautions and contradictions: While turmeric is generally considered safe for most people, there are some precautions and contraindications to be aware of:
  - Blood thinning: Turmeric may act as a blood thinner and may increase the risk of bleeding, particularly in people taking blood-thinning medications such as warfarin. It is important to talk to your healthcare provider before using turmeric if you are taking any medications that affect blood clotting.
  - Gallbladder issues: Turmeric may worsen gallbladder problems or increase the production of bile. It is recommended to avoid turmeric if you have gallstones or other gallbladder issues.
  - Gastrointestinal issues: Turmeric may irritate the gastrointestinal tract and worsen symptoms of conditions such as gastroesophageal reflux disease (GERD), stomach ulcers, and inflammatory bowel disease (IBD).
  - Pregnancy and breastfeeding: There is limited research on the safety of turmeric during pregnancy and breastfeeding. It is recommended to avoid turmeric supplements during these times and to use turmeric as a spice in moderation.
  - Allergies: Turmeric may cause allergic reactions in some people, particularly those who are allergic to ginger or other members of the Zingiberaceae family.
  - Surgery: Turmeric may increase the risk of bleeding and should be avoided before and after surgery.

It is important to talk to your healthcare provider before using turmeric, especially if you have any underlying medical conditions or are taking other medications.

Cultivation:
- Native to: Southern Asia
- Zones: 9-11
- Soil: Well-drained, fertile soil with a pH of 6.0-7.5
- Propagation: Rhizome division or seed
- Growing information and garden care: Turmeric is a tropical plant that prefers warm, humid conditions. It can be grown in containers or in the ground in areas with warm, humid climates. It requires regular watering and partial shade.
- Insects and disease: Turmeric plants are relatively resistant to pests and diseases, but they may still be affected by a few insect pests and diseases. Some of the common insects that can affect turmeric plants include:
  - Rhizome weevils: These insects can damage the roots and rhizomes of turmeric plants, leading to stunted growth and reduced yield.
  - Leaf-eating caterpillars: These pests can cause significant damage to the leaves of turmeric plants, leading to reduced photosynthesis and lower yields.
  - Scale insects: These pests can infest turmeric plants and cause yellowing of the leaves and stunted growth.
  - Whiteflies: These pests can feed on the leaves of turmeric plants, leading to yellowing and wilting.

In terms of diseases, turmeric plants are generally resistant to most fungal and bacterial diseases. However, they may be affected by some diseases such as:
  - Rhizome rot: This disease is caused by a fungus and can lead to rotting of the rhizomes of turmeric plants.
  - Leaf spot: This disease is caused by a fungus and can cause yellowing and browning of the leaves of turmeric plants.
  - Bacterial wilt: This disease is caused by bacteria and can cause wilting and death of the plant.

To prevent and manage insect pests and diseases, it is important to maintain good cultural practices such as proper irrigation, fertilization, and crop rotation. Insecticides and fungicides may also be used as a last resort if necessary.
- Harvesting and preparations: Turmeric is harvested by digging up the rhizomes (underground stems) of the plant, usually after about 7 to 10 months of growth. The rhizomes are then washed, boiled, and dried in the sun or in a drying oven. Once dried, the rhizomes can be ground into a powder or used in various preparations.

Here are some common preparations of turmeric:
- Turmeric powder: Dried turmeric rhizomes are ground into a fine powder and used as a spice in cooking.
- Turmeric tea: Turmeric powder or fresh turmeric root can be steeped in hot water to make a flavorful and healthy tea.
- Turmeric paste: A paste made from turmeric powder and water can be applied to the skin as a natural remedy for various skin issues.
- Turmeric supplements: Turmeric is also available in the form of supplements such as capsules, tablets, and tinctures. These supplements contain concentrated amounts of curcumin, the active ingredient in turmeric.

When purchasing turmeric, it is important to look for high-quality, organic sources that have been processed and stored properly to ensure maximum potency and freshness. Additionally, it is important to talk to your healthcare provider before using turmeric supplements, especially if you have any underlying medical conditions or are taking other medications.

Medicines Made with Turmeric:

Turmeric is used in a variety of medicinal preparations, including:
- Turmeric capsules and extracts: Turmeric capsules and extracts are available as dietary supplements and are used to support joint health, reduce inflammation, and support liver function.
- Turmeric tea: Turmeric tea is used as a digestive aid and to reduce inflammation.
- Turmeric paste: Turmeric paste is a topical preparation that is used to treat skin conditions, such as psoriasis and eczema.
- Curcumin supplements: Curcumin is the active ingredient in turmeric that is responsible for its medicinal properties. Curcumin supplements are available as dietary supplements and are used to support joint health, reduce inflammation, and support overall health.

What Medicines Turmeric Counteracts:

Turmeric can interact with certain medications, including blood thinners like warfarin and aspirin. Turmeric can increase the risk of bleeding and should not be used by individuals who are taking these medications without consulting their healthcare provider. Turmeric may also interact with medications for diabetes, stomach acid, and some antidepressants. It is important to talk to a healthcare provider before using turmeric supplements if you are taking any medications.

Valerian

Herbal Identification:
- Common Name: Valerian
- Latin Binomial: Valeriana officinalis
- Other Common Names: All-Heal, Amantilla, Garden Heliotrope, Capon's Tail, Setwall
- Plant Family: Caprifoliaceae
- Botanical Description: Valerian (Valeriana officinalis) is a perennial flowering plant that belongs to the Caprifoliaceae family. It can grow up to 5 feet tall and has a robust, hairy stem with opposite compound leaves, each composed of five to nine serrated leaflets. The leaves are arranged in a basal rosette at the bottom of the plant. In the summer, Valerian produces small, fragrant white or pink flowers that are clustered together in panicles. The root of the plant is the most commonly used part medicinally and is typically dug up in the fall of the second year of growth. The root is long, slender, and spindle-shaped, with a yellowish-white color on the outside and a white, spongy texture on the inside. Valerian has a distinctive, earthy odor that is often described as unpleasant.

Medicinal Properties:
- Recommended Cultivars: Valeriana officinalis is the most commonly used species, but there are some other species that are used medicinally such as Valeriana sitchensis (Pacific Valerian) and Valeriana wallichii (Indian Valerian).
- Parts Used: Root
- Taste: Bitter, pungent, earthy
- Actions: Nervine, sedative, anxiolytic, carminative, antispasmodic, hypotensive
- Energetics: Cool, dry
- Specific Indications: Valerian is commonly used to support relaxation and calmness, and to promote restful sleep. It is also used for its mild sedative and anxiolytic (anti-anxiety) effects, and is often used to ease nervous tension, stress, and mild anxiety. Valerian may also have muscle relaxant and antispasmodic properties, making it useful for treating conditions such as menstrual cramps, digestive cramping, and tension headaches. It has also been used to help with symptoms of mild depression, as well as to manage symptoms of hyperactivity and attention deficit disorders. Valerian is sometimes used as a mild pain reliever, particularly for nerve pain.

Medicinal Preparations:
Valerian can be prepared in a number of ways for medicinal use. The root of the plant is the most commonly used part medicinally and is typically prepared as a tea, tincture, or capsule. Other preparations include:
- Tea: A decoction or infusion of valerian root can be made by boiling 1-2 teaspoons of dried root in a cup of water for 10-15 minutes. This can be consumed up to three times per day.
- Tincture: Valerian root can be made into a tincture by soaking the chopped root in a mixture of alcohol and water for several weeks. The tincture can then be strained and taken in small doses.
- Capsules: Valerian root is also available in capsule form, often in combination with other calming herbs.
- Essential oil: Valerian root essential oil can be used topically in a carrier oil or diffused in a room to promote relaxation.

It is important to follow dosage instructions carefully and consult a healthcare provider before using valerian medicinally, particularly if you are taking any medications or have a medical condition.

• Ratio and Dosage Information: 1:5 (50%) tincture, 2-4 mL, three times per day; tea made from 1-2 teaspoons of dried root per cup of boiling water, steeped for 10-15 minutes, taken three times per day.

Medicinal Uses:
Valerian is primarily used for its calming and sedative effects. It is commonly used to promote relaxation and restful sleep, particularly in cases of mild insomnia.

Valerian is also often used to relieve nervous tension, stress, and mild anxiety. Its muscle relaxant and antispasmodic properties make it useful for treating conditions such as menstrual cramps, digestive cramping, and tension headaches.

Valerian may also be helpful for managing symptoms of hyperactivity and attention deficit disorders, as well as for supporting mild depression. It has been used as a mild pain reliever, particularly for nerve pain. Valerian can also be used topically in a carrier oil or diffused in a room to promote relaxation and calmness.

It is important to note that while valerian can be effective for mild to moderate symptoms of anxiety and insomnia, it is not recommended as a substitute for medical treatment for more severe conditions. It is also important to follow dosage instructions carefully and consult a healthcare provider before using valerian medicinally.

- Precautions and Contradictions: Valerian is generally considered safe for most people when used appropriately. However, there are some precautions and contradictions to be aware of:
  - Valerian may cause drowsiness, so it should not be used before driving or operating heavy machinery.
  - Valerian should not be used during pregnancy or while breastfeeding, as its safety has not been established.
  - Valerian may interact with some medications, including sedatives, tranquilizers, and anticonvulsants, so it is important to consult with a healthcare provider before using valerian if you are taking any medications.
  - Valerian may cause headaches, dizziness, upset stomach, and other mild side effects in some people.
  - Valerian can cause vivid dreams or nightmares in some people, particularly if used in high doses or for an extended period of time.
  - Valerian should not be used by children under the age of 3.

It is important to follow dosage instructions carefully and consult a healthcare provider before using valerian medicinally, particularly if you have a medical condition or are taking any medications.

Cultivation:
- Native to: Europe and Asia
- Zones: Valerian is hardy in zones 4-9.
- Soil: Valerian prefers moist, well-draining soil that is rich in organic matter. It can tolerate a range of soil pH levels.
- Propagation: Valerian can be propagated by seed or by division of the root.
- Growing Information and Garden Care: Valerian prefers partial shade to full sun and requires consistent moisture. It is a relatively low-maintenance plant, but it can be invasive in some areas. It is often grown as an ornamental plant in herb gardens.
- Insects and Disease: Valerian is relatively pest and disease resistant, but it may occasionally be affected by some common garden pests, such as aphids or spider mites. These can be treated with insecticidal soap or neem oil.

Valerian can also be susceptible to fungal diseases such as powdery mildew, particularly in humid or damp conditions. To prevent fungal infections, ensure that the soil is well-drained and avoid overwatering. If powdery mildew does occur, it can be treated with a fungicide or by removing affected leaves and improving air circulation around the plant.

Overall, valerian is a hardy and low-maintenance plant that is relatively easy to grow in the garden.

- Harvesting and Preparations: Valerian is typically harvested in the fall after the plant has gone to seed. The roots are the primary part of the plant used for medicinal purposes and should be harvested when the plant is at least two years old. To harvest the roots, carefully dig them up and clean them thoroughly. They can then be dried and stored for later use.

Valerian roots can be prepared in a number of ways, including as a tincture, tea, or capsule. To make a valerian tincture, the roots can be chopped and covered with alcohol, such as vodka, and left to steep for several weeks. The resulting tincture can be taken in small doses as needed to promote relaxation and sleep.

To make a valerian tea, the roots can be chopped and steeped in hot water for 5-10 minutes before being strained and consumed. The tea can be sweetened with honey or other natural sweeteners if desired.

Valerian capsules are also widely available and can be taken according to the manufacturer's instructions.

It is important to follow dosage instructions carefully and consult a healthcare provider before using valerian medicinally.

What medicines are made with this herb:
Valerian is commonly used in a variety of herbal remedies, particularly those designed to promote relaxation, reduce anxiety, and improve sleep. Some specific medications that may contain valerian include:
- Valerian tincture: A liquid extract made from valerian root, often used to promote relaxation and help with sleep.
- Valerian tea: A tea made from valerian root, often used to promote relaxation and reduce anxiety.
- Valerian capsules: Dietary supplements containing valerian extract, often used to promote relaxation and improve sleep.

Valerian may also be included as an ingredient in combination herbal remedies designed to promote relaxation, such as those containing chamomile, passionflower, or lemon balm. It is important to follow dosage instructions carefully and consult a healthcare provider before using valerian medicinally.

What medicines this herb counteract:

Valerian is generally safe when used as directed, but there are some medications that may interact with valerian. These include:
- Sedatives and sleeping pills: Valerian may increase the effects of sedative medications, such as benzodiazepines or barbiturates, which can cause excessive drowsiness or impaired coordination.
- Alcohol: Valerian may increase the sedative effects of alcohol, which can lead to excessive drowsiness or impaired coordination.
- Anti-anxiety medications: Valerian may increase the effects of anti-anxiety medications, which can cause excessive drowsiness or impaired coordination.
- Antidepressants: Valerian may interact with antidepressant medications, particularly those that increase serotonin levels, such as selective serotonin reuptake inhibitors (SSRIs), which can cause a potentially dangerous condition known as serotonin syndrome.

It is important to talk to a healthcare provider before using valerian or any other herbal remedies, especially if you are taking any prescription medications. They can help determine if valerian is safe for you to use and advise you on any potential interactions or precautions.

Wild Yam

Herbal Identification:
- Common name: Wild Yam
- Latin binomial: Dioscorea villosa
- Other common names: Colic Root, Devil's Bones, Rheumatism Root
- Plant family: Dioscoreaceae
- Botanical description: Wild yam, also known as Dioscorea villosa, is a climbing vine that is native to North America. It belongs to the family Dioscoreaceae, which also includes other yam species. Wild yam has a distinctive heart-shaped leaf that is approximately 10-15 cm long and wide.

The plant can grow up to 3 meters tall and produces small greenish-yellow flowers that bloom in the late summer to early fall. The flowers are dioecious, meaning that the male and female flowers are produced on separate plants. The fruit of the wild yam is a capsule that contains several small black seeds.

The root of the wild yam is the most commonly used part of the plant for medicinal purposes. The root is large and tuberous, and can be up to 30 cm in length and 10 cm in diameter. It has a light brown or beige color and a slightly sweet taste.

Wild yam has been used in traditional medicine for centuries for its anti-inflammatory, anti-spasmodic, and diuretic properties. It is also believed to help regulate hormone levels in women, which is why it is often used as a natural remedy for menopause symptoms. However, more research is needed to fully understand the medicinal properties of wild yam and its potential benefits and risks.

Medicinal Properties:
- Parts used: The roots and occasionally the rhizomes are used medicinally.
- Taste: Wild yam has a slightly bitter and astringent taste.
- Actions: Antispasmodic, anti-inflammatory, diaphoretic, diuretic, expectorant.
- Energetics: Cooling and moistening.
- Specific indications: Wild yam has been traditionally used for a variety of conditions, including menopausal symptoms, menstrual cramps, gastrointestinal issues, and rheumatoid arthritis. However, it is important to note that there is limited scientific evidence to support the use of wild yam for these indications, and more research is needed to fully understand its effectiveness and safety.

Here are some of the specific indications for which wild yam has been used:
- Menopausal symptoms: Wild yam is often used as a natural remedy for menopausal symptoms such as hot flashes, night sweats, and mood changes. This is because wild yam contains a substance called diosgenin, which is a precursor to the hormone progesterone. However, there is limited scientific evidence to support the use of wild yam for this indication.
- Menstrual cramps: Wild yam has been used traditionally to relieve menstrual cramps and other menstrual-related issues. Again, there is limited scientific evidence to support this use of wild yam.
- Gastrointestinal issues: Wild yam has been used traditionally to help with gastrointestinal issues such as nausea, vomiting, and diarrhea. It is believed to have anti-inflammatory and anti-spasmodic properties that may help to relieve these symptoms.
- Rheumatoid arthritis: Wild yam has been used traditionally to help relieve the symptoms of rheumatoid arthritis, which is an autoimmune disease that causes joint pain and inflammation. Wild yam is believed to have anti-inflammatory properties that may help to reduce inflammation and pain.

It is important to note that wild yam is not a substitute for medical treatment, and anyone with a medical condition should speak with their healthcare provider before using wild yam or any other herbal supplement.

Medicinal preparations:

Wild yam can be prepared in various ways for medicinal use. The most commonly used part of the plant for medicinal purposes is the root, which can be prepared in several ways, including:
- Tincture: Wild yam root can be made into a tincture by soaking it in alcohol or glycerin. The tincture can then be taken orally, either alone or added to a beverage.
- Capsules: Wild yam root can be ground into a powder and encapsulated for easy consumption.
- Tea: Wild yam root can be boiled in water to make a tea. This is a traditional method of preparation that is believed to help with digestive issues and menstrual cramps.
- Creams: Wild yam root can be made into a cream or ointment that can be applied topically to the skin. This is often used for menopausal symptoms, such as vaginal dryness.

It is important to note that the dosage and method of preparation may vary depending on the intended use and the individual's health status. As with any

herbal supplement, it is important to consult with a healthcare provider before using wild yam or any other herbal remedy.
- Ratio and dosage information: Dosage may vary depending on the form of wild yam being used and the specific health condition being treated.

Medicinal uses:
Wild yam has been traditionally used for a variety of medicinal purposes, although there is limited scientific evidence to support many of these uses. Some of the potential medicinal uses of wild yam include:
- Menopausal symptoms: Wild yam is often used as a natural remedy for menopausal symptoms, such as hot flashes, mood changes, and vaginal dryness. This is because wild yam contains diosgenin, which is a precursor to the hormone progesterone. However, there is limited scientific evidence to support the effectiveness of wild yam for menopausal symptoms.
- Menstrual cramps: Wild yam has been used traditionally to help relieve menstrual cramps and other menstrual-related issues. This is believed to be due to the anti-inflammatory and anti-spasmodic properties of wild yam, although more research is needed to fully understand its effectiveness.
- Digestive issues: Wild yam has been used traditionally to help with digestive issues such as nausea, vomiting, and diarrhea. It is believed to have anti-inflammatory and anti-spasmodic properties that may help to relieve these symptoms.
- Rheumatoid arthritis: Wild yam has been used traditionally to help relieve the symptoms of rheumatoid arthritis, which is an autoimmune disease that causes joint pain and inflammation. Wild yam is believed to have anti-inflammatory properties that may help to reduce inflammation and pain.
- Diabetes: Some preliminary research suggests that wild yam may have hypoglycemic properties, meaning it may help to lower blood sugar levels. However, more research is needed to fully understand this potential use of wild yam.

It is important to note that while wild yam has been used traditionally for these purposes, more research is needed to fully understand its effectiveness and safety. Anyone with a medical condition should speak with their healthcare provider before using wild yam or any other herbal supplement.
- Precautions and contradictions: While wild yam is generally considered safe when used as directed, there are some precautions and contraindications to keep in mind:
  - Pregnancy and breastfeeding: Wild yam is not recommended for use during pregnancy or breastfeeding due to a lack of safety data.

- Hormone-sensitive conditions: Wild yam may have estrogen-like effects, which may be problematic for individuals with hormone-sensitive conditions such as breast cancer, endometriosis, and uterine fibroids.
- Blood clotting disorders: Wild yam may increase the risk of bleeding in individuals with blood clotting disorders or who are taking anticoagulant medications.
- Allergic reactions: Some individuals may be allergic to wild yam, and may experience symptoms such as itching, rash, or difficulty breathing.
- Interactions with medications: Wild yam may interact with certain medications, including birth control pills, hormone replacement therapy, and blood thinners. It is important to speak with a healthcare provider before using wild yam or any other herbal supplement.

It is important to note that the safety and effectiveness of wild yam have not been fully established by scientific research. As with any herbal supplement, it is important to speak with a healthcare provider before using wild yam or any other herbal remedy.

Cultivation:
- Native to: North America
- Zones: Hardy in USDA zones 5-10.
- Soil: Wild yam prefers rich, moist soil with a pH of 6-7.5.
- Propagation: Wild yam can be propagated by seed or division of the tuberous roots.
- Growing information and garden care: Wild yam is a climbing vine that can grow up to 20 feet, so it requires a support structure to grow on. It prefers partial shade and consistent moisture.
- Insects and disease: Wild yam is generally pest and disease-resistant.
- Harvesting and preparations: Wild yam is a perennial plant that grows in various parts of the world, including North and Central America. The roots of the plant are the part that is commonly used for medicinal purposes, and they can be harvested and prepared in several ways:
  - Harvesting: The best time to harvest wild yam roots is in the fall, after the plant has gone dormant. The roots should be dug up carefully, using a spade or digging fork. It is important to leave some of the roots behind to ensure that the plant can continue to grow.
  - Cleaning: Once the roots have been harvested, they should be cleaned thoroughly to remove any dirt or debris. The roots can be washed with water and then gently scrubbed with a soft brush to remove any remaining dirt.
  - Drying: After cleaning, the roots should be dried thoroughly. This can be done by laying them out in a single layer on a clean, dry surface and

allowing them to air dry for several days. Alternatively, they can be dried in a dehydrator or oven at a low temperature.
- Preparation: Once the roots are fully dry, they can be prepared for medicinal use. This may include grinding them into a powder, making a tincture or tea, or preparing a cream or ointment for topical use.

It is important to note that wild yam should be harvested responsibly and sustainably, as over-harvesting can have negative effects on the plant and its ecosystem. It is also important to consult with a healthcare provider before using wild yam or any other herbal remedy.

What medicines are made with this herb:
Wild yam is used in several different types of medicinal preparations, including:
- Capsules and tablets: Wild yam is available in capsule or tablet form, which may contain dried and powdered wild yam root or a standardized extract of the plant.
- Tinctures: Wild yam tinctures are made by steeping the dried root in alcohol and water for several weeks. This creates a liquid extract that can be taken orally.
- Creams and ointments: Wild yam can be prepared in a cream or ointment form for topical use. These preparations are often used to relieve menstrual cramps or other types of pain.
- Teas: Wild yam tea can be made by steeping dried wild yam root in hot water for several minutes. The tea is then strained and can be consumed for its potential medicinal properties.
- Homeopathic remedies: Wild yam is also used in some homeopathic remedies, which use highly diluted preparations of the plant.

It is important to note that the effectiveness and safety of these preparations have not been fully established by scientific research. As with any herbal supplement, it is important to speak with a healthcare provider before using wild yam or any other herbal remedy.

What medicines this herb counteract:
Wild yam may interact with certain medications, including those that affect hormone levels or blood clotting. It is important to speak with a healthcare

provider before using wild yam or any other herbal remedy if you are taking any medications, to avoid any potential interactions or adverse effects.

Some specific medications that may interact with wild yam include:
- Hormone replacement therapy (HRT): Wild yam may have estrogen-like effects, which could potentially interact with HRT medications.
- Birth control pills: Wild yam may decrease the effectiveness of birth control pills.
- Blood thinners: Wild yam may increase the risk of bleeding in individuals taking blood thinning medications such as warfarin.
- Diabetes medications: Wild yam may lower blood sugar levels, which could potentially interact with diabetes medications and lead to hypoglycemia.
- Anti-inflammatory medications: Wild yam may have anti-inflammatory effects, which could potentially interact with other anti-inflammatory medications.

It is important to note that the safety and effectiveness of wild yam have not been fully established by scientific research, and it should be used with caution, particularly when taken with other medications.

Yarrow

Herbal Identification:
- Common Name: Yarrow
- Latin Binomial: Achillea millefolium
- Other Common Names: Milfoil, Nosebleed Plant, Soldier's Woundwort, Thousand-leaf, Thousand-seal, Devil's Nettle, Sanguinary, Green Arrow
- Plant Family: Asteraceae (daisy family)
- Botanical Description: Yarrow (Achillea millefolium) is a perennial herb that grows up to 3 feet tall. It has feathery, fern-like leaves that are 2-8 cm long and 1-2 cm wide, and clusters of small white, pink or yellow flowers that bloom from June to October. The flowers are arranged in a flat-topped cluster at the top of a stem and are typically 3-4 mm in diameter. The plant has a fibrous root system and a strong, slightly sweet fragrance. The leaves and stems of yarrow are covered with fine hairs that give the plant a gray-green appearance. Yarrow is often found growing in meadows, pastures, and along roadsides. It is a hardy plant that can tolerate a wide range of growing conditions and is found in temperate regions throughout the world.

Medicinal Properties:
- Parts Used: Aerial parts (leaves, stems, flowers)
- Taste: Bitter, pungent
- Actions: Astringent, diaphoretic, hemostatic, anti-inflammatory, antimicrobial
- Energetics: Cooling and drying
- Specific Indications: Yarrow has a long history of medicinal use and is believed to have many beneficial properties. Some of the specific indications for yarrow include:
  - Digestive issues: Yarrow is commonly used to improve digestion and relieve symptoms such as bloating, gas, and cramps.
  - Menstrual issues: Yarrow has been traditionally used to regulate menstrual flow, reduce menstrual cramps, and relieve PMS symptoms.
  - Wound healing: Yarrow is known for its antiseptic and anti-inflammatory properties and is often used to promote healing of wounds and skin irritations.
  - Fever: Yarrow is believed to help reduce fever by inducing sweating and promoting circulation.
  - Respiratory issues: Yarrow can be useful in treating respiratory problems such as coughs, colds, and bronchitis due to its expectorant properties.

➢ Urinary tract infections: Yarrow is sometimes used to help treat urinary tract infections due to its antibacterial and diuretic properties.

It is important to note that yarrow should be used with caution and under the guidance of a healthcare professional.

Medicinal Preparations:
Yarrow can be prepared in a variety of ways for medicinal use. Some common preparations include:
➢ Tea: Yarrow tea can be made by steeping 1-2 teaspoons of dried yarrow leaves and flowers in 1 cup of hot water for 10-15 minutes. This can be consumed up to 3 times a day.
➢ Tincture: Yarrow tincture is made by soaking the fresh or dried leaves and flowers in alcohol or vinegar for several weeks. The tincture can be taken orally by diluting it in water or juice.
➢ Salve: A yarrow salve can be made by infusing yarrow leaves and flowers in a carrier oil, such as olive or coconut oil, and then adding beeswax to create a solid consistency. This can be applied topically to wounds and skin irritations.
➢ Steam: Yarrow steam can be prepared by adding a handful of fresh or dried yarrow leaves and flowers to a pot of boiling water. The steam can be inhaled to help alleviate respiratory issues.
➢ Poultice: A yarrow poultice can be made by crushing fresh or dried yarrow leaves and flowers and applying them directly to wounds or skin irritations.

It is important to note that yarrow should be used with caution and under the guidance of a healthcare professional. The appropriate dosage and preparation will depend on the individual's health condition and other factors.

• Ratio and Dosage Information: The recommended dosage varies depending on the preparation used. Generally, a standard infusion can be made with 1-2 teaspoons of dried yarrow per cup of boiling water and steeped for 10-15 minutes. Tinctures are generally taken at a dosage of 30-60 drops up to three times daily.

Medicinal Uses:
Yarrow has been used for centuries for its medicinal properties. Some of the medicinal uses of yarrow include:
➢ Digestive Health: Yarrow can help improve digestion and relieve symptoms of indigestion, bloating, gas, and diarrhea.
➢ Menstrual Issues: Yarrow can help regulate menstrual flow, reduce menstrual cramps, and relieve PMS symptoms.

- Wound Healing: Yarrow has antiseptic and anti-inflammatory properties that can help promote wound healing and reduce inflammation in the body.
- Fever: Yarrow can help reduce fever by inducing sweating and promoting circulation.
- Respiratory Issues: Yarrow can help alleviate respiratory issues such as coughs, colds, and bronchitis due to its expectorant properties.
- Skin Issues: Yarrow can help soothe and heal skin irritations such as rashes, eczema, and psoriasis.
- Urinary Tract Infections: Yarrow has antibacterial and diuretic properties that can help treat urinary tract infections.
- Anxiety and Stress: Yarrow can help reduce anxiety and stress due to its calming properties.

It is important to note that yarrow should be used with caution and under the guidance of a healthcare professional. The appropriate dosage and preparation will depend on the individual's health condition and other factors.

• Precautions and Contraindications: Although yarrow is generally considered safe, there are some precautions and contraindications to be aware of:

- Allergic Reactions: Yarrow can cause allergic reactions in some people, especially those who are sensitive to plants in the Asteraceae family, such as ragweed, chamomile, and marigold.
- Pregnancy and Breastfeeding: Yarrow should be avoided during pregnancy and breastfeeding as it may stimulate the uterus and cause contractions.
- Blood Thinners: Yarrow may increase the risk of bleeding when taken with blood-thinning medications such as warfarin and aspirin.
- High Blood Pressure: Yarrow may lower blood pressure, so it should be used with caution by people who already have low blood pressure or are taking medications to lower their blood pressure.
- Surgery: Yarrow should be discontinued at least 2 weeks before any scheduled surgery as it may increase the risk of bleeding.
- Interactions with other Medications: Yarrow may interact with other medications, such as diuretics and sedatives, so it is important to consult with a healthcare professional before using yarrow in combination with other medications.

As with any herbal supplement, it is important to use yarrow under the guidance of a healthcare professional, especially if you have any pre-existing medical conditions or are taking medications.

Cultivation:
- Native to: Europe, Asia, and North America
- Zones: 3-9
- Soil: Yarrow prefers well-draining, sandy soil with a pH between 6.0 and 7.0.
- Propagation: Yarrow can be propagated by seed or by dividing mature plants.
- Growing Information and Garden Care: Yarrow prefers full sun and moderate moisture. It can be planted in spring or fall and should be spaced 12-18 inches apart. It is relatively low-maintenance and can tolerate drought and poor soil conditions.
- Insects and Disease: Yarrow is generally resistant to most insects and diseases. However, some common pests that may affect yarrow include:
  - Aphids: Aphids are small, soft-bodied insects that feed on the sap of the yarrow plant, causing yellowing and distortion of the leaves. They can be controlled using insecticidal soap or neem oil.
  - Spider Mites: Spider mites are tiny arachnids that feed on the underside of the yarrow leaves, causing yellowing and stippling of the foliage. They can be controlled using neem oil or insecticidal soap.
  - Leafhoppers: Leafhoppers are small, wedge-shaped insects that feed on the sap of the yarrow plant, causing yellowing and curling of the leaves. They can be controlled using insecticidal soap or neem oil.
  - Powdery Mildew: Powdery mildew is a fungal disease that causes a powdery white coating on the yarrow leaves. It can be prevented by providing good air circulation around the plants and avoiding overhead watering.
  - Rust: Rust is a fungal disease that causes orange or brown spots on the yarrow leaves. It can be prevented by providing good air circulation and avoiding overhead watering.

It is important to monitor the yarrow plants regularly and take appropriate measures to control any pests or diseases to ensure healthy growth and prevent the spread of infection to other plants.

- Harvesting and Preparations: Yarrow is usually harvested during its flowering period, which typically occurs from June to September. Here are some tips for harvesting and preparing yarrow:
  - Harvesting: Select healthy yarrow plants with well-formed flower heads. Cut the stems just above the leaves using a sharp knife or scissors.
  - Drying: Yarrow can be dried by tying the stems together in small bunches and hanging them upside down in a well-ventilated, dry area away from direct sunlight. Once dry, strip the leaves and flowers from the stems and store them in an airtight container in a cool, dry place.
  - Infusions and Teas: To make an infusion or tea, steep 1-2 teaspoons of dried yarrow leaves or flowers in 1 cup of hot water for 10-15 minutes. Strain the mixture and drink up to 3 cups per day.

- Tinctures: Yarrow tinctures can be made by soaking fresh or dried yarrow leaves and flowers in alcohol for several weeks. The resulting liquid is then strained and stored in a dark, airtight bottle.
- Poultices and Compresses: Yarrow leaves and flowers can be crushed and applied directly to wounds and bruises to help reduce inflammation and promote healing.

It is important to consult with a healthcare professional before using yarrow for any medicinal purposes, especially if you have any pre-existing medical conditions or are taking medications.

What Medicines Are Made with this Herb:

Yarrow has been used in traditional medicine for centuries and is still used in modern medicine. Here are some examples of medicines and products made with yarrow:

- Topical ointments and creams: Yarrow is used in topical preparations for its anti-inflammatory and antiseptic properties. It is often included in herbal first-aid kits and natural insect repellents.
- Digestive remedies: Yarrow is used as a digestive aid to stimulate appetite and relieve digestive discomfort, such as bloating and gas.
- Cold and flu remedies: Yarrow is used as an herbal remedy for colds, flu, and fever. It is believed to help reduce fever and relieve symptoms such as headache, sore throat, and cough.
- Wound healing products: Yarrow has been shown to promote wound healing and reduce inflammation. It is used in natural wound care products, such as salves and poultices.
- Menstrual products: Yarrow is used in some natural remedies to help regulate menstrual cycles, reduce menstrual cramps, and relieve symptoms of menopause.

Yarrow is also sometimes used in homeopathy and aromatherapy. It is important to consult with a healthcare professional before using yarrow for any medicinal purposes, especially if you have any pre-existing medical conditions or are taking medications.

What Medicines this Herb Counteract:

There are no known medicines that yarrow specifically counteracts. However, as with any herb or medication, yarrow may interact with other drugs or supplements. It is important to talk to a healthcare professional before using yarrow if you are taking any medications or have any pre-existing medical conditions.

Yarrow may increase the risk of bleeding, so it is not recommended to use it before or after surgery, or with medications that increase the risk of bleeding such as anticoagulants or antiplatelet drugs. Yarrow may also interact with medications that affect blood pressure and medications for diabetes, so it is important to consult a healthcare professional before using yarrow if you are taking these medications.

Yarrow may also cause allergic reactions in some people, especially those who are allergic to plants in the aster family, such as ragweed, chrysanthemums, and daisies. If you experience symptoms such as hives, difficulty breathing, or swelling after using yarrow, seek medical attention immediately.

Growing Herbs at Home

Growing herbs at home can be a rewarding and sustainable way to incorporate fresh, high-quality herbs into your daily routine. In addition to providing a convenient source of herbs, growing them at home allows you to control the quality and ensure that they are grown using sustainable and organic practices. To get started, it is important to set up a herb garden, choose the right herbs for your climate and region, prepare and maintain the soil, care for your herbs, and know when and how to harvest and store them. In this section, we will discuss the essential steps for growing herbs at home, from setting up a herb garden to harvesting and storing your herbs.

Setting up a herb garden

Setting up a herb garden is a fun and rewarding project that can provide fresh herbs for cooking, teas, and natural remedies. Here are some steps to consider when setting up your herb garden:

- Choose a location: The first step in setting up a herb garden is to choose the right location. Herbs require at least six hours of sunlight per day, so choose a location that receives plenty of direct sunlight. Additionally, make sure the location is easily accessible for watering and harvesting.
- Determine the size: Decide how big you want your herb garden to be. Consider the amount of space you have available and how many herbs you want to grow.
- Decide on the type of garden: You can choose from various types of herb gardens, including container gardens, raised beds, or traditional in-ground gardens. Consider the size of your space and the amount of time and effort you want to put into maintenance when deciding on the type of garden.
- Choose your herbs: Decide which herbs you want to grow in your garden. Consider your cooking and medicinal needs, as well as the climate and region you live in. Some popular herbs to consider growing include basil, thyme, rosemary, oregano, and mint.
- Prepare the soil: Prepare the soil before planting your herbs. Ensure the soil is well-drained and rich in organic matter. You can also add compost or other organic fertilizers to enrich the soil.
- Plant the herbs: Plant the herbs in the prepared soil according to their specific requirements. Make sure to space them appropriately to allow for proper growth and air circulation.

- Water and maintain the garden: Water your herb garden regularly and make sure to remove any weeds or dead foliage. Additionally, fertilize your herbs as needed to ensure healthy growth.

Setting up a herb garden can be a fun and rewarding experience. With the right location, type of garden, and herbs, you can enjoy fresh and flavorful herbs for cooking and natural remedies all year round.

Choosing the right herbs for your climate and region

Choosing the right herbs for your climate and region is crucial to ensure their growth and survival. Here are some factors to consider when selecting herbs for your garden:

- Climate: Consider the climate in your region. Some herbs prefer hot and dry climates, while others thrive in cooler temperatures with higher humidity. Determine which herbs are best suited for your climate before selecting them for your garden.
- Soil: Soil type can also affect the growth of herbs. Some herbs prefer well-drained, sandy soil, while others thrive in heavy, clay-like soil. Determine the type of soil in your region and choose herbs that are suited for it.
- Sunlight: Herbs require sunlight to grow and thrive. Determine the amount of sunlight your garden receives and choose herbs that are suited for those conditions. Some herbs require full sunlight, while others can grow in partial shade.
- Water: The amount of water your garden receives can also affect the growth of herbs. Choose herbs that are suited for the amount of water your garden receives. Some herbs require regular watering, while others can survive with less water.
- Plant size: Consider the size of the herbs you are selecting. Some herbs, like basil and mint, can grow quite large and may require more space than others. Choose herbs that are suited for the size of your garden and the amount of space you have available.
- Use: Consider how you plan to use the herbs you are selecting. Some herbs are better suited for cooking, while others are used for medicinal purposes. Determine the purpose of the herbs in your garden and select accordingly.

By considering these factors, you can choose the right herbs for your climate and region, ensuring their growth and survival in your garden. Additionally, consult with your local nursery or a gardening expert to get advice on which herbs are best suited for your area.

Soil preparation and maintenance

Soil preparation and maintenance are important factors in growing healthy and productive herb gardens. Here are some tips for preparing and maintaining the soil in your herb garden:

- Soil testing: Conduct a soil test to determine the pH level and nutrient content of your soil. This will help you identify any deficiencies and adjust the soil accordingly.
- Soil amendments: Based on the results of the soil test, you may need to amend the soil by adding compost, manure, or other organic matter to improve soil fertility and structure.
- Mulching: Adding a layer of organic mulch, such as straw or leaves, to your garden can help retain moisture and suppress weeds.
- Watering: Herbs require consistent moisture to thrive, but over-watering can lead to root rot and other problems. Water the soil around the base of the plants rather than overhead to avoid wetting the foliage.
- Fertilizing: Depending on the nutrient content of your soil, you may need to add fertilizers to your garden. Use organic fertilizers to avoid chemical runoff and to improve soil health over time.
- Crop rotation: To prevent soil-borne diseases and nutrient depletion, rotate your herb garden crops every year. Planting different herbs in the same location each year can lead to soil-borne diseases and pest infestations.
- Weed control: Regular weeding can help prevent competition for nutrients and water, as well as reduce the risk of disease and pest infestations.

By preparing and maintaining the soil in your herb garden, you can ensure healthy growth and a bountiful harvest of herbs. Additionally, consult with your local nursery or a gardening expert for advice on soil preparation and maintenance specific to the herbs you are growing.

Caring for your herbs

Caring for your herbs is essential for maintaining healthy and productive plants. Here are some tips for caring for your herbs:

- Sunlight: Most herbs require at least 6 hours of direct sunlight each day. Place your herb garden in a location that receives adequate sunlight throughout the day.
- Watering: Herbs require consistent moisture to thrive, but over-watering can lead to root rot and other problems. Water your herbs regularly, checking the soil moisture level before watering. Water the soil around the base of the plants rather than overhead to avoid wetting the foliage.

- Pruning: Regular pruning of your herbs can encourage bushier growth and prevent plants from becoming too leggy. Prune off any yellow or dead leaves or stems to encourage new growth.
- Pest control: Keep an eye out for pests such as aphids, mites, and caterpillars that can damage your herb garden. Use natural pest control methods such as companion planting, neem oil, and insecticidal soap to avoid chemical sprays that can harm beneficial insects and the environment.
- Harvesting: Regular harvesting of your herbs can promote new growth and ensure a steady supply of fresh herbs. Harvest in the morning when the essential oils are most concentrated and be sure to leave enough growth for the plant to continue to thrive.
- Fertilizing: Herbs can benefit from organic fertilizers such as compost, manure, and worm castings. Apply fertilizer according to the instructions on the package, being careful not to over-fertilize.

By caring for your herbs properly, you can enjoy a bountiful harvest of healthy and flavorful plants. Additionally, consult with your local nursery or a gardening expert for advice on caring for the specific herbs you are growing.

Harvesting and storing herbs

Harvesting and storing herbs is an essential part of maintaining a productive herb garden. Here are some tips for harvesting and storing your herbs:
- Timing: The best time to harvest your herbs is in the morning when the essential oils are most concentrated. Avoid harvesting when the plants are wet, as this can lead to mold and mildew.
- Method: The method for harvesting your herbs will depend on the type of herb you are harvesting. For leafy herbs such as basil, oregano, and mint, pinch off the top few inches of the plant, just above a leaf node. For herbs with woody stems such as rosemary and thyme, cut off the top few inches of the stem.
- Storage: Proper storage of herbs is crucial for maintaining their flavor and potency. Drying is the most common method of storing herbs, and it can be done in several ways, such as hanging the herbs upside down in a dry, well-ventilated area or using a dehydrator. Once the herbs are dry, store them in airtight containers in a cool, dark place away from moisture and direct sunlight.
- Freezing: Another method of storing herbs is freezing. Chop the herbs finely and freeze them in ice cube trays filled with water or oil. Once the cubes are frozen, store them in airtight containers in the freezer.

- Labeling: Labeling your herbs is crucial for keeping track of what you have stored and when it was harvested. Use labels to identify the type of herb, the date of harvest, and any other relevant information.

By following these tips for harvesting and storing your herbs, you can enjoy fresh, flavorful herbs year-round. Additionally, consult with your local nursery or a gardening expert for advice on harvesting and storing the specific herbs you are growing.

Growing your own herb garden can be a rewarding and enjoyable experience, and it's also a great way to have fresh herbs on hand for cooking and other uses. However, to get the most out of your herb garden, it's essential to choose the right herbs for your climate, prepare and maintain the soil, care for your plants, and harvest and store your herbs properly.

When setting up your herb garden, make sure to choose a location with plenty of sunlight and good drainage. Choose herbs that are well-suited to your climate and region, and prepare the soil with compost and other amendments to ensure optimal growth. Once your herbs are planted, be sure to water and fertilize them regularly, and keep an eye out for pests and diseases.

When it comes time to harvest your herbs, timing and method are crucial. Harvest your herbs in the morning when the essential oils are most concentrated, and use the appropriate method depending on the type of herb you are harvesting. Proper storage is also essential to maintain the flavor and potency of your herbs, whether you choose to dry or freeze them.

By following these guidelines for growing and maintaining your herb garden, you can enjoy fresh, flavorful herbs throughout the year, and even save money compared to buying herbs from the store. Whether you are an experienced gardener or a beginner, growing your own herbs is a great way to connect with nature and enhance your culinary and medicinal practices.

Preparation Methods

For centuries, herbs have been utilized for their potent medicinal properties. While the use of herbs may seem like a simple and natural solution to various ailments, it is essential to understand that the method of preparation plays a significant role in their efficacy. In this article, we delve into the world of herbal preparation methods, exploring the various techniques used to extract the healing properties of plants. From decoctions to infusions, tinctures to salves, we will examine each method and its unique benefits. By the end of this article, you will have a comprehensive understanding of how to prepare and administer herbs for maximum therapeutic effect. So, let us dive in and discover the art of herbal preparation!

Different methods of preparing herbs for medicinal use

Herbs have been used for centuries for their medicinal properties, and there are many different methods of preparing them for use. In this section, we will explore the most common methods of preparing herbs for medicinal use.

Decoctions:

Decoctions are a method of preparing herbs for medicinal use that involves simmering the plant material in water for an extended period of time. This method is commonly used for hard or woody plant material, such as roots, bark, or seeds. Decoctions are a popular way to extract the beneficial compounds from these types of plant material because the heat helps to break down the tough fibers and release the medicinal properties.

To prepare a decoction, first, select the plant material you want to use and chop it into small pieces. It is important to use a sufficient amount of plant material to achieve the desired potency of the decoction. A general rule of thumb is to use one ounce of dried herb or two ounces of fresh herb per pint of water.

Next, add the plant material to a pot of cold water and bring it to a boil. It is important to start with cold water to allow the plant material to release its medicinal properties slowly. Once the water has come to a boil, reduce the heat and let it simmer for 20-30 minutes. The length of time you simmer the mixture will depend on the type of plant material you are using and the desired potency of the decoction.

After simmering, strain the liquid and drink it while it is still warm. You can also add honey or another sweetener to improve the taste of the decoction. Decoctions can be consumed several times a day to achieve the desired therapeutic effect.

Decoctions are commonly used to treat a variety of conditions, including respiratory problems such as coughs and bronchitis, digestive issues such as diarrhea and indigestion, and to help reduce inflammation. They are also used to promote relaxation and sleep, and to help support the immune system.

It is important to note that decoctions should not be boiled for too long as this can destroy some of the beneficial compounds in the plant material. Additionally, decoctions should be stored in the refrigerator and consumed within a few days to prevent spoilage. By understanding the proper preparation and storage techniques for decoctions, you can make the most out of the medicinal properties of the herbs you use.

Infusions:
Infusions are another method of preparing herbs for medicinal use that involves steeping the plant material in hot water for a short period of time. This method is commonly used for delicate plant material, such as leaves, flowers, and soft stems. Infusions are a gentle and effective way to extract the beneficial compounds from these types of plant material.

To prepare an infusion, first, select the plant material you want to use and chop it into small pieces. It is important to use a sufficient amount of plant material to achieve the desired potency of the infusion. A general rule of thumb is to use one ounce of dried herb or two ounces of fresh herb per pint of water.

Next, bring a pot of water to a boil and then remove it from the heat. Add the plant material to the hot water and let it steep for 5-10 minutes. The length of time you steep the mixture will depend on the type of plant material you are using and the desired potency of the infusion.

After steeping, strain the liquid and drink it while it is still warm. You can also add honey or another sweetener to improve the taste of the infusion. Infusions can be consumed several times a day to achieve the desired therapeutic effect.

Infusions are commonly used to treat a variety of conditions, including anxiety, stress, insomnia, and digestive issues such as bloating and gas. They are also used to help support the immune system and to promote overall wellness.

It is important to note that infusions should not be boiled as this can destroy some of the beneficial compounds in the plant material. Additionally, infusions should be stored in the refrigerator and consumed within a few days to prevent spoilage. By understanding the proper preparation and storage techniques for infusions, you can make the most out of the medicinal properties of the herbs you use.

Tinctures:

Tinctures are a method of preparing herbs for medicinal use that involves steeping the plant material in a high-proof alcohol solution to extract the beneficial compounds. This method is commonly used for herbs that are difficult to extract using other methods, such as resinous or oily plants. Tinctures are a potent and long-lasting way to extract the medicinal properties of herbs.

To prepare a tincture, first, select the plant material you want to use and chop it into small pieces. It is important to use a sufficient amount of plant material to achieve the desired potency of the tincture. A general rule of thumb is to use one part dried herb to five parts alcohol.

Next, place the plant material in a glass jar and cover it with the alcohol solution. The alcohol should be at least 40% proof, but a higher proof is preferred as it extracts the medicinal compounds more efficiently. Shake the jar vigorously and store it in a cool, dark place for several weeks. The length of time the mixture needs to steep will depend on the type of plant material you are using and the desired potency of the tincture. Generally, a tincture should steep for at least two weeks, but some tinctures may require longer.

After steeping, strain the liquid through a fine mesh strainer or cheesecloth and store the tincture in a dark glass bottle with a dropper. Tinctures can be consumed by adding a few drops to a glass of water or taking them directly under the tongue. Tinctures can be stored for several years if stored properly in a cool, dark place.

Tinctures are commonly used to treat a variety of conditions, including anxiety, insomnia, pain, and digestive issues. They are also used to help support the immune system and to promote overall wellness.

It is important to note that tinctures are a potent form of herbal medicine and should be used with care. It is important to follow dosage instructions carefully and to consult with a healthcare provider before using any new herbal remedy, particularly if you are pregnant, nursing, or taking any medications. By understanding the proper preparation and usage techniques for tinctures, you can make the most out of the medicinal properties of the herbs you use.

Salves:

Salves, also known as balms or ointments, are a method of preparing herbs for external use. They are commonly used for skin conditions such as rashes, cuts, bruises, and insect bites. Salves are made by infusing herbs into a base of oil and beeswax, creating a thick, semi-solid substance that can be applied to the skin.

To prepare a salve, first, select the herbs you want to use and chop them into small pieces. You can use fresh or dried herbs, but dried herbs are preferred as they contain less water, which can spoil the salve. A general rule of thumb is to use one part dried herb to four parts oil.

Next, heat the oil in a double boiler and add the chopped herbs to the oil. Heat the mixture for several hours on low heat, stirring occasionally, until the oil has become infused with the beneficial compounds from the herbs. Strain the mixture through a fine mesh strainer or cheesecloth and return the oil to the double boiler.

Next, add beeswax to the oil and heat the mixture until the beeswax has melted and the mixture has become thick and creamy. Pour the mixture into jars or tins and let it cool completely before use. Salves can be stored for several months if kept in a cool, dry place.

Salves are commonly used to soothe and heal a variety of skin conditions, including minor burns, cuts, scrapes, and insect bites. They can also be used to provide relief from muscle aches and pains and to promote overall skin health.

It is important to note that salves should only be used on unbroken skin and should not be used internally. Additionally, it is important to be cautious when using salves containing herbs that may cause skin irritation or allergic reactions. Always test a small amount of the salve on a small area of skin before using it more extensively. By understanding the proper preparation and usage techniques for salves, you can make the most out of the medicinal properties of the herbs you use.

Capsules:
Capsules are a popular method of taking herbs and other dietary supplements. They are a convenient and easy-to-use way to consume medicinal herbs in a standardized and consistent dosage.

To prepare herbs for use in capsules, the herbs are first powdered using a grinder or mortar and pestle. The powdered herbs are then encapsulated using a capsule-filling machine or can be filled by hand using a capsule-filling tray.

Capsules are typically made from vegetable cellulose or gelatin and are available in various sizes. The most common sizes are 00, 0, and 1. The size of the capsule used will depend on the dosage required and the size of the herb particles.

Capsules are a popular way to take herbs because they are tasteless and odorless, making them more palatable than other forms of herbal preparations. They are also convenient and easy to take, allowing for precise dosing.

Capsules can be used to treat a variety of conditions, including digestive issues, anxiety, insomnia, and pain. They are also used to help support the immune system and promote overall wellness.

It is important to note that capsules are not suitable for all herbs, as some herbs may not be well absorbed in this form. Additionally, it is important to choose high-quality herbs and to follow dosage instructions carefully. It is always advisable to consult with a healthcare provider before taking any new herbal remedy, particularly if you are pregnant, nursing, or taking any medications.

By understanding the proper preparation and usage techniques for capsules, you can make the most out of the medicinal properties of the herbs you use. Understanding the different methods of preparing herbs for medicinal use is essential for maximizing their therapeutic benefits. Decoctions, infusions, tinctures, salves, and capsules each have their unique benefits and are used to extract the medicinal properties of different plant material. By choosing the appropriate preparation method, you can ensure that you are getting the most out of the herbs you use for medicinal purposes.

There are several methods for preparing herbs for medicinal use, each with its unique benefits and drawbacks. Decoctions, infusions, tinctures, salves, and capsules are all popular methods used to extract the medicinal compounds from herbs and make them more palatable and easier to use. Each method requires a different preparation process, and some may be more suitable for certain herbs and conditions than others. It is important to choose high-quality herbs and to follow dosage instructions carefully when using any herbal remedy. By understanding the different methods of preparing herbs, you can make the most out of their therapeutic properties and enhance your overall health and wellbeing.

Understanding decoctions, infusions, tinctures, salves, and other preparations

Decoctions

The purpose of decoctions is to extract the active ingredients from the herbs that have hard parts such as roots, bark, and seeds. Decoctions are made by boiling the herbs in water for a prolonged period, which allows the active ingredients to be released into the liquid. The heat helps to break down the tough plant material and release the therapeutic compounds.

Decoctions are often used in traditional medicine and natural healing to treat a variety of conditions such as colds, flu, digestive problems, respiratory issues, and other ailments. They are typically consumed as a hot or cold beverage and can be sweetened with honey or other natural sweeteners to make them more palatable.

The advantage of using a decoction over other herbal preparations such as infusions or tinctures is that it is more effective in extracting the active ingredients from hard plant parts. Decoctions are also a good option for people who prefer to drink their medicine rather than taking capsules or applying salves.

However, it is essential to note that decoctions can be potent, and it is important to follow the recommended dosage and consult with a qualified herbalist or healthcare provider before using any herbal preparation.

Infusions

The purpose of infusions is to extract the active ingredients from the herbs that have soft parts such as leaves, flowers, and stems. Infusions are made by steeping the herbs in hot water for a short period, which allows the active ingredients to be released into the liquid.

Infusions are often used in traditional medicine and natural healing to treat a variety of conditions such as anxiety, insomnia, indigestion, and other ailments. They are typically consumed as a hot or cold beverage and can be sweetened with honey or other natural sweeteners to make them more palatable.

The advantage of using an infusion over other herbal preparations such as decoctions or tinctures is that it is gentler and less potent. Infusions are also a good option for people who prefer to drink their medicine rather than taking capsules or applying salves.

However, it is essential to note that infusions may not be as effective as other preparations in extracting the active ingredients from certain herbs. For example, herbs with hard parts such as roots or seeds may require a decoction to extract the therapeutic compounds fully. It is important to follow the recommended dosage and consult with a qualified herbalist or healthcare provider before using any herbal preparation.

Tinctures
The purpose of a tincture is to extract the active ingredients from the herbs using alcohol or another solvent. Tinctures are made by soaking the herbs in alcohol or another solvent, which allows the active ingredients to be released into the liquid.

Tinctures are often used in traditional medicine and natural healing to treat a variety of conditions such as anxiety, depression, pain, and other ailments. They can be taken as drops or added to water or other beverages.

The advantage of using a tincture over other herbal preparations such as decoctions or infusions is that it is more potent and longer-lasting. Tinctures can also be more convenient to use than other preparations, as they can be carried with you and taken as needed throughout the day.

However, it is essential to note that tinctures may not be suitable for everyone, especially those who are sensitive to alcohol. In these cases, a glycerin-based tincture or another solvent may be used instead. It is also important to follow the recommended dosage and consult with a qualified herbalist or healthcare provider before using any herbal preparation.

Salves

The purpose of a salve is to provide a topical application of herbs for medicinal or therapeutic purposes. Salves are made by combining herbs with a carrier oil and beeswax, which creates a semi-solid mixture that can be applied to the skin.

Salves are often used in traditional medicine and natural healing to treat a variety of skin conditions such as rashes, burns, wounds, and other ailments. They can also be used to soothe sore muscles and joints.

The advantage of using a salve over other herbal preparations such as decoctions, infusions, or tinctures is that it provides a localized application of the herbs, which can be more effective for treating skin conditions or localized pain. Salves can also be more convenient to use than other preparations, as they can be carried with you and applied as needed throughout the day.

However, it is essential to note that salves may not be suitable for everyone, especially those with allergies to beeswax or certain carrier oils. It is also important to follow the recommended dosage and consult with a qualified herbalist or healthcare provider before using any herbal preparation.

Capsules

The purpose of a capsule is to provide an easy and convenient way to consume herbs or other supplements. Capsules are made by filling a gelatin or vegetarian capsule with powdered herbs or other supplements.

Capsules are often used in traditional medicine and natural healing to treat a variety of conditions such as digestive problems, hormonal imbalances, and other ailments. They are a good option for people who prefer not to consume herbs as teas or tinctures.

The advantage of using capsules over other herbal preparations such as decoctions, infusions, tinctures, or salves is that they are more convenient and can be easily consumed on-the-go. They are also a good option for people who do not like the taste of herbal teas or tinctures.

However, it is essential to note that capsules may not be as effective as other preparations in extracting the active ingredients from certain herbs. For example, herbs with hard parts such as roots or seeds may require a decoction to extract the therapeutic compounds fully. It is important to follow the recommended dosage and consult with a qualified herbalist or healthcare provider before using any herbal preparation in capsule form.

How to prepare and administer herbs for maximum efficacy

The preparation and administration of herbs can significantly impact their efficacy. Here are some guidelines to help prepare and administer herbs for maximum efficacy:

Use high-quality herbs: Always choose high-quality, fresh, and organic herbs to ensure maximum potency and efficacy.

Using high-quality herbs is essential for maximizing the potency and efficacy of herbal preparations. High-quality herbs are those that are fresh, free of contaminants, and grown using organic or sustainable farming practices.

Here are some reasons why high-quality herbs are important:
- Potency: High-quality herbs contain higher levels of active ingredients, which means they are more potent and effective in treating health conditions.
- Safety: High-quality herbs are free of contaminants such as pesticides, heavy metals, and other toxins, which can be harmful to health.
- Sustainability: High-quality herbs are grown using sustainable farming practices that minimize the impact on the environment and support local communities.
- Flavor: High-quality herbs have a better flavor and aroma, making them more enjoyable to consume.

When choosing herbs, it is important to look for reputable suppliers who prioritize quality and sustainability. This ensures that you are getting the most potent and effective herbs for your health needs.

Choose the right preparation method:
Different herbs require different preparation methods to extract their active ingredients fully. For example, roots and seeds often require decoction, while leaves and flowers are better suited to infusions or tinctures. Choose the appropriate preparation method based on the herb being used.

Choosing the right preparation method is essential for extracting the maximum therapeutic benefits from herbs. Different herbs contain different active compounds, and the preparation method used can impact the extraction of those compounds.

Here are some common preparation methods and the types of herbs they are best suited for:
- Decoction: A decoction is a method of boiling herbs in water to extract the active ingredients. Decoctions are best suited for herbs with hard parts such as roots, barks, and seeds. Examples of herbs that are commonly prepared as decoctions include ginger, licorice root, and echinacea root.
- Infusion: An infusion is a method of steeping herbs in hot water to extract the active ingredients. Infusions are best suited for herbs with soft parts such as leaves, flowers, and stems. Examples of herbs that are commonly prepared as infusions include chamomile, lavender, and peppermint.
- Tincture: A tincture is a method of extracting the active ingredients from herbs using alcohol or another solvent. Tinctures are best suited for herbs with hard or soft parts, and they can be made using fresh or dried herbs. Examples of herbs that are commonly prepared as tinctures include valerian root, milk thistle, and echinacea.
- Salve: A salve is a topical preparation made by combining herbs with a carrier oil and beeswax. Salves are best suited for herbs that can be applied topically to the skin for localized healing, such as comfrey, calendula, and lavender.

Choosing the appropriate preparation method based on the herb being used ensures that the maximum therapeutic benefits are extracted from the herbs. It is also important to follow proper preparation techniques and use high-quality herbs for maximum efficacy.

Use the right dosage:
The appropriate dosage of herbs can vary based on the herb being used and the person's individual needs. Consult with a qualified herbalist or healthcare provider to determine the appropriate dosage.

Using the right dosage of herbs is critical for ensuring their safety and efficacy. The appropriate dosage can vary based on the herb being used, the person's individual needs, and their health status.

Here are some factors to consider when determining the right dosage of herbs:
- Age and weight: Children and adults of different weights may require different dosages of herbs.
- Health status: People with certain health conditions may need to take lower or higher doses of herbs, or avoid certain herbs altogether.

- Purpose of use: The dosage of herbs may vary depending on the intended purpose of use. For example, a higher dose may be needed for treating a chronic condition, while a lower dose may be sufficient for general health maintenance.
- Preparation method: The dosage of herbs may vary depending on the preparation method used. For example, the recommended dosage of a tincture may be different from that of a tea.

It is important to consult with a qualified herbalist or healthcare provider to determine the appropriate dosage of herbs. They can take into account the individual's health status, age, weight, and other factors to recommend the optimal dosage. It is also important to follow the recommended dosage and not exceed it, as high doses of herbs can be toxic and lead to adverse effects.

Be consistent:
To achieve maximum efficacy, it is essential to be consistent with the administration of herbs. Follow the recommended dosage and administration frequency to achieve the desired results.

Consistency is key when it comes to using herbs for maximum efficacy. It is important to follow the recommended dosage and administration frequency to achieve the desired results.

Here are some tips for being consistent when using herbs:
- Set a schedule: Create a schedule for taking herbs, whether it's once a day or multiple times a day, and stick to it as much as possible.
- Use reminders: Use reminders such as phone alarms or sticky notes to help remember to take herbs at the designated times.
- Keep track of progress: Keep track of how the herbs are affecting the body, and make any necessary adjustments to the dosage or administration frequency.
- Don't skip doses: Skipping doses can disrupt the consistency of the herb's effects, so it is important to take them as recommended.

Be patient:
It may take time for the full effects of herbs to be felt, so it is important to be patient and consistent with their use.

By being consistent with the administration of herbs, individuals can ensure that they are getting the maximum therapeutic benefits and achieving the desired results.

Take herbs at the appropriate time:
Some herbs are best taken on an empty stomach, while others are better taken with food. Consult with a qualified herbalist or healthcare provider to determine the appropriate timing for taking herbs.

Taking herbs at the appropriate time can have a significant impact on their efficacy. Here are some tips for taking herbs at the appropriate time:
- Determine the best time: Consult with a qualified herbalist or healthcare provider to determine the best time to take herbs based on their intended purpose, preparation method, and any potential interactions with other medications or supplements.
- Take note of any special instructions: Some herbs may need to be taken at specific times of day or with specific foods or liquids. Follow any special instructions provided by the herbalist or healthcare provider.
- Consider the form of the herb: The form of the herb, such as a capsule or tincture, may impact the timing of when it should be taken. For example, a capsule may be best taken with food, while a tincture may be best taken on an empty stomach.
- Be consistent: Consistency in timing is important for maximizing the benefits of herbs. Set a regular schedule for taking herbs and stick to it as much as possible.

By taking herbs at the appropriate time, individuals can ensure that they are getting the maximum therapeutic benefits and avoiding any potential interactions or adverse effects. It is important to always follow the recommendations of a qualified herbalist or healthcare provider when it comes to the timing and administration of herbs.

Store herbs properly:
Proper storage of herbs is essential to maintain their potency and efficacy. Store herbs in a cool, dark place away from moisture and direct sunlight.

Proper storage of herbs is essential to maintain their potency and efficacy. Here are some tips for storing herbs properly:
- Choose the right container: Store herbs in airtight containers made of glass or ceramic. Avoid plastic containers, as they can allow moisture to build up and affect the quality of the herbs.

- Store in a cool, dark place: Store herbs in a cool, dark place away from moisture and direct sunlight. Heat and light can cause herbs to lose their potency and efficacy.
- Label and date: Label each container with the name of the herb and the date of purchase or preparation. This will help keep track of the freshness of the herbs and avoid using stale herbs.
- Keep away from strong odors: Herbs can absorb strong odors from other foods and spices, so it is important to store them away from strong-smelling items such as onions and garlic.
- Keep out of reach of children and pets: Store herbs in a safe place that is out of reach of children and pets.

By storing herbs properly, individuals can ensure that they maintain their potency and efficacy for longer periods and avoid any potential risks associated with using stale or contaminated herbs.

Consult with a qualified herbalist or healthcare provider: It is essential to consult with a qualified herbalist or healthcare provider before using any herbal preparation to ensure maximum efficacy and avoid any potential side effects.

Consulting with a qualified herbalist or healthcare provider is essential to ensure the safe and effective use of herbal preparations. Here are some reasons why consulting with a qualified herbalist or healthcare provider is important:
- Safety: Some herbs can interact with medications or have potential side effects, so it is important to consult with a qualified herbalist or healthcare provider to ensure that the chosen herbs are safe for use.
- Efficacy: A qualified herbalist or healthcare provider can recommend the most appropriate herbs and preparation methods for a specific health condition, ensuring that the herbs used are effective for the intended purpose.
- Individualized recommendations: A qualified herbalist or healthcare provider can provide individualized recommendations for the dosage and administration of herbs based on an individual's unique health needs, medical history, and other factors.
- Quality control: A qualified herbalist or healthcare provider can provide guidance on how to select high-quality herbs and ensure that they are prepared and stored properly to maintain their potency and efficacy.
- Monitoring and follow-up: A qualified herbalist or healthcare provider can monitor an individual's response to herbal preparations and provide follow-up recommendations as needed to ensure optimal results.

In summary, consulting with a qualified herbalist or healthcare provider is essential for safe and effective use of herbal preparations, as they can provide personalized guidance on herb selection, preparation, dosage, and administration to achieve maximum efficacy and avoid any potential risks.

By following these guidelines, you can prepare and administer herbs in a way that maximizes their potency and efficacy.

Herbs can be used for a variety of purposes, including improving overall health, treating specific health conditions, and relieving symptoms of various ailments. To achieve maximum efficacy when using herbs, it is essential to use high-quality herbs, choose the appropriate preparation method, use the right dosage, be consistent with administration, take herbs at the appropriate time, and store herbs properly. Additionally, consulting with a qualified herbalist or healthcare provider is crucial to ensure the safe and effective use of herbs, as they can provide individualized recommendations and monitor an individual's response to herbal preparations. By following these guidelines, individuals can enjoy the full benefits of using herbs for their health and wellbeing.

Safety Considerations

While herbal medicine can be a safe and effective alternative to conventional medicine, it's important to be aware of potential side effects and interactions with other medications. Some herbs may have contraindications for specific conditions or should not be taken in certain situations. It's crucial to seek professional advice before using herbal remedies, especially if you have a pre-existing medical condition or are taking prescription medication. This section will cover some of the safety considerations to keep in mind when using herbal medicine.

Potential side effects of herbal medicine

While many herbs are generally safe to use, they can still have potential side effects. Some common side effects of herbal medicine include:

- Allergic reactions: Just like with any medication, herbs can cause an allergic reaction in some people. Symptoms may include itching, hives, swelling, difficulty breathing, or anaphylaxis.
- Digestive issues: Some herbs can cause digestive issues such as nausea, vomiting, diarrhea, or constipation.
- Dizziness or drowsiness: Certain herbs may cause dizziness or drowsiness, especially if they have a sedative effect.
- Interference with other medications: Herbs can interact with other medications, including prescription medications, over-the-counter medications, and supplements. This can cause side effects or reduce the effectiveness of the medication.
- Photosensitivity: Some herbs can cause photosensitivity, making your skin more sensitive to the sun and increasing your risk of sunburn or other skin damage.

It's important to be aware of these potential side effects and to talk to a healthcare provider before using any herbal remedy, especially if you have a pre-existing medical condition or are taking prescription medication.

Interactions between herbs and conventional medications

Herbs can interact with conventional medications in a variety of ways, including:

- Increasing or decreasing the effectiveness of medication: Some herbs can increase or decrease the effectiveness of conventional medications. For

example, St. John's wort, which is commonly used for depression, can reduce the effectiveness of some antidepressant medications.
- Causing side effects: Some herbs can cause side effects when taken with conventional medications. For example, taking the herbal supplement ginkgo biloba with blood thinners can increase the risk of bleeding.
- Interfering with drug metabolism: Some herbs can interfere with the metabolism of certain medications, leading to higher or lower levels of the drug in the body. This can cause side effects or reduce the effectiveness of the medication.
- Interfering with absorption: Some herbs can interfere with the absorption of certain medications, reducing their effectiveness. For example, calcium supplements can interfere with the absorption of some antibiotics.

It's important to talk to a healthcare provider before using any herbal remedy, especially if you are taking prescription medication. They can help you understand any potential interactions and advise you on the best course of action. It's also important to let your healthcare provider know about any herbal supplements or remedies you are taking, as they may need to adjust your medication dosage or recommend an alternative treatment.

Contraindications for specific herbs and conditions

Contraindications refer to situations where certain herbs should not be used due to the potential harm they may cause to a person's health. It is essential to be aware of these contraindications and avoid using herbs that may cause harm, especially if a person has a pre-existing medical condition or is taking medication. Some common examples of contraindications for specific herbs and conditions include:
- Blood-thinning herbs such as garlic, ginkgo biloba, and ginger should not be used by people taking blood-thinning medications such as warfarin, as they may increase the risk of bleeding.
- Herbs such as licorice root, ephedra, and ma huang should be avoided by people with high blood pressure, as they can increase blood pressure and exacerbate the condition.
- St. John's wort, an herb commonly used for depression, can interact with certain medications such as antidepressants, birth control pills, and blood thinners, reducing their effectiveness.
- Herbs such as valerian, kava, and passionflower, which are commonly used for anxiety, can interact with sedatives and other medications that cause drowsiness, increasing the risk of excessive sedation.

- Herbs such as comfrey, which contain pyrrolizidine alkaloids, should be avoided as they can cause liver damage.

It is important to consult with a qualified herbalist or healthcare provider before using any herbal remedy to ensure that the herb is safe to use and will not interact with any medications or pre-existing medical conditions.

Importance of seeking professional advice before using herbal remedies

While herbal remedies can be effective and safe when used properly, it is essential to seek professional advice before using them to avoid any potential harm or interactions with medications.

Professional advice can come from a qualified herbalist or a healthcare provider who is knowledgeable in herbal medicine. Here are some reasons why seeking professional advice is important:

- Safety: Certain herbs can interact with medications, cause allergic reactions, or have toxic effects when taken in large doses or for extended periods. A professional can help you understand the potential risks and side effects of herbs and guide you on the appropriate dosage and administration.
- Efficacy: A professional can help you choose the right herbs and preparation method based on your individual needs and health concerns. They can also provide guidance on the appropriate duration of treatment and monitor your progress to ensure maximum efficacy.
- Individualization: Herbal remedies should be tailored to an individual's specific needs and health conditions. A professional can take into account your medical history, current medications, and other factors that may affect the use of herbal remedies.
- Quality: The quality and source of herbs can affect their potency and safety. A professional can help you choose high-quality herbs from reputable sources to ensure maximum efficacy and safety.

Seeking professional advice before using herbal remedies is important to ensure their safety, efficacy, individualization, and quality. It is particularly important if you are pregnant, nursing, or have pre-existing medical conditions or are taking medications.

While herbal remedies can offer numerous health benefits, it is important to be aware of the potential side effects and interactions with conventional medications. Certain herbs may also be contraindicated for specific health conditions or populations. Seeking professional advice from a qualified herbalist or healthcare provider is crucial to ensure the safe and effective use of herbal remedies. By taking these safety considerations into account, individuals can make informed decisions about incorporating herbal medicine into their healthcare regimen.

Conclusion

Incorporating herbal medicine into your healthcare routine can provide a multitude of benefits. First and foremost, herbs can be used to treat a wide range of health conditions, from minor ailments to chronic illnesses. Many people find that using herbal remedies can help to improve their overall health and wellbeing, while also reducing the need for conventional medications with potential side effects.

Herbs are also often more affordable and accessible than conventional medications, making them a viable option for those with limited financial resources or limited access to healthcare. Additionally, using herbs can empower individuals to take control of their own health and become more self-sufficient.

Another benefit of incorporating herbal medicine into your healthcare routine is the potential for fewer adverse reactions and interactions with other medications. Because herbs are natural substances, they are less likely to cause negative side effects or interact with other medications in harmful ways.

Using herbs can provide a more holistic approach to healthcare, taking into account not just physical symptoms but also emotional, mental, and spiritual aspects of health. By focusing on treating the whole person rather than just the physical symptoms, herbal medicine can help to promote overall wellness and balance in the body.

Incorporating herbal medicine into your healthcare routine can provide numerous benefits, including improved health and wellbeing, affordability, accessibility, fewer adverse reactions and interactions with medications, and a more holistic approach to healthcare.

The world of herbal medicine is vast and constantly evolving, with new research and discoveries being made all the time. As such, it is important to continue learning and exploring the world of herbs and their medicinal uses.

By staying up to date with current research and new developments in herbal medicine, you can broaden your knowledge and understanding of the potential health benefits of different herbs. You can also learn how to use herbs safely and effectively, and become better equipped to make informed decisions about your healthcare options.

Moreover, by exploring the world of herbal medicine, you can gain a deeper appreciation for the natural world and the healing power of plants. You may also discover new and innovative ways to incorporate herbs into your daily life, such as by growing your own herbs, making herbal remedies at home, or trying new herbal products and supplements.

The world of herbal medicine offers a wealth of potential health benefits and opportunities for exploration and learning. By incorporating herbs into your healthcare routine and continuing to learn and explore the world of herbal medicine, you can take an active role in your own health and well-being and enjoy the many benefits that herbs have to offer.

References and Further Reading

A comprehensive list of resources for further study and research on herbal medicine

1 American Botanical Council - A nonprofit organization that provides education and research on the medicinal use of plants.

2 United Plant Savers - A nonprofit organization dedicated to preserving native medicinal plants and their habitats.

3 National Center for Complementary and Integrative Health - Part of the National Institutes of Health, this center provides research-based information on complementary and alternative medicine, including herbal medicine.

4 Herbal Academy - An online educational resource for herbalism courses, workshops, and articles.

5 American Herbalists Guild - A professional organization for herbalists that promotes education and research on herbal medicine.

6 The Journal of Herbal Medicine - A peer-reviewed journal that publishes research on the medicinal uses of plants.

7 "The Complete Herbal" by Nicholas Culpeper - A classic reference book on herbal medicine, first published in 1653.

8 "Medical Herbalism: The Science and Practice of Herbal Medicine" by David Hoffmann - A comprehensive guide to herbal medicine, including its history, pharmacology, and clinical use.

9 "The Modern Herbal Dispensatory: A Medicine-Making Guid"e by Thomas Easley and Steven Horne - A practical guide to making herbal medicines, including tinctures, salves, and teas.

10 "The Herbal Medicine-Maker's Handbook: A Home Manua"l by James Green - A beginner-friendly guide to making herbal preparations at home, including recipes and safety guidelines.

11 "Rosemary Gladstar's Medicinal Herbs: A Beginner's Guide" by Rosemary Gladstar - A popular introductory book on herbal medicine, including information on growing and using herbs.

12 "A Modern Herbal" by Margaret Grieve - A two-volume reference book on herbal medicine, first published in 1931, that includes botanical descriptions, medicinal uses, and historical information.

13 "The Earthwise Herbal: A Complete Guide to Old World Medicinal Plants" by Matthew Wood - A guide to the medicinal uses of plants from the Western herbal tradition, including information on energetics and constitutional types.

14 "The Way of Herb"s by Michael Tierra - A comprehensive guide to herbal medicine, including information on diagnosis, treatment, and preventive health care.

15 "Botanical Medicine for Women's Health" by Aviva Romm - A guide to using herbs for women's health concerns, including menstrual problems, menopause, and reproductive health.

Additional books, articles, and websites for those interested in exploring herbs and their medicinal uses in greater detail

Here are some additional books, articles, and websites for those interested in exploring herbs and their medicinal uses in greater detail:

Books:
- "The Herbal Medicine-Maker's Handbook: A Home Manual" by James Green
- "The Herbal Apothecary: 100 Medicinal Herbs and How to Use Them" by J.J. Pursell
- "The Complete Medicinal Herbal: A Practical Guide to the Healing Properties of Herbs" by Penelope Ody
- "The Earthwise Herbal: A Complete Guide to Old World Medicinal Plants" by Matthew Wood
- "Rosemary Gladstar's Medicinal Herbs: A Beginner's Guide" by Rosemary Gladstar
- "The Modern Herbal Dispensatory: A Medicine-Making Guide" by Thomas Easley and Steven Horne
- "Herbal Antibiotics: Natural Alternatives for Treating Drug-Resistant Bacteria" by Stephen Harrod Buhner
- "Alchemy of Herbs: Transform Everyday Ingredients into Foods and Remedies That Heal" by Rosalee de la Forêt

Articles:

- "Herbal Medicine: Biomolecular and Clinical Aspects" published in the National Institutes of Health's National Center for Biotechnology Information
- "Herbs at a Glance" published by the National Center for Complementary and Integrative Health
- "Herbal medicine: Where to start" published by Harvard Health Publishing
- "The Power of Herbs for Preppers Series" by Lisa Bedford on The Survival Mom website
- "Herbs for Health" section on Mother Earth News website

Websites:
- American Botanical Council (www.herbalgram.org)
- United Plant Savers (www.unitedplantsavers.org)
- The Herbal Academy (www.herbalacademy.com)
- Herb Society of America (www.herbsociety.org)
- International Herb Association (www.iherb.org)
- The Plant Medicine School (www.plantmedicineschool.com)
- Herbalists Without Borders (www.herbalistswithoutborders.weebly.com)

General Recipes

Tinctures

1 Simple Herbal Tincture:
2 Ingredients:
- Dried herb of your choice
- 100-proof vodka or other alcohol of your choice

Instructions:
- Fill a jar with the dried herb, leaving about 1 inch of space at the top.
- Pour the alcohol over the herb until it covers the herb by 1-2 inches.
- Close the jar tightly and shake it well.
- Store the jar in a cool, dark place for 4-6 weeks, shaking it every day or so.
- Strain the tincture through a cheesecloth or fine mesh strainer and store it in a dark glass bottle.

Herbal Tincture with Multiple Herbs:

Ingredients:
- Dried herbs of your choice (2-3 types)
- 100-proof vodka or other alcohol of your choice

Instructions:
- Combine the dried herbs in a jar, filling it about 2/3 of the way full.
- Pour the alcohol over the herbs until it covers them by 1-2 inches.
- Close the jar tightly and shake it well.
- Store the jar in a cool, dark place for 4-6 weeks, shaking it every day or so.
- Strain the tincture through a cheesecloth or fine mesh strainer and store it in a dark glass bottle.

Fresh Herbal Tincture:
Ingredients:
- Fresh herb of your choice
- 100-proof vodka or other alcohol of your choice

Instructions:
- Chop the fresh herb finely and fill a jar about 2/3 of the way full.
- Pour the alcohol over the herb until it covers it by 1-2 inches.
- Close the jar tightly and shake it well.
- Store the jar in a cool, dark place for 2-3 weeks, shaking it every day or so.
- Strain the tincture through a cheesecloth or fine mesh strainer and store it in a dark glass bottle.

Note: The ratio of herb to alcohol may vary based on the herb being used and the desired potency of the tincture. It is best to consult a reliable herbal reference or an experienced herbalist for guidance on the appropriate ratio.

Decoctions:
Here is a general recipe for making a decoction:

Ingredients:
- 1 ounce (28 grams) of dried herb or 2-3 ounces (56-85 grams) of fresh herb
- 1 quart (946 milliliters) of water

Instructions:
- Bring the water to a boil in a stainless steel or glass pot.
- Add the herbs to the pot and reduce the heat to low.
- Cover the pot and simmer the herbs for 20-45 minutes, depending on the herb.
- After simmering, strain the decoction through a fine mesh strainer or cheesecloth to remove the herb solids.
- Allow the decoction to cool before transferring it to a clean glass jar.
- Store the decoction in the refrigerator and use within 2-3 days.

Note: Decoctions are typically used to extract medicinal properties from tougher plant parts such as roots, bark, or seeds. If using fresh plant material, you may need to increase the amount used compared to dried material. Additionally, some herbs may require a longer or shorter simmer time, so it's important to do your research on the specific herb you are using.

Infusion

Here's a general recipe for making an herbal infusion:

Ingredients:
- 1-2 tablespoons of dried herbs or 2-4 tablespoons of fresh herbs
- 2 cups of water

Equipment:
- Pot with lid
- Strainer
- Mug or jar for serving

Instructions:
- Bring 2 cups of water to a boil in a pot.
- Place the herbs in a strainer and place the strainer in a mug or jar.
- Pour the boiling water over the herbs and cover with a lid.
- Let the mixture steep for 15-30 minutes, depending on the herb.
- Remove the strainer and discard the herbs.
- Enjoy your herbal infusion hot or cold.

Note: The amount of herbs and steeping time may vary depending on the specific herb and desired strength. It's always best to research the individual herb and adjust accordingly.

Salves

Here is a general recipe for making an herbal salve:

Ingredients:
- 1 cup of herb-infused oil (olive oil, coconut oil, or almond oil)
- 1 oz of beeswax
- Essential oils (optional)

Instructions:
- Make the herb-infused oil by gently heating 1 cup of your chosen oil with 1-2 tablespoons of dried herbs (or 2-4 tablespoons of fresh herbs) in a double boiler for 1-2 hours. Strain the oil through cheesecloth or a fine-mesh strainer to remove the herbs.
- In a separate double boiler, melt 1 oz of beeswax.

- Once the beeswax is melted, slowly add the herb-infused oil to the mixture, stirring continuously until well combined.
- Optional: add a few drops of essential oils for fragrance and additional benefits.
- Pour the mixture into small containers, such as jars or tins, and allow to cool and solidify completely before use.

Note: The ratio of oil to beeswax can be adjusted to create a softer or firmer salve, depending on your preference.

Balm

Here's a general recipe for making an herbal balm:

Ingredients:
- 1 cup herbal infused oil (you can use any carrier oil such as olive oil, coconut oil, almond oil, etc.)
- 1 ounce beeswax
- 15-20 drops of essential oil (optional, for fragrance and added benefits)

Instructions:
- In a double boiler, melt the beeswax over low heat.
- Once the beeswax is melted, add the herbal infused oil and stir until everything is combined.
- Remove from heat and add essential oils (if using) and stir well.
- Pour the mixture into small glass jars or tins and let it cool until it solidifies.
- Label the jar or tin with the name of the balm and the date it was made.
- Store in a cool, dry place.

To use, simply apply a small amount of the balm to the affected area as needed.

Poultice

Here's a general recipe for making an herbal poultice:

Ingredients:
- 1/2 to 1 cup of dried or fresh herbs (depending on the size of the poultice)
- Hot water
- Cheesecloth or muslin cloth
- Optional: carrier oil (such as olive oil or coconut oil)

Instructions:
- Finely chop or grind the herbs in a mortar and pestle or food processor.
- Place the herbs in a bowl and add enough hot water to create a paste-like consistency.
- Optional: Add a few drops of carrier oil to the mixture and stir well.
- Cut a piece of cheesecloth or muslin cloth to the desired size for your poultice.
- Spread the herbal paste onto the center of the cloth, leaving a small border around the edges.
- Fold the cloth in half to cover the herbal paste.
- Apply the poultice directly to the affected area and hold it in place with a bandage or wrap.
- Leave the poultice on for 20-30 minutes or as directed by your healthcare provider.
- Remove the poultice and discard the used herbs.

Note: The specific herbs used in the poultice will depend on the intended use and desired effects. It's important to consult with a qualified herbalist or healthcare provider for guidance on choosing the appropriate herbs for your needs.

Juice

Here is a general recipe for making herbal juice:

Ingredients:
- Fresh herbs of your choice
- Water
- Lemon or lime juice (optional)
- Honey or other sweeteners (optional)

Instructions:
- Wash the herbs thoroughly and chop them into small pieces.
- Add the chopped herbs to a blender or juicer.
- Add enough water to cover the herbs and blend or juice until the mixture is smooth.
- Strain the mixture through a fine mesh strainer or cheesecloth to remove any solids.
- Add lemon or lime juice and sweetener, if desired, to taste.
- Serve the herbal juice immediately, or refrigerate it for later use.

Note: The amount of water and herbs used can vary depending on the type of herb and desired strength of the juice. It is recommended to start with a small amount of herb and adjust the recipe accordingly. Also, consult with a healthcare provider before consuming any herbal juice, especially if you have any medical conditions or are taking medications.

Tea

Here is a general recipe for an herbal tea:

Ingredients:
- 1-2 teaspoons of dried or fresh herbs (depending on strength and preference)
- 8-12 oz of boiling water
- Optional: honey or lemon to taste

Instructions:
- Bring water to a boil in a kettle or on the stovetop.
- Place the herbs in a tea infuser or directly in a teapot.
- Pour the boiling water over the herbs and let steep for 5-10 minutes.
- Remove the tea infuser or strain the herbs from the liquid using a fine mesh strainer.
- Add honey or lemon to taste, if desired.
- Serve hot and enjoy!

www.ingramcontent.com/pod-product-compliance
Lightning Source LLC
LaVergne TN
LVHW081316060526
838201LV00006B/181